PSYCHOLOGY IN SPORTS
Methods and Applications

Richard M. Suinn
Colorado State University
Fort Collins, Colorado

 Burgess Publishing Company
Minneapolis, Minnesota

Consulting Editor: Robert D. Clayton, Colorado State University

Cover Design: Adelaide Rita Trettel

Editorial: Wayne Schotanus, Marta Reynolds
Copy Editing: Jim Wicklatz
Art: Joan Gordon, Adelaide Rita Trettel, Lynn Guilfoyle Dwyer
Production: Morris Lundin

Copyright © 1980 by Burgess Publishing Company
Printed in the United States of America
Library of Congress Catalog Number 79-55482
ISBN 0-8087-3532-2

Burgess Publishing Company
7108 Ohms Lane
Minneapolis, Minnesota 55435

0 9 8 7 6 5 4 3

*To those who strive to excel in sports, and
to those who strive to know in sports*

CONTENTS

FOREWORD viii

PREFACE ix

Part One • Concepts in Sports Psychology 1

PRINCIPLES IN SPORTS PSYCHOLOGY 3

Selected Psychological Considerations in Sport **4**
— *William P. Morgan*

Coaching Decisions and Research in Sport Psychology **19**
— *Bryant J. Cratty*

Psychology and Sports Performance: Principles and Applications **26**
— *Richard M. Suinn*

MOTIVATIONAL VARIABLES 37

Motivation in Sport **40**
— *Robert N. Singer*

Achievement Training **56**
— *Robert N. Singer and Robert Hilmer*

Using Applied Behavior Analysis for Altering Motivation **63**
— *Brent S. Rushall*

A Behavioral Assessment of Motivation **73**
— *David Youngblood and Richard M. Suinn*

What Can Psychology Offer to the Athlete and the Coach? **78**
— *Dorcas Susan Butt*

The Unconscious Fear of Success **86**
— *Bruce C. Ogilvie*

The Way of the Runner: An Examination of Motives for Running **90**
— *David Pargman*

Citizens' Racing Is More Than Fun **99**
— *Dick Taylor*

EMOTIONAL STATES: AROUSAL 102

Emotional Arousal and Motor Performance **103**
— *Joseph B. Oxendine*

On the Brink of Catastrophe **112**
— *Dorothy V. Harris*

Psychosocial Factors in Athletic Injuries: Development and Application
of the Social and Athletic Readjustment Rating Scale (SARRS) **119**
— *Steven T. Bramwell, Minoru Masuda, Nathaniel N. Wagner, and
Thomas H. Holmes*

EMOTIONAL STATES: AGGRESSION 124

Aggression and Sport: Two Theories **125**
— *Ruth E. Tandy and Joyce Laflin*

Violence and the Coach **129**
— *Robert Corran*

Effects of Viewing Aggressive Sports on the Hostility of Spectators **133**
— *Robert L. Arms, Gordon W. Russell, and Mark L. Sandilands*

PERSONALITY VARIABLES 143

Personality Dynamics and Sport **145**
— *William P. Morgan*

Psycho-Social Study of Outstanding Female Athletes **156**
— *Eva K. Balazs*

Sport Personality Assessment: A Methodological Re-examination **163**
— *J. Stuart Horsfall, A. Craig Fisher, and Harold H. Morris*

Kid Sports: A Den of Iniquity or a Land of Promise? **169**
— *Rainer Martens*

Part Two • The Personal View 177

Olympics—The Personal View **179**
— *Phil Gunby*

After the Golden Moment **202**
— *William Johnson*

What Makes a Champion? **212**
— *Lones W. Wigger, Jr., Hershel L. Anderson, James P. Whitaker, and
Bonnie D. Harmon*

Part Three • Applications 225

COACHING VARIABLES 227

The Gymnast's Perception of the Coach: Performance
Competence and Coaching Style **229**
— *Joe Massimo*

Hurting, Winning, and Preparing **238**
— *Barbara Zaremski*

How to Ruin an Athlete **247**
— *Byron Richardson*

Use of Groups to Improve Athletic Performance **250**
— *David Nesvig*

Psychology of Coaching **261**
— *Cal Botterill*

Goal Setting and Performance **269**
— *James D. McClements and Cal Botterill*

MENTAL STATES 280

Attentional Focus—Self-Assessment **281**
— *Robert M. Nideffer*

Psychological Techniques for the Advancement of Sports Potential **291**
— *Maurie D. Pressman*

The Mind of the Marathoner **297**
— *William P. Morgan*

BEHAVIORAL STRATEGIES 304

Body Thinking: Psychology for Olympic Champs **306**
Appendix A: Muscle Relaxation Exercise **310**
Appendix B: Psychological Preparation on Competition Day **313**
— *Richard M. Suinn*

Improving Athletic Performance through Visuo-Motor Behavior Rehearsal **316**
— *John F. Lane*

The Loneliness of a Long-Distance Kicker **321**
— *Robert W. Titley*

An Application of Biofeedback and Self-Regulation Procedures with
Superior Athletes: The Fine Tuning Effect **328**
— *Betty J. Wenz and Donald J. Strong*

Cognitive-Behavioral Skills in Golf: Brain Power Golf **334**
— *Daniel S. Kirschenbaum and Ronald M. Bale*

Psyching the College Athlete: A Comprehensive Sports Psychology Training Package **344**
Appendix: Mahoney-Avener Gymnast Questionnaire **351**
— *Philip R. Spinelli and Billy A. Barrios*

ISSUES IN SPORTS PSYCHOLOGY 356

Ethics in a Highly Visible Environment: Consultation and Intervention
with Athletes and Athletic Teams **357**
— *Robert W. Titley*

Applied Psychology in Major College Athletics **362**
— *Wayne Lanning*

FOREWORD

It is generally agreed that American athletes are as well prepared physically as any group of athletes in the world. Their psychological preparation, however, is often inadequate. This is a matter of concern to the Olympic coaching staff and also to coaches at all levels of competitive athletics.

Psychology in Sports is an important contribution to the holistic development of participants in the athletic arena. Dr. Suinn has selected articles by recognized authorities, and has organized them to provide a logical synthesis of theory and practice. The aim is to elucidate principles that will enable athletes to cope better with the competitive experience. This goal has been admirably achieved, and in the final section of the book one perceives how the transition from idea to action, from technical jargon to workable application, is accomplished. *Psychology in Sports* is the book for coaches and athletes, prepared by a psychologist who knows their needs by virtue of having lived and worked with them at all levels of competition.

Kenneth Foreman
Head Coach, United States Olympic Team/Athletics Women 1980

PREFACE

Psychology in Sports—by no means a new topic, but with a new and more useful approach to the topic—is the result of a desire to reach one aim: to bring together not only findings but also applications. Scientific findings are reported primarily through articles that either carefully summarize current knowledge or represent special contributions. Care has been taken to emphasize writings that avoid the language of the laboratory and statistical jargon, but which nonetheless were written by researchers of known rigor. Since even the best articles do not give the flavor of new methods being used by consulting sports psychologists, this book also includes a group of writings on applications. The authors were encouraged to offer concrete illustrations of psychological training methods drawn from actual interactions with athletes and coaches. However, to insure that only sound applications would be presented, methods were selected only if they were based upon accepted psychological principles. This blend of findings and applications should appeal to any reader interested in both the scholarly and the applied aspects of sports psychology today. In addition, several articles have been included to highlight athletes and competitors themselves, and, although they do not pretend to offer findings or applications of psychology, these reports offer more personal views of Olympic-class athletes.

The search to achieve this aim was an exciting one, since it took some new approaches. First, a systematic attempt was made to identify the leading sports psychologists in North America. Eventually the search included nearly all of the prominent contributors who have shaped the field, who have researched the topic extensively, or who have been successful as consultants to world-class teams. The next step was a review of the literature, to find articles that offer knowledge or applications, but which have meaning and immediate use and yet fit into what we know about sound psychological principles. Articles were examined for their coverage of diverse issues and diverse applications, ranging from motivation to violence and from goal setting to imagery rehearsal. The views and recommendations of coaches are represented here, and writings that offer ideas and challenges to coaches were also selected. Finally, a number of original articles were revised by their authors and other materials were edited to achieve the basic aim of the book.

The book is organized into three parts. Part I, *Concepts in Sports Psychology,* gives the reader a comprehensive overview of certain important basic topics. The involvement of psychology in sports comes from a traditional interest in areas such as personality, emotional states, motivation, and individual psychology and testing. Major contributions have been made in studies of the personality characteristics of competitive athletes, and through the understanding of successful athletes comes an understanding of how certain human qualities influence performance, not only of competitive athletes, but also of recreationally oriented participants in sports.

The articles included in Part I are either outstanding summaries of knowledge in the area or writings that offer an important perspective. This part is organized into five sections.

Principles in Sports Psychology. This section includes the best writings that define what sports psychology is, what its role involves, what contributions can be expected, and how psychological principles translate into performance. These articles draw conclusions from research or attempt to organize information into a coherent conceptual form.

Motivational Variables. This section approaches the concept of motivation from a variety of directions. The articles here introduce principles governing motivated performance, some conceptual theories converted to actual programs, measurement methods, and attempts to provide an understanding of what constitutes being motivated. Motivation is often a difficult subject to understand, mainly because motivation is an inferred state, not a directly observed one. What is observed is performance, from which a level of motivation is estimated.

Emotional States: Arousal. This section begins with the broad concept that both high and low arousal states influence performance. Further views are presented about the heightened arousal state, which can be labeled *stress*. Currently, the analysis is that some stress is useful for most individuals, that high stress may be sought by some individuals attracted to certain sports, but that undue stress can have detrimental effects.

Emotional States: Aggression. This section confronts the societal concern regarding the possible impact of aggression in sports. Do athletics contribute to increasing violence as athletic heroes model aggressive behavior? Are youngsters being trained in violent actions as they participate in sports that demand aggressivity? On the other hand, is it possible that sports permit the release of aggression and thereby serve as an outlet to reduce aggressive reactions? The articles in this section offer data and insights into these various issues. Although they will not provide simple answers, these articles should provoke useful thought and discussion.

Personality Variables. This section covers the topic that has perhaps been reported on and and studied the most in the history of sports psychology. What psychological or social profiles characterize a successful athlete? Are there different traits that predict success in different sports? Some scholarly summaries of the vast literature on personality are presented here. Also included are some important cautions about care that needs to be taken in drawing conclusions from test data.

Part II, *The Personal View,* calls attention to the most crucial factor in athletic performance, the athlete as a person. While Part I emphasizes the scientifically relevant data on performance, Part II provides a more personal tone, with the reflections of Olympic medalists and other champions on their outlooks as world-class athletes. In one sense, these reports of athletes' experiences are not truly psychology, since no attempts have been made to examine them in the manner of that discipline. In another sense, as these writings provide an experiential sharing, they represent a form of psychology-in-sports. Competing on a national or an international level is certainly a rare experience; winning a medal in such competition is even more unusual. Yet, there are some common threads that are important, even for those of us who are recreational participants, since exercise and sports of all levels share features and experiences in common. More and more, sports is being viewed in a more holistic fashion, which includes the importance of genetic or ability factors, training or learning experiences, and psychological or personalistic characteristics. Part II variously highlights different factors as they entered into the final peak achievements of champion performers.

Part III, *Applications,* is the result of a widespread search for materials that properly convey the applications of psychological approaches. Historically, psychology has undertaken the tasks of either psychological testing of athletes or laboratory studies of factors influencing performance. Deriving from the traditional strengths of the discipline, these have been the strongest areas of sports psychology. The weakest area has been the designing of programs for training competitors to perform at maximal levels and programs for skill acquisition. It is not surprising that the literature search for this part of the book turned up few articles. Nearly all of the articles here are previously unpublished papers or recent presentations. The lack of laboratory data on the programs described here should not discourage careful examination of the articles. In various ways, the programs have been field-tested, since they were designed with the special needs of current competitors in mind. Visuo-motor behavior, for example, seemed to produce field results at the 1976 Winter Olympic Games and was then verified under laboratory conditions. The applications included in this section illustrate similar, seemingly valid programs with the hope that careful research and laboratory evaluations will eventually follow.

Certain trends seem apparent in these programs. First, training, as opposed to therapy, is the orientation. The programs are designed to enhance strengths rather than to treat emotional conflicts. Second, these programs emphasize self-control or self-regulation models. This means that athletes are trained in techniques that can be self-initiated and permit better self-control over psychological and physical states. Third, some programs aim at improvement of performance without the traditional limitation that psychology should deal with psychological factors rather than physical performance factors. For example, imagery rehearsal training has been applied, not simply to improve psychological factors (such as confidence or aggressivity), but also to improve physical or behavioral factors (such as reaction time or the ability to achieve a smoother flow on the course). Finally, the programs all appear to reflect techniques developed on something more than trial-and-error experiences. Highly specific psychological and behavioral principles form the foundations out of which these applied methods arise. Without such foundations, applications would be risky at best. With a basis in psychological principles, athletes and coaches can be assured that psychological consultants are scientifically grounded and are not technicians blindly applying a formula.

Part III is organized into four sections.

Coaching Variables. The articles in this section are directed to coaches or are about coaching as a factor that influences performance. A coach's values, behaviors, standard-setting, and perceptions directly influence performance as heavily as the coach's instructions. These articles offer insights into and findings about the role of the coach as a performance variable.

Mental States. While preceding sections discuss emotional states, this section covers various applications related to mental states. The direct effects of mental states such as attentional (concentration) or thought processes are nearly an untapped area, and yet it is clear that lapses in concentration influence performance and that, similarly, thoughts can enhance or reduce tolerance of pain. The use of hypnosis as a device for understanding mental states is also an issue of application. Although brief, this section may be the most intriguing, as it presents discussions of little-understood mental states and methods.

Behavioral Strategies. This section offers a number of programs developed from behavioral psychology. These strategies emphasize stress management, visualization methods for skill enhancement, principles involved in slumps, use of thought control as a positive step, and biofeedback for assessing relaxation skills. This section presents many programs that have not been described in print before, but all have been field-tested with subjects at various levels of sports.

Issues in Sports Psychology. This section covers some crucial issues that must be addressed in any application of services. As the field of sports psychology expands and the number of programs grows, ethical considerations must be confronted. We are dealing with people and their lives. On the one side are the rules that should govern the actions of sports psychologists and anyone offering services in the field. On the other side are the expectations that a psychological consultant must be prepared to consider in order to serve effectively. Both topics are discussed in this section.

This book is the product of many persons' efforts in different ways. I gratefully acknowledge the efforts of the authors who submitted original articles or permitted reprinting their materials in this book. The very quality of the reputations of the authors is invaluable in certifying the value of these materials. Appreciation is also due to the journals, periodicals, and proceedings editors that gave permissions to reprint authors' works. Special thanks are due to Wayne Schotanus for his personal aid in the final process and to Dr. Robert Clayton for his interest and efforts on behalf of the manuscript. Unusual appreciation is offered to Joanne T. Moran for her extraordinary work, always effective and always there, and to Susan Suinn, who carefully read the manuscript. Finally, recognition should be given to the athletes, competitive and recreational, who revealed something of themselves for this book, sports, and sports psychology.

Richard M. Suinn
Fort Collins, Colorado

CONCEPTS IN SPORTS PSYCHOLOGY

Part One

PRINCIPLES IN SPORTS PSYCHOLOGY 3

Selected Psychological Considerations in Sport **4**
— *William P. Morgan*

Coaching Decisions and Research in Sport Psychology **19**
— *Bryant J. Cratty*

Psychology and Sports Performance: Principles and Applications **26**
— *Richard M. Suinn*

MOTIVATIONAL VARIABLES 37

Motivation in Sport **40**
— *Robert N. Singer*

Achievement Training **56**
— *Robert N. Singer and Robert Hilmer*

Using Applied Behavior Analysis for Altering Motivation **63**
— *Brent S. Rushall*

A Behavioral Assessment of Motivation **73**
— *David Youngblood and Richard M. Suinn*

What Can Psychology Offer to the Athlete and the Coach? **78**
— *Dorcas Susan Butt*

The Unconscious Fear of Success **86**
— *Bruce C. Ogilvie*

The Way of the Runner: An Examination of Motives for Running **90**
— *David Pargman*

Citizens' Racing Is More Than Fun **99**
— *Dick Taylor*

EMOTIONAL STATES: AROUSAL 102

Emotional Arousal and Motor Performance **103**
— *Joseph B. Oxendine*

On the Brink of Catastrophe **112**
— *Dorothy V. Harris*

Psychosocial Factors in Athletic Injuries: Development and Application of the Social and Athletic Readjustment Rating Scale (SARRS) **119**
— *Steven T. Bramwell, Minoru Masuda, Nathaniel N. Wagner, and Thomas H. Holmes*

EMOTIONAL STATES: AGGRESSION 124

Aggression and Sport: Two Theories **125**
— *Ruth E. Tandy and Joyce Laflin*

Violence and the Coach **129**
— *Robert Corran*

Effects of Viewing Aggressive Sports on the Hostility of Spectators **133**
— *Robert L. Arms, Gordon W. Russell, and Mark L. Sandilands*

PERSONALITY VARIABLES 143

Personality Dynamics and Sport **145**
— *William P. Morgan*

Psycho-Social Study of Outstanding Female Athletes **156**
— *Eva K. Balazs*

Sport Personality Assessment: A Methodological Re-examination **163**
— *J. Stuart Horsfall, A. Craig Fisher, and Harold H. Morris*

Kid Sports: A Den of Iniquity or a Land of Promise? **169**
— *Rainer Martens*

PRINCIPLES IN SPORTS PSYCHOLOGY

Dr. William P. Morgan has worked with U.S. Olympic and U.S. national rowing and wrestling teams, has been involved with world-class runners, and has served as a consultant for the Institute on Aerobics Research. He is professor and director of the Sport Psychology Laboratory at the University of Wisconsin. This article identifies five concepts that define and summarize the role of sports psychology. These concepts derive from Morgan's review of the research literature. Thus, the reader will be familiarized with basic concepts and also with actual findings from important sports psychology studies.[1]

Dr. Bryant J. Cratty has worked with the U.S. Figure Skating Coaches Association and with coaching programs in swimming and skiing at the Squaw Valley Olympic Training Center. As an athlete at UCLA, he lettered in water polo and gymnastics, and he has coached for over 15 years. He is the recipient of a commendation from the French Association for Sport Psychology and is professor of kinesiology at UCLA. This article shows the relationship between certain basic psychological principles, such as transfer of training, and their meaning for performance. The author focuses on the role of sports psychology in the design of practice workouts and in human relations.

Dr. Richard M. Suinn has been the team psychologist for the U.S. Olympic and U.S. national nordic ski teams and the U.S. Olympic biathlon team. In this capacity, he traveled with the teams to the 1976 Winter Olympic Games and provided on-site services. He has been a consultant to the U.S. national pentathlon team, the U.S. Marksmanship Unit, and the U.S. national alpine ski team, and he is a psychological coordinator for the U.S. women's track and field teams. He developed the term visuo-motor behavior rehearsal *for his method of using relaxation and imagery training for athletic performance. He is professor of psychology and head of the Department of Psychology at Colorado State University. This article gives an analysis of the component parts of performance and proposes that the selection of a psychological training method, such as biofeedback or imagery rehearsal, is determined primarily by how the performance problem is analyzed.*[2]

---

[1] *Other articles by Morgan appear on pages 145-155 and 297-305.*
[2] *Other articles by Suinn appear on pages 306-315 (in collaboration with David Youngblood) and 73-77.*

Selected Psychological Considerations in Sport

William P. Morgan

The primary purpose of this paper is to present a series of psychological concepts which hopefully can be employed in the daily work of sports medicine physicians, coaches, trainers, and physical educators. The concepts to be presented were derived through research conducted by my colleagues and myself over the past 8 yr. This work has involved rather diverse samples including young age group and university level athletes as well as world class performers. In addition, the role of physical fitness in the development and maintenance of mental health has been evaluated in normal middle-aged male and female subjects as well as emotionally disturbed children and adult psychiatric patients. It is on the basis of this background that the present paper has been constructed. Each concept is followed by a brief review of selected literature, a statement pertaining to implications, and a concluding commentary.

Concept 1. Athletes from Various Subgroups Differ on a Variety of Psychological States and Traits

This particular point has been demonstrated in numerous studies over the past two decades, and the interested reader will find detailed reviews in recent chapters by Kroll (1970) and Morgan (1972)[1] as well as earlier reviews by Cooper (1969) and Cofer and Johnson (1960). It has also been noted, however, that even though athletic subgroups have characteristic profiles (e.g., wrestlers are extroverted and marathoners are introverted), highly successful athletes from given subgroups may not fit the group stereotype.

Indeed, Morgan and Costill (1972) found that one of the most successful marathoners in the history of the Boston Marathon possessed a psychological profile which would normally characterize the world class wrestler (Morgan 1968). While such individual exceptions have been noted in most of our work, the fact remains that athletes from various subgroups differ on a variety of psychological

William P. Morgan. Selected psychological considerations in sport. *Research Quarterly* 45 (1974):374-390.

[1]See this article in a shortened version on pages 145-155. —Ed.

states and traits. This point of view has been reinforced by the recent investigation of Morgan and Johnson (1978) who studied the MMPI profiles of all entering freshmen athletes at the University of Wisconsin for the years 1960 through 1964. They also randomly selected 100 nonathletes from each of the five freshmen classes for comparative analysis. The athletes were found to differ from the non-athletes on various MMPI scales in each class. Furthermore, consistent differences were found between certain of the athletic subgroups, and these differences were generally replicated across the five classes. The complete findings of this investigation will be published in detail in another paper.

Implication. Athletes from various subgroups as well as athletes within a given subgroup possess different personality structures. Therefore, they presumably have different psychic needs and should be handled in a personalized fashion. Application of psychological methods to groups will likely be just as ineffective as the prescription of medication on a group basis; that is, personalized needs must be taken into account. A further implication is that those individuals responsible for an athlete's care and treatment must be thoroughly acquainted with the athlete's personal history. Also, any decision about treatment must be based upon input from as many sources (e.g., coach, trainer, physician, perhaps teammates, and the athlete himself) as possible. This point was reinforced during the 7th South East Asian Pacific (SEAP) Games on the occasion of Nor Azhar Hamid's record shattering performance of 2.12 m (6'11.5") in the high jump. In responding to his failure to break the 7-ft barrier, Nor stated, "My target was a gold for Singapore and this I achieved—seven feet was only a dream" (Ryan and Kovacic 1966).

While one might be tempted to classify Nor's reply as a rationalization, it might also be proposed that it reflects sound goal-setting judgment on his part. That is, he left the SEAP Games with a gold medal around his neck; the pride of his countrymen; the respect of his fellow athletes as well as his athletic contemporaries throughout the world; and, equally as important, had bolstered his confidence at achieving his "dream" of a 7-ft jump. Of course, had he jumped 7 ft in the 7th SEAP Games, Nor would have been forced to strive for greater heights in the forthcoming Asian Games. The danger inherent in such a feat would have been the possibility of peaking too early in preparation for the Montreal Olympics. It will be recalled that Pat Matzdorf of the University of Wisconsin set the World Record in the high jump during 1972, but he was unable to even qualify for the U.S. Olympic Team later that same year. My clinical impressions, as well as conversations with coaches, team physicians, trainers, and athletes suggest that Nor and Matzdorf possess comparable personality structures. Readers interested in the psychology of goal-setting and self-imposed limits in athletics should refer to the discussion of the "fear of success phobia" described by Ogilvie and Tutko (1966). Conversations with the team physician, physical therapist, and dentist who treated Nor the day of and the day following his record performance revealed a complex psychobiologic mosaic centering around the experience of pain. While professional confidence would be violated if the details were disclosed, it is fair and reasonable to simply say that Nor's performance was associated with a significant psychic component.

Conclusion. It is absolutely imperative that all persons concerned with the athlete be made aware of the need to manage athletes on a highly individualized basis. Put another way—you must know your athlete(s). Also, decisions concerning training intensity and duration as well as goal-setting should be based upon *objective* input from the coach, trainer, team physician, and consultants such as exercise physiologists, sport psychologists, or psychiatrists where possible.

Concept 2. High Level Performers in Athletics Are Characterized by Psychological Profiles Which Generally Distinguish Them from Lower Level Performers

This particular viewpoint is not supported by all exercise scientists working in the area of personality. This matter has been reviewed in detail by Morgan (1972) in a recently edited volume, however, and the data included in that discussion is sufficient to simply state here that the failure to find psychological differences between athletes of differing ability levels reflects methodological problems to a great extent. For example, most of the literature in this area reports on attempts to make distinctions with psychometric scales designed to measure psychological *traits* rather than *states*.[2] State theory would appear to be more efficacious from an intuitive standpoint, and recent research (Morgan et al. 1973; Morgan 1979) has provided support for the superiority of state theory. A second major problem with the majority of research in this field has been that inventions such as the 16 PF have been widely employed, but these scales do not contain psychometric correction scores. That is, the bulk of the null findings in this area of study should be viewed cautiously since investigators have historically failed to employ safeguards such as (1) lie, (2) guess, or (3) random response scales. At any rate, the reader should understand that the author's position here has not been met with widespread agreement.

In one of our first investigations it was noted that wrestlers participating in the 1966 World Championships were characterized by extroversion and stability when taken as a single composite (Morgan 1968). When the Canadian, South African, and U.S. wrestlers were examined separately, however, a different picture emerged. In these tests, the South African contingent scored significantly higher on the neuroticism-stability dimension. This may well have been a cultural factor, however, and one should be extremely sensitive to cultural differences when employing psychometric devices.

This investigation supported the viewpoint that high-level competitors are both extroverted and stable. Furthermore, it seems fair to state that stability is a prerequisite for high-level performance. It was also found in this study of high-level wrestlers that extroversion was significantly correlated with success as measured by final placement in the 1966 World Tournament. More recently, it has been demonstrated that extroversion is not a requirement for success in all sports. For example, Morgan and Costill (1972) have reported that marathoners score low on extroversion and are generally characterized as tending toward introversion. This finding is illustrated in Figure 1 which graphically depicts marathoners as introverts and wrestlers as extroverts. Nevertheless, it will be noted that both of these athletic subgroups are still characterized by stability.

Reinforcement of concept 1 seems appropriate here since we are talking about group averages and profiles. While it is safe to generalize and state that world-class marathoners are introverted and world-class wrestlers are extroverted, one must not lose sight of the importance of individuality. For example, one of the best marathoners we have evaluated was an extrovert; and, conversely, one of the best wrestlers tested was found to be an introvert. Extroversion is also correlated with a variety of other factors which are important in the athletic domain. For example, Ryan and Kovacic (1966) have found that contact athletes have higher pain tolerance than noncontact athletes, who in turn have higher pain tolerance than nonathletes. Ryan and Foster (1967) later demonstrated that such groups could be distinguished on the basis of perceptual style (augmentation-reduction) as well. Further, pain tolerance, an important factor in many sports, is high in the extrovert and low in the introvert. As would be expected, contact athletes score high on extroversion, whereas, noncontact athletes

---

[2]See the article by Horsfall, Fisher, and Morris on pages 163-168. —Ed.

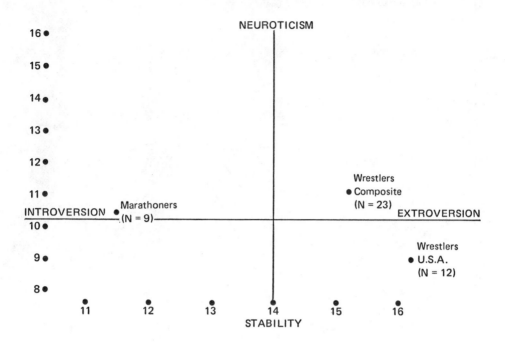

Figure 1. Extroversion-introversion and neuroticism-stability for world-class wrestlers and marathoners as measured by the Eysenck Personality Inventory

score lower on this factor (Morgan and Johnson 1978). The reader is referred to Eysenck and Eysenck (1962) for a thorough discussion of extroversion-introversion and neuroticism-stability as well as the method of measuring these two psychological traits.

The 1972 Olympic Freestyle Wrestling Team was by far the most outstanding team ever fielded by the United States. They won a total of 6 Olympic medals among the 10 participants. It was possible to test these 10 Olympians as well as the 30 athletes who were eliminated in the final trials. Psychological testing of the 40 aspirants for the team was performed prior to the final selection process which consisted of round-robin wrestle-offs in each weight class. The results of this investigation (Morgan et al. 1973) are summarized in part in Figure 2. It should be noted that the Olympians (successful group) scored lower on tension, depression, fatigue (psychic), and confusion and higher on psychic vigor. A substantial number of the unsuccessful wrestlers also exhibited high lie scores; therefore, L-corrected profiles are presented as well. The correction revealed that suppression of anger scores occurred for the unsuccessful athletes, although none of the remaining differences were of significance. The differences in tension, vigor, and confusion were regarded as significant, and it should be noted that the profiles for successful and unsuccessful wrestlers alike differed markedly from the published norms for college males. The important point here is that the Olympians and unsuccessful athletes differed on a number of psychological variables.

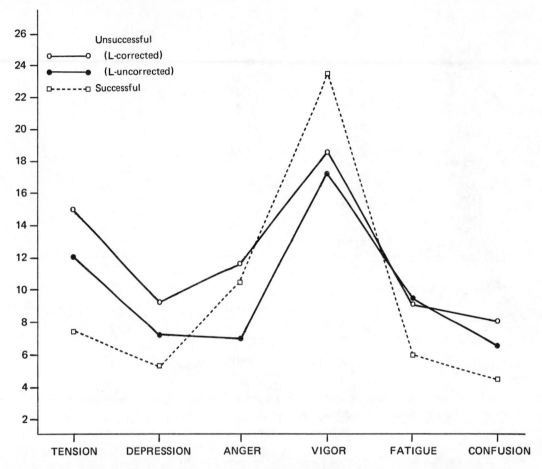

Figure 2. Psychological characterization of Olympic wrestlers (successful) and wrestlers who failed to make the team (unsuccessful) as measured by the Profile of Mood Scores. Raw scores are plotted on the ordinate, and the unsuccessful group's profile is presented both with and without an L-score correction.

Throughout all of this research one question remains unanswered. Are the differences between (1) athletic subgroups, (2) high- and low-level performers, and (3) athletes and nonathletes the result of athletic participation or did these differences exist from the outset? Put another way, are these group differences due to heredity or environment? This is an important question since it bears on the matter of selection and prediction. This author has previously proposed that these differences can be largely attributed to genetic factors (Morgan 1972; Morgan 1974a). Space does not permit an exhaustive discussion of this topic, and the reader is therefore referred to the original presentation of this hypothesis (Morgan 1972). It should be stated, however, that this viewpoint is based upon theoretical considerations to a greater extent than empirical evidence. One pioneering study has been performed by Lukehart (1969) who tested a group of 12- and 13-yr-old boys prior to their decision to become members of an organized sports team. The findings of Lukehart's study (Lukehart 1969) are portrayed graphically in Figure 3. It will be noted that those boys who elected to join the team (American football) were significantly more extroverted than those who elected not to participate (nonathletes). Also, he retested both groups following the first year of competition and found these differences to have remained unchanged. It will be noted, however, that these athletes and non-athletes did not differ on neuroticism at either point. It would be predicted from Eysenckian theory that the athletes would be more extroverted than the nonathletes from the outset of their careers, and athletic competition would not be expected to modify this trait. This, of course, is precisely what Lukehart (1969) found to be the case. The work of Yanada and Hirata (1970) offers additional support for the genetic or gravitation-mortality model. They found that athletes who dropped out of their sport clubs at the University of Tokyo were more depressed, neurotic, and hypomanic than those who remained. Hence, selective mortality (drop outs) also supports the genetic argument.

Implication. Since athletes of differing ability levels are characterized by different psychological profiles it would seem appropriate to pursue at least two avenues in attempting to counsel and advise athletes regarding sport adoption as well as in selecting and developing national teams. First, one might attempt through screening to identify athletes with desired profiles; and, second, behavior modification might then be attempted where appropriate. Of course, an individual must be careful that the self-fulfilling prophecy is not permitted to operate in the first instance, and it should be emphasized that no attempt at behavior modification should be attempted by persons without appropriate training in clinical psychology or psychiatry. Also, any decision regarding team selection or attempts at behavior modification should be arrived at on the basis of input from the athlete, coach, trainer, team physician, and other appropriate consultants where necessary.

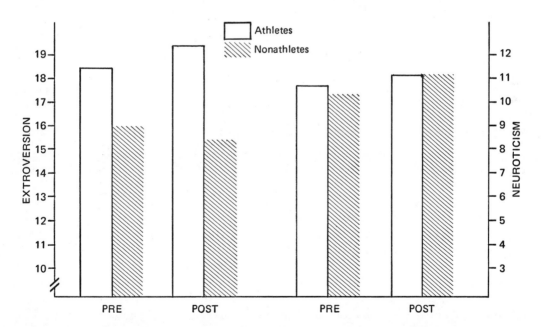

Figure 3. Extroversion-introversion and neuroticism-stability of young males who elect to become involved in organized football and those who elect to be nonathletes as measured by the Junior Eysenck Personality Inventory

Based upon a discriminant function analysis of successful and unsuccessful oarsmen representing five separate classes at the University of Wisconsin, Morgan and Johnson (in preparation) recently proposed a mental health model for use in predicting success in oarsmen. This model was tested out by Morgan (1979) in a recent investigation. They tested the 60 candidates for the 1974 National Rowing Team; and, employing the above model (Morgan 1979), they attempted to predict who would make the team. Their predictions were accurate in 70% of the cases. This, of course, means that psychological states and traits played an important role in predicting whether or not a given oarsman would make the team. It should be emphasized, however, that this particular model was far from perfect, having an error rate of 30%. In other words, one would certainly not want to rely on psychological data alone in the selection of athletes. While this point probably seems rather obvious, it is not accepted by all contemporary sport psychologists.

Conclusion.   Successful athletes tend to be extroverted with the major exception to this generalization focused around the case of the marathoner and long distance runner who tend toward introversion. Outstanding athletes possess stable personalities in terms of the neuroticism-stability dimension, and it is unlikely that unstable athletes can perform at a high level on a consistent basis. In behavioral-state terms the successful athlete tends to be less anxious, depressed, and confused as well as possessing more psychic vigor than the unsuccessful athlete. On the other hand, we have consistently observed world-class wrestlers, oarsmen, and marathoners who were anxious, depressed, confused, and lacked psychic vigor. Therefore, the generalization being advanced is made with reservation. It is also noteworthy that athletes with "ideal" profiles frequently do not win berths on national and Olympic teams. This is understandable in view of the fact that 10 or 15 individuals are frequently selected from a sample of 100 or 200 aspirants.

Concept 3. Attempts to Elevate Anxiety ("Psych-up") and Reduce Tension States Should Be Used Cautiously and Employed on a Personalized Basis

While coaches frequently employ "pep talks" as a means of "energizing" their teams, there is little or no evidence to suggest that such practices are of any value in the competitive situation. There is, however, considerable evidence from research studies involving the matter of anxiety states and motor behavior of both a simple and complex nature. Martens (1973) has reviewed this literature in detail, and it seems that the evidence is equivocal. That is, there is evidence which suggests that anxiety plays a role in performance of motor skills, but there is an equal amount of evidence suggesting it does not.

Actually, this issue is not unique to sport. It represents a continuing controversy in psychology which has been waged for at least the past 20 yr. There are essentially two theoretical views which have been advanced. The first is the Drive Theory which holds that increases in drive level are thought to be linearly associated with increments in performance. Drive level can be translated to mean anxiety, hence, as anxiety increases one would predict increases in performance. A second theoretical position, and one which tends to conform more consistently with everyday experience, is the inverted-U concept or Yerkes-Dodson Law. This position holds that increases in anxiety will be followed by increments in performance up to a given point, following which further increases in anxiety will result in performance decrements.

While it is difficult to state with certainty which of these viewpoints coaches generally subscribe to, it is fairly clear that a large proportion of coaches employ a variety of techniques (e.g., pep talks, punishment, threats, etc.) in their attempt to increase tension states ("psych-up") in their athletes.

A thorough review of this matter by Martens (1973) reveals that neither the drive theory nor the inverted-U concept is supported by an impressive body of evidence. We have conducted a series of investigations bearing on this question, and they will be reviewed to further elucidate the role of anxiety in sport.

First of all, it should be pointed out that exercise *per se* has the effect of reducing state anxiety. Therefore, any benefit to be accrued from elevating precompetitive anxiety states would presumably be short lived since subsequent physical activity would reduce anxiety. This viewpoint is consonant with the common observation that precompetitive tension in the form of nervousness, stomach upset, excretory frequency, dry oral mucosa, and so on, passes almost immediately upon the initiation of competition. Again, it should be kept in mind that activity alone is capable of reducing anxiety. This point is illustrated in Figure 4. It will be noted that anxiety increased slightly following exercise in these 40 adult males (Morgan 1973). A reduction in state anxiety was observed, however, following 30 min of recovery which also included a shower. Hence, the shower following exercise may have played a role in the associated anxiety decrement. This possibility was not substantiated, however, in a subsequent investigation involving 15 adult males who completed psychological inventories immediately before, immediately following, and 30 min following vigorous physical activity. It will be noted in Figure 5 that this group experienced significant decrements in anxiety immediately following exercise as well as after the shower. These findings have been replicated in a series of investigations, and it is now fairly certain that vigorous exercise *per se* will reduce state anxiety in high-anxious as well as normal adult males and females (Morgan 1973).

Of course, there are many factors which might regulate precompetitive anxiety states. For example, the practice of "making weight" which is so common among certain athletes, especially wrestlers, has been found to decrease state anxiety. This is illustrated in Figure 6 where it will be seen that a 4% loss of body weight was associated with a significant decrement in anxiety (Morgan 1968).

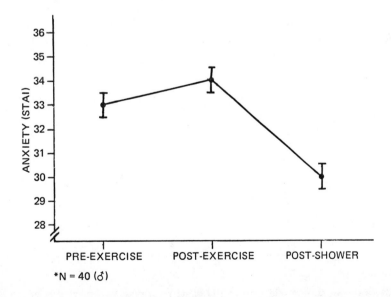

Figure 4. State anxiety of 40 adult males (1) prior to, (2) immediately following, and (3) 30 min following a vigorous 45 min workout as measured by the Spielberger scale

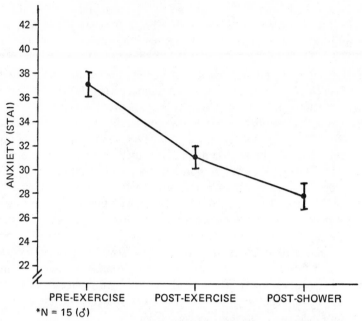

*N = 15 (♂)

Figure 5. State anxiety of 15 adult males (1) prior to, (2) immediately following, and (3) 30 min following a vigorous 15 min workout as measured by the Spielberger scale

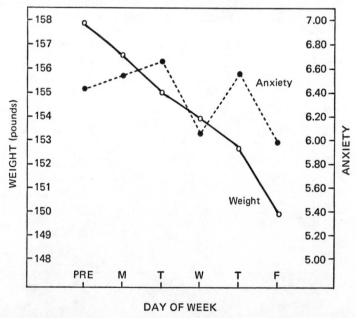

DAY OF WEEK

Figure 6. Alteration in state anxiety and body weight during a 1 wk period in which college wrestlers lost 4% of their body weight. State anxiety was assessed with alternate forms of the IPAT 8-Parallel-Anxiety-Battery.

In another study designed to evaluate state anxiety of college wrestlers prior to both difficult and easy matches, it was found that significant *decrements* in anxiety took place 1 hr prior to competition as contrasted with corresponding control levels (Morgan 1970*a*). Furthermore, the state anxiety level of the opposing team was also assessed prior to the difficult match, and they were found to possess a similar level of anxiety. These findings are graphically portrayed in Figure 7. It is emphasized that the anxiety or drive state of the winners did not differ from that of the losers when assessed precompetitively.

In a somewhat related investigation Langer (1966) assessed the anxiety of a college football team approximately 3 hr prior to each of 10 football games as well as during preseason workouts. Langer also employed coaches' ratings of performance for each game. He found that a shift in anxiety from a low score to a "more moderate game day score" was essential for good performance. It is also important to note that Langer found large fluctuations in pre-game anxiety to be detrimental to performance. In other words, the better football players were able to "work themselves up" to a consistent level for each competition. In view of the fact that team success did not covary with anxiety, being "up" or "down" for a given game was apparently of no practical value.

More recently, Moran and Hammer (1974) evaluated the state anxiety of wrestlers from four different colleges (1) at the beginning of the season as well as (2) 4 hr before, (3) 1 hr before, and (4) immediately following competition in a state tournament. The findings are illustrated in Figure 8. It

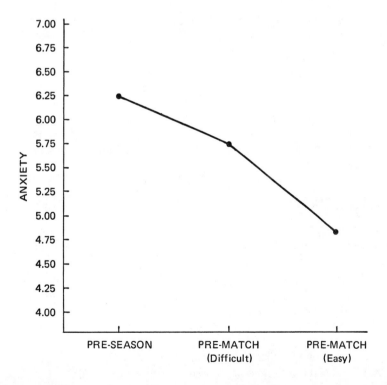

Figure 7. State anxiety of college wrestlers (1) in preseason, (2) prior to a difficult match, and (3) prior to an easy match as measured with alternate forms of the IPAT 8-Parallel-Anxiety-Battery

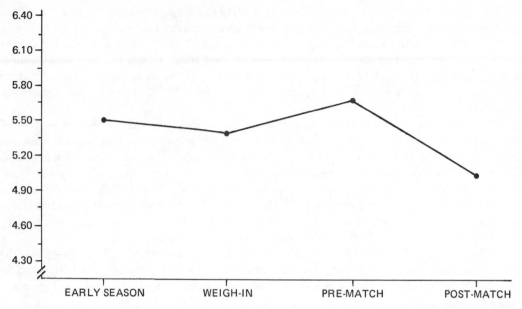

Figure 8. State anxiety of wrestlers (1) at the beginning of the season as well as (2) 4 hr before, (3) 1 hr before, and (4) immediately following competition as measured with alternate forms of the IPAT 8-Parallel-Anxiety-Battery

will be noted that the overall anxiety level was not altered between the early season and weigh-in period (4 hr prior to competition) which took place some 2 mo later. Hence, 2 mo of training and dual competition apparently did not alter the state anxiety of these athletes. It will be noted, however, that anxiety increased significantly 1 hr prior to competition which is in direct disagreement with the earlier findings presented in Figure 7.

Of course, the former example represented dual competition during the regular season, whereas, the latter was associated with round-robin competition in a state tournament. Such conditions are obviously inherently different in a variety of ways. It will be noted in Figure 8 that a significant reduction in anxiety took place postcompetitively. It should also be emphasized that the data points in Figure 8 represent the average for the four teams. The data were expressed in this fashion because the four teams *did not differ at any point!* That is, the preseason, pretournament, and posttournament anxiety levels of the first, second, third, and fourth place teams did not differ. Hence, anxiety did not apparently play a role in success or failure. A similar finding was noted in an earlier study (Morgan 1970*a*). Furthermore, if the data are grouped according to high- and low-anxious athletes disregarding team affiliation, the same picture emerges. That is, anxiety does not appear to be a critical factor.

Referring back to Figure 2 which illustrates the profiles of Olympic wrestlers as well as wrestlers who failed to make the team, it will be noted that the successful wrestlers scored lower than the unsuccessful wrestlers on the tension-anxiety variable prior to competition. Both groups also scored somewhat lower than the published norm under these precompetitive conditions. This finding suggests that, if anything, success is dependent upon *low state anxiety*. A recent investigation involving national calibre oarsmen generally supported these findings (Morgan 1979).

Implication. The practice of attempting to increase performance levels by altering precompetition anxiety states seems to be a questionable practice; and, at best, such attempts must be made cautiously and on an individualized basis.

Conclusion. Anxiety levels of winning and losing teams do not seem to differ either before or following competition. Physical activity *per se* has a direct influence on reducing anxiety, and therefore successful attempts to elevate anxiety precompetitively would presumably be reversed very rapidly once vigorous physical activity was initiated.

Concept 4. Mental Health Plays an Important Role in Athletic Success, and It Is Quite Likely That "Emotional First Aid" Following Competition Is Just as Important as Physical First Aid

Coaches have historically been concerned with the psychological preparation of their athletes for competition. This preparation has frequently taken the form of pep talks and various other techniques thought to possess motivational value. The previous section raises the question of whether such techniques are of any value whatsoever, and existing evidence implies that the answer is no. On the other hand, a neglected, and probably far more important consideration, is the athlete's postcompetitive psychological state. While coaches have historically attempted to get their teams "up" for competition, there is little published evidence to suggest they attempt to bring them "down." On the other hand, there is some evidence which suggests that win or lose athletes return to normal psychological levels postcompetitively (see Figure 8).

At any rate, it is reasonably clear that strains, sprains, and fractures are treated immediately or shortly following their occurrence, whereas, months may pass before any attention is given to serious psychological problems (Carmen, Zerman, and Blaine 1968; Pierce 1969). Furthermore, certain psychological ailments common among athletes are never even detected much less treated. As with the case of physical injuries, preventive measures and early detection procedures should be employed. It is especially important that team physicians, coaches, and trainers "sensitize" themselves to the potential existence of psychological problems. Dismissing an athlete's problem as a "head problem" does not solve anything. It should also be noted that "emotional first aid" should not be limited to the athlete who experiences obvious failure. Indeed, the mediocre athlete who suddenly is catapulted into the spotlight following a record-setting performance is probably in need of more scrutiny than the occasional failure. The reader interested in gaining additional insights into the matter will find the papers by Carmen, Zerman, and Blaine (1968), Little (1969), and Pierce (1969) to be of particular value.

Implication. Athletes should not be left to their own psychological resources following either successful or unsuccessful competition. The coach should talk with his athletes following competition with the aim of ego strengthening in the case of traumatic failure as well as counsel and "insulation" following record-setting performances. The athlete should not be left to crawl off and nurse his physical wounds, nor should he be expected to completely manage his psychological trauma either. Indeed, he is probably less likely to possess the resources necessary for adaptation in the latter situation.

Conclusion. Coaches should pay careful attention to the postcompetitive psychological condition of their athletes. It is also reasonable to state that psychological stability is a prerequisite for consistent success in the high-level athlete. Successful athletes who are *truly* neurotic are the exception rather than the rule.

Concept 5. There Is Frequently a Lack of Congruence between the Athlete's Conscious and Unconscious Motives

It is not uncommon for an athlete to set a record and subsequently be unable to replicate his performance or even come close to it for that matter. This sometimes occurs despite the fact that the athlete verbalizes his willingness to "do anything" in order to achieve his previous level of performance. There is, however, frequently a lack of congruence between the athlete's conscious verbalization and his unconscious motivation.[3] This particular point of view is illustrated in one of our recent hypnoanalytic cases which will now be summarized (Morgan, Nagle, and Ryan 1972).

The athlete was a 21-yr-old college distance runner at the time of the evaluation. He had previously established a school and conference record in the 3-mi run, but he was unable to match this performance or even come close. Indeed, he was frequently not even capable of completing races. The athlete's coach interpreted his failure as reflecting a lack of desire and willingness to "put out." The athlete on the other hand felt the coach was not offering him the necessary instruction to regain his previous performance high. At any rate, the runner was willing "to do anything" to perform well once more. The runner was examined by the team physician and found to be perfectly healthy. There was no medical explanation for his poor performance. He was next examined by an exercise physiologist and found to have a maximal aerobic power of 70 ml/kg which compares favorably with the aerobic power of distance runners and marathoners described by Morgan and Costill (1972).

The runner's previous record performance in the 3-mi run was calculated to have taken place at about 96% of his maximal aerobic power. While others have noted that runners can work at such a percent of maximum in similar races, such a performance across a 3-mi course is obviously demanding to say the least. The runner's psychological profile suggested normality in all respects. He, however, possessed the characteristics of the world-class wrestler to a greater extent than those of a distance runner. He was extroverted rather than introverted and scored high on hypnotizability. Subsequent sessions revealed that he was capable of entering a deep trance during which he could age-regress to earlier periods.

Under deep hypnosis the athlete was age-regressed to the day of his championship performance and requested to describe the entire race. He was able to visualize this event quite clearly, and after a very short period he began to experience "pain in the side" as well as respiratory discomfort. He explained that he could not continue the race because of the intense pain. It should be recalled that he was running at about 96% of his maximum capacity. Just as he began to terminate the race a group of his teammates appeared and exhorted him to "kick." He explained that he could not let his teammates down, and he was therefore able to continue and the pain was no longer noticeable. The pain returned later in the race, however, and he again decided to quit the race only to experience a double-visual hallucination on the horizon consisting of two television sets. He was depicted on one set as if the race were being televised (it was not), and his parents appeared on the other monitor. They, in turn, were thought to be viewing his run on their own television set. He was unable to carry out his plan to stop because of these "complications" and within a short period of time he felt as though he was in a vacuum. He could not feel any wind resistance, nor could he sense his feet hitting the ground. He described the conclusion of the race in which his chest hit the tape as being a very "weird" experience.

---

[3] See the article by Ogilvie on pages 86-89. —Ed.

The runner elected to have posthypnotic recall for all of these events during the waking state. When asked if he cared to continue with the program of "insight training" he responded that he would prefer to give the matter some additional thought. He subsequently elected not to continue "insight training" (hypnoanalysis). Presumably he had gained the necessary insight he lacked earlier. His running did not improve, but his understanding of his inability to replicate his previous record apparently did. That is, the record race was extremely painful, and he had apparently repressed this experience from his conscious awareness. This repressed perceptual experience was "replayed" during hypnosis, however, resulting in the athlete electing not to continue delving into the matter. Of course, it would have been quite simple to construct "cognitive strategies" during hypnosis with an aim toward dissociation of pain during running competition in the waking state. Since the athlete did not wish to pursue such avenues, however, "the case was closed."

Implication. A significant discrepancy may exist between an athlete's stated desires and his "actual" (unconscious) attitude toward record-setting performance.

Conclusion. The coach and physician must look beyond the athlete's past performances and current conscious verbalizations. The essence of "failure" is best understood within a psychobiological framework which relies upon such specialties as sports medicine, exercise physiology, and sport psychology.

Summary

Five concepts to be kept in mind while attempting to understand the psychological determination of athletes and their preparation for competition have been presented. These concepts have been specified and elaborated upon, implications delineated, and conclusions presented. The position which has been outlined emphasized the totality of man and the necessity of coach, trainer, psychologist, physiologist, and physician working in concert as a multidisciplinary team.

References

Carmen, L. R.; Zerman, J. L.; and Blaine, G. B., Jr. 1968. Use of the Harvard psychiatric service by athletes and nonathletes. *Mental Hygiene* 52:134-137.

Cofer, C. N., and Johnson, W. R. 1960. Personality dynamics in relation to exercise and sports. In *Science and medicine of exercise and sport,* ed. W. R. Johnson, pp. 525-529. New York: Harper.

Cooper, L. 1969. Athletics, activity and personality: A review of the literature. *Research Quarterly* 40:17-22.

Eysenck, H. J., and Eysenck, S. B. G. 1962. *Manual for the Eysenck Personality Inventory.* San Diego: Educational and Industrial Testing Service.

Kroll, W. 1970. Personality assessments of athletes. In *Psychology of motor learning,* ed. L. E. Smith, pp. 349-367. Chicago: Athletic Institute.

Langer, P. 1966. Varsity football performance. *Perceptual and Motor Skills* 23:1191-1199.

Little, J. C. 1969. The athlete's neurosis—A deprivation crisis. *Acta Psychiatrica Scandinavica* 45:187-197.

Lukehart, R. 1969. The effect of a season of interscholastic football on the personality of junior high-scool males. *Abstracts of the American Association of Health, Physical Education and Recreation* 5:122.

Martens, R. 1973. Trait and state anxiety. In *Ergogenic aids and muscular performance,* ed. W. P. Morgan. New York: Academic Press.

Morgan, W. P. 1968. Personality characteristics of wrestlers participating in the world championships. *Journal of Sports Medicine and Physical Fitness* 8:212-216.

——.1970*a*. Pre-match anxiety in a group of college wrestlers. *International Journal of Sport Psychology* 1:7-13.

——.1970*b*. Psychological effect of weight reduction in the college wrestler. *Medicine and Science in Sports* 2:24-27.

——.1972. Sport psychology. In *The psychomotor domain,* ed. R. N. Singer. Philadelphia: Lea and Febiger.

——.1973. Influence of acute physical activity on state anxiety. *NCPEAM Proceedings* 76:113.

——.1974*a*. Exercise and mental disorders. In *Sports medicine,* ed. A. J. Ryan and F. L. Allman, Jr. New York: Academic Press.

Morgan, W. P. 1974*b*. Psychology of sports competition. In *Sports medicine,* ed. A. J. Ryan and F. L. Allman, Jr. New York: Academic Press.

Morgan, W. P. 1979. Prediction of performance in athletes. In *Coach, Athlete, and the Sport Psychologist,* ed. P. Klavora and J. Daniel. Toronto: University of Toronto School of Physical and Health Education, Publications Division.

Morgan, W. P., and Costill, D. L. 1972. Psychological characteristics of the marathon runner. *Journal of Sports Medicine and Physical Fitness* 12:42-46.

Morgan, W. P., and Hammer, W. M. 1974. Influence of competitive wrestling upon state anxiety. *Medicine and Science in Sports* 6:58-61.

Morgan, W. P., and Johnson, R. W. 1978. Personality characteristics of successful and unsuccessful oarsmen. *International Journal of Sports Psychology* 9:119-133.

Morgan, W. P.; Nagle, F. J.; and Ryan, A. J. 1972. Psychobiologic interpretation of "failure" in sport. American College of Sports Medicine, Philadelphia.

Morgan, W. P.; Nagle, F. J.; Serfass, R. C.; Alexander, J. F.; and Hellickson, R. O. 1973. Psychobiologic correlates of success in candidates for the 1972 Olympic wrestling team. American College of Sports Medicine, Seattle.

Ogilvie, B. C., and Tutko, T. A. 1966. *Problem athletes and how to handle them.* London: Pelham.

Pierce, R. A. 1969. Athletes in psychotherapy: How many, how come? *Journal of American College Health Association* 17:244-249.

Ryan, E. D., and Foster, R. L. 1967. Athletic participation and perceptual augmentation and reduction. *Journal of Personality and Social Psychology* 6:472-476.

Ryan, E. D., and Kovacic, C. R. 1966. Pain tolerance and athletic participation. *Perceptual and Motor Skills* 22:383-390.

Yanada, H., and Hirata, H. 1970. Personality traits of students who dropped out of their athletic clubs. *Proceedings of the College of Physical Education,* University of Tokyo, no. 5.

Ziegelaar, R. 1973. Golden Nor delights the fans. *The Straits Times,* 3 September, p. 24

Coaching Decisions and Research in Sport Psychology

Bryant J. Cratty

It is not unusual to hear coaches in various sports complain that they fail to ascertain just how research in psychology can help them work with their teams. This irritation has been echoed for years by educators from a number of disciplines, many of whom also fail to perceive the existence of helpful bonds between principles derived from research and their daily interactions with classroom children.

Researchers might give several answers to the practitioner requesting exact guidelines. Some might turn their heads away and mutter that basic research, after all, is the most useful kind since it can, and frequently does, lead toward the solution of a multitude of problems. Another scholar emerging from his laboratory might point out the differences between basic and applied research and grant the practitioner at least a portion of his time to pursue applied problems confronting the coach.

Little of this, however, is helpful to the mentors of football, basketball, and swimming. They are confronted with frequent problems, and are forced to make a number of decisions when planning their seasons, conducting practice sessions, and while competition is underway. As a game or meet progresses the coach must not only make qualitative and quantitative judgments concerning his athletes' group performance but must also evaluate the quality of the hundreds of decisions each of his players may be called upon to make. Player and coaching decisions must be made rapidly and are influenced by both the unique traits of individual athletes and by the specifics of sports situations. It is little wonder that a coach declares, "I found little in a textbook of the psychology of physical activity that was of help to me in my coaching," when he encounters only abstract theorizing and/or statements concerned with the obvious, often caged in psychological jargon.

It is believed, however, that a thorough analysis of just how research in sports psychology may affect, aid, or otherwise influence the decisions of coaches depends first upon deciding what types of decisions coaches must make. A second step is to explore the degree to which various types of clinical and experimental research has or has not provided information leading toward more productive decision-making behavior. It is also important to keep in mind that many things one does on an athletic field (or in a classroom) need not be substantiated by reference to a research article in some

Bryant J. Cratty. Coaching decisions and research in sport psychology. *Quest* 13 (January 1970):46-53.

obscure journal . . . some things just "make sense." At the same time all research findings do not necessarily need to point toward the solution of practical problems.[1]

The decision-making behavior of coaches may be placed upon a time continuum. For example, decisions about the planning of a season and practice periods might be placed in one category, while judgements arising from practice situations and games could form a second. A third category could contain the decisions made during the game at the time of its evaluation.

Another categorical arrangement could arrange decisions at various levels. One type could be compiled dealing with the mechanics of conditioning, practice schedules, intensity of workouts, etc.; a second, with decisions centering around inter-personal relationships between the team members themselves, and the coach and his charges. Another part of the latter category could involve judgments of team strategy, personnel selections, and the like.

In the following pages, decisions of several kinds as well as the quality and quantity of the available research affording reasonable guidelines within each sub-division are analyzed. Two types of decisions will be dealt with, each containing two sub-divisions. Neither of the categories is mutually exclusive; the arrangement was formulated for convenience and clarity.

In outline form, these decisions appear as follows:

I.   Decisions about Training Sessions
    A.   Decisions on the arrangement of practice to elicit optimum performance in complex skills.
    B.   Decisions to encourage maximum effort leading toward the assumption of strength and/or endurance qualities.
II.   Decisions about Inter-Personal Relations
    A.   Decisions between the coach and his players, dealing with individual differences in personality traits and motivational values.
    B.   Decisions to encourage optimum group effort by manipulating human relations between the team members.

PRACTICE SESSIONS

It is believed that tne greatest help afforded by the experimental literature revolves around information outlining helpful ways to elicit maximum skill. The research literature on transfer of training, massing versus distributing practice sessions, and the like has been summarized by several writers within the past five years and reasonably sound guidelines have been formulated (Cratty 1967; Knapp 1964; Oxendine 1968; Singer 1968). For example, material seems to indicate that the coach may impede motor learning by scheduling practice sessions too close together in time, and/or by over-teaching, thus not permitting a skill to be assimilated.

Research on transfer indicates that while so-called coordination drills, though not directly resembling the athletic skill(s) they are designed to improve, may indeed create some kind of general motor learning set. To optimize transfer from practice to competition, one should also attempt to exactly replicate game conditions in practice.[2]

---

[1] The writer was once asked to speak upon the topic, "The Helpful Nature of Useless Research."

[2] Sport psychologists in Europe have at times gone to the extreme of broadcasting crowd noises into practice sessions to accustom athletes to the stressful effects of a hostile audience. [See also the article by Suinn on pages 26-36. —Ed.]

Sagacious coaches familiar with the literature on transfer, or perhaps just acting instinctively, thus attempt to replicate all the possible competitive circumstances. A waterpolo coach will drill his team in the 20 or 30 ways in which a player may legally proceed across the tank with a ball. A track coach may withhold his guidance for a period of time from his top athletes who may later find themselves truly isolated in top level Olympic or regional competitions; while a swimming coach may discard the rhythmic interval training for simulated races in which swimmers are asked to catch up, or avoid being caught by a teammate (Vanek and Cratty 1969).

To elicit maximum effort from athletes, the literature indicates that practice sessions should first of all be as interesting and novel as possible, perhaps varying in content from day to day. More mature athletes may be further motivated by planning their own workouts. Furthermore, research indicates that if the athletes obtain exact knowledge concerning the intensity and duration of a practice session they are less likely to slow down on their initial efforts; if no or incorrect information is afforded, they are likely to save themselves for the most rigorous practice imaginable (Cratty 1967).

Research findings which might aid the coach in formulating more productive practice sessions are, however, frequently contradictory. Thus, the coach must formulate helpful operating principles by inserting his intellect between the research findings and the situation in which he finds himself. Furthermore, such data are often based upon the performance and learning of laboratory tasks having little resemblance to athletic skills. On the other hand, to ignore the principles of transfer of training which have been clearly formulated in innumerable studies, to induce boredom in athletes by over-teaching, or to deceive today's intelligent and sophisticated athletes concerning the nature and purposes of their workout are indicative of a coaching "mind" probably leading to competitive efforts somewhat short of success.

HUMAN RELATIONSHIPS

Far less definitive are research findings affording guidelines when working with the unique personalities and inter-personal relationships on athletic teams. By their nature, people in groups are difficult to study. Innumerable variables, including childhood experiences and motivational factors beyond the control of the researcher, contaminate many so-called scientific investigations of the interaction of two or more individuals performing some kind of motor task. Within this study area, far fewer investigations are found than in those dealing with more measurable parameters present as a single individual sits alone before a pursuit rotor in a laboratory.

The coach may also make decisions about human relations; for example, the placement in adjacent positions of players he feels may "work together" well, the selection of a team captain, and the arrangement of levels of competition. At another level, he may make rather subtle decisions concerning how to deal with a "difficult to coach" athlete or how to speak when attempting to settle differences arising between players on his team.[3] Furthermore, in the future, coaches of teams commanding large budgets may have to decide whether or not to employ a full- or part-time psychologist to evaluate and to clinically deal with athletes.

It is believed that present studies of the personalities of groups of athletes are of relatively little help to the coach. Many have employed extremely limited samples, and at times, the assessment

[3] An interesting narrative of the manner in which a psychologist dealt with an Olympic Team is found in Vanek and Cratty (1969, Chap. 11, "Olympics, Mexico City, 1968").

methods and evaluative instruments have been poor. In general, this research illustrates that the personalities of athletes are highly variable and much of the time resemble the personalities of populations of nonathletes. Only when one delves within specific sports and often within sub-divisions of a sport (i.e., sprinters within a track team) are significant personality trait differences uncovered.

When the personality trait scores of large groups of athletes are compared to those of nonathletes, however, few differences in mean scores emerge. At the same time, it is difficult to determine whether or not: the personality traits of athletes are molded by the culture in which they compete, the sport has somehow contributed to the personal characteristics revealed, or (which is most likely) that individuals of a given personality type (i.e., determined, hard-minded, aggressive) seek outlets in specific sporting activities.

The most useful narrative of which I am aware is the excellent book by Biesser (1967). Among the vivid lessons presented which might be heeded by coaches is the suggestion that the sudden termination of sports participation in an individual's life may require rather marked personal adjustments calling for the aid of a psychologist or psychiatrist. All coaches reading this text become better able to aid their athletes in this transition.

Among the more valuable techniques outlined in the literature through which a coach, with the help of qualified psychologists, might learn about his team members has been described by Rushall in a series of lectures and papers (unpublished). With the help of a computer program and through use of scores from the Minnesota Multiphasic Personality Index administered to each team member, he obtained a "print out" describing the probable reactions of an individual to various situations. For example, the description will state that "It is likely that . . ." and continue to describe that the individual may react well under stress, and a similar list of descriptions. The program continues by stating that "It is probable that . . ." and a similar list of descriptions is presented. Additional personality profiles of the athletes are contained under the headings "It is unlikely that . . ." and "It is highly probable that . . ."

Although such an approach might seem superficial, mechanistic, or downright inhuman to some, it is believed helpful to the coach needing a rather rapid survey of a rather large group of athletes. The university or high school coach who must rapidly assess 50 to 80 players during the beginning of the season (or during spring practice) could well devote an hour or so of team time to this type of evaluation. Even more information might be available if subsequent assessments were carried out periodically during the season, i.e., during pre-season, mid-season, and following the final contest of the year. A major university football team utilizing Rushall techniques enjoyed a remarkably successful year, posting a win and loss record far superior to that achieved in its recent history. Although a number of factors obviously contributed, the coach was highly enthusiastic about recommending this type of assessment.

In a recent paper Rushall describes how a coach, using assessments of individual differences in personality traits, might shape individual behavior by recourse to conditioning techniques taking the form of social reinforcement for desired behavior and negative reinforcement for undesirable behavior. Although Rushall's paper is interesting, it is doubtful that the kind of stultified human relationships developing from such a "rigged" and clumsy type of athlete-player relationship would result in desirable changes. However, most coaches unconsciously follow the principles outlined by Rushall as they deal with their athletes.[4]

---

[4]See the article by Rushall on pages 63-72, the article by Horsfall, Fisher, and Morris on pages 163-168, and the article by Nesvig on pages 250-260. —Ed.

Manipulation of relationships between team members is often difficult, if not impossible, for the coach. He is of course not always aware of the quality and type of interactions and problems arising between team members since it is impossible to directly observe them at places other than the athletic field.

When attempting to make decisions affecting team performance, the research literature offers evidence supporting several interesting principles. For example, research in Germany with rowing teams and in America with basketball teams indicates that there is probably an optimum amount of intra-group hostility (or tension) which is productive of the best team effort. If a player at times expresses open dissatisfaction with the actions of his teammates, it may be a healthy sign that he is more concerned with winning than with maintaining the friendship of one of the less able team members (Vanek and Cratty 1969). It is apparently important that an athlete's need for winning is paramount to his needs for team friendships and affiliations. Teams, whose members value "good fellowship" too highly, may achieve such a feeling at the cost of winning.

Thus, a coach should not always be concerned when he observes clashes of temperament. If the goal is to be successful and to win when possible, this type of intra-group hostility may at times be inevitable. Of course, it is not desirable that the amount of inter-personal tension exceeds reasonable bounds. Research in small-group interaction is equally clear in suggesting that if such an excess is present, a great amount of potential "leadership energy" may have to be expended to deal with it. Whereas, with a minimum of intra-group tension, the leader may focus upon more productive aspects.

With the aid of a trained psychologist, the coach may also mold his team into a more compatible and productive unit. Inspection, for example, of a socio-gram in which group affiliations are diagrammed could afford insights into team coalitions and the presence of social isolates, either of which may be potentially harmful or helpful to team effort. A recent text outlines interesting research suggesting that the manner in which a team interacts on the playing field (i.e., who passes the ball to whom most of the time) may be reflected in the questions upon which a socio-gram is based (i.e., "Who is your best friend . . . less liked teammate?", etc.). Additional research of this nature may provide even more important insights for the coach making decisions about team membership (Vanek and Cratty 1969).

During the 1968 Olympics, components of at least one national team with the help of a clinical psychologist, engaged in psychodramas. With trained leadership, this serious type of "role playing game" could be potentially helpful. While the coach should not personally undertake this potentially destructive psychological exercise, the benefits derived from such a baring of feelings may be of important assistance to the mentor as he attempts to modify the behavior of his team and to adjust his own manner of interacting with his athletes.

SUMMARY

Only a sampling of research findings potentially useful to coaches are herein summarized. Numerous other guidelines may also be helpful. For example, the research dealing with arousal tension and activation affords insights into the individual manner in which athletes may be activated and/or deactivated by others and by themselves prior to and during athletic contests. This literature makes obsolete the traditional emotional exhortation applied to large groups of athletes and still practiced by some coaches. Reference to this material should encourage the coach to react to the individual dimension of human personality.

Research dealing with the personality of the coach himself should also be helpful to coaches seeking to improve their personal effectiveness. This type of investigation might encourage some coaches to become more flexible in their assessments of new practices and in dealing with individual differences among athletes (Loy 1968; Loy 1969).

The athletic instructor, reviewing the principles that writers have derived from the research, may, however, face several dilemmas. Traditionally, coaches are decisive, and decisiveness in leaders (whether in war or in stressful athletic competition) is probably a desirable trait. A number of exact, precise, and rapid decisions must be made continually during the practice sessions and during competition. At the same time, the research literature seems to abound with contradictions, ambiguities, and numerous courses of actions to follow in apparently similar situations. The coach cannot, and should not, thumb through the pages of the latest psychological journal or the "how to handle hard-to-handle athlete books" now appearing with more frequency on the bookshelves prior to making the innumerable judgments called for during the average football afternoon.

At the same time, material directly appropriate to the athletic coach—writings considered as dealing with sport psychology—are often superficial. Not only is there little which can be considered as sound scientific work, but what is available is often based upon rather questionable clinical judgments or contains investigations with methodologies and findings which might be seriously questioned (Vanek and Cratty 1969).

It is believed, however, that the presently available material affords several classifications of operating principles which contemporary coaches might consider:

1. Reference should be made to the literature on learning principles to formulate sound guidelines for the spacing and content of practice sessions.

2. Motivation should be enhanced by encouraging athletes to participate in workout planning, and by arranging novel workout schedules daily.

3. Individual differences in motive structure, personality traits, and arousal levels should be accommodated for in the manner in which the athlete is dealt with on a personal basis, and in the way in which he is prepared for competitive efforts.

4. The coach should seek the help of a qualified psychologist when attempting to assess the personality traits of team members, and/or to plot the social structure of the team. Professional aid should also be enlisted when dealing with athletes with marked problems of personal adjustment, and/or when engaging in potentially disruptive attempts to understand team interactions via a psychodrama or some similar group experience.

5. The coach should be sensitive to the emotional health of his charges, not only during their competitive careers, but during the time they no longer may participate. The athletic mentor should not only train his charges for optimum performance during their younger years, but should also seek to instill long-range goals to aid the athletes in preparing for a productive life following termination of competition.

REFERENCES

Beisser, A. 1967. *The madness in sports.* New York: Appleton-Century-Crofts.
Cratty, B. J. 1967. *Movement behavior and motor learning.* Philadelphia: Lea & Febiger.
Knapp, B. 1964. *Skill in sport.* London: Routledge & Kegan Paul.

Loy, J. W., Jr. 1968. Sociopsychological attributes associated with the early adoption of a sport innovation. Worcester, Massachusetts: The Journal Press.

——. 1969. Social psychological characteristics of innovators. *American Sociological Review.*

Oxendine, J. 1968. *Psychology of motor learning.* New York: Appleton-Century-Crofts.

Rushall, B. The relationship of personality variables to participation, levels of performance, and success in football. Unpublished studies, Bloomington, Ind.

——. An investigation of the relationship between personality variables and performance categories in swimmers. Unpublished studies, Bloomington, Ind.

——. Some applications of psychology to swimming. Unpublished studies, Bloomington, Ind.

Singer, R. N. 1968. *Motor learning and human performance.* New York: The Macmillan Company.

Vanek, M., and Cratty, B. J. 1969. *Psychology and the superior athlete.* New York: The Macmillan Company.

Psychology and Sports Performance: Principles and Applications

Richard M. Suinn

This paper offers a way of conceptualizing psychological aspects of competition and shows the relation between how you analyze an athlete's performance and what you recommend. The focus is some current psychological approaches used in the U.S. and abroad, which include autogenic training, cognitive strategies, meditation, biofeedback, stress management training, and visuo-motor behavior rehearsal.

Figure 1 represents the basic concept that athletic performance can be considered a product of aptitude and the strength of an acquired skill. In other words, one's level of performance is influenced by innate ability combined with what one has gained through learning, experience, and training. We are interested in what influences skill acquisition. As noted, skill can be considered a result of the strength of correct athletic responses, the ability to transfer these from practice to competition conditions, and the ability to eliminate or at least control incorrect responses.

CORRECT ATHLETIC RESPONSES

Correct responses can be analyzed to include isolated motor responses, preparatory or arousal responses, adapting responses, linking responses, and cognitive or thought responses. This package of various types of responses fitted together forms the correct motor skills demanded in performance.

Isolated motor responses are the physical actions learned and shaped through coaching, such as the technique of the leg drive, the downhill tuck position, the squeeze of the trigger, or the full extension of the arm.

Preparatory or arousal responses are "psyching-up" preparations, traditionally recognized by athletes as important and only now coming under study by psychologists.[1] In some cases, these responses are equivalent to the warming-up exercises that are used to prepare the muscles to perform. Arousal levels can be influenced by physical steps or by psychological steps. Taking a number of runs on a course can stimulate one's competitive drive just prior to the event. The simple action of talking to another competitor about a forthcoming race, meet, or game can start the adrenaline flowing. In some sports, such as weight lifting, psychological methods can be used as competitors mentally

---

[1] See the article by Oxendine on pages 103-111.

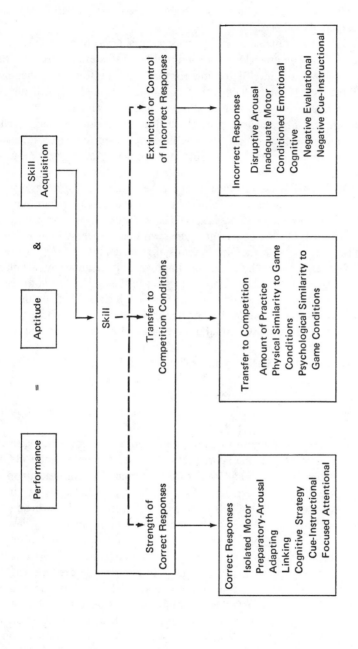

Performance = Aptitude & Skill Acquisition

Skill

Transfer to Competition Conditions

Strength of Correct Responses

Extinction or Control of Incorrect Responses

Correct Responses

Isolated Motor
Preparatory-Arousal
Adapting
Linking
Cognitive Strategy
Cue-Instructional
Focused Attentional

Transfer to Competition
Amount of Practice
Physical Similarity to Game Conditions
Psychological Similarity to Game Conditions

Incorrect Responses

Disruptive Arousal
Inadequate Motor
Conditioned Emotional
Cognitive
Negative Evaluational
Negative Cue-Instructional

Figure 1. Factors affecting sports performance

attempt to dominate the weights. I know of a national team fencer who successfully whipped himself into extreme anger to sharpen his reflexes.

I should quickly point out that preparations can cause arousal levels to move in either direction, psyching up or psyching down. The crucial step is for an athlete to carefully assess his or her level prior to a performance: if the arousal level is too low for maximum performance, then psyching-up steps are introduced; if the level is too high, then psyching-down is called for. Athletes need to be encouraged to check their levels routinely and to know themselves well enough to catch the signs associated with optimal arousal. Signs can be general, such as the feeling of being ready, but an athlete can also discover more specific signals, such as those reflected in heart rate, warmth in an extremity, thoughts that are occurring, how controllable such thoughts are, or even time of awakening in the morning.

Preparatory responses appear also to include what has been called *self-efficacy*, meaning one's personal expectation of success, or confidence. Self-efficacy can vary from competition to competition, especially if the event involves competing against a new opponent or against different course conditions. However, it may well be that confidence grows with each success so as to become more and more generalized. Also, success can be defined in terms of goal statements.[2] An athlete can define a subgoal of bettering his or her last times by a fraction, improving on standings by one place, or even being more fluid or more aggressive or calmer (important goals in themselves but not necessarily tied to times or scores). If the athlete sets these subgoals just far enough ahead that continuous improvement and effort are required, but not so unrealistically far ahead that they are unreachable, then the corresponding success builds self-efficacy. Often an athlete in a slump has unconsciously set the goal of returning within one practice session to midseason winning form—after a slump that has taken perhaps weeks or months to develop! Setting more realistic and achievable subgoals that can still be seen as steps towards a winning form can help. Another facet of self-efficacy is, not simply the expectation of success in performing, but the sense of being ready to perform. Once again, this may be simply a more specific version of arousal level. We have been experimenting with training athletes in the feeling, physical and mental, of being ready.

Adapting motor responses are a factor in sports that require a motor action as a reaction to another event. A tennis player must emit the appropriate response, depending upon the opponent's serve—wide, down the line, top spin, flat, and so forth. An alpine skier must adapt to the slalom course as each gate rapidly appears. The strength of W. T. Gallwey's philosophy of "inner tennis" appears for this type of response. Recall that Self 1 is the mind directing the body in an instructional or evaluational way and that Self 2 is the body taking over its own performance. I believe that Self 2 should indeed take over in adapting responses, almost as reflexes take over. Self 1 is important and should not be discounted. Typically, the process of analyzing, thinking about an event, telling oneself what to do, comes during the acquisition or practice stage. In practice, before an event, it is useful to analyze the course, one's opponent, or technique flaws that need correction. Then is the proper time for the mind to work closely in instructing the body, so that later the body can take over. I agree that, once competition begins, Self 2 takes over and Self 1 becomes an observer. The role of Self 1 in competition itself is generally limited to strategy—"Avoid giving him pace on the ball," "Look for that fifth gate"—or what we call *attentional variables*. What *Inner Tennis* has revealed is the ambiguity in most training programs. Many instructions have nothing concrete for an athlete to

---

[2] See the article by Rushall on pages 63-72, the article by Botterill on pages 261-268, and the article by McClements and Botterill on pages 269-279.

hold on to. Saying "You need to improve your timing" or "You're not watching the ball" may sound like giving concrete instructions, but they do not show the player how to achieve, as real goal-evaluative statements should do. Gallwey, in *Inner Tennis* (1976), proposed that the solution is the elimination of evaluation and Self 1's emphasis on instruction in what is right or wrong, with an emphasis instead on Self 2 and what feels proper. But it seems to me also valid to improve Self 1's instructions and to regard Self 1 as appropriately placed in the acquisition or practice sessions or in the postgame analyses. One can improve on the ambiguities of Self 1's instructions by directing athletes to do certain things to achieve a goal statement, rather than stating the goal as if it were the instruction. It is one thing, for example, to say to a person, "Relax!" and another thing to train the person in a muscle relaxation exercise that can be used under stress situations.

I include linking responses among the factors that influence performance to acknowledge that some sports require a flow of movements in which one move determines or sets the stage for the following one. Figure skating and gymnastics routines fit this category. There is a chain of responses that smoothly lead from one to another. In a sense, the rhythm sought by racers in a slalom course is an example of linking responses. Sometimes linking responses become important when they are introduced into an event. In work with members of the U.S. Olympic biathlon team, the problem was presented of how to insure making the correct turns in a relay event. In this event, a competitor skis into a rifle range, fires in the prone position at a target, and then skis to a trail, which eventually loops back to the range; this time, the standing position is used, and the competitor then skis onto a different trail. Any hesitation about which trail to ski at the choice point means critical time lost. To train for this event, imagery rehearsal (visuo-motor behavior rehearsal)[3] was used to practice linking responses as follows: the phrase "last round fired prone—up and to the left trail by the fence" was repeated until the behaviors were firmly linked together. Then the mental rehearsal shifted to "last round fired standing—up and to the right trail by the bridge." These scenes had the advantage, not only of practicing linking responses, but also of relying upon visual cues (the fence or the bridge) to enhance the correct response. The technique worked so well that one of the participants had dreams all night about "prone to the fence trail . . . standing to the bridge trail"!

Cognitive responses, or thought processes,[4] also form a crucial influence on performance. These include strategy, cue-instructional responses, and focused attentional responses. As indicated earlier, strategy is important in many sports—what line to take in a downhill course, how conservative a gymnastics routine to undertake (depending upon your standing), what weakness to exploit in one's tennis opponent. Cognitive factors can also involve what I call *cue-instructional responses*. By this I mean that a thought or a word can be used as a cue to trigger a desired response. For some persons, cue-instructional thoughts can enhance or maintain performance, e.g., if the words *calm and steady* have been associated through training with the reduction of competition stress. The cue can actually produce a pattern of actions rather than a single behavior, as when an alpine skier thinks, "Attack the course," and this triggers leaning, tips forward, greater effort, speed retention, and emotional arousal, all in the same instant. The key to cue-instructional responses is the amount of practice in associating the desired response with the cue. Nearly any word or symbol can become a trigger if it is paired often enough with the response, whether it is the word *fire!* paired with the movement of firing through a starting gate or whether it is the 7- symbol I used once to cue controlled relaxation

---

[3] See the article by Suinn on pages 306-315, the article by Lane on pages 316-320, and the article by Titley on pages 321-327.
[4] See the article by Kirschenbaum and Bale on pages 334-343 and the article by Morgan on pages 297-303.

in members of a ski racing team (we even had this symbol taped on the backs of the protective downhill helmets—on the backs so that team members riding behind on the chair lift could benefit from seeing the cue).

Focused attentional responses refer to the ability to narrow one's attention[5] and thoughts to the task at hand. Data suggest that successful performance is associated with the experience of being fully aware and tuned into the relevant parts of an event. The audience, distracting conditions, weather, equipment, internal doubts, prior errors—all seem to be outside this focus of attention, as though an impenetrable shield were erected. Where is the attention? It seems to focus more on the experience than on technical details, perhaps on Self 2 rather than on the intellect, on the involvement in doing rather than on the how-to-do or the what-to-do or the how-am-I-doing. In sequencing events that require linking responses, there is some reason to believe that the attention is on the next sequence, not the current move. So a gymnast might be experiencing a focus on the next move, the slalom racer on the next series of gates. Once again, this may reflect a method by which the mind can be active and involved without interfering with the body's current movements.

TRANSFER OF RESPONSES FROM TRAINING TO COMPETITION

In the original analysis (Figure 1), the next variable involved in skill is the transfer of correct responses from practice to competition conditions. Practicing a skill must occur in conditions that are as close as possible to game conditions. This encourages the transfer of the skill. Coaches are fully aware of athletes who are superior in practice but who somehow never do well in competition. Many variables are different in the real tournament, race, or meet. Physical variables can be different, and so can psychological ones. Differences in scores in a match or point standings are added to the situational demands. Facing certain competitors as opponents is also a new dimension.

The rule is that practice makes perfect, the more similar the practice demands are to the game demands. Some professional tennis players do not simply practice their serves; instead, they practice serving to Nastase with the imagined score of 30-40. If the event is one in which an athlete has no control over adverse conditions, then practice should take place in adverse weather or under poor course conditions. Basketball players are never asked in a game to shoot a free throw after a five-minute rest; hence they practice free throws *after* a full afternoon or running, not while they are fresh and rested.

INCORRECT RESPONSES

Finally, skill is influenced by incorrect responses, which interfere with performance. Incorrect responses can be disruptive arousal, inadequate motor responses, conditioned emotional responses, or various cognitive responses. Disruptive arousal can involve any deviation from the optimal arousal level.[6] A level that is too low leads to a "flat" performance, lacking drive, falling short of a full commitment. A level that is too high involves being hypertense and disrupts coordination, including the timing and display of adaptive and linking responses. Too high a level also leads to a greater sense of fatigue and energy consumption.

[5] See the article by Nideffer on pages 281-290.
[6] See the article by Bramwell et al. on pages 119-123.

Inadequate motor responses, of course, represent flaws in basic technique and occur if an athlete has been poorly trained in the technique of a sport. If one views progress towards superior skill as a gradual increase of correct skills with a gradual decrease of deficient actions, then the importance of eliminating inadequate responses becomes clear. Inconsistency in performance sometimes (but not always) can be attributed to the recurrence of a deficient motor response. Because of poor instruction earlier, a promising athlete can have acquired many bad habits or technique problems that are as strongly ingrained as is the good technique. Sometimes these habits are so strong that an athlete is completely unaware of a flawed action, as in the case of a ski jumper who did not realize that his arm lifted on one side while in flight: he "knew" it happened because he saw it in films, but he was not actually aware of it at the moment it was occurring. Occasionally, the technique of deliberately practicing the incorrect movement is helpful to introduce body awareness. Videotape playback is useful in some ways but may prove ineffective if a bad habit has been overlearned to the point that the athlete has lost awareness. Experiments with body awareness training programs are being conducted to help sensitize athletes and perhaps to improve body control.

An incorrect response can be a result of conditioned emotionality. We know that a negative emotional reaction can be conditioned in humans; this is how we acquire a reflexive hand withdrawal at a stove when someone shouts "That's hot!" and how we experience a quick anxiety when we hear "Look out!" A negative emotion or an avoidance or a self-protective behavior is stirred in certain situations, which originally did not create these reactions. An injury can lead to the development of such an association: the next time the athlete faces the same or similar circumstance, there may be an automatic holding back. Unusual competition conditions can stir unique emotional responses; the Olympic games hold such a prominent place in our values that they precipitate unusual reactions. In some cases, the stimulus is another competitor. For example, Franz Klammer, of the Austrian team, whose very name conjured up anxiety, was aided by stories of specially made skis, which were to give him an even more insurmountable advantage (and which he decided not to use because they had not been tested). An accumulation of experiences can foster a conditioned aversive response. One of the major problems of slumps is the emotional buildup of tension, depression, loss of confidence, and confusion.

Just as cognitive variables can play a useful role, so can they play a disruptive role in performance. Negative thoughts, low self-efficacy, and statements of doubt can interfere with functioning. Such negative evaluational or negatively toned thoughts tend to cue responses that are incompatible with correct skills. Since thoughts can have an impact on behavior, negative thoughts certainly have an impact. There is a real difference between objective evaluational thoughts and negative evaluational ones. Athletes can appraise their chances of success and then go out and do their very best. This appraisal is more an intellectual exercise, devoid of negative influence and maybe even having some positive effects. In contrast, a negative evaluational thought triggers negative emotions and disruptive actions that prevent the body from releasing its previously rehearsed skill. For some athletes, cue-instructional responses can become negative as well: instead of serving to precipitate desired responses, the cue-instructions prompt disruptive responses. For example, an athlete who continues to say, "Remember, don't make an error!" can inhibit muscle coordination and commit numerous errors. It has been my principle in the use of imagery rehearsal always to practice correcting an error, so that the body *experiences* the correct response, and hence it is not necessary to *remind* oneself about what needs to be done. Instructors are fully aware that it is generally more desirable to emphasize "Do this" as opposed to "Don't do that."

TRAINING METHODS

In the final part of this paper, I will tie some of the topics previously discussed to training methods. It should be obvious that a deficiency in a basic motor skill is easily handled by a coaching staff, since this falls under the common area of technique. What we might add is the question of whether the deficiency is in an isolated motor skill, an adapting motor response, or a linking motor response. As mentioned earlier, if a linking response is weak, then training would emphasize connecting the last response of a chain with the first response of the next chain of responses. Thus, when the athlete does *this*, the immediate response is *that* (recall the imagery used in preparing the biathlon competitors). If adapting responses are deficient, then the practice would emphasize the external cue that demands a response from the athlete, such as a wide serve. In linking responses, it is the athlete who emits a response that is the signal for going on to the next response; in adapting responses, the athlete must wait for an event to be presented.

Psychological training for arousal depends upon whether a higher or a lower level of arousal is sought. For athletes who need an increase, autogenic training with an emphasis on changing and controlling bodily sensations ("feeling strong and alert") can be appropriate. Biofeedback to increase pulse rate can be applicable for those who are responsive to heart rate. Sometimes, behavioral methods are useful,[7] as in exposing oneself to stimulating cue conditions (for those who respond to the excitement of an audience, a brief walk among spectators can generate the desire to perform well). Music with a beat can be a helpful procedure. Sometimes, for a cognitively oriented person, just to watch someone else competing increases a sense of readiness. For athletes who feel that a lower level of arousal is needed, various relaxation exercises are useful, such as deep muscle relaxation, with or without muscular or thermal biofeedback equipment.[8] Audio cassette tapes for relaxation are available (from the author). We have obtained some preliminary data suggesting that such techniques can permit an athlete to reduce heart rate or respiration (see Figures 2 and 3). For those who are disposed towards mind-quieting methods, meditation and yoga center the attention. And, for others, simply relying upon a repeated routine helps to settle (such as awakening at the same hour, dressing in the same way, reading a certain type of material, preparing equipment—everything done exactly in the same order and at a predictable pace). Just being aware of one's arousal level and knowing of a step to optimize this level may be in itself a major factor in feeling ready.

Self-efficacy is still being studied in terms of methods for its improvement. It may be important to investigate the relative value of using mental rehearsal to practice *perfection* versus *coping*. Others have suggested that better performance can be obtained if the rehearsal includes coping with less than perfect conditions. For example, we have used visuo-motor behavior rehearsal with alpine skiers, who were to ski a slalom course where "something unexpected" was to happen, but who were told, "You are to quickly adjust to it." The concept of goal setting mentioned earlier can be a useful means of assuring the continuing buildup of self-efficacy. Slumps can be reversed by a form of goal setting. Often, in slumps, an athlete tries many, many different solutions, randomly moves from one idea to another, becomes more frustrated, and with building frustration grows even more confused and discouraged. First, the goal of instant recovery must be replaced with the more realistic goal of systematic elimination of steps that do not work, thereby gradually narrowing down the area where the problem lies. This attitude suggests that the failure of a possible solution provides helpful

[7] See the article by Suinn on pages 306-315.
[8] See the article by Wenz and Strong on pages 328-333.

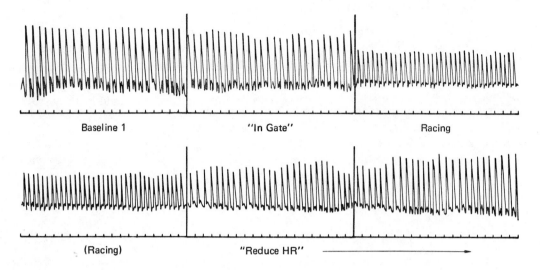

Figure 2. Athletic imagery and heart rate. During the stress of racing in imagery, heart rate increased, as it would in real life. At the end of the racing scene, the athlete was instructed to relax and reduce the heart rate; as the figure shows, some reduction did occur.

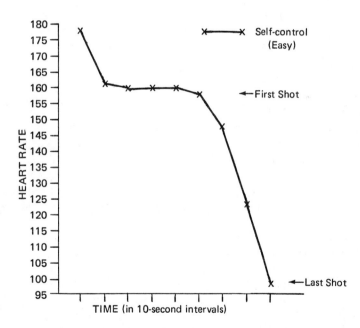

Figure 3. Heart rate after exercise of Olympic biathlete. A biathlete must ski with maximum effort and then slow down to shoot calmly on a rifle course. This biathlete was trained to begin slowing down the physiological state before the first shot. On an actual course, an initial reduction was shown, followed by a stabilization of heart rate as the athlete shifted to aiming the rifle, followed by further decrease in heart rate.

information rather than a source of frustration, for it helps to narrow the field. One type of attempt at a solution should be tried at least twice before it is discarded. Second, straightforward signs of progress should be identified ahead of time, so as to be noticed when they occur. The sign can be one's feeling more comfortable in a movement, feeling more fluid, or feeling as though the body is taking over again or that accuracy or speed is returning. I have sometimes used pacing techniques, if rhythm is a part of the sport, as in the stride for cross-country skiing. A pacing technique is simply a rhythmical pacer, such as music to ski to. In many cases, tension control techniques, such as relaxation training, are useful to prevent further motor inhibition. In some circumstances, a slump can be broken by introducing responses that are incompatible with an inhibitory response. For example, a wrestler went into a slump, which led to his losing. The more he lost, the more cautious he became, and this led to even more losses. Soon he felt constricted in his wrestling moves, in contrast to the free and spontaneous style of his successful days. My program was that, at the starting signal, he should deliberately swing his hands and his entire arms in broad, sweeping movements, with rapid and quick taps to his opponent's body. Such gross and wide moves are incompatible with inhibitory, close-to-the-body, "freezing" movements, which were characterizing his slump. As his movements became looser, his body was able to return to its freer style.

Cognitive problems sometimes plague athletes. The thought "What would happen if . . ." or "Can I make it to the finish?" or "Don't make that mistake again, you've already lost points (time)" can disrupt even the most competent person. A variety of cognitive approaches have been used. One method is based upon the principle that two thoughts cannot exist in the same space at the same time. By this approach, one substitutes a different thought, which has been prepared ahead of time and practiced. This thought can be one that is relevant, but it is positive instead of negative, such as "In a moment I *will* finish and then I can relax." Alternatively, the substituted thought can be completely irrelevant, used simply to eliminate an undesired thought; for example, some marathon runners construct houses, do mathematical calculations, or pretend to be trains as means of distracting themselves from boredom or pain. Some cognitive strategies involve self-instruction for solutions, for example, "You're trying too hard; relax and get the rhythm." Finally, cognitive restructuring has often been suggested. In restructuring, a different and more positive perspective is placed. For example, one athlete looks forward to pain since "I know then that I'm putting out to my maximum." A gold-medalist marksman brightens up with adverse wind conditions: "It will help me, since I'm ready for it and the others are not." Similarly, one can either react to a fault on the first serve with the thought "I only have one more serve; I'd better be careful and not double fault" or restructure this into "My first serve told me something about the range; now I can really count on hitting the next one!"

If conditioned emotionality interferes with performance, counterconditioning or self-control methods can be used. Desensitization is a method combining imagery rehearsal with relaxation. An athlete visualizes a scene involving, for example, an injury but with an emphasis on retaining controlled muscle relaxation. Through this pairing, a new association develops, which replaces the previous negative emotion. This method has been useful in reducing "butterflies" and nervousness in starting gates and even in enabling athletes to confront other competitors without being psyched out. Anxiety management training (AMT) is another method for developing control over stress reactions.[9] By this method, athletes are trained to recognize early physical-muscular signs of tension buildup, through the use of imagery. Next, they are trained in deep muscle relaxation. Finally, the

---

[9]See the article by Spinelli and Barrios on pages 344-355.

program increases their ability to use the relaxation method as an instant means for eliminating tensions wherever or whenever they might occur.

One final mention needs to be made of our use of visuo-motor behavior rehearsal (VMBR), an imagery rehearsal technique I first introduced to training skiing competitors in about 1971. We have some evidence that VMBR is on a continuum of imagery, with thinking about an event on one end and realistic dream imagery on the other end. VMBR seems nearest to the reality end, with the imagery being so clear and vivid as to reproduce visual, tactual, auditory, motor, and even emotional reactions. In a comparison of EMG muscle responses, the records of one skier closely reproduced the course he was "skiing" through VMBR, whereas no muscle activity occurred when he was asked to "think about" skiing that same course (see Figure 4). Because of this characteristic, VMBR has been a useful method for identifying what happens under game conditions and for practicing for transfer to game conditions. In the former approach, an athlete uses VMBR to rerun a race to determine the source of an error. The athlete can then rerun the race, in imagery, but correcting the error. In the latter approach, VMBR is used as a means of practicing the correct moves for a coming event. Members of an alpine ski team, for example, use VMBR after course inspection to gain "experience" in running that course. VMBR was used at the 1976 winter Olympics to allow skiing the course just minutes before the event.[10] This type of mental rehearsal can be used to practice technique, to practice strategy, to practice a general approach (e.g., being aggressive), to prepare so well for a difficult part of a course that the right moves are ingrained, to build confidence, or just to obtain a sense of being familiar with the course by reason of rehearsing it so often. Early findings of a recent study funded by the AAU Women's Track and Field Development Subcommittee and the U.S. Olympic Committee suggest that VMBR can be used to lower physiological effort needed by endurance athletes (see Figure 5).

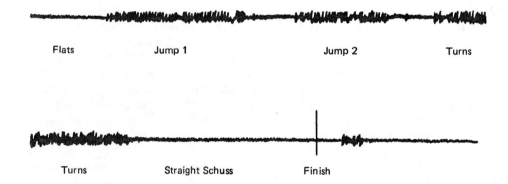

Flats   Jump 1   Jump 2   Turns

Turns   Straight Schuss   Finish

Figure 4. EMG for downhill racer. The EMG measure of muscle activity was attached to the legs of the athlete, whose muscle reactions peaked at various moments in the imagery corresponding to times at which extra muscle involvement would be expected in real life on such a course. Where the imagery scene involved a jump, for example, the corresponding EMG recording showed intense leg activity.

[10] See the article by Suinn on pages 306-315.

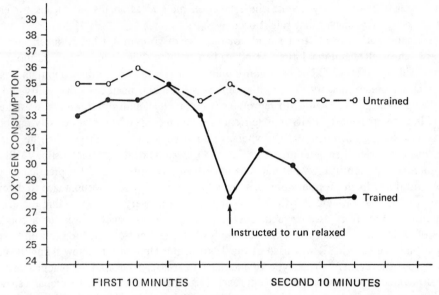

Figure 5. Oxygen consumption for a trained athlete and an untrained athlete under work load of 65% anaerobic threshold. The trained athlete was trained with VMBR to adopt controlled relaxation during running. Both athletes used the same amount of energy under the same work load for the first 10 minutes, but, after using the VMBR method, the trained athlete reduced energy consumption.

The major point of this paper is that it is possible to conceptualize sports performance into various component parts and that such an analysis gives direction for the application of a variety of psychological methods. Training programs then become tailor-made to the particular component that needs attention. Further, the conceptualization points out that different athletes have different needs, some being more influenced by cognitive factors, others more by arousal levels, others more by emotional factors. Psychological methods, to be useful, must first be appropriate for the person and for the situation. Furthermore, such methods require that athletes carefully assess their personal needs and then train with the appropriate method enough to have good control over its application. Psychological techniques, whether biofeedback or VMBR or meditation, demand training in the same way that weight exercises require a commitment to a program. The payoffs are high; psychological methods enable the athlete to finally use an integrated approach to performance, combining physical aptitude with coaching instructions and fine-tuned by physical training and psychological conditioning.

REFERENCE

Gallwey, W. T. 1976. *Inner Tennis.* New York: Random House.

MOTIVATIONAL VARIABLES

Dr. Robert N. Singer has been sports psychology coordinator on the Sports Medicine Committee of the U.S. Olympic Committee and has served as a consultant to the American Swimming Coaches Association, the Professional Golf Association, and the Cincinnati Reds baseball team. He "started in every baseball and basketball game" during his student days at Brooklyn College, has played in tournaments in tennis and handball, and was on the coaching staff in basketball at Ohio State University. This article calls needed attention to the diverse factors that influence motivation and provides a definition of motivation in terms of its effects. The author outlines some important principles and assumptions governing motivation and offers some recommendations, based on psychological principles, for increasing motivation.[1]

Coach Robert Hilmer has been a head coach for high school track, baseball, and basketball teams. In basketball, his teams have a record of 230 wins and 83 losses over a 15-year period. He has worked on psychological programs in stress management and achievement training. He has served as head coach for the Iowa All-Star game and is head basketball coach at Forest City (Iowa) Community High School. This original article, written in collaboration with Singer, is a direct product of some of the basic psychological principles outlined in the latter's preceding article,[2] and it shows how theory and applications work together. Accepting the notion that achievement motivation can be learned, the authors state the theory and then illustrate, with an actual case, how this theory was put into practice.

Dr. Brent S. Rushall has been the team psychologist for the Canadian Olympic swimming team and Olympic wrestling team, the Canadian World Aquatic Championships, the Commonwealth games swimming teams. He has been a consultant to Ski Canada, the Canadian Water Skiing Association, the Canadian Diving Association, the U.S. Volleyball Association, the National Hockey League, and the Canadian Amateur Basketball Association. He was an all-American athlete in rugby, participated in competitive rowing, surfing, kayaking, and took part in the Canadian national team trials in rugby. He has had coaching experience with swimming, rugby, rowing, and track and field teams at various levels. He is professor in the School of Physical Education and Outdoor Recreation at Lakehead

[1] Another article by Singer, in collaboration with Robert Hilmer, appears on pages 56-62.
[2] See pages 40-55.

University. This article presents basic principles from behavioral psychology. Emphasizing the role of positive reinforcement and applied behavioral analysis, the author illustrates the principles through actual examples. In this article, motivation is used as a topic to demonstrate the place of behavioral analysis.

David Youngblood has coached AAU diving teams in Texas, was the diving coach for Colorado State University, and currently is the aquatics director and swimming coach at Katy (Texas) High School. As a student at the University of Texas, he was a competitor in diving. This article reports on a collaborative study between Youngblood and Suinn,[3] which sought to develop a questionnaire to identify motivational factors. The questionnaire differs from traditional motivational scales in that it measures factors that have immediate meaning to a coach or athlete. It assumes that higher performance can be motivated if the incentives or rewards are individualized for each athlete; e.g., a training program that emphasizes conditioning would have more appeal to an athlete high on category 6, the Fitness and Health motivational factor. The questionnaire seeks to identify such individual motives.

Dr. Dorcas Susan Butt has been a successful tennis player, having been the captain for the Canadian Federation Cup team, having played at Wimbledon, and holding several Canadian championships. She has been the vice-president of the Canadian Tennis Association. She has consulted with swimming teams and with tennis players. She is associate professor of psychology at the University of British Columbia. This article proposes that certain motivational styles can be identified among athletes. Using case examples, the author shows how different profiles of aggression, conflict, competence, competition, and cooperation factors are associated with performance. Through her choice of profile factors, she bridges the two areas of motivation and personality.

Dr. Bruce C. Ogilvie has been a consultant to various U.S. Olympic teams, to 12 National Football League teams, to 13 professional baseball teams, and to 4 professional basketball teams. He is currently retired, having been professor in counseling and psychology at California State University, San Jose, where he received recognition as "Outstanding Professor." This article approaches athletic performance from a psychodynamic motivational perspective, emphasizing unconscious motives. From this view, the author hypothesizes five syndromes that can develop from stresses as an athlete becomes successful.

Dr. David Pargman has been involved in research at Florida State University, with varsity athletic teams from all sports, ranging from track to football to tennis. He lettered in cross-country track, has coached, and still competes as a distance runner. He is a fellow of the American College of Sports Medicine and is professor of movement science at Florida State University. This article, on motivation for running, presents the hypothesis that addiction, or dependence, is involved for some and that commitment, or dedication, explains why others run. Continuing along the theoretical vein, the author speculates on some biochemical (as opposed to psychological) explanations for running, including the concept that running involves stimulus seeking. Of the articles in this section, Pargman's is at once the most speculative and the most intriguing.

Dick Taylor was a member of the U.S. biathlon team that placed fourteenth in the 1961 world championships, a member of the 1964 Olympic team, and captain of the Dartmouth College ski team. He has worked as a coach with members of the U.S. ski team's development team. He is the

---

[3] *Other articles by Suinn appear on pages 26-36 and 306-315.*

regional coach for the U.S. nordic cross-country ski team and director of the Devil's Thumb Cross-Country Ski Center, and he is nearing the completion of a doctoral degree. In his approach to coaching, he has combined technical knowledge with a concern for the humanistic needs of competitors. This article reflects the viewpoint of a competitor and a coach, in contrast to the previous articles, most of which were written by psychologists. Taylor attempts to communicate the subjective reasons that make sports attractive to participants. He discusses such motives with the example of cross-country skiing, which offers both high-level competitive events and events for recreational participants (aptly called citizens' races).

Motivation in Sport

Robert N. Singer

Athletic accomplishments can be attributed to many factors working together in an ideal "intermix," but none are referred to with more reverence and less understanding than what the more avid sports enthusiasts refer to as "the mind and the heart." Others have coined the synonymous phrase, "the will and the guts." The urge and the ability to achieve is due in part, no doubt a great part, to those many recognized and intangible processes that encompass the previous and present motivational states of the athlete.

Physical characteristics, sense acuity, perceptual and decision making processes, acquired skills, and developed abilities structure the human system for preparation for competition. The optimal state of arousal encourages the structure to function in a desirable way. But emotions and attitudes translated into motivational force accomplish more than this. They were responsible for the athlete's selection of a particular sports activity over other possible activities at some point in his or her life. They influenced the decision to persevere and practice at it over many years and under trying conditions, even though other alternate activities were always available. In fact, we might suggest that motivation is responsible for:

1. selection of and preference for some activity
2. persistence at the activity (duration of training)
3. intensity and vigor of performance (effort)
4. adequacy of performance relative to standards

Consequently, motivation affects the past history of the athlete and any particular contest performance. Behaviors must be considered during the pre-season, the actual competitive season, the pre-event, and the actual event. As we will see, motivational processes need to operate in dissimilar forms for the different purposes of each situation. Furthermore, optimal motivation levels need to be considered relative to the nature of each athlete and each activity.

Robert N. Singer. Motivation in sport. *International Journal of Sport Psychology* 8 (1977):1-22.

BASIC ASSUMPTIONS

Assumption Number 1

Performance at any one time = motivation (affect and expectancy) x capabilities (genetics and learning)

In this formula we can observe that the athlete's actual performance is certainly dependent upon relevant hereditary characteristics that serve to predispose one for achievement. Heredity sets the boundaries or the framework of the human system. Yet there is always much room for improvement. Practice, quality practice that is, allows the athlete to more truly realize potential. Previous experiences influence the development of skills, abilities, knowledge, and tactics.

But excellence in performance is also a function of the affective domain of behaviors. These include attitudes, feelings, arousal level, and expectations. It is here that psychology and sport are most obviously meshed. Psychological preparation helps the athlete to produce according to his capabilities. The training of the athlete with regard to such psychological variables, along with training that promotes organic efficiency, physical development, knowledge and strategies, and specialized skills, will result in the behaviors observed in competition.

Assumption Number 2

Degree of learning = performance level (when ideal motivation is present and normal body homeostatic conditions prevail)

The best and most widely used indicant of learning is performance. However, performance fluctuates for a variety of reasons, among which are health and nutrition factors, fatigue, and the influence of drugs. It also fluctuates with varying degrees of motivation. With reinforcement or rewards, expectations fulfilled, or other sources of motivation, performance is more apt to truly indicate learning level. With the absence of personal or externally-set incentives, behavior is likely to be at its worst.

The classic example of the need in a situation for the presence of reinforcement-motivation to demonstrate the true learning level is indicated in Figure 1. The concept of latent learning was clearly demonstrated in this case. Learning occurs during repeated experiences but reinforcement-motivation is necessary for it to be revealed through some measure of behavior. In the illustrative investigation, three groups of rats received a series of trials to learn to traverse a maze. The speed recorded from beginning to end to where a goal box was located was the performance measure, presumably indicating the learning that had occurred. Group I received reinforcement (food in the goal box) every day. Group III did not experience food until the fourth day, Group II until the eighth day. Groups II and III did not appear to be learning the task until reinforcement was introduced. Within one or two subsequent trials, their performances were comparable to that of Group I. Learning had occurred during the previous trials, but some situational variable, in this case the presence of food which served as a reinforcement-motivator, was necessary to produce performance changes reflecting true learning.

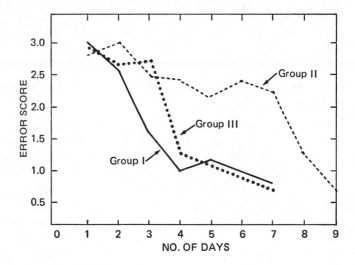

Figure 1. Latent learning and performance. (From Blodgett, H. C. 1929. The effect of the introduction of reward upon the maze performance of rats. *University of California Publications in Psychology* 4:113-134).

Assumption Number 3

Theoretical constructs can adequately describe performance at any one time as a function of motivational presence: Drive Theory vs. the Inverted-U Hypothesis

When the behavioristic school of thought was in its prime, and the noted psychologist Clark Hull shaped research efforts through his mathematical equations that attempted to quantify learning and behavioral potential, his concept of "drive" indicated the linear relationship of arousal (motivation) to performance. His concepts were geared to describe all types of learning. Contemporary researchers have tended to find fault with drive theory as applied to motor behaviors. Instead, they have tended to support the tenets of the inverted-U hypothesis as more applicable for an explanation of movement-oriented performances. A monotonic relationship is predicted between level of performance and arousal here, with optimal arousal presumably associated with best performance and too little or too much arousal resulting in poorest performances. Borrowed from the old Yerkes-Dodson law (1908), reformulated by Duffy in the form of "activation theory" in the early 1960's, it seems to hold true in a variety of situations.

Yet it may be possible to use both ideas to explain different forms of circumstances in sports. Where extreme effort or persistence is required, drive theory offers a useful explanation. With activities that involve complexity in sequential coordinated movements, controlled and perhaps flexible response patterns to changing and unpredictable situations, the inverted-U hypothesis is applicable. This "best" motivation is a function of task characteristics (see Figure 2).

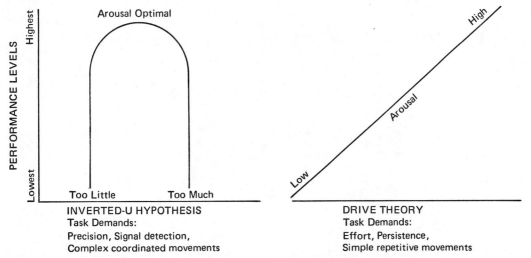

Figure 2. Drive theory compared to the Inverted-U Hypothesis. (From Singer, R. N. 1975. *Myths and truths in sports psychology.* New York: Harper & Row.)

Assumption Number 4

Personal characteristics, situational variables, and task dimensions interact to suggest the optimal motivation to be imposed and/or generated

The demand characteristics of the activity have been partially discussed previously, and it was shown how its dimensions suggested ideal arousal states. Situational or environmental factors surrounding the to-be-performed event may contain stimuli with arousal properties, as perceived by the athlete. The presence of spectators, the words of the coach,[1] the contest conditions, and other variables are associated with potential arousal dynamics. Owing to the nature of individual differences in personality, each athlete may react differently to particular situational factors and the nature of the activity. Anxiety level, resistance to specific stressors, and perception of locus of control (internal vs. external) on performance outcome are good examples of personal characteristics that must be considered in relation to motivation. Figure 3 illustrates the relationship of variables just discussed.

A Dynamic Overview of Motivation as Related to Performance

Motivation and its relation to cumulative performance is even more complicated than has been described so far. Perhaps John Atkinson, through over 25 years of work in the area, has contributed as much as anyone in suggesting the dynamic interplay of the myriad of variables influencing cumulative achievement.

Figure 4 presents the variety of factors determining the learning of and performance in a particular activity. Briefly summarized, genetic factors and experiences in those early formative years set the stage for later performance potential in specific tasks. Personal characteristics (e.g., personality,

---

[1] See the article by Corran on pages 129-132, the article by Massimo on pages 229-237, the article by Zaremski on pages 238-246, and the article by Richardson on pages 247-249. —Ed.

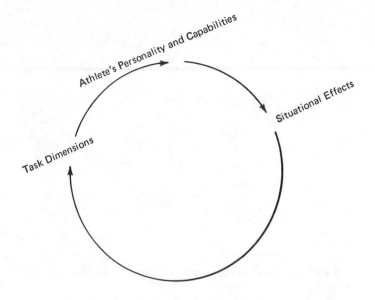

Figure 3. The interactive, dynamic process affecting performance

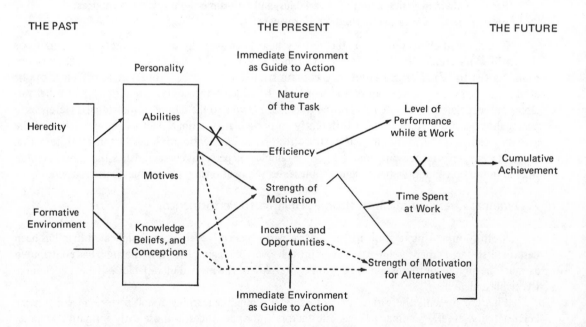

Figure 4. Atkinson's model of motivational factors and achievement. (From Atkinson, J. W. 1974. Motivation and ability. Paper presented at 18th International Congress of Applied Psychology, Montreal, 28 July-2 August 1974.)

abilities, etc.) influence activity preferences, dedication to sustain practice, and capability to achieve. Highest levels of persistent motivation are prerequisite to sustained practice at one task to the exclusion of other possible involvements. Environmental and situational variables greatly affect the quality and quantity of practice. Cumulative achievement, the end result, is a function of previous experiences, developed potential, and the ability to apply the appropriate level of motivation during the actual athletic contest.

It is possible to examine sources of motivation in four categories. Overlap exists and the classifications are not pure. But the identification of motivational sources by category is convenient in that such a scheme suggests situational structuring by some external source (e.g., a coach of an athletic team) to help athletes realize their greatest potential through the application of principles of motivation. Therefore, let us consider personal variables, societal influences, task dimensions, and possibilities for situational modification.

PERSONAL VARIABLES

1. Under, Over, and Expected Achievers. Competitive performance is a function of capability level and motivation as associated with (*a*) persistent prior practice in the sport and (*b*) present feelings and arousal compatible with the situational event. True levels of capability are not realized if the current motivational state is inappropriate.[2] An under-achiever, the athlete who achieves worse in the contest than expected from practice performances is probably unable to activate or control the arousal mechanisms to a desirable degree. By the same token, the over-achiever, the athlete who produces more than expected in actual competition, may be demonstrating a reversed arousal affect. Consistent performance between practice sessions and actual contests imply consistent motivational response to each.

Academic achievement is often evaluated in the form of a written or oral test. Many students feel that their test scores and course grades do not truly reflect the information mastered by them over a period of time. These students are no doubt poor test-takers; that is, they have an inability to cope emotionally with testing.

2. Instrumental satisfiers. Each preceding satisfying experience[3] related to the activity often leads to a favorable disposition to that activity. Personal motivation is sustained or enhanced. The effect is encouraging to the continuation of practice over a long period of time. Improved athletic accomplishments and feelings of self-satisfaction are instrumental in determining activity preference, additional practice, and greater skills learning.

3. Level of Aspirations: Situation Evaluated → Expectations Produced → Performance Output. The goal level expected, hoped for, or accepted in any endeavor represents an athlete's level of aspiration. Previous successes and failures in related experiences, present evaluations in terms of probabilities of achievement, and realistic or unrealistic appraisals influence aspiration levels. In turn, goal level affects performance yield.

[2] See the article by Butt on pages 78-85 and the article by Ogilvie on pages 86-89. —Ed.
[3] See the article by Taylor on pages 99-101. —Ed.

4. Need to Achieve. The degree of felt need to accomplish is not a generalized trait but is specific to each activity and situation. The need to achieve in a particular activity reflects the motivational strength of that ability, and the level of this need influences risk-taking, the sustenance of practice, and momentary performance.

5. Need for Social Approval. Activity preference and achievement is related to socio-cultural factors, and actual societal expectations and pressures as well as perceived social expectations bear upon motivation and behavior.

6. Need to Avoid Failure or to Avoid Success. Both of these types of needs are anxiety-producing; both are associated with motivation and performance. Fear of failure can produce improved skills but it also limits risk-taking and best potential for success in sports with demand characteristics associated with taking chances or altering intended behaviors in unexpected circumstances. Fear of success limits achievement, for it is possible to wish to reject the responsibilities and prestige that migh accrue with elevated skilled performance.

7. Future Orientation. The continual undertaking of activities may depend on the future goals of a person. Being oriented to distant accomplishments is encouragement to practice those activities perceived as leading to the realization of these accomplishments.

8. Locus of Control. Individuals may perceive their chances of success as dependent upon internal or external factors. An athlete possessing an internal locus of control feels that his or her accomplishments are influenced through personal efforts. The athlete is master of his own fate, so to speak. The athlete with an external locus of control perceives the situation as having chance outcomes. His performance would be influenced by luck, environmental factors, and other variables external to his own efforts and abilities. It would appear that the degree of motivation associated with overcoming fate or energizing perceived capabilities might differ, with an internal locus of control the more desirable of the two.

9. Extrinsic and Instrinsic Motivation. It is possible to be primarily motivated to practice and achieve for reasons associated with materialistic goals (e.g., praise, prestige, money) or personal satisfaction and self-realization. Rewards are incentives to perform and produce. Likewise, self-fulfillment is an inspiration to participate and accomplish. Extrinsic and intrinsic forms of motivation probably operate together in many situations, with one of the more dominant of the two.[4] In other words, the athlete may find the experience of competition to be personally rewarding as well as socially and monetarily beneficial. It is possible for external sources of motivation to lead to internal sources, where rewards encourage one toward task selection and an increasing number of goal-directed activities, and then the experience of satisfaction and fulfillment occurs, is repeated, and dominates the wish to participate and succeed. It appears as though intrinsic rather than extrinsic forms of motivation encourage greater persistence at an activity and may in the long run lead to better athletic performance.

[4] See the article by Youngblood and Suinn on pages 73-77. —Ed.

10. Self-image. An athlete's concept of himself, the extent to which contentment and confidence are exhibited, will depend upon a variety of personal experiences. A positive valence toward oneself provides a necessary impetus toward action. Such feelings will probably be represented by the level of aspiration decided upon prior to competition. The personality structure of the athlete, experiences and successful performances, and the reaction of others directed toward him, will be most influential in the development of self-image. Continual criticism and rejection can transform the sensitive athlete with tremendous potential from realizing this potential to the classification of an under-achiever.

SOCIETAL VARIABLES

1. Cultural Influences. The environment in which we grow up shapes our attitudes and behavioral patterns in obvious or subtle ways. Life styles, activity preferences, and achievements are unique from country to country, from culture to culture. Hockey is extremely popular in Canada. It is the ambition of many youngsters there to become outstanding hockey players, for prestige and notoriety are associated with prowess in hockey. Consequently, as soon as children can walk, they skate. Leagues for all age levels and skills levels have been formed.

Football (soccer) is intensely played and universally observed throughout Europe. Americans are enamoured with football, basketball, and baseball, among other sports. Differences among cultures with regard to approval and recognition for activity preferences, participation, and proficiency become apparent as we witness the behavioral patterns and accomplishments unique to those people representing a particular culture.

2. Social Expectancies (Sub-cultural, Familial, and Peer Group Influences). Within a given culture or country, sub-cultures exist. Communities offer their own environments which influence the behaviors of inhabitants. Even friends or the family can exert a powerful effect in directing behaviors. A person does not operate in a vacuum and in a sense, "freely" forming attitudes, making preferences toward activities, and becoming motivated to achieve in certain endeavors.

The expectations of a group, whether it be family, associates, community, or society, play a forceful role throughout the lifespan of the person. Some people are less susceptible and conforming than others. Social approval, nevertheless, is a goal searched for by the majority. As in any activity selection, the type of sport and level of participation of the athlete can be traced to a variety of socio-cultural variables.

ACTIVITY DIMENSIONS

1. Complexity. As was pointed out earlier, the intricacies of an activity in terms of simple versus complex demands on the performer is very much related to the degree of motivation appropriate for optimizing performance potential. Sporting events placing relatively few cognitive, perceptual, and finely and continually coordinated movement demands on the athlete require the highest level of arousal and vice-versa. Self-generated or regulated arousal compatible with the activity reflects the learning of emotional discharge appropriate for skilled performance.

2. Physical Demands. More "pure" physical tasks require highest degrees of activation. Strength, speed, endurance, or explosive power is generated best under such conditions.

3. Appeal. Unique and interesting activities can help to generate enthusiasm and motivation. Implications for varying the structure of practice sessions are obvious.

4. Relevance and Meaningfulness. The more meaningful practice routines are perceived by the athlete in helping to contribute to personal and team goals, the greater the motivation to perform well and to persevere. Even though specified practice activities are known by the coach to be appropriate and necessary, the athlete must be convinced as well (involvement of cognition and affect).

SITUATIONAL VARIABLES: CONSIDERATIONS FOR TRAINING

The identification of various personal, societal, and activity considerations with regard to motivation is helpful in designing appropriate instructional and training strategies increasing probabilities of optimizing each athlete's motivation and performance. The motivational properties of any activity and situation can be influenced through subtle or direct training techniques. The following list of considerations is by no means exhaustive.

1. Help athletes to set personally high but attainable and specific goals

Level of aspiration is related to performance. Many athletes can and do establish realistic and high performance goals; others do not. Since goal level will reflect past successes and failures in similar situations, and are in turn interpreted according to absolute or relative standards, it is quite necessary for the athlete to view his performances within a realistic framework according to personal development and potential as well as to the nature of each competition. By ensuring the athlete's rational interpretation of each performance, there is less chance of his performing badly in a future situation due to loss of motivation because of (*a*) overconfidence and an unrealistically high interpretation of past performances; or (*b*) underconfidence and an unrealistically low appraisal of past performances.[5]

When preparing for each new competitive event, the athlete might be directed to strive for a personal goal that is 10 percent greater than before. This percentage could be translated to a particular time for a running or swimming event. It is relatively easy to do in certain sporting events, much more difficult in complex activities that require actively coordinating team efforts and in which performance contributions can be made in a variety of ways, directly measurable or virtually impossible to determine. To the extent any situation allows, performances should be translated in the form of specific and expected outcomes. Figure 5 indicates the importance of this procedure.

These goals provide the athlete with something concrete to direct his energies toward. Since goals are specified, they can be evaluated. Specific analyses of performance are useful in that such information can be used to restructure training programs, if necessary.

[5] See the article by McClements and Botterill on pages 269-279. —Ed.

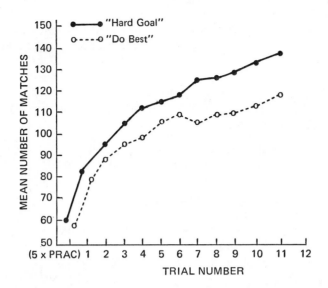

Figure 5. Learning curves demonstrating the importance of specific, high, but attainable goals. (From Locke, E. A., and Bryan, J. F. 1966. Cognitive aspects of psychomotor performance: The effects of performance goals on level of performance. *Journal of Applied Psychology* 50:286-291.)

2. Supply appropriate reinforcement and feedback (knowledge of results) to athletes about their performances

Positive reinforcement refers to any stimulus that tends to increase the probability of the occurrence of a response. A coach's comments or some form of reward are good examples of reinforcement.[6] Feedback, or knowledge of results, is information about one's performance that could be useful in adjusting, controlling, or regulating it. In most athletic situations, a sufficient amount of feedback is present to provide adequate information to the athlete during or at the termination of performance. In other cases, supplementary feedback would be helpful.

Reinforcement, feedback, and motivation are not synonymous terms, and have been operationally defined as distinct constructs by psychologists. However, there are many circumstances when the same cue or event will possess reinforcing, feedback, and motivating properties. Shaping desired athletic behaviors in the correct direction can be accomplished efficiently and effectively with the wise deployment of reinforcers and feedback. A careful analysis of the activity would suggest any need for additional feedback (verbal cues, comments, visuals, etc.). The nature of the athlete's performance would possibly suggest any need for special feedback, and of course this could assure informational, directional, and/or motivational properties.

Reinforcement in the situation can come in a variety of ways, although a typical example would be the coach's comments to the athlete during or after performance. Words of praise can go a long way. The coach's reactions to the athlete's performance demonstrate an interest and concern for him. Motivation can be elevated in this manner.

[6]See the article by Rushall on pages 63-72. —Ed.

The strategic employment of reinforcement schedules is another consideration. It is apparent that not every athlete can be immediately reinforced upon the execution of every act, nor should such have to be the case. Consequently, random and unpredictable schedules are affective in facilitating the acquisition of skills.

3. Special strategies should be used to maximize motivation for training perseverance and to optimize pre-event motivation

The intense and long period of time that is devoted by the athlete to prepare for the first competitive event of the seasonal sport oftentimes requires an unbelievable amount of devotion and sacrifice. The maintenance of top-quality practice under such conditions is mandatory if the athlete is to progress as quickly as possible in realizing his athletic potential. Practice sessions should be as interesting and personally rewarding as possible.[7]

Drills might be varied. Possibilities for personal achievement and the development of a positive self-image must be available. Principles of reinforcement and feedback can be applied. In short, a variety of situational factors can be modified to influence the motivational level of the athlete throughout the pre-season training.

With regard to pre-event motivation, a careful analysis of situational demands and each athlete's personality will result in guidelines for a path of action. The under-aroused athlete must be recognized and stimulated. Verbal techniques are typical, but it requires a sensitive coach to know his or her athletes. A more usual circumstance is the over-aroused athlete. If the forthcoming competition is at all meaningful to the athlete, certain patterns of anxiety will be demonstrated. Too much anxiety and arousal may be detrimental to performance.

The highly skilled athlete learns self-regulation for the activity when such behavior is appropriate. Where this is not occurring, it may be necessary for the athlete to learn how to relax or for someone to assist him just prior to performance. Popular in Europe, especially the Eastern European countries, are autogenic training programs, self-regulatory programs (similar in principle to biofeedback programs), and the use of hypnosis. The most ideal situation is when the athlete can learn how to identify when too much tension is present and then to self-regulate his internal systems appropriately. Even transcendental meditation is being popularly endorsed by some outstanding athletes as a means of obtaining complete and fulfilling relaxation in a brief time period which in turn is supposed to maximize the energies for impending task demands. Pre-event considerations for optimal activation levels are currently being researched and hopefully we will know more about this area in the near future.

4. Practice situations should simulate contest situations when possible

The arousal effects of contest competition is usually far greater than those associated with training. More experience with the stressors of competition will enable the athlete to cope with them. Not only might practice conditions simulate event conditions, but every opportunity for each athlete to experience some moments of contest competition will be beneficial in learning to control and regulate emotions. The effective use of emotions needs to be learned as is the case with skills and information.

---

[7] See the article by Singer and Hilmer on pages 56-62 and the article by Richardson on pages 247-249. —Ed.

5. Individual athletes should be understood and respected for their individual differences

No application of induced motivation can be made intelligently without regard for individual differences among athletes. It is true that certain principles concerning motivation can and should influence procedures used by the coach. There are general guidelines alluded to earlier which can be most helpful in dealing with athletes collectively. But a sensitivity to dissimilarities among athletes with respect to personalities, values, reactions to incentives and situations, and the like, will enable the coach to treat each athlete as needed.

6. The coach should do everything possible to help to develop the self-confidence and self-concept of each athlete

The motivation for an athlete to persevere and to achieve will depend on the kinds of reinforcement he has had and felt relative to previous experiences. A positive and realistic image of oneself is related to motivation and performance potential. Coaches are often guilty of berating athletes, of being negative to them. Some athletes are emotionally tougher, and will respond sufficiently to the Darwinism type of approach that imposes a survival of the fittest model. Many others are quite sensitive and can be literally destroyed by heartless coaches.

It is amazing to see so many talented athletes who do not perform according to capabilities due to a loss of motivation which was affected by a loss of self-confidence. Positive reinforcement is a valuable tool for the dramatic improvement of an athlete's self-image. Experiencing successes also helps immeasurable. Situations and athletes should be compatible in that the possibility of achievement is present on various occasions. Achievement does not necessarily have to be evaluated in terms of victory. Performance according to previous performances and potential can also indicate a form of personal achievement.

7. The Hawthorne effect or placebo effect hold implications for training

From 1926 to 1939 a series of studies were conducted at an industrial plant demonstrating the beneficial effects on worker output of various situational and environmental changes. Worker output was increased when it appeared that a special interest was taken in their environmental settings. The implications for athletics would be the consideration of coaches for varying training situations and for paying more attention to each athlete.

The placebo effect on behavior is more complex, perhaps due to the difficulty in defining the word placebo. A placebo in medical terms is any inert substance with no real known value. It is administered with the understanding that it is supposed to help a patient in some specified way. The psychological value of the placebo has been demonstrated repeatedly in many situations. It often works like the real thing. In more recent years, the interpretation of the word placebo has been expanded considerably to cover any contrived situation which the learner or performer believes will be of some value in fulfilling objectives, but which in fact should not. Deception can work if a person is truly deceived.

For instance, the commonly-held belief in the value of a steak prior to an athletic contest is without scientific verification. Yet the athlete may psychologically react in such a way as to perform better because he thinks he is supposed to after the steak meal. The placebo effect of the food is thereby demonstrated. Coaches, according to their imaginations, can contrive many circumstances in which a placebo effect would be attempted. The more the athlete is convinced of the value to be derived, the more possible the beneficial psychological effects will be noted.

Yet there is a moral question that must be raised here. Is it defensible for a coach to utilize a placebo substance or situation which he knows contains no known real value and proceed to deceive an athlete? What happens if and when the truth is discovered by the athlete? Although the positive psychological effects of placebos which influence the behavioral reactions of those administered them can be realized, we must come to grips with the moral issue involved. It can be argued that the most important need is to obtain the greatest performance yield from the athlete. As long as there is no physical danger, the procedure might be defensible. It is not my aim to take a stand on the use of placebos in sport, but merely to indicate their potential impact on athletic performance. There are many sound medical reasons for the use of placebos instead of drugs to relieve pain. Their use for improved athletic performance can be viewed as an extension of the same problem or a completely different matter.

8. Leadership style should reflect the outstanding qualities of the coach, be compatible with the situation, and believed in by the athletes

There has been no reported success in attempting to identify the psychological profile of recognized outstanding leaders, be they coaches or in some other line of responsibility. Authoritarians or democratically-oriented people can accomplish equally well, each under the right circumstances. One of the major ingredients in situations is the confidence in and respect for the coach felt by the athletes. Coaches with dissimilar leadership styles, with unique communication and tactical procedures, can be and have been successful. Much, of course, depends on the quality of the athletes. But from a psychological point of view, the "frame of reference" in which the coach is held by the athletes will reflect his ability to motivate them to adhere to training guidelines, to perform conscientiously and qualitatively, and to produce desirable behaviors in competition.

What works for one coach may not work for another coach. What works for one coach in one coaching position might not work in another coaching position. Situations, personnel, timing, and sound coaching principles delivered in a manner as to be supported by the sportsmen are involved in determining the ability of a leader to influence the performance of athletes. Outstanding leaders assume many forms. Some are aggressive and intense. Others are reserved and tactful. Some demand strong control and authority. Others are more humanistic and less demanding.

Consideration must also be given to cultural differences and the societal forces operating in a given point in time. Acceptable and even desirable features of a leader vary accordingly. It is little wonder that a coach with a particular personality profile might be more effective in one era or one culture than another. Whatever his personal traits, the productive coach is one who knows how to develop skills, organize group cohesiveness, and to motivate all athletes to perform to the best of their capabilities.

9. Training programs and practice procedures should be meaningful to the athlete

"Enabling" activities, those which will facilitate the progress of the athlete to realize goals oriented toward the future, constitute the contents of practice. If these activities are interpreted by the athlete as relevant to the achievement of these goals, motivation will be increased and practice sustained in an enthusiastic manner. Perhaps it might be a good idea for the coach to explain to the athlete the rationale behind certain training procedures, especially if it appears that some resistance might be exhibited. In an era where authority figures are being questioned more and more, and youth are encouraged to think, analyze, and question, a "do as I say" attitude in sport does not work as universally as was the case years ago.

Enabling activities are only as meaningful as perceived by the athlete who must perform them. Intensity and duration of practice will be partially reflected by the favorable attitudes held by the athlete toward the training procedures. An understanding of the importance of them encourages the athlete to practice conscientiously.

10. Intrinsic motivation is preferable to extrinsic motivation in most athletic activities

There are many sources of extrinsic motivation that a coach can supply in athletic situations. A variety of reward systems are available and in fact are used in various sports. Even without the coach's intervention, it is indeed probable that many athletes are involved in sport for reasons that might be categorized as extrinsic sources of motivation.

For typical complex athletic events, nonetheless, it would appear that the development of intrinsic motivation will lead to more satisfying long-lasting results. Feelings of fulfillment, expression, and involvement will probably inspire the athlete to greater heights over a longer period of time than participation and competition for more materialistic gains. The preponderance of excellent athletes most likely receive both internal and external benefits from their chosen sport. One can achieve a sense of fulfillment as well as bask in the glories of fame and prestige. Nonetheless, favorable disposition toward the activity for personal, "idealistic" purposes would seem to be a strong and compelling force to continue conscientious training over a great span of time. In societies that seem to encourage the selection and demonstration of behaviors according to heavy reward systems, it is difficult to sustain motivation and best performances. A heavy dependence on rewards to influence the nature and type of athletic behaviors is not as desirable as the emittance of behavior that is self-generated for personally rewarding reasons. Figure 6 illustrates extrinsic and intrinsic sources of motivation.

Skilled performance may be defined in part as the ability to perform under self-regulation and direction rather than under the heavy reliance on external sources and environmental cues. It may also reflect a change from dependence on extrinsic sources of motivation to internally-generated sources. Extrinsic incentives may operate effectively to affect the attitudes of someone toward an activity and to stimulate an interest in it. The motivation to train may also occur. But ideally, the major force of action should change from extrinsic to intrinsic. Even more ideally, the primary initial rationale for undertaking an activity would be because of its intrinsic value to the participant.

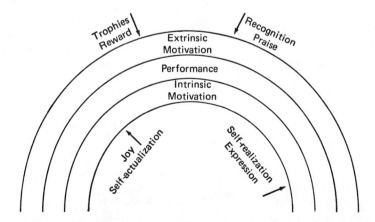

Figure 6. The interaction of extrinsic and intrinsic sources of motivation

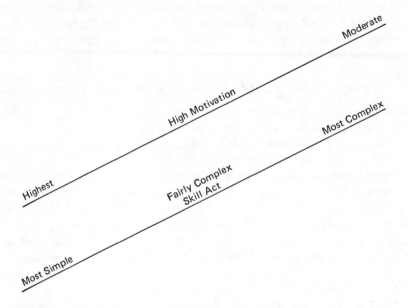

Figure 7. Level of motivation related to the difficulty level of activity

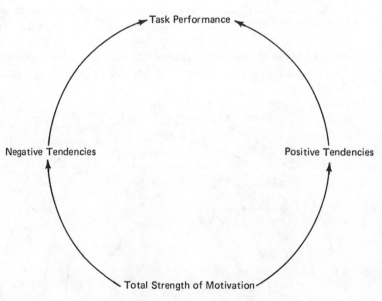

Figure 8. The total strength of motivation

11. The relationship of coactors and spectators to the performance of the athlete should be understood

Social facilitation theory was formulated in an attempt to explain the expected effects of the presence of others on one's behavior. The situation, from an arousal or motivation point of view, may not be the same when performing alone versus performing with others or in front of others. Social facilitation theory suggests that social effects tend to dampen the performance of the lowly skilled and to raise the performance of the more highly skilled. In other words, the relatively skilled athlete translates social situations as energy sources for better performances.

Practice conditions can be improved on occasion through social interactive processes, as coactors serve to inform, reinforce, and motivate each other. Competitive and cooperative situations oftentimes result in better performances than alone conditions.

The damaging arousal effects of spectators on the athlete's efforts do not appear with his increased skill and familiarity with such situations. Prior experiences performing with spectators present permit the athlete to be more resistant to potential negative influences on behavior. The stress of the competition, including meaningfulness of the contest and social-emotional conditions surrounding it is coped with by the superior athlete and even used to his advantage. Emotional control and direction (optimal level of motivation for the specific activity and situation) is learned or has to be learned.

TRUE LEVEL OF ABILITY: A SUMMARY

An attempt has been made to show that performance at any given time will reflect not only previously developed capabilities but the ability to energize the motivational level appropriate for the task and the situation. [A simplified example is found in Figure 7.]

The total strength of the motivation present within an individual may be considered as a conflict between positive and negative behavioral tendencies related to the situation (Figure 8). For example, the need to achieve and need to gain social approval may be balanced to some degree by the need to avoid failure or need to avoid success. Motivational strength is greatest when the positive valences far outweigh the negative ones. The result is persistent training to reach high and possibly distant future-oriented goals.

Personal, societal, activity, and situational factors operate in a complex manner to influence motivation and subsequent performances. Sources of motivation have been identified. Suggestions for influencing the average person or the individual have been made. Since, in fact, appropriate arousal may be the difference between coming closer or further from realizing the performance potential, or between winning or losing in competition, the psychology of motivation warrants serious analysis by the dedicated coach and athlete.

Achievement Training

Robert N. Singer and Robert Hilmer

Personal motives influence behaviors in a variety of ways. Due to past experiences and present expectations, athletes respond differently in similar situations. That aspect of personality that has been termed *motivation,* or more particularly, the *motive to achieve,* is responsible for:

1. the selection of one activity over another activity with regard to participation;
2. the effort expended within the activity;
3. the persistence demonstrated at an activity; and
4. the momentary quality of performance in an activity.

As we can see, motives influence decisions, and in turn, practice is more effective and efficient in activities when athletes are highly motivated for this purpose. In turn, it can be expected that skill will be improved and that athletes will develop more favorably in the sport of interest. But not all athletes reveal the same motives. Nor are they developed to the same extent. Furthermore, a person can show a high achievement motive for one activity and not for another activity.

Characteristics have been identified that are associated with those people who have been termed high achievers. Through an analysis of their behaviors, it then becomes possible to formulate notions about the training of others who do not demonstrate these same behaviors. If we can assume that achievement demonstrated in any given situation is reflected by capabilities and motivation, then we can readily deduce the importance of understanding motivation and how to improve the need to achieve in those who are apparently poorly motivated for special activities and responsibilities.

If we were to review the research in the past 20 years in which individuals designated as high need achievers were analyzed, we would make the following observations.[1] Those who have a high need to achieve:

1. demonstrate an extremely high persistence at tasks;
2. demonstrate exceptional quality in performance;
3. complete tasks at a high rate;
4. are task rather than person oriented;

[1] See the article by Singer on pages 40-55. —Ed.

5. take reasonable risks and enjoy stress;
6. like to take personal responsibility for their actions; and
7. like to have knowledge of the results of the activity in which they are involved (to judge capabilities in order to develop them further).

A recognition of these characteristics associated with a high need to achieve allows us to analyze others in order to develop such attributes within them if in fact they are not present. More specifically, it has become more apparent in recent years that the traditional approach of merely placing individuals into athletic training programs is an insufficient basis for assuming reasonable improvement. The same has been found to be true in industry and business. Productivity does not necessarily improve because procedures and policies are dictated. There are ways in which motives can be improved in order for work output and personal development to occur in a more desirable manner. Let us identify some of the key characteristics of an effective program that might be used to improve the achievement motive in those who are not well motivated.

ACHIEVEMENT TRAINING

If we are trying to change performance and practice habits, then we might first explore ways of influencing cognitive (knowing) and affective (feeling) behaviors.[2] People like to be aware of those reasons why they should change their behaviors. Intellectualizing the experiences and attempting to modify attitudes would seem to be a better approach than merely dictating training procedures. If they are going to be a part of a program, athletes would naturally want to know what it will do for them, why they should be involved in it. It is through an interactive process that a rationale can be developed, ideas exchanged, understandings improved, and attitudes changed.

Somehow, responsibility for performance must be borne by the participant (athlete) rather than the leader (coach). Personal decision-making and a perceived personal control over the situation will lead to a greater commitment. Once an understanding has been reached as to the value of a particular program, procedures can then be agreed upon as to how many goals may be attained. Let us state some of the principles more specifically with regard to improving the achievement motive:

1. Discussions between athletes and coaches should be held as to the purposes of a particular program.[3] Communication channels should be open and conducive to an exchange of ideas. The goal is to increase understandings and to modify attitudes.
2. Working together, the athlete should set specific, high, but attainable goals in the program under the guidance of the coach.[4] These should be long term as well as short term, with the short term goals providing the enabling activities in order to attain long term goals. The athlete knows that he has a role in the decision-making process and establishes personal goals.
3. Procedures to achieve the goals should be explored. As means are identified to achieve goals, the coach can help the athlete determine if the program can realistically help to

---

[2] See the article by Suinn on pages 26-36. —Ed.
[3] See the article by Nesvig on pages 250-260. —Ed.
[4] See the article by Botterill on pages 261-268. —Ed.

achieve the goals. In case there is incongruity between the program and the goals, either the goals should be lowered or the program intensified. Once again, this occurs through a mutual process of exploration and decision-making.

4.   Once the program has been determined, personal records of progress should be maintained.[5] These are good for motivational purposes.

5.   Wherever possible, feelings of self-confidence and self-image should be enhanced. Much depends on the relationship of the coach to the athlete. Reinforcement and communication processes can do much to help the participant gain the necessary self-confidence.

6.   There should be a constant reevaluation of the progress and achievement rate of the athlete. Perhaps goals will have to be shifted upward or downward or programs modified, depending upon situations. A continual evaluation of progress is a necessity.

These, then, are the principles of a sound achievement training program. If they are adhered to, we would expect the athlete's attitudes and performance to improve dramatically. The view here is that achievement can be reflected primarily through the interactive process, and both the coach and the athlete need to be involved in such a way as to establish a working relationship towards the establishment and realization of goals. The command or dictatorial process has inherent flaws in it. On the other hand, allowing the participant free rein in the decision-making process is also a frivolous activity. Yet, a fruitful relationship between the participant and leader can emerge with careful planning and thoughtfulness. These procedures, unfortunately, are not recognized and advocated or utilized in a sufficient number of situations. Hopefully, the recognition of an achievement orientation will lead to specially designed programs to enhance motives and productivity.

We would like to present an athletic situation here where achievement motivation procedures were actually used, in case the preceding discussion seems too idealistic and not practical enough.

A CASE STUDY

This case study involves the Forest City, Iowa, high school basketball team during the 1973-74 school year. The preceding year the team had a 10-11 record with three sophomores in the starting line-up. The team had won 9 of its last 14 games. Without the three best players the sophomore team finished the season with a 15-3 record. The coaching staff viewed the forthcoming season with cautious optimism. Although Forest City had four returning lettermen, other strong teams had returning personnel as well. Two teams had made it to the state tournament and had three of their top six players back. The previous conference champion also had three of the top six athletes returning. Another strong team had eight returning lettermen. The Forest City coaching staff felt it would be possible to play very well and finish anywhere from first to fifth in the conference standings.

The early stages of the season caused some concern on the part of the coaching staff as there seemed to be a "missing spark" that separates a good team from an outstanding team. This was true in practice as well as in games. However, the team did win its first four games. Then in three of the next four games the team was defeated rather easily by the stronger teams. Admittedly the

---

[5]See the article by Rushall on pages 63-72. –Ed.

squad could have conceivably played well and have had the same record. The head coach still was very concerned about the lack of hustle, or that something extra, that means so much to a team's performance.

After Christmas vacation and just before the third defeat occurred, the head coach gave each player a questionnaire to fill out and hand back in an attempt to explore the attitudes and feelings of the players. Before these were returned to the coach, the practices progressed much better and the crisis appeared to be over. As a result the coach at first viewed the questionnaires with only casual interest. But the next game was the third humiliating defeat that the team suffered.

The coaching staff held an emergency meeting after the game to discuss the situation to determine a course of action to get the team back on the road to success. After six hours of deliberation the coaching staff decided that it was necessary to select a starting five based on hustle alone although there were eight ball players of nearly equal ability. It was felt that the main problem confronting the team was to eliminate mental errors that had been present. The questionnaires were examined and it was decided to treat any one opinion as important regardless if only one player expressed this opinion or if all did.

These were opinions present in all of the questionnaires. All players indicated they thoroughly understood everything they were doing. Yet all at one time or another had committed mental errors. It seemed as if they took turns committing blunders that were costly to the team's success. It was difficult to find any item of consistency in the player opinions; very seldom did more than two or three of them answer any one question the same way. There was only one element of consistency. The players listed goals that were individually oriented. They indicated that lack of teamwork and hustle were major problems. Eight players indicated they were not ready mentally for practice each day; they were not motivated or had no confidence in themselves. The coaching staff decided to attack the problem of motivation.

During the following weekend the head coach visited the homes of the athletes and talked with the athletes and their parents in an attempt to uncover any additional information that might help. The athletes who were not at home met with the coach individually before the next week of practice began. The question posed to the athletes was: what can be done to get things turned around? None seemed to have an answer, tending to blame themselves and the squad as a whole for lack of hustle. Some admitted that they were thinking more of themselves than the team. Most wanted a starting five and this was about all they requested of the coaching staff. It might be of interest to note that after the move was made to form a starting five, those athletes who had been playing a lot and suddenly found themselves benched more of the time weren't so sure a starting five was a good idea any more.

The key to the situation seemed to be the player with the most natural ability. At the time he was the leading scorer, leading rebounder, and leading shooter percentagewise. However, he did best in games against the weak teams and didn't perform well against the stronger teams. Some researchers might have described him as a poor competitor. Others may have used the term *success phobia* to indicate his lack of achievement in key situations. The head coach felt he had not worked as hard as the rest of the squad for one reason or another. The athletes individually had indicated they wanted the starting five selected on the basis of hustle rather than potential ability. They were asked to list the five players who had hustled the most up to that point in the season excluding themselves. The opinions of the players concurred with those of the coaching staff. The best athlete was not included on the starting five. He was told this at the home visitation since the coach waited to visit him last and knew that the players and coaching staff had agreed on the starting five.

The next week in practice the coaching staff initiated a campaign in motivation. The first thing was to hold a team meeting before the first practice of the week. The coach mentioned some of the opinions that had been expressed in the questionnaires without mentioning names and asked for any other suggestions that the players might have had. He indicated the coaching staff would form a starting five based on the criteria the squad had set. Some players had felt the poor school spirit was a factor in the situation. The coaching staff challenged the players to develop that school spirit themselves with an exciting and successful brand of basketball and to quit feeling sorry for themselves, indicating that this was going to be the attitude of the coaching staff itself.

No longer in the conference championship race, the team and coaches established the goal of using the rest of the season in preparation for tournament play. By the way, Forest City had won only one district tournament in 20 years. The coach then had the squad elect a leader for the rest of the year. The coach requested that team members sit together in a special section during the preliminary sophomore game on nights of home games. Perhaps the most successful action taken in regard to the team as a whole was to create a Mau Mau Squad composed of players who had not seen much game action. This unit was in charge of squad preparation and morale. They were given special jerseys to distinguish it from others in practice. They were instructed to tape numbers on their jerseys matching the numbers of players on the team Forest City was to play next. This unit was to run the other offenses and defenses during the week.

The coach had his wife call the families of the players inviting them to the next game and asking them to sit in a special parent's rooting section right behind the players' bench. The sophomore coach, who was also the head football coach, rounded up athletes from other sports to form a special Go-Go Spirit Club. The only instructions were to make constant noise from opening whistle until final buzzer at the games. They were encouraged to sit as a unit in the front row of the bleachers facing the squad from across the floor. It is of interest to note that one of the leading figures in the Go-Go Spirit Club was a player that had quit during the third week of practice after having nailed down one of the starting berths.

The emphasis that week in practice was on positive motivation structured around practices designed to be fun first, learning second. It was a satisfying week of practice, with mistakes made from over-hustling rather than not hustling. After the game on Friday night the coach also initiated another procedure known as the Unity Circle. Immediately following a game when all the players and coaches had reached the locker room they grouped together in a circle clasping hands in the middle. Each individual spent 30 seconds of silent thought concerning the opportunity for group experience in athletics. The coach concluded the ritual by asking the players if they were proud to be a member of the team. After the response he asked if they can get ready for the next week of practice. This experience seemed to provide the players with a feeling of group achievement or failure rather than individual success or failure. Especially after defeat, it left the players with a more positive feeling and less of a feeling of frustration as they departed from the locker room for the weekend.

For the remainder of the season, the team was very difficult to beat. The player with the most ability hustled and played his way back into the line-up and did not let up once. His attitude carried over into other school activities and he seemed to exhibit self-fulfillment in his many activities. The only defeat suffered by the team up to tournament play came when it was weakened physically. One game was lost during a flu epidemic, and three others were lost when the best player and one other starter were injured. Even then the scores against strong teams were close. Not once did the athletes use the injuries as rationalization for defeat. During the week of the flu epidemic the team voted to play the game even though four starters had missed at least two of the four practices. Two teams had previously postponed games with Forest City because of the flu. Forest City won the district tournament and came within two games of getting to the state tournament. Eight lettermen returned for the next season.

The next year, 1974-75, virtually the same players finished third in the state tournament with a 23-1 record. One player from the team played during the following season, 1975-76, and Forest City High School finished 21-3, with a state championship. The team used many of the same techniques that were innovated the year before. Some other techniques found to be successful during the past few years are the following:

1. Each player is given a chance to perform with the first team in practice at least once or twice during the three weeks before the first game. This gives each player an opportunity to demonstrate that he knows the offensive system and defensive alignments in a setting where he has teammates who are competent, too.

2. The assistant coaches are given the opportunity to develop the structure of their program with the head coach. Each coach helps determine the goals of the program at his level as well as determine how his techniques can contribute to the over-all goal of the varsity game. Forest City High School has found that this results in goals that are designed to make basketball a meaningful experience to each athlete, rather than to simply win ball games. The assistants tend to show a great desire to contribute in any way that they can to an effective program.

3. As the season progresses the coaching staff makes sure that those who are not starters know in what situations they will most likely play. An example from this past season is that there were three reserve guards who were called on in different situations. One was very quick on defense and, if the opponents had a hot outside shooter, he went into the game. Another player could penetrate well on offense and, if the defense was forcing the offense to the outside, he played. A third sagged well and helped effectively on defense; if help was needed on a big man inside, this guard played. Each player knew he might not play much for three games, depending on the opponents. Or he might play quite a bit a given night. This prevented any misunderstandings as to why one went in first on a particular night and another went in first on a different night.

4. The coaching staff uses a post-season form to give to the players at the end of the season. These forms show the player where he fits into the program for the next year. The first part of the form deals with the player's strengths, the next part deals with things the player needs to work on to improve his skills, and the third shows him where he fits into the staff's plans for the coming season. It is hoped that this can provide intrinsic motivation for the players to work hard in the off season.

5. Another technique deemed effective this year was to discuss the team's weaknesses in the open rather than to try not to mention them. The greatest weakness was the press offense. Other teams pressed Forest High very effectively early in the year, with zone and man-to-man presses. In drills to overcome this problem not one player was found who could dribble up the floor easily in a one-on-one situation. Alternative techniques were tried to remedy the situation, and it was to some degree.

6.   Finally, after a loss the coaches and players sit together on the bus or in the locker room to discuss the problems encountered. The players' opinions and views are very important to the coaching staff as to preparation for the same team in the future.

CONCLUDING REMARKS

It is just as important to teach athletes *how to learn* and to perform as what to learn and to perform. Spirit and morale are tied together with motivation. The right atmosphere can bring out the best in anyone.

The coaching staff at Forest City High School attempted to involve all the players in making decisions affecting the team. The players did not exist at the mercy of the coaches. Realistic personal and team goals were established. All players contributed, in their own way, to the good of the team.

Every attempt was made to have everyone think positively. Personal and team evaluations were continually made throughout the season, with everyone taking their share of the responsibilities.

It is imperative to remember that performance reflects learning and motivation. Even previous learning, resulting in a certain skill level, is dependent upon motivation for selection of, perseverance at, and effort in an activity. Present motivation mirrors attitudes, expectations, attributions, and arousal level. Is there any doubt of the necessity to encourage athletes and coaches to become achievement-oriented, but within an environment that encourages the total development of all concerned?

Using Applied Behavior Analysis for Altering Motivation

Brent S. Rushall

THE PRINCIPLES FOR ALTERING MOTIVATION

The first decision for coaches to make is to determine the behaviors which are important in their sports. This is rarely done as long-term plans and system designs are a rarity in sports. However, coaches have to be able to answer the question "to motivate athletes to do what?"[1] The implication of this decision process is not difficult when the behaviors already exist in the athletes' behavior repertoires. When they do not exist or need to be altered the coach first has to develop or alter the behaviors. The procedures for doing these are called shaping strategies and are discussed elsewhere (Rushall and Siedentop 1972).

The second decision for coaches is to determine when each of the following behaviors should occur. There will be some behaviors such as rule-following behaviors, attending behaviors, task-completion behaviors, etc. which need to be emitted whenever they are appropriate across many situations. There are others which should only be performed under certain circumstances, e.g., maximum efforts, forehand drives, a lay-up. Athletes need to be taught to discriminate the environmental cues which signal that an appropriate behavior should be performed. Thus, what and when behaviors are to be performed need to be determined before trying to effect behavior control.

The first principle for effecting control is that behaviors should be positively reinforced (rewarded) to cause an increase in response rates.[2] It should be noted also that persons behave to avoid and escape noxious events (negative reinforcers). For this discussion, only positive reinforcement will be considered.

The scope of positive reinforcers which are significant for individuals usually far exceeds those comprehended by a coach. There now exists a measurement/reporting procedure which indicates those circumstances and events which occur in the sports environment which function as positive

Brent S. Rushall. Using applied behavior analysis for altering motivation. An invited address presented at the Annual Conference of the North American Society for the Psychology of Sport and Physical Activity, Ithaca College, 24 May 1977.

[1] See the article by Botterill on pages 261-268 and the article by Singer and Hilmer on pages 56-62. —Ed.

[2] The reader is referred to the text *The development and control of behavior in sports and physical education* by B. S. Rushall and D. Siedentop (1972) for a full treatment of behavior control.

THIS LIST DESCRIBES THE ASPECTS OF PERFORMANCE AND PERFORMANCE INFORMATION THAT THIS SWIMMER WOULD LIKE TO OCCUR WITH REGARD TO HIS/HER SWIMMING.

HAVING HIS/HER TIMES IMPROVE CONTINUALLY IN TRAINING.

GETTING AS MUCH INFORMATION AS POSSIBLE ABOUT SWIMMING, E.G. HOW TO TRAIN, THE CORRECT TECHNIQUES, HOW TO PREPARE FOR RACES, ETC.

RECEIVING FREQUENT INDICATIONS (AT LEAST ONCE A DAY) AS TO WHETHER HE/SHE IS OR IS NOT IMPROVING.

KNOWING THE TIME FOR EVERY REPEAT THAT IS SWUM IN TRAINING.

KNOWING HIS/HER PROGRESS AND IMPROVEMENT IN EVENT TIMES, ACCUMULATED TRANING MILEAGE AND TECHNIQUES.

* *

THE FOLLOWING ITEMS ARE ALSO MOTIVATORS FOR THIS INDIVIDUAL-

HAVING HIS/HER NAME APPEAR IN NEWSPAPERS AND PRESS RELEASES AND ANNOUNCED ON RADIO OR ON TELEVISION.

BEING ABLE TO TRAVEL AWAY TO MEETS.

RECEIVING MEDALLIONS AND RIBBONS FOR RACING.

* *

THE FOLLOWING CHARACTERISTICS DESCRIBE THE ASPECTS OF COMPETITION THAT ARE LIKED BY THIS SWIMMER-

BEING ABLE TO PLACE FREQUENTLY IN RACES.

INDIVIDUAL RACES ARE CONSIDERED TO BE MORE IMPORTANT THAN RELAYS.

COMPETITION IS USED MAINLY TO DETERMINE WHETHER HE/SHE HAS OR HAS NOT IMPROVED.

HAVING RACE TIMES IMPROVE MOTIVATES THIS INDIVIDUAL TO TRAIN MORE AND HARDER.

COMPETING ITSELF IS ENJOYABLE ALTHOUGH PLACING IN RACES DOES NOT OCCUR VERY FREQUENTLY.

Figure 1. A sample page of a computer output of the motivational events which are significant for the examped individual

reinforcers for each athlete. This is derived from the use of environment specific behavior inventories (Rushall 1975*c*) and a computerized analysis service.[3] The analysis lists the social circumstances, forms of performance information, aspects of training and competition, material rewards[4] and self-control factors which are positively reinforcing for each athlete. An example of some computer output is contained in Figure 1. This analysis provides the coach with a recipe of the significant events which occur in the sport that can be used to reinforce behaviors.

[3]Sport Science Associates, 376 Algoma Street North, Thunder Bay, Ontario. An analysis costs $10.00 per individual.
[4]See the article by Youngblood and Suinn on pages 73-77. —Ed.

It is also possible for coaches to experiment with events and to see if they function as positive reinforcers. Rushall and Siedentop (1972) categorized events as being social, performance information, material, and internal and suggested their use as reinforcers (Figure 2). It is also possible to mix qualities of these events, for example producing a consequence containing both social and performance information characteristics, to produce a very strong reinforcer. New events (novelty) and preferred activities (things the athlete really likes to do) also serve as reinforcers in certain circumstances.

TYPE OF REINFORCER	EXAMPLES
Social	Coach—"very well done," signaling a correct response, providing attention and approval
	Peer—congratulating after a performance, encouragement, peer approval
	Public display—performance boards, recognition of achievement
Material	Candy, tokens, points, marks out of 10
Performance	Time, goal achievement, criterion performance, hitting a target, performing to accuracy, correct feeling, improvement in time
Internal	Watching others being rewarded, achieving a personal goal, meeting a performance standard

Figure 2. A reinforcer classification scheme as indicated by Rushall and Siedentop (1972)

The discussion of reinforcers is quite involved and the reader is referred to the Rushall and Siedentop text (1972) for further information and elucidation on the topic. Coaches need to increase the amount of positive reinforcement that is supplied to athletes contingent upon their performance of specific behaviors.

In applying positive reinforcement two points should be kept in mind. First, it is necessary to produce periodic negative reinforcement rather than to attempt only positive reinforcement. A ratio of 1:4 is a good "ball-park" figure for the frequency of the two. Second, do not ascribe both negative and positive qualities to the same events. It has been observed that at one stage of a training session athletes have been made to do more push-ups as punishment for not executing a play effectively. This also occurs with situps, extra laps, stair runs, etc. The inconsistency factor in operating this way decreases one's potential for achieving effective control.

The second principle for gaining control is to effect a greater frequency of provision of positive reinforcement. This can emanate from two sources, the coach and noncoach entities. When the coach considers himself or herself to be a valuable source of reinforcement he/she should attempt to concentrate on and maximize this form of behavior because it is the most important coaching behavior although one of the least emphasized.

It should be realized that the logistics of the coach:athlete ratio of most sporting environments is such that a coach's effect is diluted often to the point where it becomes ineffective. The provision of adventitious group rewards and acknowledgments (such as "Good work, team" and "That's the way to go," etc.) has no permanent effect of any consequence on the performances of individual athletes. Coaches must concentrate on providing *individual* positive reinforcement. A coach can alter his/her behavior to supply more reinforcement more effectively. That is, coaching effectiveness can be elevated by increasing the quantity and quality of positive reinforcement. For the sake of simplicity it is necessary to differentiate between rewards and performance information. Rewards indicate approval of or the adequacy of a behavior. Performance information indicates aspects of the behavior.

Whenever a coach sees a good behavior or execution of a task he/she should reward it. In teaching this is often termed as utilizing a *teachable moment*. The main point is to supply the reinforcement immediately after the desirable behavior has been observed. The greater the number of rewarding behaviors emitted by the coach the greater is his/her potential for effect although in my opinion this will still remain relatively low.

The quality of rewarding behavior can be increased if the coach is able to emote more and to vary the characteristics of the rewarding behavior. Figure 3 indicates some of the parameters of good coach or teacher behaviors which serve as reinforcers. The figure is termed a reinforcer synthesizer because by varying the ingredients in different combinations a coach can have a virtual limitless arsenal of rewarding behaviors. This is important because most coaches are very limited and invariant in their rewarding behaviors. With practice at implementing these features and a conscientious endeavor to increase the frequency of reward a coach can upgrade his/her coaching performance.

Performance information is necessary for indicating the level of adequacy of a behavior. It is provided usually for the level of effort, skill level, execution of tasks, performer interaction, work volume, and amplitude of response. When a reward and performance information are combined in that order the athlete is motivated to do the behavior again in accordance with the new information, i.e., it is repeated or altered in some way. The reasons for combining both reward and performance information are (1) the performance information alone is explanation or direction and does *not* motivate, and (2) good elements in the behavior are rewarded while only those which need to be changed are indicated and subsequently altered.

A coach should concentrate on the following behaviors to alter his/her effect on the motivation of athletes.

1. Increase the frequency of rewards.
2. Increase the quality of rewards.
3. Increase the frequency of rewards in combination with performance information.
4. Increase the quality of rewards in combination with performance information.

Coaches can enhance the quantity and quality of reinforcement within the sport situation by increasing the sources of reinforcement. It appears that coach-oriented environments generally feature low motivational effects. What motivation exists is maintained by the trial-and-error circumstances that occur in the environment, the majority of which are weak in their reinforcing strength. To support this contention it is worthwhile to consider a study by McKenzie (1972).

KEY WORDS		VOICE MODULATION	GESTICULATION	PROXIMITY	SUBJECT
Top notch	Out of this world	Pitch up	Wave arms	Touch	Individual
Capital	A1	Pitch down	Punch air	Close	Sub-group
First class	Grand	Volume up	OK sign	Medium	Group
First rate	Beautiful	Volume down	Clap	Distant	
Magnifique	Incredible	Pitch high	Smile		
Stupendous	Unbelievable	Pitch low	Nod		
Superlative	Fantastic	Volume high	Pat on back		
Good	Proud	Volume low	Squeeze		
Super	Superb	Pronunciation slow	Thumbs up		
Fabulous	Splendid	Emphasis	Point		
Amazing	Magnificent		Arm around shoulders		
Far out	Terrific				
Dynamite	Great				
Phenomenal	Marvellous				
Tremendous	Wonderful				
	Gorgeous				

Figure 3. A reinforcer synthesizer

A comparison was made between coach-controlled and athlete-controlled organization effects on the behaviors of swimmers. A number of conditions were compared, (1) normal training circumstances, (2) training sessions where the two coaches in charge concentrated solely on providing praise and reproof to the exclusion of other coaching behaviors, and (3) the employment of a behavior game where the swimmers provided consequences for each other's behaviors. Figure 4 illustrates the responsiveness of the athletes to the three different conditions. Under normal training circumstances each of four swimmers displayed inappropriate behaviors. When the coaches concentrated solely on positive and negative consequences for the swimmers' behaviors there was a noticeable effect. However, when the swimmers employed a behavior game and were responsible for controlling each others' behaviors the effect was most striking and far more effective than the other two conditions. As a matter of fact when the athlete-controlled situations were removed the control over the swimmers' behaviors was less evident. The point behind this illustration is that when the consequences of behavior are frequent (as assumed in the athlete-controlled condition) behavior control is more effective.

It is proposed that coaches increase the amount of reinforcement in sport situations by utilizing sources of control other than just the coach. As exampled above, athletes should be taught how and when to provide reinforcement for each other. Athletes should also be taught how to reinforce themselves through objective self-evaluation of all the performance aspects of their sport (self-reinforcement). Increasing the athletes' awareness of the task-orientations of training will increase the amount of performance information that can be derived from the coach, peers, and the athletes themselves. Finally, the coach can be more effective in control by providing more frequent quality consequences if reinforcers are administered to small homogeneous groups or individuals rather than to the total group.

Effective motivation can be increased if the coach alters the social situation of the training program from coach-oriented group control to athlete/coach-oriented individual control situations. The quality and quantity of positive consequences will be increased under these altered circumstances. Consequently, the sport situation will be more motivating for more behaviors than is possible in the commonly observed restricted coach-centered circumstances.

Increasing the rate of positive reinforcement in order to alter the levels of motivation is important for the initial stages of change. To be most effective the supply should be continuous, i.e., every occurrence of the behavior should be reinforced. However, it can soon be realized that this would be impossible for all individuals, doing all behaviors in normal sporting circumstances. Once again the logistics of such a situation would become overwhelming but not nearly so in the proposed "enriched" reinforcement environments as opposed to the traditional coach-oriented environments. The answer to this problem is to provide reinforcement continuously (for every response) in the initial stages of alteration and then to make multiple responses dependent upon varied occurrences of reinforcement.

The provision of continuous positive reinforcement (+CRe) requires some organizational changes. Some alternatives are:

1. The coach as the source of +CRe would have to devote blocks of time to individuals or small homogeneous groups to the exclusion of others in the sporting group. This is not as difficult as it might appear particularly if positive reinforcement emanates from sources other than the coach to maintain the on-going behaviors of the athletes not attended to by the coach.

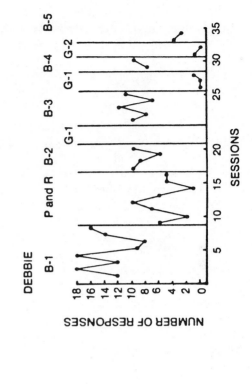
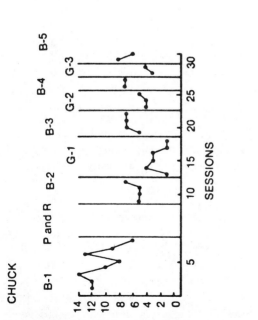

2.   Devise technologies which supply continuous reinforcement. An example of such a device was the program board discussed by McKenzie (1972), McKenzie and Rushall (1974), Rushall (1975*b*), and Rushall and Pettinger (1969). A further example of a device for providing continuous evaluative information (reward plus performance information) was described by Rushall (1975*a*).

Another device was used to shape the stability of a sculling boat. An alarm system is activated when the craft is tilted to a pre-set angle. This signals the sculler that his balance is unsatisfactory. In this application the sculler attempts to avoid the original angle of the tilt. The angle of instability is gradually reduced in each training session. The balancing of the craft is gradually shaped to an acceptable level. Normally, this performance characteristic has to be taught by a coach over a long period of time (perhaps two months or more). In this situation not only is the coach relieved of this task (the device teaches the sculler) but the time period is reduced to a few days. . . .

3.   Teach athletes how to evaluate and reinforce their own behaviors. This requires some attempt at educating athletes about their sport and appropriate self-analysis methods.

4.   Coordinate the program training session to have every member evaluating each other and themselves on the same behavioral content as in a behavior game.

What is required to generate +CRe is an honest attempt to remove the organizational inertia which is so prevalent in sports today. This can be facilitated by having a systematic development program which extends over a considerable period of time. It is better to think small in terms of the amount of control that is sought rather than to do too much at one time. The provision of +CRe will increase the rate of occurrence of behaviors. Once the behavior is occurring frequently enough it then becomes a problem of establishing persistent responding.

The principle of applied behavior analysis that involves developing persistent responding also produces responding for a low pay-off rate. The procedure for doing this is called *stretching the schedule of reinforcement.* Stretching the schedule first requires the intermittent missing of reinforcements for adequate behaviors. Gradually, more and more reinforcements are omitted until the athlete performs many behaviors for a single reinforcement, i.e., a low pay-off rate. The implementation of this stretching in the circumstances of coaching is an art. If the schedule is stretched too quickly the response rate will decrease as the behavior will be partly extinguished. It is better to be too conservative rather than too hurried in this stage of development. An example of stretching the schedule to produce intermittent reinforcement that maintained a response was provided by Smith (1973) in modifying the behaviors of a swimming coach.

The development of maintenance schedules may not be necessary in some circumstances. With the use of program boards in swimming reinforcement was continuous and self-generated. It was found that the motivated rates of training behaviors were maintained after two months of continuous use without any sign of diminution (McKenzie 1972). Similar observations were made with the performance information device for balance that was discussed above. It appears that when continuous reinforcement is self-generated and based on objective measurements, the persistency of the response rate is very enduring without having to stretch the schedule. There are vast amounts of performance information which are intrinsic to activities that always are available with sporting behaviors.

There is a problem concerned with relying on contrived positive reinforcement. Consider what would happen if devices did not function or the individual responsible for the +CRe was not in attendance. The source of reinforcement would be removed and the control program would not be in effect. Thus, for attaining total control, it is important that the sources of reinforcement be altered in the final stages. The sources should occur *naturally* in the environment.

One of the easiest sources of reinforcement to use to produce persistent responding is self-evaluation. When an individual is able to evaluate his/her behaviors and to determine their adequacy then that source of reinforcement will always be available under all circumstances. This, then, is the final principle for producing an altered state of motivation, relinquishing control to naturally occurring reinforcements. The implication of this for the coach is that athletes have to be taught how and when to evaluate behavior and to adopt standards for decision making.

Self-evaluation and control[5] can be augmented by procedures and sources which occur consistently in the sports environment (the coach, peers, public displays). Ideally, a coach would engineer a dual situation for all forms of reinforcement when a behavior is supported by a stretched schedule. The two circumstances would be to self-reinforce and/or be reinforced externally. This would guarantee reinforcement which would be contingent upon responding under the new motivated conditions.

The alteration of motivated states requires a number of decisions and procedures to be followed. They are:

1. Determine the behaviors to be motivated.
2. Determine an implementation schedule for change.
3. Enrich the quantity, and sources of positive reinforcement.
4. Continuously reinforce the target behavior to produce the desired rate of occurrence.
5. Stretch the schedule of reinforcement until varied amounts of multiple responding are necessary for reinforcement to occur.
6. Transfer the reinforcement to naturally occuring consequences.
7. Repeat steps 4 through 6 until the implementation schedule is completed.

CONCLUSION

Applied behavior analysis will produce better coaching and teaching effects. Its use of observable and measurable elements which produce principles and procedures for altering behavior makes it appropriate for practitioners. Applied behavior analysis is the most effective method for achieving behavior control and development.

This presentation consisted of two emphases. The first part enumerated the basic postulates underlying operant psychology to justify its scientific and functional value. The second part briefly indicated the application of the functional relationships which have resulted from the scientific inquiries into behavior. The application embraced the altering of motivation in sports situations. The scope of the application was to consider the control potential of the environment for achieving that end. . . . That could be termed *extrinsic motivation*.

[5] See the article by Spinelli and Barrios on pages 344-355 and the article by Suinn on pages 26-36. —Ed.

REFERENCES

McKenzie, T. L. 1972. Effects of various reinforcing contingencies on behaviors in a competitive swimming environment. Unpublished M.Sc. thesis, Dalhousie University.

McKenzie, T. L., and Rushall, B. S. 1974. Effects of self-recording contingencies on improving attendance and performance in a competitive swimming training environment. *Journal of Applied Behavior Analysis* 7:199-206.

Rushall, B. S. 1975a. Applied behavior analysis of sports and physical education. *International Journal of Sport Psychology* 6:75-88.

——. 1975b. A motivational device for competitive swimming training. *Swimming Technique* 11:103-106.

——. 1975c. Environment specific behavior inventories: Developmental procedures. In *Proceedings of the IV Congrès de la Fédération Européene de Psychologie des Sports et des Activités Corporelles,* Edinburgh, 1975.

Rushall, B. S., and Pettinger, J. 1969. An evaluation of the effect of various reinforcers used as motivators in swimming. *Research Quarterly* 40:540-545.

Rushall, B. S., and Siedentop, D. 1972. *The development and control of behavior in sports and physical education.* Philadelphia: Lea and Febiger.

Smith, K. C. 1973. The modification of a competitive swimming coach's behavior. Unpublished M.Sc. thesis, Dalhousie University.

A Behavioral Assessment
of Motivation

David Youngblood and Richard M. Suinn

The measurement of motivation is one of the leading interests of coaching staff seeking the help of psychology. Motivational level is considered one of those intangibles, powerful enough to make the difference between success and failure, yet so ambiguous as to defy assessment. Attempts to identify the motivational structure of an athlete have usually depended upon instruments which measure personality structure, from which inferences are made about motivation. This reflects the state of psychological testing today in that the test for directly measuring motivation is nearly non-existent. An even greater problem is the lack of assessment instruments designed for athletes.[1] Although a few are available, the results are usually reported in terms which still tend to reflect traditional views of motivation developed by psychologists. Our approach was aimed at designing a scale which measured factors that would have direct meaning for coaching staff, specifically, factors which could readily be translated by coaches into actions on their part which would be expected to touch the motivational characteristics of their athletes. For, after all, identifying the motivational characteristics of an athlete is important only if this leads to some answer to the question of "What can we do about it?"

The first step was a preliminary listing of needs which might be involved in an athlete's choosing to be in athletics. Another requirement was that the list involve needs that would have meaning for coaches without requiring the services of special consultation with a psychologist. Through the combined efforts of the senior author (a swimming and diving coach) and the second author (the head of the psychology department), such a list was generated. This list was then submitted to 17 psychology faculty, 22 coaches in the athletic department, and 16 members of the physical education faculty who had prior participation or experiences in coaching. These individuals were asked to further add to the list based upon their experiences.

A final list of 19 categories was developed. Within this framework, five specific subcategories were identified which defined more clearly the motivational factors involved. For example, social approval was the first category. This was in turn subdivided into parental social approval, peer social approval, social approval from opposite sex persons, social approval from same sex persons, and approval from coach. Table 1 shows each of the categories and subcategories. Finally, each of the subcategories was converted into a question to be answered in a test format. We administered

[1] See the article by Horsfall, Fisher, and Morris on pages 163-168 and the article by Rushall on pages 63-72. —Ed.

Table 1. Motivational Categories

Category 1: Social Approval

a.   Parental approval
b.   Peer approval
c.   Opposite sex approval
d.   Coach approval
e.   Same sex approval

Category 2: Competition

a.   Against time
b.   Against fellow team members
c.   Competing rather than practicing
d.   Against rival teams
e.   Defeating specific competitors

Category 3: Self-mastery

a.   Mentally push yourself farther
b.   Achieve control of mind over body
c.   Feeling more in control of body movements
d.   More control of personal emotions
e.   Learn new skills

Category 4: Life Style

a.   Family participation
b.   Habit
c.   Lack of something better to do
d.   Introduced to activity at early age
e.   Parents decided for you

Category 5: Fear of Failure

a.   Critical comments from others
b.   What others might say
c.   Self-criticism
d.   Finish in last place
e.   How others view your performances

Category 6: Physical Fitness and Health

a.   Feel healthier
b.   Increased muscle tone
c.   Keep in good shape
d.   Greater physical strength
e.   Sense of physical well-being

Category 7. Friendship and Personal Associations

a.   Fellow team members
b.   Meeting other competitors at contests
c.   Meeting other teams' coaches
d.   Meeting athletes of other sports
e.   Meeting famous athletes

Category 8: Success and Achievement

a.   Achieve more in practice
b.   Being a participant in an important contest
c.   Achieve in training periods
d.   Achieve personal goals
e.   Setting higher levels of achievement

Category 9: Tangible Payoffs

a.   Athletic scholarship
b.   Travel
c.   Extra awards (extra coaching, equipment, etc.)
d.   Athletic awards
e.   Chance for better life (job, money, etc.)

Category 10: Recognition

a.   By peers
b.   By the public
c.   By younger persons
d.   By older persons
e.   By special people

Category 11: Intimidation/Control

a.   By the coach giving instructions
b.   By the coach being angry
c.   By the coach directing your training
d.   By the coach criticizing severely
e.   By the coach telling you exactly what to do

Table 1 (continued)

Category 12: Heterosexuality

a. Being more attractive to the opposite sex
b. Dating because of athletics
c. Athletics having positive effect on social life
d. Getting more dates
e. Being dated because you are an athlete

Category 13: Competing Conditions/Crowds

a. Competing before a large enthusiastic audience
b. The crowd focusing on your event
c. Being viewed as the "favorite"
d. Crowd watching you only
e. Competing with lots of noise and fanfare

Category 14: Independence/Individuality

a. Deciding your own training schedule
b. Practice alone
c. Few rules/requirements about training
d. Help coach decide training schedule
e. Viewed as an individual or team member

Category 15: "Family"

a. "Family" belonging in team situations
b. Being able to talk to athletic personnel
c. Athletic personnel being a substitute family
d. Confide in athletic personnel
e. Close relationship with coaches, teammates, etc.

Category 16: Emotional Release

a. Competing bringing sense of calmness
b. Letting your feelings take action
c. Feeling exhilarated
d. Being in athletic situation being pleasing
e. "Let it all hang out" in athletic competition

Category 17: Status

a. Others view you as more important
b. Others put you on a higher level
c. Others look up to you
d. Others treat you with more respect
e. You feeling more important

Category 18: Self Direction/Awareness

a. Getting a focus in life
b. Greater sense of confidence
c. Knowing better what direction to follow
d. Feeling better about yourself as a person
e. Feeling you are "special"

Category 19: Understanding Reasons

a. Coach explains purpose of your training
b. Coach explains reasons for changing your techniques
c. Coach explains reasons for training regulations
d. Coach explains his directives
e. Coach explains his actions regarding your competing

the final test under two formats, a yes-no format and a rating scale format. Under the first, the questions required a yes or no answer, e.g., for measuring parental social approval, the question was worded "Do your parents show an interest in your sports activities?" Under the rating format, the athlete was required to rate the importance of the item in influencing "your willingness to turn out for the team, to practice, to continue swimming for the season, to perform at a high level, to try harder." Results of both formats were studied separately to see which provided the most usable approach.

The next phase of our study involved soliciting the cooperation of competitive teams and their coaching staffs. Collaboration was obtained from the members and coaches of the Colorado State University and University of Colorado women's swimming and diving teams, with a total of 25 athletes participating. The help of the coaching staff was obtained to validate the motivational scale, for although the items seem to make sense on the surface, some external source of validation was needed to prove that the instrument measured motivational levels. Towards this purpose, the coaches were asked to assign their own rating of each of their athletes, based upon their direct observations and without any knowledge of the test results. For further interest, these coaches were asked to complete ratings at four different times in the season: at the beginning of the season just following training (rating 1), after about two weeks of competition (rating 2), within about two weeks of the end of the season (rating 3), and following the regional championships (rating 4).

The results were gratifying. In general, the total scores showed significant correlation with coaches' ratings of motivation, with the yes-no format being somewhat better in predicting the coaches' ratings across the season. This format also seemed to provide for greater likelihood that the answers obtained from the athletes would remain stable, as evidenced by the higher reliability data. A very intriguing set of findings was also found when the specific motivational categories were examined. As the reader will recall, some 19 motivational categories were used, ranging from Social Approval to Emotional Release. When the scores from each of these categories were separately compared with coaches' ratings of motivation taken during each of the four time periods, some interesting results were obtained. Under the yes-no format, the categories of Fear of Failure and Emotional Release predicted motivational level during rating period 1 (just at the end of training), while the category Life Style was most associated with motivation during periods 2 and 3 (during the competitive season), and the categories of Social Approval and Competition best correlated with motivation during the rating period 4 (right after the regionals). When the data from the rating scale format were examined, the categories Self-Mastery, Recognition, Intimidation/Control, Emotional Release, and Status were significant for rating period 1; Intimidation/Control for periods 2 and 3; and Competition, Self-Mastery, Achievement, Recognition, Intimidation/Control, Heterosexuality, Crowds, Emotional Release, and Status, were significant for period 4. What does this mean? It could reflect the different and changing motives which influence an athlete across the competitive season. Thus, the athlete who works the hardest during training and prior to team selection may be the one experiencing a fear of failing, a desire for self-mastery, recognition and status. Once the season begins, after the team has been selected, and during the great pressure from competing daily activities such as studies and social life, the athletes that work the hardest may be responding to different factors entirely. These seem to be life style and intimidation/control. Life style needs to be explained to understand its contribution. It is a category introduced by the second author from his observations of national and Olympic team members in another study. As a consultant to such teams, he has test results covering several years. A striking finding is the lack of consistency of scores on achievement scales. Although a natural premise is that Olympic qualifiers should score high on achievement motivation (and some did nearly take the top of the scale), a number showed very low scores. In examining the total social histories for such athletes, it seemed that life style served as important a role.[2] Specifically, high levels of performance might be expected where the competitor was raised in competition from youth, such that athletic competition became a way of life. This is similar to those who began jogging

---

[2] See the article by Pargman on pages 90-98, the article by Balazs on pages 156-162, and the article by Gunby on pages 179-201.

for health reasons and who then discover that running has become so much a part of their lives that the idea of quitting is aversive, even for a day.

Getting back to the data of this study, it would seem reasonable that a life style of competing becomes predictive of motivational ratings during the long and often dreary competitive season. The other category that turned up, Intimidation/Control, also becomes sensible if one supposes that the glamour of athletics begins to fade during the season itself. At this point, the establishment of directives and control from the coaching staff may be just what is needed to spur the athlete on.

The other side of this study is the possible meaning of the results for coaches. It is true that the results offer hope that the instrument may be a simple but useful way of assessing motivational level: the higher the total score, the higher the motivation of the athlete. However, the more important impact could be the implications of the various categories for a coach in interactions with a particular athlete. Although not directly studied, the 19 categories could be examined for the particular profile they suggest for individual athletes. For example, one competitor might show peak scores on categories 2-3-14 (Competition, Self-Mastery, Independence), but low values on 1-10-11 (Social Approval, Recognition, Intimidation/Control). This might be interpreted to mean that the athlete is self-motivating, and that the coach would not be expected to or need to offer external encouragement. If the profile were reversed, then the coach might take this to be a sign that extra time devoted to the athlete could pay off in heightened performance. In essence, the 19 categories were selected because they imply something about how a coach might best approach an athlete to increase motivational responsiveness. Often the assumption is made that a personal pep talk from the coach will be responded to by all team members. In some cases, this may be the result; but in other cases, it may have less impact since it overlooks the individuality of the athlete. Using the profile approach, the coach might instead elect to offer personal support for that athlete characterized by high Social Approval scores, discuss the rival competitor with the athlete high on Competition, inquire about the personal or career development of the athlete with high emphasis on Family, set and plot training goals for the competitor who emphasizes Success and Achievement, take special efforts to introduce the athlete to new persons during events where the score is highest on Friendship, be open to discussing personal feelings about life and its resolution through athletics for the competitor high on Self-Direction, or present detailed explanations for the athlete who indicates that Understanding Reasons is of great importance in accepting training or coaching suggestions. In sum, examining the athlete's specific answers may provide the coach not only with insights regarding what moves the individual competitor on his/her team, but also insights into what the coach can do to enhance performance and to make competition and training more and more meaningful to the athlete as a person.

A word of caution: this report is based upon a study that can only be considered preliminary since it was on a small group, and restricted to swimmers. The results appear promising, but much more needs to be accomplished before the instrument can be offered as a valid test of motivational level and used as a selection device. It is even questionable whether *any* psychological test should be used as the sole means for such decisions as team selection; at best, the test can only serve as one facet of a broader approach. On the other hand, questionnaires such as the one reported here can serve other purposes even while validation studies are still ongoing. Specifically, the questionnaire can be used as a kind of interview guide to develop insights about an athlete. In a sense, the recommendations previously about the profile approach may be viewed in this manner.

What Can Psychology Offer to the Athlete and the Coach?

Dorcas Susan Butt

The editor of this volume has asked me to describe some applications of psychological concepts for athletes and coaches. I will therefore describe the theory and the approach which I have used when consulting with people in sport along with some of the specific suggestions which I have made.

There are two basic premises from which I have worked. The first is that the achievement of high athletic performance should never take precedence over the psychological and personal growth and development of an athlete. Although athletic achievement and personal growth are not incompatible, they often become so when athletes are pushed or forced by others or by themselves beyond their level of physical or personal maturity.[1] The second point is that figures peripheral to the athlete (coaches, parents, psychologists, medical advisors) should all remember that it is the athlete who is performing in the contest and not the advisor. Similarly, psychologists should remember they are not coaches. Just as some coaches may kill the personal experiences of some athletes, so can some psychologists destroy the unique relationship of the athlete with the coach. A constructive coaching relationship is essential between the athlete and the coach for the development of the athlete and particularly for the achievement of peak performance. I am reminded here of a national gymnastics coach who was asked how he controlled the anxiety of gymnasts who faced a difficult vault alone for the first time. His response: "I say, 'Look, you fool, you are not making the vault, I am making it. Just do as I say. I am making this vault.' " Such a coaching style, if repeated over time, could well rob the athlete of the intrinsic feedback accompanying skill development and impede progress. Similarly, a psychologist with all the answers (for example, with a rigid training schedule) who steps into an existing relationship between a coach and an athlete could destroy the spontaneity of that coaching relationship.[2] I refer to a relationship in which an admired coach projects an image or role for the athlete and at the same time molds the skill necessary for the athlete to reach that potential. With these two premises stated—first, that the personal fulfillment of the athlete takes precedence over performance and, second, that the pschologist complements and never replaces the existing roles within the sports arena—one is at least positioned to help by applying psychology in the field of sport.

[1] See the article by Zaremski on pages 238-246, the article by Richardson on pages 247-249, and the article by Titley on pages 357-361. —Ed.
[2] See the article by Lanning on pages 362-367. —Ed.

THEORY AND CONCEPTS

A schematic representation of sport motivation has been outlined elsewhere (Butt 1973; Butt 1976). Briefly it is suggested that there are four levels of sport motivation: biological, psychological, social, and secondary reinforcements (which may be external or internal). The basic life energy of the first level, the biological, may be channelled into the service of aggression, conflict, or competence motivation on the second level, the psychological, and these motivations will be present to a greater or lesser extent in any individual. Each of these energy models of psychological motivation (aggression, conflict, and competence) has extensive theorizing behind it in the works of Konrad Lorenz (1966), Sigmund Freud (1961), and Robert White (1963) respectively. The ideas of all have been modified and extended but remain basic to an understanding of motivation.

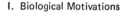

LEVELS OF MOTIVATION

I. Biological Motivations

II. Psychological Motivations

III. Social Motivations

IV. Reinforcements as Motivations

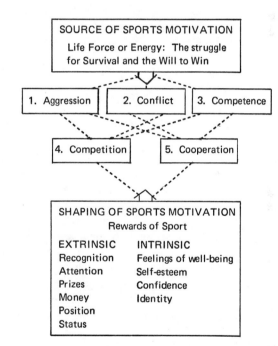

Figure 1. The motivational components of sport. (Adapted from Butt 1976, p. 2.) Motivation in sport evolves from two major sources or influences: biological motivation and the reinforcements conferred through the sports enterprise. Psychological motivation is represented in the three basic energy models of aggression, conflict, and competence. The solid arrows and the dotted arrows indicate greater and lesser degrees of connection thereafter. Aggressive motivation and conflict are most likely to lead to competitive social motivation and, to a lesser extent, to cooperation. Competence motivation is most likely to lead to cooperative social motivation. Both the competitively and cooperatively motivated will be affected by the reinforcements of sport. The external rewards will usually be most important to the competitor, however, and the internal rewards to the cooperator.

Enlarging on the implications of the foregoing styles for athletics, we offer the following brief descriptions. The *aggressive athlete* has much energy and thus appears to be eager, active, and impulsive. If frustrated the aggressive athlete is quick to find fault with others and may verbally or physically attack them. The *conflict ridden athlete* (Freud used the term *neurotic*) is unhappy, often complaining, full of excuses, and slow to fulfill his or her promise. If such athletes do achieve prominence, their self-absorption and moods are often a bane to coaches and fellow athletes. The *competence oriented athlete* tends toward maturity and self insight. Intrinsic feedback from skill development and mastery lead to joy in sport. There is a constant seeking of new levels of excellence and of new challenges.

It is the writer's theory that in the third level of motivation in sport, that of social motivation, competitive motivations will tend to evolve from aggression and conflict patterns on the psychological level while cooperative motivations will tend to evolve from competence on the psychological level. Both competitive and cooperative motivations are also heavily influenced by social reinforcements (level four). The *competitively motivated* will want to win at any costs over an opponent, in order to achieve external rewards such as money, recognition, and status. The *cooperatively motivated* will be rewarded more by feelings of self-fulfillment, confidence, and well-being.

However, as the dominant social values of many of our institutions endorse and foster competitions in which there are only winners and losers, even the competence oriented athlete must force himself or herself to be somewhat competitive. On the other hand the aggressive and conflict oriented athletes must gain some competence feedback from performance or become even more socially frustrated than they currently find themselves. Finally, a competitive person may also be encouraged to be somewhat cooperative if only in conforming to a set of rules or in becoming a member of a team. For all these reasons a moderate correlation may be expected between aggression and cooperation, between conflict and cooperation, and between competence and competition.

I have recently (1978 [in press]) developed short scales to measure the sport motivations of aggression, conflict, competence, competition, and cooperation. The use of these measures has yielded preliminary support for the descriptive model above and for the association of competence feedback with excellence in sports performance.

How may competence motivation be encouraged? As a first step I believe it is sufficient to introduce the various motivational constructs to coaches and athletes for discussion, often along with their own profiles on the scales. When athletes and coaches seriously discuss their feelings and experiences in sport, most recognize the rewards of competence and can identify personal or situational events which prevent them from experiencing it and hence from developing in sport. Two examples of how such discussions might occur follow. One demonstrates applications of the foregoing ideas to the cases of individual athletes, while the second refers to the use of a group consultation.

SUGGESTIONS FOR INDIVIDUAL ATHLETES: EXAMPLES

Variations in the needs of athletes and their relationships with coaches are infinite. Every case is unique. Therefore psychological measures will never replace the coaches' or the athletes' continual need to evaluate and experiment with their own attitudes, goals, and training procedures. However, psychological measures can open areas for discussion and thought so that athlete and coach can work more closely and effectively together. I have always given psychological information to coaches and athletes in the form of "ideas" with which they might experiment rather than in the form of "facts" with proven success.

I have administered the *Sports Protocol,* which contains measures of the constructs previously described, to many atheltes representing various sports, age levels, and abilities in Canada, Great Britain (with Dr. June Redgrove of Middlesex Polytechnic), and Japan (with Mr. Yoshiyuki Matsuda of Tsukuba University). Through the protocol, participants are asked to use a sport or leisure activity as a base and to answer whether during the last month while participating or competing they have ever felt: strong? (aggression), guilty for not doing better? (conflict), happier than you have ever been? (competence), like trying to win a prize? (competition), or like sharing ideas or strategies with someone? (cooperation). There are 10 such items for each scale to which participants answer yes or no. Item content is based upon behavioral descriptions (Butt 1976, pp. 1-60) of athletes representing high levels of each motivation component.

The profiles of three female athletes follow. They have been specifically altered in order to make individual identification impossible without altering the actual scores of the participant.

The athlete represented in Profile 1, a one-time national champion, shows a basically constructive pattern of motivations with some qualifications. Competence motivation is her highest score, showing she receives a good amount of intrinsic feedback in the form of happiness and well-being from her sports performance. Aggression and competition are second in importance, showing that she uses her energy and drive to come out ahead of others. This will cause her frustration when she does not succeed. Conflict is low, which is good, while cooperation is also low. Because she feels little affiliation with her sports group (low cooperation), this athlete may be unmotivated to persevere in in her sport should she face a series of personal setbacks and fail to win. The low conflict score is borne out by a very positive general personality profile (not reported here) which features strong feelings of well-being, family support, and personal integration into social mores and customs. In such an athlete one would encourage and reinforce the competence orientation and try to channel her strong social commitments into the athletic milieu (hence increasing cooperation). At present she shows a familiar North American pattern of identity with a commitment to family and social values but little empathy or need for others outside her immediate family.

Profile 1. Track: A national champion
Female: Aged 20

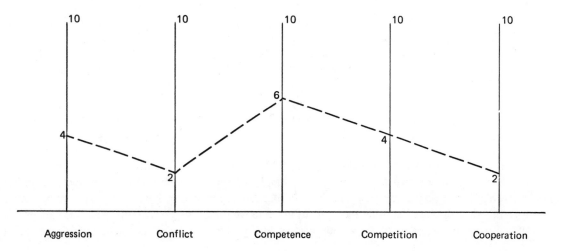

Profile 2. Badminton: A problem profile in a very talented athlete
Female: Aged 13

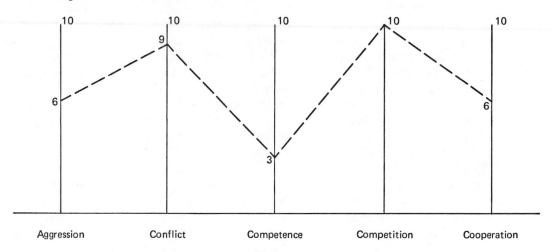

| Aggression | Conflict | Competence | Competition | Cooperation |

Profile 2 highlights conflict and competition. The athlete has very unhappy feelings when participating in sport (guilt, weeping, fatigue, moods, nervousness) and at the same time feels competitive pressure to outdistance others. As might be expected, she also feels aggressive toward her team members and opponents, while cooperation, although endorsed, is lower. The endorsement of cooperation is a very positive feature because the girl identifies with the sports group; however, the very low endorsement of competence is a serious concern. The athlete's family background provides an explanation for the profile. It features a broken parental relationship of much concern to the girl, while at the same time both parents push her to succeed in sport. In general mood the girl describes herself as unhappy. Such a profile, in a girl of recognized high athletic ability, would suggest a coaching strategy focused upon developing the girl's awareness of feelings of competence in sport. In addition the coach would show acceptance of her and genuinely lessen pressure upon her to perform. At the same time her ability and achievements should be supported and appreciated. Discussion with the athlete should be directed toward her high endorsement of conflict. Why are unhappy feelings experienced in sport and what can be done to lessen them while increasing more positive ones? Can the coach help? Can the team help? It is likely both could alleviate the pressure this girl feels in that sport is already compensating in her life for the disappointment she feels over the failure of the parental relationship.

The gymnast represented in Profile 3, who withdrew from her club shortly after responding to the *Sports Protocol* (but before intervention), raises interesting questions for coaches. When such an individual is identified as a possible withdrawal, how much time should or can a coach give toward keeping the athlete motivated and in the program? This girl says she is going to give up because her coach gives her a hard time and her parents (especially her mother) push her to do well. She is rated by her coach as of moderate ability. She endorses many unhappy feelings in her sport motivation (conflict). She is somewhat angry (aggression) and expresses few experiences of competence in her sport. She is not very competitive but is high on cooperation, evidently satisfying some of her needs for affiliation through the other members of her club whom she enjoys and cares for. Such an athlete should have the opportunity for weekly discussions in a group with a coach during which individual

Profile 3. Gymnastics: An athlete who withdrew from an organized competitive program
Female: Aged 12

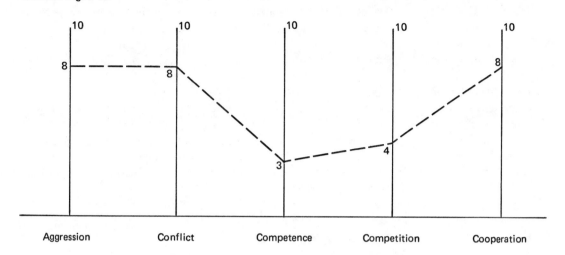

and group goals and purposes are discussed. If this girl's needs for affiliation are satisfied through the club, it may be that new horizons of intrinsic feedback (competence) from her own performance could be opened up for her over time. She might therefore be saved from dropping out of the program and become an important source of support to the other members of the club (even though she is not of high ability). However, it is worth noting, in keeping with our original assumptions, that, if such an athlete chooses to drop out of her sport after self-examination, then such a decision should be supported by all. She should leave her club or group with the understanding that the program will again be available to her if she feels she can benefit from it in the future.

SUGGESTIONS FOR GROUP TRAINING: AN EXAMPLE

In response to a request from the coaches of a swim club, who wished to explore the use of psychology in their coaching, I administered the *Sports Protocol* and the *Personality Research Form* (Jackson 1974) to the club members. The swim club was a well-organized, hard-driving, competitive club led by well-trained and competent coaches. Members ranged in age from 7 to 16 and were swimming up to three hours a day, 10 or 11 months a year, training for meets. In consideration of time and space I will deal only with the suggestions made for the adolescent group of swimmers, aged 12 to 16. In this group the major concerns of the coaches were the low motivation levels of swimmers and dropouts from the club. The motivational problem was one of the members' not being as highly motivated and eager as the coaches would have liked. Dropouts were few but disappointing to the coaches and therefore of significance.

Important information for coaches can result from placing some very simple questions to athletes. The present group, for example, were asked if they had ever considered giving up their sport and why. In addition they were asked to write down the best thing about their coach and the worst thing (or what they would like their coach to do differently). They were asked to describe their own ambition in sport and the part played by their parents in their club involvement.

Over 8 out of 10 adolescent swimmers had considered giving up their competitive sport involvement. Their major reason for doing so was that swimming took time away from friends, schoolwork, and interests and activities. These adolescents stated a major concern of young athletes in training. How can the drive for competitive excellence be tempered with the need to develop and to grow in other areas? This is a problem to which there is no simple solution. If the adolescent finds the challenge of developing other competencies greater than the challenges and competence feedback experienced in his or her chosen sport, motivation will subside and continuation will be in doubt. An unmotivated youngster continuing in a program under the pressure of parents and/or coach is not in a constructive situation. On the other hand, the parent or coach encouraging a motivated athlete over a plateau or difficult time when other attractions interfere with development is to be encouraged. Each athlete and coach must come to his or her own decision about how much time will be devoted to developing sports competence, and only the closest of understandings and communications can allow them to come to the best decision. Discussion with the coach and others in the group will lead to clarification in such situations for the athlete.

In general the personality profiles of the teenaged swimmers showed a high need for spontaneity, fun, and free play (in contrast to the very regimented training schedule they were following). In addition a significant number showed extreme sensitivity to, and were quite threatened by, people in their environment. Both of these factors might be considered a feature of adolescence but become especially significant in examining relationships with coaches. The best thing about a coach as seen by the swimmers was the coach's support, understanding, and attention to the individual needs of the athlete. The coach's efficiency as a trainer, technician, and teacher of athletic proficiency ranked second but far lower.[3] The worst things about coaches were lack of patience, not showing concern for the individual, and yelling or embarrassing the athlete in front of the group. All of these findings are of great importance. First, it is important to note that all persons invested in the club (athletes, coaches, and parents) agreed and recognized that swimming excellence in competitive situations was of prime importance. However, the athletes were also saying that this must not be given priority over the personal needs of the athletes as individuals. Second, a strong need to develop competence in a free swimming situation was indicated in the personality profiles and free responses of the swimmers.

In discussion with the coaches we therefore offered several suggestions for their consideration. It was noted that, in dealing with adolescent athletes, one is working with what are often turbulent times for the individual and therefore more time might be spent on psychological development than when one is dealing with preadolescent or postadolescent athletes. Variations in behavior, moods, and self-concerns are best expected when dealing with adolescents, rather than treated as exceptions. In order to deal with this I suggested one of the coaches meet with small groups of athletes (about eight) for a short weekly discussion of personal concerns and swimming goals. Second, it was suggested (on the basis of individual responses and profiles) which athletes could be pushed and worked hard because they would continue to experience competence from their training and which were telling us that they were sensitive, worried, and did not want to be pushed in the current direction. It was suggested that different features might be emphasized in the training of each of these groups. Third, it was suggested that brief free periods be interspersed in the training program along with additional variety in order to meet the strongly expressed needs for spontaneity, experimentation, and fun. Fourth, it was suggested that parents be given monthly access to coaches in a brief conference so that their needs, questions, and concerns could be dealt with. Fifth, suggestions were made on the psycho-

---

[3]See the article by Massimo on pages 229-237 and the article by Nesvig on pages 250-260. —Ed.

logical needs of each swimmer (along the lines of the examples given in the previous section). Finally, the coaches were encouraged to keep up their very effective work with the swimmers in that their organization, stress on team cooperation, and enthusiasm (along with their coaching techniques) were excellent. It was apparent that an overwhelming majority of club members appreciated their efforts and their abilities.

This report serves as a brief introduction to one method of applying psychological principles to the development and growth of individuals and groups through sport.

REFERENCES

Butt, D. S. 1973. Aggression, neuroticism and competence: Theoretical models for the study of sports motivation. *International Journal of Sports Psychology* 4:3-15.

———. 1975. Towards psychological competence and social cooperation as sports motivations. In *Readings in the psychology of sport*, ed. H. T. A. Whiting, 2:51-62. London: Kimpton Publishers.

———. 1976. *Psychology of sport: The behavior, motivation, personality and performance of athletes.* New York: Van Nostrand Reinhold.

———. (In press.) Short scales for the measurement of sports motivation. *International Journal of Sport Psychology.*

Freud, S. 1961. *The ego and the id.* In *The standard edition of complete works of Sigmund Freud*, ed. J. Strachey, vol. 19. London: Hogarth Press. Originally published in 1923.

Jackson, D. N. 1974. *Personality Research Form manual.* London, Ont.: Research Psychologists Press.

Lorenz, K. 1966. *On aggression.* New York: Harcourt, Brace and World. Originally published in 1963.

White, R. W. 1963. *Ego and reality in psychoanalytic theory: A proposal regarding independent ego energies.* Psychological Issues, New York: International Universities Press.

The Unconscious Fear of Success

Bruce C. Ogilvie

Research into the potential negative factors associated with high-level athletic performance is now being conducted in many parts of the world.[1] Most of the valuable psychological insights into the emotional constituents that influence athletic achievement are based upon depth studies of a select number of individuals who have sought counseling. This paper explores a number of the major psychological reactions to high-level athletic competition. The subjects who have contributed to our knowledge about the negative emotional reactions to athletic success represent members of the U.S. Olympic Team, professional athletes, and athletes from every major college sport.

The success-phobia syndrome has a number of common elements, each of which individually or all of which collectively could produce emotional reactions to inhibit or interfere with top physical efficiency. It is not implied that this psychological block can be reduced to only a few major aspects, but these aspects represent the range of typical reactions with which the authors have had clinical experience. It is not the intent of this paper to suggest that these emotional reactions are in any way mutually exclusive. It has been our finding that one of them will have the central role in determining the form that failure will take.

The typical human reactions of the athletically gifted male to the severe stress of physical excellence have been found to be related to the following causal factors. Each of these has been found to be a direct reflection of parental training and of other environmental influences. Success can breed the following syndromes:

A. a growing sense of social and emotional isolation
B. guilt feelings about self-assertion or overt suggestion
C. the habitual use of rationalization to protect the athlete from having to face the reality of his true physical potential
D. unconscious feelings of resentment as a reaction to exaggerated external demands for excellence (usually by a parent)
E. an unconscious fear of old traditions or old idols; an unconscious fear with regard to supporting the emotional weight of success or being the record-holder.

Bruce C. Ogilvie. The unconscious fear of success. *Quest* 10 (May 1968):35-39.

[1] See the article by Butt on pages 78-85, the article by Bramwell et al. on pages 119-123, and the article by Pressman on pages 291-296. —Ed.

Each of these characteristic responses to athletic stress has its basis in specific forms of social learning. All are the products of parental attitudes and other environmental conditions which reinforce negative factors which in turn contribute to ways of feeling and behaving that inhibit true physical excellence. Rather than capitalizing upon the positive aspects of the developing motor skill, there is a continued focusing upon its imperfections or upon the length of time necessary to learn it. This type of training environment conditions the athlete to develop an exaggerated awareness of possible failure at the expense of wholesome concern with possible success. Guilt, rationalization, and resentment over parental demands for excellence best typify the athlete's response to the negative reinforcement. The burden of isolation, the fear of old traditions or idols, and the emotional weight of success are special forms of athletic stress that affect only those approaching greatness. These stresses will require that the individuals have adequate preparation in order that they not be immobilized by their effects.

Here is a brief description of the unique psychological and sociological features of each of the foregoing stress syndromes. Syndrome A is the effect of the ever increasing stress of social and emotional isolation. The prospective great must adjust to a subtle form of increased resentment by former friends and associates. The response of these persons to the athlete as he moves away from his social group is conditioned by the unconscious fear that he will outgrow his need for their friendship. They begin to imagine or project the feeling that the athlete has outgrown his need for whatever contribution his friends have made to his life. Rather than remain anxiously in doubt about how the athlete feels, they unconsciously create situations which they can use as confirmation of their feelings that eventually they will be rejected. In the life of the professional athlete we are constantly reminded of this by the marital conflict that often accompanies sudden success. The wife is often one of the first to question her meaning and value in terms of the new life into which her mate is being catapulted. Often just when the athlete needs the most continuous form of emotional support, he finds that it is being withheld. Therefore, he feels isolated.

An intimate feature of this stress is the possessiveness of the fans who become identified with a particular athlete. They have a natural tendency to place him on a pedestal and then expect him to exhibit superhuman personality traits. This phenomenon only increases his sense of loneliness. Spectator expectations are always unrealistic, and yet many great athletes have unconsciously attempted to meet the fans' idealized standards, eventually to collapse under this unreasonable burden.

In the case of syndrome B, we find those athletes who develop unconscious guilt feelings in response to the necessary "wholesome aggression" which is essential for athletic success. These men tend to be reliving old childhood fears associated with childish forms of aggression. In a very real sense they have developed an overscrupulous conscience with regard to hostile or aggressive feelings. These feelings are often so deeply repressed in their personalities that defeating an opponent often results in feelings of depression rather than elation. Somehow they must punish themselves for allowing natural aggressive tendencies to be expressed in an overt form. In their social training their teachers or parents have conditioned them to equate anger, hostility, aggression, and even dominance with being evil or bad. Almost every truly great athlete we have interviewed during the last four years, representing every major sport, has consistently emphasized that "in order to be a winner you must retain the killer instinct." Each of these men had to discover for himself that winning takes an aggressive, dominant spirit. Each found that he had to be emotionally free to become self-assertive and not be haunted by conscious or unconscious fears that such behavior may cause him to be socially rejected.

Syndrome C is a most subtle form of fear of success and has its roots deep in the early developmental history. The athlete who uses excessive rationalization is one who dares not place his ability on the line or even face the reality of his true potential. He is still bound by his parents' attitudes to define in specific ways the limits of his tolerance for the stress of competition. Basically his social conditioning over-emphasized the pain of failure at the expense of the pleasure of success. Rewards or recognition for partial success or moderate improvement are absent from his life experience. The only social reward or positive parental recognition has been for winning or for showing excellence. Any performance short of these standards has been treated as failure. Often the parent communicates this attitude by his failure to respond to any performance which has not reached the parent's arbitrary standard of achievement. The end effect of such social conditioning is a personality structure with an inordinate fear of failure. The athlete unconsciously internalizes an unrealistic standard for human performance, and he studiously avoids the conscious experience of failure. He, therefore, learns to overdevelop his powers of rationalization and unconscious denial. He becomes expert at avoiding the ultimate truth by developing self-deceptive ways of justifying the quality of his performance. This is frequently expressed by falsely denying the meaning of success or victory. Somehow, in some way, the "moment of truth" is avoided in order not to have to face the reality of an absolute test of ability and then to be made to feel unworthy.

Syndrome D has a number of complex features, only a few of which can be discussed in a paper of this length. There are certain records and athletic standards that have become as awe-inspiring to competitors as religious symbols are to priests. There are individual athletic greats who inspire a type of admiration that borders upon worship. These two facts have considerable significance in the lives of a number of young athletes who have used each as a source of motivation in their own teaching. These standards and greats come to represent the ultimate goal which the athlete internalizes as his ideal of what he will become. The youthful competitor retains these motivational standards over such a span of years that considerable anxiety tends to develop when his ability reaches a point where the former standard or idol can be challenged. In order to set new standards it is necessary to develop a healthy arrogance towards the old ones. Athletes like Bannister, who was the first to defy all distance traditions, cannot be inhibited by an unconscious respect for the former standard, a respect that is based upon fear. They must feel a genuine sense of having every right to the prize which they have made such a great personal sacrifice to obtain.

Syndrome E is a reaction to the responsibility of being first or being the champion. Very few individuals seem able to identify with the negative side of the ledger when we discuss the cost of high-level athletic success. To be in possession of the record places one in the position of being for the rest of one's athletic life a potential failure. Every audience, every fan, every representative of the press expects each old record to be exceeded at each new performance. Now excellence becomes the universal standard. Any performance below a record is treated by most spectators with resentment. They often behave as if the athlete had somehow cheated them out of their just reward. This was best exemplified by the spectators during an Eastern swimming meet who actually booed the performance of a member of the swimming Hall of Fame. Their reaction was to the fact that not only did he fail to set a new world record, but he had the audacity to place second. This is a reality of crowd behavior of which every great athlete we have interviewed is most acutely aware. It is not surprising to find that some men with the potential for greatness state that the immediate rewards of success are not sufficiently great to sustain them in the face of the threat of crowd rejection.

SUMMARY

The authors review the five most frequent causes of success-phobia which they have observed in clinical practice during the past twelve years: fear of social and emotional isolation; guilt with respect to self-assertion or aggression; unconscious fear of expressing one's potential; fear of old idols or traditions; and disinclination for the burden of success. Each of these fears may operate independently or con-jointly with one or more of the others. Each is the result of social conditioning. The unconscious fear of isolation, guilt over aggression, and the threat of old standards are psychological blocks which respond well to counseling. The exaggerated use of rationalization is much more resistant. This protective mechanism is too deeply ingrained and rationalization is too readily available as an escape from the threat of failure. Since men in this category never consciously accept failure, re-education becomes a special problem. They are never able to change those features of their personalities which they are either unable or unwilling to accept about themselves.

It is strongly recommended that those who demonstrate physical giftedness receive special psychological attention. This is of particular significance when athletic greatness is imminent. The athletes who have gained insight into the negative side of greatness will be able to protect themselves against it.

REFERENCES

Antonelli, F. 1963. *Psicologia e psicopatologia dello sport.* Rome.
——. 1966*a*. Psychopathology and psychotherapy in sporting phenomena. *Journal of Sports Medicine and Physical Fitness* 6 (June):108-110.
——. 1966*b*. Sport and psychic fitness. Paper presented at the International Congress, Prague, August 1966.
Cagigal, J. M. 1966. Introduction to a personology of sport. *Congress of Sports Psychology,* Barcelona, August 1966.
Ogilvie, B. C., and Tutko, T. A. 1963. Unable to be first. *Track and Field News* 16 (September):10.
——. 1966*a*. Success phobia. In *Problem athletes and how to handle them,* pp. 88-106. London: Pelham Books.
——. 1966*b*. Build a winning psychology. *Golf Digest* 17 (November):32.

The Way of the Runner:
An Examination of Motives for Running

David Pargman

They tread rhythmically and relentlessly in all sorts of weather, at almost any time of day or night. They are young, old, male, female, of various physical endowments and socio-economic persuasions. They move resolutely and rigorously, some with flowing grace, others struggling clumsily and desperately. Their feet strike city streets as well as rural byways. They are runners.[1]

Currently, our nation appears to be in throes of a running madness. Sporting goods shops report phenomenal sales of running footwear and equipment, and a 1977 Gallup poll reports that about 25 million persons (11% of American adults) run or jog regularly. Magazines such as *Runner's World* and *Running Times* proliferate with rapidly rising circulations. Popular periodicals such as *Psychology Today, Newsweek,* and *Time* frequently include articles dealing with one aspect or another of running or jogging. Books about and for runners are now on the lists of best-sellers.

Recently in Los Altos Hills, California, joggers created an unusual dilemma for the town council as well as a new twist to the classic machine-versus-environment controversy. Motorists had registered somewhat heated complaints about traffic tie-ups and congested roads caused by more than 100 runners galloping 4 or 5 abreast through streets presumed by some citizens to be the exclusive domain of the automobile. The council, however, was pressured by a large number of vociferous runners, who rallied at the meeting and caused a proposal intended to outlaw street jogging of 2 or more runners to be tabled.

What is the substance of this craze? Is running a fad destined for short-order expiration, like the hoola-hoop? Will its wildfire growth continue until millions more shuffle, dart, and scamper along our pathways, roads, and city pavements?

Figuratively and metaphorically we have been running for countless decades. We run for political office; run at the mouth; run a business; run a fever; run up a bill; or run around with men or women. But millions of us are now actually carrying out the mechanical, locomotor act of running and, moreover, doing it with high frequence and fervor. Why?

Primitive man ran after quarry or from dangerous animals of lower order. Obviously, he had no alternatives. The ancient Greeks used runners to carry messages from one community to another. Evidently, barefoot humans could traverse certain terrain more unobtrusively and efficiently than mounted riders or messengers in horse-drawn carts and chariots. Supposedly, the contemporary

---

[1] See the article by Morgan on pages 297-303. —Ed.

Olympic marathon event is a throwback to the valiant efforts of the runner-messenger Phidippides, who carried to the citizens of Athens news of the Greeks' victory over the Trojans on the plains of Marathon. Thus, utilitarian factors understandably accounted for man's early and historic engagement in running. But why the apparent fascination with this seemingly unnecessary activity today? No Olympic medal, college scholarship, or professional sport contract entices most of today's die-hard harriers. Nonetheless, their number is legion. What are the dynamics of this rapturous interest in running? Are answers to be found in principles of human psychology?

DIFFERENT RUNNING TYPES: A-D VERSUS C-D

To begin with, my speculation is that serious, regular runners or joggers (I use the terms interchangeably although I appreciate performance differences between the two) may be located on a continuum according to the nature or strength of their motivation for running. One end of the continuum may be designated *addiction* or *dependence;* the other, *commitment* or *dedication.* Although the word *addiction* has largely been replaced by *dependence* (Worick and Schaller, 1977), which in turn may be used to refer to physical as well as mental or psychological conditions, both terms are applied herein to identify one pole of the proposed continuum. Collectively, they suggest a psychological and physiological reliance upon regular sustained running, to the extent that a withdrawal syndrome is suffered when continuation of the regimen is interrupted for more than 24 or 36 hours. As is the case with all continua, most values do not fall precisely at either end, but somewhere in between. However, in this proposed model, it is assumed that all who run regularly belong toward one end or the other of the continuum; that is to say, if they run with regularity they must be either dependent or committed. Despite similar ostensible characteristics, such as running on a daily basis or feeling good after the run, which tend to encourage a standardized descriptive psychological profile of all those who jog, runners vary in their motivations for running. Those who are truly psychologically hooked or trapped by the experience fall toward the addicted end of the hypothesized range, and those who are but volitionally pledged to running fall toward the other end. I believe that examination of this hypothesized polarity will be helpful in understanding the way of the runner, or "What makes Janie jog and Robert run?" Runners are not like the proverbial rose. All do not smell as sweetly, and not all are powered by the same motivations. This is obvious from their descriptions of the meaning and importance of running, which we have been recording and analyzing at Florida State University for approximately three years.

I suspect that individuals in the addicted-dependent (A-D) part of the continuum tend to participate with comparatively less psychological awareness and intellectual understanding about their running than do committed-dedicated (C-D) runners. When A-D runners attempt to explain their immoderate enthusiasm, they tend to emphasize perceived exhilaration and joy. Their focus is usually not upon motivational or causal factors. The A-D runner describes his/her need to participate purely in terms of affect or emotions generated by the run as well as feelings experienced before and during it. Rarely is inquiry made about reasons for the run beyond description of a strong inner force crying out to be satisfied. Furthermore, A-D types make reference to withdrawal symptoms when the need to run is unsatisfied. Their only relevant realization is that if they don't run they feel unwell.

On the other hand, the very high priority attached to running by committed-dedicated (C-D) participants, has a broader intellectual and more rational basis. These individuals run for reasons that may best be described as pragmatic. Their goals are designed to satisfy very basic and practical needs.

C-D types make no claim for euphoric, mind-bending, esoteric, Zen-like experiences. They do not report mental spinouts or long periods of dissociation from the run in order to focus their thinking upon problems or topics of their own selection. Real-life reinforcers support their conception of the run as a positive, supportive experience. For example, their physician may have suggested regular physical exercise due to overweight or a problematical cardiovascular condition. The C-D type runner has a reason for running and is aware of it and understands it. Eventually, blood pressure is lowered, stored fat is metabolized, and the body becomes firm—all a consequence of running. The C-D runner is encouraged and gratified, and the running effort is reinforced. Waving neighbors and passing motorists also provide recognition and respect for the C-D individual and thereby, in no insignificant way, assuage some of the exhaustion, aching tendons, and weary bones felt during the run. The C-D runner revels in the knowledge that his/her store of courage is sufficient to enable perseverance through a predetermined and self-imposed dose of pain and stress. But he/she does not necessarily love the run and may very well not even look forward to it. It is accepted and integrated into the runner's day because it is rational in terms of a calculated strategy. Among other things, this type of runner may require peer admiration in order to support a self-image of athlete-competitor and vigorous, healthy person. Whatever the reasons for running, C-D runners seem to be aware of them. They run because running is important in some recognizable, logical, and often salubrious way, irrespective of the extent to which their perception is psychobiologically correct. For such individuals, running is prescriptive in a manner similar to physical therapy done by one abandoning an immobilizing cast for a fractured limb. The orthopedic physician prescribes rehabilitative movements which are to be done regularly. Pleasure and joy are not relevant objectives and are not pursued or realized. For the C-D runner, the run is far from the highlight of the day and may be anything but joyful, although satisfaction may be derived upon its completion. Such gratification probably takes the form of relief fostered by the awareness that the experience is over, as in the case of the college student who finishes a final exam. Pleasure is felt, irrespective of the quality of the experience; it is simply over, and that in itself is gratifying.

Because it is rigidly imposed upon the day's schedule, the run or anticipation of it may actually produce a form of pre-run anxiety in the C-D person. If the run is sacrificed due to unforeseen impediments, the runner may feel guilt. Insecurity about the ability to maintain self-discipline or fulfill requirements of an important plan may arise. The C-D type thereby offends his/her own sense of intellectual integrity and may be compelled to confront a self-perception of weakness and wishy-washiness. Consequently, unlike the A-D counterpart, the C-D runner does not necessarily view the run as a pleasurable experience. Realistically, he/she may even feel relief when circumstances such as inclement weather, injury, or professional or familial crisis prevent its execution.

The typical child studying music and the C-D runner may be compared with reference to motives about involvement in their respective activities. More often than not, a child practices an instrument daily because a parent has so instructed or demanded. The requirement is supposedly levied in the child's best interest, and motivation for practice is thereby externally provided. It is uncommon that a young child's enthusiasm for repetitive performance of scales and musical exercises is maintained at a high level for appreciable periods of time. Although practice is not necessarily physically painful, for many children it is undoubtedly viewed as a deterrent to more entertaining and pleasurable activities, such as playing games and watching television. For all too many kids, practicing the violin, flute, or piano is tantamount to doing homework; it *must* be done, and derivation of pleasure is not anticipated as a direct outcome. Joy and pride may develop from feedback deriving from admiring observers who praise and reinforce both child musician and committed runner after having witnessed a few practice sessions or runs. But, to the C-D runner, the jog is very often a chore, something to be accomplished because of a self-promise to do it.

THE C-D—A-D SHIFT

Is a positional shift on the proposed continuum likely? May committed individuals who don shorts and running shoes daily over months and perhaps years move toward the addicted end of the continuum? According to psychiatrist William Glasser, the author of *Positive Addiction* (1976), the answer is yes. Glasser maintains that not all addictions are bad or negative; that some are growthful, fulfilling, and psychologically supportive; and, moveover, that running is one such positive experience to which we may become addicted. Glasser (1978) believes that a naturally occurring chemical called *enkephalin,* which is secreted by the brain, may be responsible for causing a condition he calls "positive addiction to running." He says that running a minimum of four days a week for 45 minutes, for at least a year, accelerates the production of enkephalin to the extent that its presence in the body is addicting. Deprivation from running causes withdrawal symptoms akin to those associated with substances such as morphine. In other words, the brain's reaction to this supposedly valuable physical and mental activity (running) is to release a "pleasure factor," enkephalin, upon which the central nervous system becomes dependent. Maintenance of the daily running program and perhaps increasingly greater doses of running (longer runs) are then necessary to satisfy the addiction. Thus, Glasser ascribes a chemical, rather than a mental, basis to running addiction.

Glasser's hypothesis is predicated upon the research of Professor Solomon H. Snyder (1977), of the Johns Hopkins University School of Medicine, who suggests that enkephalin inhibits the excitation of certain brain cells which play important roles in the perception of pain and emotions. It is an opiatelike substance and may therefore induce a euphoric state.

If indeed biochemical factors underlie addiction to running, then the conscious and rational decisions to embark upon a regular regimen of running serve as a precipitator of the so-called positive addiction. The addiction state must have a beginning point. But, once it has begun, the system is regulated by neurochemical mechanisms proposed by Glasser, and volitional cognitive processes (decision making) become subordinate to biochemical mediation. The runner uncontrollably becomes addicted although he/she may originally have begun as a dedicated decision-maker with an awareness of a personal need for physical exercise (C-D type). But, as attractive as it may appear, Glasser's hypothesis falls short of being unassailably wholesome. First, Glasser assumes that enkephalin production increases in response to stress (running). This has not been established in humans, much less in runners. Furthermore, it has not been determined that enkephalin levels are atypically elevated in those who have been running on a long-term basis. Second, if enkephalin production is indeed increased by stress, then all runners, including the C-D type, would be or would eventually become addicted. In runners who do not enjoy the activity, the discomfort caused by the run or its anticipation would stimulate enkephalin production; in runners in whom a very pleasant run and its joyful anticipation prevails, enkephalin production would also increase, since stress is defined as any imbalance in the homeostatic condition, irrespective of its positive or negative nature. Preparation for pleasurable activities, such as a party, a sexual encounter, or a ride on the roller coaster, may account for a tilt in homeostasis just as significant as the news that one's wallet or purse has been lost. (The term *eustress* has been coined by Bernard [1968] to refer to pleasant stress.)[2] Therefore, all those who have been running regularly for a prolonged period would develop addiction. But this does not appear to be the case. Not all those who run regularly seem to be A-D types.

At Florida State University, my graduate student Michael Sachs and I have queried many hard-core regular runners with self-reported running histories of a minimum of 2 miles per day, five days a week, for at least a year. Most run considerably more than 2 miles per day. We questioned them as to their perceived motives for running. Our structured, tape recorded interviews with some of the runners addressed the occurrence and frequency of mentally spinning-out or altering consciousness; transcending the body; dissociation during the run; and other claims said to be related to running addiction. Very few subjects reported experiencing these effects, but most described a sense of physical well-being brought about by running. Many reported a good workout to be invigorating and refreshing, and such findings are in keeping with observations made by Baekeland and Lasky (1966); Brunner (1969); Gary and Guthrie (1976); Graham (1966); and McPherson et al. (1967). At a recent clinic dealing with psychology and running, Sachs asked the following question of the audience of about 40 runners: "How many of you have actually experienced the 'runner's high' or euphoria while running?" Only 4 responded affirmatively to the question.

If Glasser's hypothesis is correct and the addiction producing chain of events which he proposes does occur, then it assuredly does not happen in all cases. At least, not all regular runners are reporting that they are addicted. One alternate possibility is that all are but that many are not aware of it or deny it in very much the same fashion that a large number of alcoholics deny their dependence upon alcohol. However, my guess is that very few runners actually belong at the extreme A-D end of the continuum or even close to it, where consciousness alteration, mid-run euphoria, and biochemical addiction supposedly prevail.

Physiological considerations may very well be important clarifiers of the A-D type runner. If enkephalin is not a causal factor, then perhaps another chemical agent is. To say the least, regular running causes the development of abilities to cope with physiological demands of running which are categorically referred to as *tolerance*. Vigorous physical activity produces within the body a number of biochemical and physiological adaptations, and running, in particular, may cause immediate effects such as elevated respiratory rate, increased heart rate, and higher blood pressure. Long-term training effects include a more efficient cardiovascular system, greater endurance, stronger muscles, and a trimmer waistline. While such training does not necessarily produce exercise dependence per se, it may very well lay the groundwork for its development as long as the intensity causes certain physiological reactions indicative of a considerable amount of physical stress. Some of the reactions stemming from exercise deprivation smack of withdrawal symptoms very similar to those described in the drug literature. These symptoms, which may have biochemical underpinnings, include feelings of anxiety, restlessness, discomfort, and irritation. Similar responses may be reported by both A-D and C-D runners, but, in the case of the former, a biochemically related withdrawal syndrome may be present rather than a more psychologically oriented one. However, since I believe that among regular runners there are at least as many of the C-D type as there are A-D types, it seems important to emphasize psychological considerations which may also explain the motives of runners.

[2] See the article by Harris on pages 112-118. —Ed.

PSYCHOLOGICAL THEORIES WHICH MAY EXPLAIN MOTIVATION
FOR RUNNING

Among numerous categories of theories which attempt to explain why individuals behave as they do, some emphasize *stimulus seeking*. Essentially, these theories hypothesize a spectrum of activation or arousal ranging from deep sleep to extreme effort or great excitement. Somewhere between these two extremes is an optimal range of arousal for which an individual is suited.[3] There also exists a desirable level of stimulus-input which accounts for optimal arousal. Furthermore, an individual learns to react in a manner which tends to maintain optimal arousal by increasing or decreasing stimulation. One acquires an understanding of the things or activities needed, thereby rejecting some and pursuing others. In this way, boredom or overstimulation is avoided through behaviors which tend to maintain satisfactory arousal.

We know that the effects of arousal are mediated by anterior, superior aspects of the reticular formation (the reticular activating system, RAS), which exerts an excitatory influence upon the organism's behavior (Guyton 1971). The RAS is subject to an extremely wide variety of afferent impulses (e.g., touch, pain, temperature changes, olfactory and auditory influences, hormonal and chemical changes, drugs). Counterbalancing efforts (antagonistic to the excitatory influences of the RAS) are mediated by medullary function and the posterior, inferior part of the reticular formation as well as by various cortical functions. Therefore, for each of us, arousal or excitation may be defined as a balance between RAS and cortical activity. Humans are highly motivated and driven toward seeking optimal levels of arousal. Slight deviations in one direction from the desired range in the arousal continuum produce sensations of pleasure, and changes in the opposite direction are aversive or unpleasant.

Ironically, a level of arousal which is too low for an individual may cause irritability which is aversive to the point that the organism experiences excitation or increased arousal. This may actually result in reduced cortical inhibition of the RAS and subsequently produce a stimulating effect. Perhaps this mechanism underlies the feeling of increased need to exercise which A-D runners report after being restricted to a low-stimulating environment for a relatively long period of time (the feeling that we must get away from the desk or out of the classroom and onto the roads or track).

Sharon Burgess (a former graduate student of mine) and I recently (1977) made some interesting observations from our study of 90 males (ages ranging from 20 to 50 years) who ran or swam with varying degrees of regularity. At the time when we were preparing for this study, I had not yet developed the idea for an A-D–C-D continuum and therefore, perhaps somewhat naively, categorized all regular exercisers (minimum of five days a week) as "exercise dependent." Our study revealed that all regular exercisers and occasional exercisers (those who swam or ran, but not for a minimum of five days a week) scored significantly higher on the Stimulus Seeking Scale (SSS) and the Thrill and Adventure Seeking Scale (TA) and lower on the Eysenck Personality Inventory Neuroticism Scale (N) than nonexercisers. It remains unclear whether thrill and adventure seeking, a form of stimulus seeking, is a motivating force in the intensity and/or frequency of exercise involvement, since the differentiation was between all exercisers, regardless of frequency per week, and nonexercisers. Perhaps regular runners require greater amounts of sensory input which may be gained through physical activity. A high need for TA stimuli in A-D exercisers may explain the so-called withdrawal symptoms

---

[3] See the article by Oxendine on pages 103-111. —Ed.

reported when they are deprived of their accustomed run. It may be that only a vigorous, sustained physical activity such as running which generates large amounts of stimuli satisfies their high TA need.

Although the etiology of stimulus-seeking tendencies is unclear, both genetic and environmental factors probably interact to produce certain stimulus-seeking preferences. Running itself may be a cause or a result of higher TA-seeking tendencies in A-D runners. Some individuals may be genetically predisposed to respond to kinesthetic stimuli with an adjustment toward arousal, while others may experience a disruption in their arousal level. If heredity plays a large part in stimulus-seeking preferences, this might indicate that individuals low in TA may not be good candidates for regimens of regular sustained running. Their stimulus needs in the external sensation category could be low, and physical activity beyond their personal requirements would result in unpleasant overstimulation which they might learn to avoid. If, on the other hand, running increases TA requirements, it is likely that those who are encouraged to participate in this form of physical activity at an early age are those who will develop high TA-seeking tendencies and continue to participate in strenuous physical activity throughout their lives.

An additional finding in the study done with Burgess was that exercise participant groups scored significantly lower on *neuroticism* (N) than did nonexercisers. The well-known British psychologists Eysenck and Eysenck (1969) have reported that high-scoring individuals tend to be emotionally over-responsive and frequently complain of minor somatic upsets, such as headaches, digestive troubles, insomnia, and backaches. Such individuals also report many worries, anxieties, and other disagreeable feelings. Low-scoring individuals, by contrast, are emotionally stable, not as likely to worry, become upset over minor frustrations, or suffer minor psychosomatic disorders. Perhaps this, at least in part, lends support to the claim by runners that a feeling of well-being accompanies participation in vigorous physical activity. Other researchers have noted higher levels of emotional stability in physically active people (Ismail and Trachtman 1973; Sperling 1942).

Burgess and I were unable to determine whether lower neuroticism was the result or the cause of exercise participation in our study. Possibly, only persons with low levels of neuroticism seek out and participate in activities such as running or swimming. On the other hand, regardless of their original level of neuroticism, persons who embark on an exercise program may derive some psychological benefit resulting in increased emotional stability.

Yet another theoretical construct which may help to clarify motivation for running is Petrie's *augmentation-reduction model.* Petrie (1967) describes the reducer as one who benefits from the intense stimulus of physical activity. Reducers tend to diminish and augmentors incline to exaggerate incoming stimuli. E. D. Ryan's work (1969) supports Petrie's theory. Ryan observed that contact sport athletes (e.g., wrestlers and football players) possess characteristics of the reducer. A group of subjects who expressed a dislike for participation in athletics demonstrated augmentor characteristics. Athletes in noncontact sports were found to be located between the extremes of reducer and augmentor. Reducers are apparently gratified by more vigorous and stressful activities, in contrast to the more sedentary experiences sought by augmentors. Although application of Petrie's theory to A-D and C-D running is quite speculative, it is appropriate to include her construct within this discussion because it deals with the mediation of stimulation strength. For example, A-D individuals may tend toward the reducer end of Petrie's model.

The last of the psychological considerations discussed here which may bear upon motivations for running is the *opponent-process theory of motivation* proposed by Solomon and Corbit (1973).

It is one of many constructs referred to as *derived motives* (D'Amato 1974). This model is based upon a concept of motivational homeostasis which has been in circulation for some time and emphasizes the notion that motivation is acquired. In effect, the opponent-process theory says that the mechanisms striving to restore hedonic balance to an out-of-kilter system may generate an effect which is quite the opposite of what was intended and hence the term *opponent*. The opponent-process needs time to be effectuated, and so there occurs a delayed implementation of this second-order affect. However, in time, it gains in strength and ultimately dominates the object of the initial stimulus input. For it to be well established, numerous elicitations of the effect must occur.

To use an illustration offered by Solomon and Corbit (1973; 1974), parachutists seem to be "stunned" after experiencing their first few leaps from the moving airplane. They are quite fearful and terrified before jumping, but, after a number of trials, during which time the "opponent" gains in potency, the fear and terror give way to feelings of exhilaration and euphoria. Subsequent jumps continue to reinforce the positive feelings, and ultimately the jump is associated with very positive and joyful emotion. Increased frequency of the first state enforces the strength of the second. This model may be applicable to both positive and negative affect states, and therein lies its relevance to the entire issue of A-D and C-D running. The regular runner endures the discomfort or even pain of the demanding physical experience (in this case the negative affect) in order to arrive at the pleasure of the feeling produced at its termination. The runner volitionally and masochistically initiates an aversive primary condition in order to achieve the joy and satisfaction of the secondary state. Thus, the so-called hedonic balance is restored by proceeding from a relatively aversive condition to one which produces euphoria. In brief, the individual is not habituated to running but rather to the pleasure provided by its cessation and the restoration of the equilibrium which is depleted during its occurrence.

As increased numbers of individuals turn to running in order to exercise, escape from the day's tribulations, or simply recreate, sweeping allegations about the therapeutic value of the run are put into circulation. We would do well to consider underlying motivational dynamics in terms of legitimate existing psychological theory. There are too many myths and grandiose claims about running. As is the case with any behavior experienced by a large number of persons, the causal factors vary considerably. Not all joggers run due to the same or even similar motives.[4]

[4]See the article by Youngblood and Suinn on pages 73-77. —Ed.

REFERENCES

Baekeland, F. and Lasky, R. 1966. Exercise and sleep patterns in college athletes. *Perceptual and Motor Skills* 23:1203-1207.

Bernard, J. 1968. The eudaemonists. In *Why man takes chances,* ed. S. Z. Klausner. Garden City, N. J.: Doubleday.

Brunner, B. C. 1969. Personality and motivating factors influencing adult participation in vigorous physical activity. *Research Quarterly* 40:464-469.

Burgess, S. S., and Pargman, D. 1977. Stimulus seeking, extroversion and neuroticism in regular, occasional and non-exercisers. Unpublished manuscript.

D'Amato, M. R. 1974. Derived motives. *Annual review of psychology* 25:83-106.

Eysenck, H. J., and Eysenck, S. B. 1969. *Personality structure and measurement.* London: Routledge & Kegan Paul.

Glasser, W. 1976. *Positive addiction.* New York: Harper and Row.

——. 1978. The positive addiction experiment. *Starting Line* 2 (March):2.

Graham, M. F. 1966. *Prescription for life.* New York: Van Rees Press.

Guyton, A. 1971. *Function of the human body.* Philadelphia: W. B. Saunders.

Ismail, A. H., and Trachtman, L. E. 1973. Jogging the imagination. *Psychology Today* 6:78-82.

McPherson, B. D.; Paivio, A.; Yuhasz, M.; Rechnitzer, P.; Pickard, H.; and Lefcoe, N. 1967. Psychological effects of an exercise program for post-infarct and normal adult men. *Journal of Sports Medicine and Physical Fitness* 7:95-102.

Petrie, A. 1967. *Individuality in pain and suffering.* Chicago: University of Chicago Press.

Ryan, E. D. 1969. Perceptual characteristics of vigorous people. In *New perspectives of man in action,* ed. R. C. Brown and B. J. Cratty. Englewood Cliffs, N. J.: Prentice-Hall.

Snyder, S. 1977. Opiate receptors and internal opiates. *Scientific American* 236 (March):44-56.

Solomon, R., and Corbit, J. 1973. An opponent-process theory of motivation II: Cigarette addiction. *Journal of Abnormal Psychology* 81:158-171.

———. 1974. An opponent-process theory of motivation I: Temporal dynamics of affect. *Psychological Review* 81:119-145.

Sperling, A. P. 1942. The relationship between personality adjustment and achievement in physical activity. *Research Quarterly* 13:351-363.

Worick, W. W., and Schaller, W. E. 1977. *Alcohol, tobacco and drugs: Their use and abuse.* Englewood Cliffs, N. J.: Prentice-Hall.

Citizens' Racing Is More Than Fun

Dick Taylor

Some exult in the phenomenon as a celebration of native human robustness, others look furtively for a place to hide, lest they too be caught in this monument to mass hysteria, St. Vitus's dance played out on skis—citizens' racing. The same contagious enthusiasm which has gripped foot running has caught cross-country skiing. Both sports are adventures into personal mobility and endurance, and simply the numbers of participants undertaking such an elemental venture into themselves compels one to seek some kind of explanation.

I am aware that speculation about the motivation for a regular weekend calorie burn may not seem quite reverend; analysis might rob racing of its mystery and therefore its attraction. Yet the reasons for racing are various enough to allow each skier not only to find his own preference for charging through the woods but also to qualify, even refute, the reasons of his fellows who are also trying to figure themselves out. There is room for the spiritualists and the iconoclasts, the budding jocks and the artistes of sweat, the seekers of grace and the stallions of snow-lit meadows out to steam and stomp in the sunshine. It can be said in advance that athletes—real and pseudo athletes, egomaniacs or mortifiers of the flesh—do not fit a single mould. As research has proven (Ogilvie and Tutko 1971), athletes include all the types of human body and psyche, are no more happy or sad than human beings in general. What makes mass sport so engaging, to do and to think about, is that a various crowd is coming together to do the same thing. To one the race means an electric, shiny blue, skin-tight, all-around dazzling, dimple-winking stretch racing suit; to another, modest dancing duds; to another, a splendid hair shirt. The common denominator remains the presence of skis, boots, and poles; with reverence for them, for the pleasure of moving well, and for the righteous hunger they produce (moral credits for those whose altar is the icebox), I would offer some thoughts on the motivations for citizens' racing, winter's more benign divine insanity.

The importance of play in culture has long been recognized *(Homo ludens: A study of the play element in culture,* by Johan Huizinga, is a good start). Whether the form of play be serious or light-hearted, cards, dance, courting, sports, poetry, or telling tall tales, the blessings are similar: an artificial theater or field in which workaday time is cancelled and free movement and open thought can take off without the stricture of social norms, production pressures, or the conventions upon which the institutions of our culture were founded and persist. Citizens' racing also is apart from professional pretentions, demands, or goals, separate from past and future. No racer can have a moral measure taken of him, nor can he absolutely succeed or fail. Finishing position and stopwatch time make for fleeting comparisons, part of the game, but, like a racing number, do not mark the human or social substance of each individual. These numbers do not even have the circumstantial relevance of, say, a social security number or a license plate. In short, as in all play, citizens' racing is given to each runner for himself or herself, for what each may seek or find in the way of strength or frailty, fear and daring, surprise or predictability—the peculiar combination of everything each of us is.[1]

Perhaps this is the chief attraction: the race is a ritual, a highly compacted human existence situation defined within the limits of graceful movement and the subleties of stress. In no situation other than sport are the demands so concentrated, the rewards (in the sense of instant feedback) so quick. You feel yourself strong or weak, surging and dying, winning and losing, yet without the comforts of logical cause and effect: dying a little may tap an unknown strength and thus be winning. There is no delusion or division in this totally present creature, only the acceptance and use of everything, everything sharp and visible at every movement of the race. Energy and rhythm melt body and psyche together, waking the senses, releasing the speed. Each is totally vulnerable and totally assertive.

The heightened sense of identity and total awareness available in sport, particularly in a stress-endurance sport such as cross-country racing, has lead some observers to regard sport as the yoga of the western world. With the rise of consciousness disciplines like transcendental meditation, est, Gestalt therapy, and Zen (whether they are approached with integrity or with the cheaper magic of pop psychology) has come the recognition that there is a sort of insight, repose, and clarity in articulate movement, that the body is not simply the profane package of an imprisoned intelligence but rather the substance of awareness itself. The Puritan fear of the flesh is rejected, or simply outgrown, in sport (though cynics might contend that sport allows a sublimation of sexual drives and is therefore functionally Puritan—the ultimate cold shower). At the same time, the fervor of a fitness program and the pleasant, warm, and reflective use of the weekend's race have their own spiritual dimension. There is a fullness, a compactness, and yet a compelling simplicity in articulate stress movement which produces a sense of inner balance and resource. The flesh is no longer rejected; it becomes the prime idiom of efficient animal movement and flow with what existence is present at any given moment.

The sense of flow is another essential attraction of racing. A combination of directional grace with a sense of inner balance, of increased concentration with natural relaxation, results when one's physical and psychic elements, accepted together for as much or as little as they are, are strangely converted into a power source. All these elements limit the runner, to be sure, but they also sustain him through the repose of acceptance and the intensity of fascination. It is this inner combination of repose and intensity which determines speed and efficiency (grace) down the track. The feeling is at once soothing and compelling, frightening and freeing, and, above all, addicting.

The acceptance levels of racers are great indeed and are focused most pointedly at pain or stress. Frequently it is thought that performance levels will be raised in relation to how successfully pain is accepted as part of our total creature situation. You cannot beat pain down; you accept it, and in doing so convert it into an open-ended resource (however dark like a cave) to be investigated. Runners who become fascinated with pain go the deepest into pain without loss of their sense of flow, and they are then able to tap the experience of pain as an energy source.[2] It is in this manner that

---

[1] See the article by Gunby on pages 179-201 and the article by Johnson on pages 202-211 for further personal insights from and about athletes. —Ed.
[2] See the article by Morgan on pages 297-303. —Ed.

the intensity of their fascination comes as both an expansion of self and a breakthrough increase in speed.

Why do I dwell so on what may seem esoteric stuff for elite racers? Because it applies to citizens' racers as well. The excitement of citizens' races is that the experience, particularly inner experience, of elite racers is amply available to anyone who decides to put on a number on a Sunday afternoon. For the elite racer as for the citizen racer, the physical-psychological condition in relationship to mobility and stress is basically the same. In any run it is natural for us to move quickly to the front edge of our strengths. What is left, the space we look at and attempt to move more deeply into, is our frailty. Our acceptance of that forward space is the measure of our curiosity about optimum human possibility. The enthusiasm and peculiar dignity of citizens' racing derives from the quiet honesty of accepted limits and from running into and beyond them in the company of others. Perhaps in this sense the sustenance of citizens' racing comes less from absolute comparisons of one relative to another than from a shared sense that all are relatively more alive from having "died" a little and well. The experience of expanded personal potential and relativity with (rather than to) other humans is both profound and rare. A play context of competition generates a deeper sense of belonging, to oneself and to a community. Self-confirmation happens simultaneously with a community venture—a total reward.

A final idea about why such a reward in sport may be so prized by us, and more and more so in recent years. In 1964, Herbert Marcuse analysed man's position in an advanced industrial society in a book called *One-Dimensional Man.* He described how man *(homo faber,* man the fabricator) had begun by inventing machines to help him extend his native capabilities. His ultimate dependence upon machines soon produced an ironic and dehumanizing switch: instead of machines functioning as the object and tools of man's talent and dreams, man became the object of the machines' massive potential and specific constraints. His energies were channeled and compartmentalized to fit the demands of the more productive mechanical producer. Man switched from the subject making and using technology to the object governed by that same technology, and this process left him progressively more alien to human potential and the experience of fullness and a unique personal profile. What makes mass participation in sport so intriguing is that it gives back that sense of personal profile. *Homo ludens,* man at play, recovers the mystery and daring which are elemental to a full personal sense of being alive, frail but surviving. The Sunday ritual of endurance ultimately makes a winner of everybody, each to himself a modest hero.

REFERENCE

Ogilvie, B. C., and Tutko, T. A. 1971. Sport: If you want to build character, try something else. *Psychology Today* 5 (October):60-63.

EMOTIONAL STATES: AROUSAL

Dr. Joseph B. Oxendine has played collegiate football, basketball, and baseball and played professional baseball for three years in the Pittsburgh Pirates farm system. He has been a coach for high school athletics and is now dean of the College of Health, Physical Education and Recreation, Temple University. This article points out that there is an optimal level of arousal that enhances performance in sports, and it cites the possible differences in levels for different sports. This view sets the stage for the articles that follow, with the suggestion that arousal that is too high or too low can cause problems.

Dr. Dorothy V. Harris has served on the U. S. Olympic Committee's Sports Medicine Committee, has worked with the U.S. women's field hockey team, and has consulted with a variety of women's varsity teams (including fencing, tennis, and basketball) at the Pennsylvania State University. She is a past president of the North American Society for Sport Psychology and Physical Activity. She lettered in high school basketball and in collegiate basketball, field hockey, swimming and diving, lacrosse, and tennis. This article suggests that persons may become involved in sports activity as a means of obtaining increased emotional arousal and, in particular, stress. Thus, tension arousal may be experienced by some as a positive state rather than an interfering state.

Dr. Steven T. Bramwell played football for the University of Washington and established several records. He is the team physician for the University of Washington's football squad and director of the Division of Sports Medicine in the Department of Orthopedics at the University of Washington Medical School. Dr. Minoru Masuda is professor of psychiatry and behavioral sciences at the University of Washington and a long-time recreational skier. The late Dr. Nathaniel N. Wagner was professor and director of clinical training in the Department of Psychology at the University of Washington. Dr. Thomas H. Holmes participated in track in college and is now professor of psychiatry and behavioral sciences at the University of Washington. This article presents a counterbalance to the previous writing. Whereas Harris shows that stress is not all bad, these authors show that stress is not all good, either. This article reports on a study relating susceptibility to injury and the general life stresses facing an athlete. In tandem, this and the article by Harris lead to the conclusion that an optimal level of arousal—neither too low nor too high—is most suited to enhancing performance (the point is also made in the lead article, by Oxendine).

Emotional Arousal
and Motor Performance

Joseph B. Oxendine

One of the most widely accepted principles of human behavior is that people perform best when "motivated." This principle is validated when keenly interested children exhibit greater enthusiasm and performance on school tasks than less interested children. Highly excited individuals performing unexpected feats or attaining unusual levels of performance is further evidence. However, empirical evidence seems to indicate that high levels of excitement interfere with efficiency in certain activities. In one situation, therefore, a high level of motivation may place the individual at a distinct advantage, whereas, at another time a person so stimulated would be hindered. The relationship between arousal and performance is a complex one and does not appear to follow a straight line. This paper will investigate several aspects of this phenomenon.

WHAT IS EMOTION?

One difficult problem in analyzing the arousal-performance question is that of defining and categorizing human emotion. The terms "motivation," "excitement," or "arousal," though often used interchangeably may imply different things to different individuals. When one speaks of emotional arousal he may be referring to one or a combination of the following "negative" conditions: fear, anger, anxiety, jealousy, embarrassment, disgust, boredom, or rage. "Positive" states may include: joy, elation, ecstasy, interest, happiness, and love. The list is limited only by one's vocabulary and point of view. Although the emotional states result from different situations, the physiological response of the individual is often similar. Certainly, there is a high degree of overlap in both physical and psychological reactions to many of the indicated conditions.

Since it is not yet possible to establish distinct lines of demarcation between the various terms describing emotion, perhaps the most useful approach is to describe emotion on the basis of level of arousal or activation. In this way the emotional state may be placed on a continuum from high to low activation as follows: excited, alert and attentive, relaxed, drowsy, light sleep, deep sleep, coma, and death.[1] Different levels are reflected in physiological changes which are controlled by the automatic

Joseph B. Oxendine. Emotional arousal and motor performance. *Quest* 13 (January 1970):23-32.

[1] See the article by Pargman on pages 90-98. —Ed.

nervous system. Extensive investigation of the physiological response was carried out by Cannon in 1929, and more recently by Hanson (1967), Husman, Hanson, and Walker (1968), Johnson (1949), and Scubic (1955). Woodworth and Schlosberg (1963) present a thorough description of the known responses. Heart rate, blood pressure, muscle tension, respiration, galvanic skin response, and many other bodily functions have been identified as being sensitive to changes in emotional arousal.

In this discussion, emotional arousal will refer to those conditions in which one's "normal" physiological functions have been intensified.

AROUSAL AND MOTOR PERFORMANCE

Any effort to develop generalizations regarding the role of emotional arousal and motor performance must consider several factors. According to Cratty (1968), Husman (1969), and Oxendine (1968) the optimum level of arousal varies with the particular motor task, i.e., different tasks require different levels of arousal for most effective performance. In addition, the optimum arousal state varies from person to person. For example, high anxiety versus low anxiety, extraversion versus introversion, and experience versus nonexperience are some of the individual variables making it difficult to establish definitive guidelines for all persons. Furthermore, even for the same person the optimum level would be expected to vary somewhat from day to day. This principle is supported by Lewin's "Life-Space" concept which indicates that individuals respond to situations according to both internal and external stimuli.

Despite the limitations presented by the task and the individual variables, an effort will be made to generalize on the basis of research and literature available. The Yerkes-Dodson Law,[2] now more than a half century old, can be used as a point of reference. According to this Law, complex tasks are performed better when one's drive is low while simple tasks are performed better when drive is high. Therefore, drive which is either too great or too low for a particular task may result in impaired performance. It is assumed here that "drive" is somewhat related to motivation or arousal. There is abundant empirical research evidence to support this widely accepted generalization, and, in addition, several plausible explanations have been offered. Nevertheless, the Law fails to answer many questions for the teacher or athletic coach interested in gaining more specific guidelines for the conduct of his activities. For example, when the Yerkes-Dodson Law is used, there is a question of which tasks are "complex" and which are "simple." Furthermore, what is "high drive" and "low drive"? With the uncertainty and latitude inherent in the Law, the researcher or the practitioner can explain any results on the basis of the task being either complex or simple or the level of drive being either high or low, whichever seems to support the results in a given situation. Such reflective explanations, however, are of little value in predicting performance. Though offering a rough guide as an explanation of emotional arousal and performance, the Yerkes-Dodson Law is inadequate in terms of today's needs.

On the basis of research evidence, scientific literature, and empirical observation the following generalizations are offered on the arousal-performance topic:

1. *A high level of arousal is essential for optimal performance in gross motor activities involving strength, endurance, and speed.*

[2] See the article by Singer on pages 40-55. —Ed.

2. *A high level of arousal interferes with performances involving complex skills, fine muscle movements, coordination, steadiness, and general concentration.*
3. *A slightly-above-average level of arousal is preferable to a normal or sub-normal arousal state for all motor tasks.*

Arousal Effects on Strength, Endurance and Speed

As an example of the positive relationship between arousal and physical *strength,* the following incident is cited by Oxendine (1968, p. 173):

> *The following case was described in a newspaper a few years ago. A man, after having jacked up his station wagon to change a tire in his driveway, was called into his house. Moments later, one of his children, who had been observing the proceedings ran into the house to tell his father and mother that the car had fallen off the jack and on another child. Both parents ran outside, and the quick-thinking father immediately began resetting the jack in order to lift the car off the child. The mother, seeking more immediate results, took hold of the car and manually lifted it so that the child could crawl out from under! So great was the strain that, in the process, a bone was broken in her back. Certainly, this feat was outside the expected performance possibilities of the woman, who was described as average in size.*

Most persons can recall unusual feats of strength when persons have been confronted with emergency situations. These incidents run the gamut from "superhuman" actions by men during war to little old ladies carrying refrigerators downstairs and outside a burning house.

D. L. Johnson (1965) reported that subjects with induced motivational techniques made significant gains in strength, whereas, a nonmotivated group did not. One technique which simulated the competitive aspects of an athletic contest increased strength scores to a greater degree than other motivational techniques. Johnson further reported that subjects with below average strength and subjects with above average strength made similar improvements under conditions of motivation. Gerdes (1958) found that motivated subjects increased performance in pull-ups and push-ups.

On the basis of research and observation, there is every reason to believe that a very high arousal state will result in most extraordinary strength performances. Therefore, the gymnast performing an "iron cross," the weight lifter pressing a heavy weight, or the student doing a leg lift with a dynamometer—each would do his best if greatly aroused.

As an example of the relationship between arousal and *endurance,* I am reminded of the following personal incident which occurred approximately three years ago. I was nearing the completion of a three mile run which ended with a long uphill climb through a wooded area and the customary painful level of fatigue had become very evident. Suddenly, out of the brush sprang two large Weimaraner dogs, noticeably unhappy, and, in fact, exhibiting a high level of unwarranted hostility. After about 15 seconds of stressful uncertainty, I was rescued by the owner. As I resumed jogging I realized that not only had my pace increased but there was a total absence of any sensation of fatigue. I could not attribute the sudden burst of energy to the 15 second "rest."

Cannon (1929, p. 226) cites the case of John Colter who along with a companion was seized by a group of Indians in Montana in 1808:

Colter was stripped naked; his companion, who resisted, was killed and hacked in pieces. The Chief then made signs to Colter to go away across the prairie. When he had gone a short distance he saw the younger men casting aside everything but their weapons and making ready for a chase. Now he knew their object. He was to run a race, of which the prize was to be his own life and scalp. Off he started with the speed of the wind. The war hoop immediately arose; and looking back, he saw a large company of young warriors, with spears, in rapid pursuit. He ran with all the speed that nature, excited to the utmost, could give; fear and hope lent a supernatural vigor to his limbs, and the rapidity of his flight astonished himself. After nearly three miles his strength began to wane. He stopped and looked back. Only one of his pursuers was near. The Indian rushed towards him, attempting to cast his spear and fell headlong. Colter seized the spear, killed his enemy and again set out, with renewed strength, feeling, as he said to me, as if he had not run a mile.

Fatigue results in an increase in the threshold of a muscle and, thus, motor responses become slower. During fatigue, muscle thresholds increase from 100 percent to 200 percent and occasionally much higher in situations involving extreme amounts of work. Muscles usually return to their normal condition in 15 minutes to two hours of rest. Cannon (1929) reported research in which fatigued animals were injected with adrenalin immediately after the cessation of long work periods. He reported that animals with threshold increases of 150 percent had this decrement cut in half within five minutes as a result of the adrenalin. Rested animals did not increase their muscle response time with the injection of adrenalin. He concluded, therefore, that the injection of adrenalin had a counter action on the effects of fatigue.

While it is unlikely that Indians, Weimaraners, or injections of adrenalin will be used as a regular means of increasing endurance in sports participants, it does seem clear that situations eliciting strong emotional arousal will result in significant endurance gains.

Incidents seeming to show a positive relationship between fright, anger, or other forms of arousal and *speed* are within the experiences of most persons. Unfortunately, in these situations accurate measures of speed are not usually made. Whereas, feats of strength are usually verifiable, it is rare that anyone is available to clock frightened people over a measured course. Nevertheless, the belief remains that a child being chased by either a bully or a ghost will run faster than when told by the teacher to "run as fast as you can." In experimental situations, a relationship between movement speed and motivation has been shown by Gerdes (1958), Miller (1960), Henry (1961), and Strong (1963). Thus, there is ample reason to assume that sprinters will run faster and swimmers will swim faster if highly aroused.

AROUSAL EFFECTS ON COMPLEX AND FINE CONTROLLED MOVEMENTS

Numerous situations can be cited from sports in which highly motivated or aroused individuals performed less well on complex tasks. The typical young baseball pitcher who becomes highly excited in a tense game situation is less likely to throw strikes than in practice or a routine game situation.[3] Similarly, erratic or subpar performance in a high pressure situation may be expected from the basketball player shooting a free throw, a gymnast in a balancing routine, or a diver attempting a fancy dive. Frequent interference in activities requiring complex and controlled movements appear to support the Yerkes-Dodson Law.

The interference effects of high emotional arousal appear to have greater detrimental effects on tense or highly anxious persons than on those less anxious. Carron (1965) reported that a shock stresser (electric shock from a constant current electronic simulator) had a detrimental effect on high anxious male college students in a *balancing* task, whereas low anxious subjects were unaffected. Late in the learning period, however, the detrimental effect of the stresser on high anxious subjects was lessened. In reviewing several research studies in this area, Carron concluded that in tasks of low difficulty, high anxious subjects were found to be superior to low anxious subjects. However, in *tasks of high difficulty,* low anxious subjects proved superior. Stress seemed to be particularly detrimental when persons were largely unacquainted with a particular activity. However, experience in the activity tended to reduce the adverse effects of stress. Bergstrom (1967) reported that experienced airplane pilots performed less well on a *complex motor task* during stressful conditions. The stressful situation used was distracting flashing lights and the performance of a secondary task along with the main task. Bergstrom reported that the human pilot can perform extremely difficult and complex tasks in a calm laboratory situation or a simulated cockpit. When the system is airborne, however, the pilot's performance seriously deteriorates as a result of the stress. Pinneo (1961) reported that as tension increased so did the errors in a complex tracking task.

In a study of *steadiness,* Eysenck and Gillen (1965) reported that high drive subjects performed at an inferior level to low drive subjects in a hand steadiness test. Basomity, Karchin, and Otken (1955) found a decrement in performance in hand steadiness following the administration of adrenalin, and Hauty (1954) reported an increase in fine tremor after the administration of a stimulant drug. Several authors report that muscle tension and tremor is a normal characteristic of increased tension. Such tension may easily result in the inability of the pass receiver in football to catch the ball. The same may be true for the basketball player attempting to catch the ball or retrieve a rebound, or the field hockey player unable to exercise the typical "give" with the stick when receiving the ball.

Husman (1969) states that as emotion goes up, functioning *intelligence* goes down. Of course, effective intelligence is an important factor in athletic contests, not to mention I.Q. tests and performance in general daily routine. However, rising emotion and declining intellectual functioning is probably not a straight line relationship. That is, there is no evidence to indicate that an emotional state slightly above normal is less effective than a "normal" or even below average level. Nevertheless, there is little question about the distracting effects of extreme levels of emotion on any type of performance involving reasoning powers. Such interference may be particularly harmful when the performer is in an activity requiring quick thinking or fast decision making. Extreme examples of this interference occur when the individual "freezes" or "goes blank."

EMOTIONAL AROUSAL AND PERFORMANCE IN SPORTS

Research dealing with the role of emotional arousal in ordinary sports activities is sparse. Some studies have attempted to determine the level of arousal associated with participants in different

---

[3] See the article by Lane on pages 316-320. —Ed.

sports without determining the relationship between that level and subsequent performance. Other studies specifically designed to relate arousal to performance level usually consider the team as a whole to make a generalization about a particular sport. One of the few studies in this specific area was conducted by Harmon and Johnson (1952) who found that a major college football team played its best game of the season when aroused to the highest level. On the other hand, the team performed poorest when the arousal level was at the lowest state. However, to generalize that a football player performs best when he is most highly motivated is a rather crude generalization. The game of football is so varied and complex that optimum emotional arousal for the different skills may vary from near the norm line to extreme high levels. For example, the offensive guard or tackle required to block the individual straight across the line will probably exhibit speed and power most effectively if he is motivated to the highest possible degree. On the other hand, the open field runner is required to exhibit agility, balance, and judgment in direction as well as good running speed. Therefore, a moderate level of arousal may be most helpful. Finally, the quarterback when throwing a pass, and the field goal kicker would probably perform best at a low level of arousal so that they relax and focus their attention on the task at hand and, thus, make the accurate and rather delicate responses necessary for success. For the performance of individual tasks in football, therefore, it appears that different levels of arousal would be ideal for players at different positions.

Without adequate research relating emotional arousal to specific sports skills, suggestions as to the most appropriate level for different sports activities are speculative. Nevertheless, Table 1 includes a summary of suggestions regarding the optimal arousal level for the typical participant in a variety of sports activities. These are based on some reflections on the research and opinions which relate to the components necessary for performance in the activities listed.

In Table 1, the #5 level refers to extremely high levels of excitement approaching "blind rage" while the #1 level suggests a condition only slightly more intense than a normal relaxed state. Skills are placed on the scale at a point seeming to reflect the needed ingredients for excellent performance. That is, those activities high on speed, strength, or endurance needs but low on complexity, fine muscle control, and judgment are placed nearer to #5. Those activities placing high priority on fine muscle control and coordinated movements but low on strength and speed are placed nearer to #1. Of course, many skills require a combination of these several factors and, thus, fall somewhere in between #1 and #5. For example, the boxer, though needing the strength, speed, and endurance afforded by high emotion must devote attention to analyzing his opponent's moves and figuring out a way of maximizing his own strengths while exploiting his opponent's weaknesses. In addition, he must protect himself. Consequently, the boxer who becomes unduly angry or "loses his head" is an easier target for the more composed boxer. Similarly, the sprinter in a short race is likely to lose some efficiency at the start of the race and during the first few steps if a state of extreme tension exists at the starting blocks. However, in a slightly longer race, i.e., 200 yards, the negative effects of extreme tension would be minimized while the benefits (speed and endurance) would be maximized. For longer races such as a mile or greater, there is a tendency for the highly aroused runner to throw caution to the winds, fail to pace himself, and tire badly near the end of the race.[4]

For an activity such as golf putting, an extreme level of arousal is often devastating. The golfer is likely to putt the ball much too strongly because of his general muscular tension or, on the other hand, much too easily, because of his fear of overputting. The same holds true for other skills emphasizing accuracy and precision. I have never known a basketball coach to say to a young player who

---

[4]See the article by Suinn on pages 26-36 for the use of relaxation in distance running. –Ed.

Table 1. Optimum Arousal Level for Some Typical Sports Skills

LEVEL OF AROUSAL	SPORTS SKILLS
#5 (Extremely excited)	Football blocking and tackling Performance on the Rogers' PFI test Running (220 yards to 440 yards) Sit up, push up, or bent arm hang test Weight lifting
#4	Running long jump Running very short and long races Shot put Swimming races Wrestling and judo
#3	Basketball skills Boxing High jumping Most gymnastic skills Soccer skills
#2	Baseball pitchers and batters Fancy dives Fencing Football quarterback Tennis
#1 (Slight arousal)	Archery and bowling Basketball free throw Field goal kicking Golf putting and short irons Skating figure 8's
0 (Normal state)	

has just missed an important free throw, "You did not try hard enough." Rather, most problems arise when individuals try too hard.

ESTABLISHING THE DESIRED AROUSAL LEVEL

Understanding the optimal level of arousal for each activity is only part of the information needed to make effective use of emotions in motor skills. Also needed is a means of determining the arousal level of an individual or group at a particular time, and further, the ability to alter it. Each of these topics is appropriate for a major investigation. Only a brief overview will be presented here.

Since emotional arousal as considered in this discussion is reflected in physiological responses, the only accurate means of determining one's condition is by the measurement of these responses. Usually this requires the use of some equipment of varying degrees of sophistication. Several experimental psychology books including the one by Woodworth and Schlosberg, *Experimental Psychology* (1963), describe procedures used in the measurement of most responses related to emotional arousal. However, experienced athletic coaches and physical education teachers have developed ways of making empirical judgments as to whether an individual is "up" for an impending event. In 1929, Cannon described a highly aroused football player as "sitting grimly on a bench, his fists clenched, his jaws tight, and his face the grayish color of clay." Today's football coaches recognize these and other behaviors as being characteristic of the highly aroused player.

Changing arousal state in the desired direction requires an understanding of some basic principles of psychology and skill in using certain techniques.[5] Most texts relating to the psychology of behavior or teaching devote large portions to these processes. The following techniques have been used in practical and experimental situations to raise the level of arousal for participation in motor activities: competition (challenges), praise and reproof, rewards and punishment, "pep" talks, music, and hypnosis. Ironically, most of these have been used both to heighten and to lower the level of arousal. For example, in one situation music with a stirring, rhythmic beat and with increasing intensity may be used to raise one's general level of excitement. In another situation, soft or soothing music may be used to calm overly excited participants prior to competition. A great deal of research is essential before refinement can be made in the use of these or other techniques for promoting the desired arousal level of athletic participants.

[5] See the articles by Suinn on pages 26-36 and on pages 306-315. —Ed.

REFERENCES

Basomity, H.; Karchin, S. J.; and Otken, D. 1955. The evocation of anxiety and performance changes under minimal doses of adrenalin. *American Psychologist* 10:388.

Bergstrom, B. 1967. Complex psycho motor performance during different levels of experimentally induced stress in pilots. In *Emotional stress*, ed. L. Levy. New York: American Elsevier.

Cannon, W. B. 1953. *Bodily changes in pain, hunger, fear and rage.* 2d ed. Boston: Charles P. Branford.

Carron, A. B. 1965. *Complex motor skill performance under conditions of externally induced stress.* M.A. thesis, University of Alberta.

Cratty, B. J. 1968. *Psychology and physical activity.* Englewood Cliffs, N.J.: Prentice-Hall.

Eysenck, H. J., and Gillan, P. W. 1964. Hand-steadiness under conditions of high and low drive. In *Experiments in motivation,* ed. H. J. Eysenck. New York: Macmillan.

Gerdes, G. R. 1958. The effects of various motivational techniques on performance in selected physical tests. Unpublished Ph.D. dissertation, Indiana University.

Hanson. D. 1967. Cardiac response to participation in little league baseball competition as determined by telemetry. *Research Quarterly* 38:384-388.

Harmon, J. M., and Johnson, W. R. 1952. The emotional reactions of college athletes. *Research Quarterly* 23:391-397.

Hauty, G. T. 1954. *The effects of drugs upon the components of hand steadiness.* USAF School of Aviation, Report No. 5.

Henry, F. M. 1961. Reaction time-movement time and correlations. *Perceptual and Motor Skills* 12:63-67.

Husman, B. F. 1969. Sport and personality dynamics. NCPEAM *Proceedings,* Durham, N.C., January 1969.

Husman, B. F.; Hanson, D.; and Walker, R. 1968. The effect of coaching basketball and swimming upon emotion as measured by telemetry. Paper presented at Second International Congress of Sport Psychology, Washington, D.C., November 1968.

Johnson, B. L. 1965. *The effects of applying different motivational techniques during training and in testing upon strength performance.* Ed.D. dissertation, Louisiana State University.

Johnson, W. R. 1949. A study of emotion revealed in two types of athletic contests. *Research Quarterly* 20:72-80.

Miller, L. A. 1960. The effects of emotional stress on high school track and field performance. Unpublished master's thesis, University of California, Los Angeles.

Oxendine, J. B. 1968. *Psychology of motor learning.* New York: Appleton-Century-Crofts.

Pinneo, L. R. 1961. The effects of induced muscle tension during tracking on level of activation and on performance. *Journal of Experimental Psychology* 62:523-532.

Skubic, E. 1955. Emotional response of boys to little league and middle league competitive baseball. *Research Quarterly* 26:342-352.

Strong, C. H. 1963. Motivation related to performance of physical fitness tests. *Research Quarterly* 34:497-507.

Woodworth, R. S., and Schlosberg, H. 1963. *Experimental psychology.* Revised ed., pp. 133-191. New York: Holt, Rinehart and Winston.

On the Brink of Catastrophe

Dorothy V. Harris

Only in play and sports can an individual who creates artificial obstacles, pursues contests, and tempts fear achieve full toleration. (Klausner 1968)

In this age of greater leisure time, what determines the choice of becoming sedentary or physically active? What motivates man to participate? Why do many choose to be sedentary in spite of the better health, fitness, strength, relaxation, and other outcomes known to occur with participation? Although there is research-supported knowledge of why man *should* play, it appears that man does not play primarily for health and fitness. Therefore, there must be other reasons; however, very little is known about why man *does* play. It is possible that needs of which the participant is unaware are being gratified.

With sport such a dominant aspect of American life, investigators are not content with knowing what sport does physiologically for the participant but also are questioning why man plays and participates in the sports that he does. Recently, investigators have wrestled with definitions, with classifications, with the rationale, and with attempts to explain this involvement. Some writers have been content with Huizinga's somewhat general approach to the discussion of play; others have continued to reduce the generalization to more fundamental components through the process of classification and development of other conceptual models.

CLASSIFICATION OF SPORTS AND GAMES

Caillois (1961) produced the first comprehensive and logical classification of games and sports. His paradigm is based on both the description and the behavior of the game. The four categories included in his paradigm are: AGON (competition), ALEA (chance), MIMICRY (simulation), and ILINX (vertigo). Caillois' paradigm attempted to order and classify sport but failed to supply a category for many activities within his flexible framework.

McIntosh's (1963) consideration of Caillois' classification also found it lacking. Consequently, he developed a classification determined by the motive and the nature of the satisfaction which the

Dorothy V. Harris. On the brink of catastrophe. *Quest* 13 (January 1970):33-40.

sport provided the participant rather than by the activity itself. His first category included those sports in which the participant could "prove" himself better than others either singly, in pairs, larger groups, or teams. The second category was comprised of combat sports or those activities requiring physical contact with the opponent or with equipment. Conquest sports were placed in the third category; challenge is provided by the environment or the situation rather than by individual or group opponents. A fourth category included those physical activities that express or communicate feelings and ideas through movement but are not considered sport or activities where one can demonstrate superiority.

Social anthropology has made several contributions to the classification of sports and physical activity. Games and physical activities have been classified as to whether the activity was primarily concerned with physical skill, with strategy, or with chance (Roberts, Arth, and Rush 1959). Investigators concluded that: (*a*) the games of physical skill are related to environmental conditions and are possibly associated with mastery of both self and environment, (*b*) the games of strategy are related to social systems and to the mastery of the social system, and (*c*) the games of chance are related to religious beliefs and are associated with mastery of the supernatural. In general, the conclusions support the psychoanalytic theory that games are exercises in mastery.

Another study was concerned with relating types of games adults preferred to their child-training pattern experience and economic status (Sutton-Smith, Roberts, and Kozelka 1963). It was concluded that games of strategy were stressed for the value of obedience and preferred by upper status groups and women who had had such a child-training experience. Games of chance were associated with routine-responsibility experience patterns and were found among the lower status groups and among women. Games of physical skill were associated with high achievement training and were popular among upper status groups and among men.

Efforts have just begun to produce a framework for characterizing physical activity as some type of social-psychophysical phenomenon. The value of physical activity that participants perceive suggests that such phenomenon can be reduced to more specific components. One such component is concerned with the possibility of a common motivation to participate in activities that may be classified as *eustress-seeking*.

EUSTRESS (PLEASANT STRESS)

Eustress is associated with adventure, excitement, and thrilling experiences and is considered as a pleasant type of stress as opposed to the painful, unpleasant type of stress (dys-stress) studied by Selye and his followers. Both types may be voluntary.

Bernard (1968) described eustress as fun and as having the capacity to enhance vital sensations. Eustress "turns one on" and, in the process, releases energy. She suggested that if knowledge of how to make activities eustressful is acquired, ways to motivate more people to participate may be found. The study of eustress-seeking may provide the key that will unlock part of the mystery of human motivation and provide support for a curriculum change for physical education. It is quite possible that eustress may be a factor in physical activity that "turns on" many individuals. This possibility may exist to the extent that properly directed physical activity could be a substitute for many of the current efforts to "turn on" through spiritual media, drugs, trance-states, etc. In general, stress-seeking may be defined as behavior structured to amplify the individual's level of involvement. The work of Petrie (Petrie 1960; Petrie, Collins, and Soloman 1960; Petrie, Holland, and Wolk 1963; Petrie,

McCulloch, and Kazdin 1962) and of Ryan (Ryan 1969; Ryan and Kovacic 1966) and their discussion of the athletic participation of the augmenter and the reducer support the theory of sport participation being classified as stress-seeking.

Characteristics of Eustress

Experiences of a limited duration are characteristic of eustress. Stresses sought are those associated with a proximate climax and tend to occur in a context that is the antithesis of routine, boredom, stability, and sameness; without confrontation, excitement dwindles. Sports and physical activities without intrinsic eustress usually have to add a competitive element to attract eustress-seekers. Thus, some means of comparison, of keeping score, and of testing oneself are essential.

Seeking a symbolic or a physical challenge that motivates the searcher to become actively involved is called stress-seeking according to Klausner (1968). Both types of stress-seekers (the symbolic and the physical)[1] share many common characteristics: both approach the task rationally, both tend to repeat the difficult challenge or continue to seek new and greater ones, and both tend to be egocentric. Participants in sports and other activities may be seekers of physical challenges and of stressful situations.

Recognition has been given to the fact that some individuals strive to raise their tension levels rather than maintain homeostasis. The paradox observed in the stress-seeker, that of seeking painful, stressful situations rather than avoiding them, may be resolved by the fact that pleasure and pain are both drawn from the same reservoir of underlying excitement. How else can one explain the mixture of joy and fear of a child's first trip down a long slide and the resulting excitement, or that combination of anxiety and thrill of diving from a three-meter board the first time? Experiencing this combination of pain and pleasure may well be the motivating factor involved in repeating stressful situations. That some individuals seek this type of stress for its own sake and enjoy the process is obvious in the literature and research. Why one seeks or avoids stress is a complex question; why man plays is also a complex question. It is possible that the answer to both is quite similar.

Individual differences in stress-seeking appear justified. If a continuum of stress-seeking-avoiding can be envisioned, individuals would be placed all along it from one extreme to the other. Stress-seeking varies in degree and nature both within a given culture or subculture and from one culture to another.

The role that stress-seeking plays in the motivation of man to participate in physical activities has yet to be determined. In many activities the stress is clear, apparent, and freely sought. The process of transferring anxiety or fear into pleasure composes the very essence of participation. To understand how and why this occurs is to understand why one participates.

Factors Influencing Eustress-Seeking

Several factors are to be considered when evaluating eustress-seeking as a motivator to physical activity:

Human Physical Energy. The amount of human energy available for eustress-seeking determines how much one may utilize. Klausner has shown that stress-seeking in parachuting is related to individual differences in human physical energy. He classified jumpers as "thrilled" and "tempered" and

---

[1] See the article by Pargman on pages 90-98. —Ed.

described the former as more energetic, less accident-prone, and having a lesser sense of danger. Fear adaptation is more active among the "thrilled" and more passive among the "tempered." Bernard suggested that if the individual differences that Klausner found among sky divers were so great, then the differences in human energy available to them and to others who find more sedentary forms gratifying must be much greater. Those who get their satisfaction vicariously must evidence even greater differences. This possibility remains to be explored.

Klausner pointed out that eustress may be more than energy-consuming; it may be energy-mobilizing. He suggested that eustress-seeking may release energy for constructive social activities. Most people have far more energy resources than they realize. This has been demonstrated many times in emergencies when individuals accomplish feats never dreamed possible.

Age is related to available energy. Youth has more energy than that required for the routine of living. This may partially explain the relationship of physical activities to age. The young average age of participants in riots, demonstrations, street fights, gang wars, etc. may be explained by the energy available for eustress-seeking. The available amount of human energy may also explain why lower classes, who have to expend tremendous energy for a living, seek their eustress through vicarious forms. The reported relationship between social class and sports participation may possibly be explained by the difference in energy levels that may exist among classes. The possibility also exists that utilization of energy through directed physical activities may leave too little energy to become involved in socially undesirable behavior. Much more research is needed on the role vigorous activity may play in affecting positive behavioral patterns.

Class. Historically the class-bound nature of eustress is characteristic. Lower classes, restricted in opportunities, have had to seek challenges in adventure and excitement differing from the upper classes. Ghetto areas may provide eustress-seeking through riots, street fighting, brawls, etc. when no other outlets are available. Providing constructive outlets for all classes may serve to meet the needs in a positive manner. Current studies are investigating the social climbing that may occur through select sport participation.

Sex. The male has traditionally been the stress-seeker; adventure, excitement, and the thrill of battle have been the male prerogative. The American culture provides and approves stress-seeking activities for the male, but few for the female. There is no reason to suspect that women are any less stress-seeking than men. Because of the physical difference in size and strength, most women seek their excitement and eustress in other ways.[2] Physical education should provide for activities which meet this need. Boys have grown up testing their physical strength, their bodily skill, and their courage while girls traditionally have needed no such assurance. With the cultural trend toward unisexualism, there may be reason for change in the physical education curriculum, especially for women.

Stress-Seeking Vicariously

Vicarious eustress may be created by words, by music, by pictures, by symbols; it may also be created by observing bodily actions of others in spectator sports. These sports, such as automobile racing, bull fighting, boxing, and competitive sports of all kinds have supplied and continue to supply eustress to both participants and to millions of spectators. Evidence of the amounts of energy generated through vicarious eustress can be observed universally with the trouble officials have in trying to prevent fights from breaking out during and after competitive events. Research is not available to

---

[2]See the article by Balazs on pages 156-162. —Ed.

support the theory that active participation in eustress activities would eliminate vicarious eustress-seeking.

OTHER SUPPORTING THEORIES

Steinhaus (1961) expressed the theory that youngsters who grow up with over-protective parents who say, "No, no, no!" each time the youngster attempts to explore, to climb, to venture close to the "brink of catastrophe," will produce offspring unwilling to take risks in adult life. In contrast, those youngsters allowed to take risks and who enjoy challenges serve as the "doers" in society. Klausner suggested this when he said that a good population of risk-takers enhanced the possibility of economic development.

Russell, in his *Reith Lectures* of 1948 argued that there is savage in each person that must find some outlet compatible with the culture. He suggested that sports competition might provide this outlet for such competition does not occur enough in the lives of most individuals. He further added that men must compete for superiority and that sports contests yielding seemingly useless results are the best solution. On the other hand, the results do matter; if not, they would not satisfy man. Victory or defeat is never for all time as the participant will live to challenge once again.

Morris (1967), in his discussion of "Exploration," outlined rules which could easily serve as principles of eustress. He stated that the function of exploration was to provide the participant with greater awareness of his environment and his relationship to it. All through life each person carries on complex and specialized forms of exploration and experimentation. Through training as performers and observers, Morris felt that individuals could sensitize their responsiveness to the tremendous exploratory potential that these pursuits offer. Eustress-seeking can be classified as a type of exploration or testing and has the potential of providing many rich experiences. Morris supported Steinhaus' theory when he suggested that if a child fails to explore, to experiment, to join in these experiences as a child, then similar experiences will be difficult, if not impossible, as an adult.

Lorenz (1966) stated that sport can educate man to a conscious and responsible control of his fighting behavior. While his topic was aggression, he suggested eustress-seeking activities as an outlet for the aggressive tendencies of man. He further suggested that the difficult forms of sport, particularly those demanding cooperation and dangerous undertakings, provide the challenge and the outlet that man needs.[3] Proper channeling should direct man toward desirable positive behavioral patterns and provide opportunities for meeting these needs.

Bernard said that in societies where all energies are not devoted to survival it can be assumed that energy will be available for pleasure. If this assumption is correct, then it does not have to be asked why they seek eustress, but what factors determine the form of eustress-seeking taking place?

Resenthal, Professor of Preventive Medicine at the University of Illinois College of Medicine and Medical Director of the Research Foundation, has spent several years theorizing about danger as a way of joy (see Furlong 1969). He reported that participants of "risk-exercise" (fox hunting, bull fighting, polo, mountain climbing, etc.) described a sense of exhilaration, of feeling euphoric. He concluded that the experience of the creative person is exhilarating, but that there is always tension at one level or another; while experiencing lightheartedness they are beset with doubts and uncertainties. Participants of risk-exercise experience an exhilaration without fear, doubt, or uncertainty.

---

[3] See the article by Tandy and Laflin on pages 125-128. —Ed.

Individuals who participate in nonrisk sports and activities experience physiological benefits and an uplift in spirit but not to the same degree. Rosenthal believes that the popularity of risk-exercise may indicate the degree of conflict within the society and within the individual. He stated that the basic premise of risk-exercise is that calculated risks, both physical and mental, are essential to the well-being of man. The feeling experienced in demanding risk-exercise are so great that one becomes addicted in that he must go back and experience it again.

Rosenthal stated that we now have enough evidence that this exhilaration response does exist with involvement in risk-exercises. The mechanisms responsible for this reaction are yet to be discovered but it is important for each individual to realize that participation in risk exercise can offer sensations that are at the extreme end of the human elation continuum.

Each of these writers has alluded to the fact that man has demonstrated needs which may be identified as eustress needs. Each has suggested that these needs may be met through some means of positive direction of energies and abilities. Physical education may better serve to meet these needs if efforts are directed toward understanding the motivating factors behind man's action and restructuring programs to more adequately meet these needs.

CONCLUSION

Sports and participation in physical activity appear to serve as one of the few socially accepted avenues left for eustress-seeking. Many of our young people have joined the civil rights movement; others, the Peace Corps; and still others, the hippies; or resorted to drugs and other stimulants. This still leaves many who turn to crime, to rioting, and to violence in their quest. The problem is one of channeling and providing suitable modes of expression; not suppressing this eustress-seeking. The professions of physical education and recreation should be vitally interested in researching this area as they are in the best position to expand the positive potential of stress-seeking.

Man's longing to fly, to go to the moon, to jump farther, to climb higher, all attest to his need to flirt with danger. This joy of being on the "brink of catastrophe"; this need to encounter danger, to master it, to repeat this mastery until it loses the danger; and then go to further challenges, supports man's need for this eustress-seeking. How else can the excitement of the "near misses" that are so often experienced in sports be explained? The games of "chicken," "I dare you," and others also support this need. Skiing is an excellent example. Many participants admit this as part of the intrigue of skiing. Participants in other activities, such as white water canoeing, also verbalize pleasure as flirting with danger, of being on the "brink of catastrophe" in explaining why they enjoy participation. For Jean-Claude Killy, as for many others, skiing was only one of an assortment of thrills; when that was mastered, new and more dangerous activities had to be found. Continued participation in an activity must be emotionally exciting including both fear as well as enthusiasm. Anticipation of these emotions may well be part of the original motivation for participation.

It may be that the common motivation to participate in many sports and physical activities is eustress-seeking. The flirt with disaster, the sudden release of tension, and the surge of exhilaration that follows may well be the sensation each is seeking. Everyone appears to have an instinctive need to pit himself against some force that is out of his control, to find out what sort of person he is under stress, and to fight natural forces (Musselman 1961). This whole area needs research to focus the direction of physical education programs toward meeting the psychological and social needs of mankind. To do this, greater understanding of why man plays and what motivates him is needed.

REFERENCES

Bernard, J. 1968. The eudaemonists. In *Why man takes chances,* ed. S. Z. Klausner. Garden City, N.J.: Doubleday.

Caillois, R. 1961. *Man, play, and games.* New York: Free Press.

Furlong, W. 1969. Danger as a way of joy. *Sports Illustrated* 30 (27 January):52-53.

Klausner, S. Z., ed.1968. *Why man takes chances.* Garden City, N.J.: Doubleday.

Lorenz, K. 1966. *On aggression,* trans. M. K. Wilson. New York: Harcourt, Brace and World.

McIntosh, P. C. 1963. *Sport in society.* London: Watts.

Morris, D. 1967. *The naked ape.* New York: McGraw-Hill.

Musselman, V. 1961. The White House Conference on Children and Youth—The challenge to program. In *Selected papers presented at the forty-second National Recreation Conference.* New York: National Recreation Association.

Petrie, A. 1960. Some psychological aspects of pain and the relief of suffering. *Annals of the New York Academy of Science* 86:13-27.

Petrie, A.; Collins, W.; and Soloman, P. 1960. The tolerance for pain and for sensory deprivation. *American Journal of Psychology* 73:80-90.

Petrie, A.; Holland, L.; and Wolk, I. 1963. Sensory stimulation causing subdued experience: Audio-analgesia and perceptual augmentation and reduction. *Journal of Nervous and Mental Disease* 137:312-321.

Petrie, A.; McCulloch, R.; and Kazdin, P. 1962. The perceptual characteristics of juvenile delinquents. *Journal of Nervous and Mental Disease* 134:415-421.

Roberts, J. M.; Arth, M. J.; and Rush, R. R. 1959. Games in culture. *American Anthropologist* 61:597-602.

Ryan, E. D. 1969. Perceptual characteristics of vigorous people. In *New perspectives of man in action,* ed. R. C. Brown, Jr., and B. J. Cratty. Englewood Cliffs, N.J.: Prentice-Hall.

Ryan, E. D., and Kovacic, C. R. 1966. Pain tolerance and athletic participation. *Perceptual Motor Skills* 22:383-390.

Steinhaus, A. H. 1961. Class lecture notes, George Williams College.

Sutton-Smith, B.; Roberts, J. M.; and Kozelka, R. M. 1963. Game involvement in adults. *Journal of Social Psychology* 60:15-30.

Psychosocial Factors in Athletic Injuries: Development and Application of the Social and Athletic Readjustment Rating Scale (SARRS)

Steven T. Bramwell, Minoru Masuda,
Nathaniel N. Wagner, and Thomas H. Holmes

Athletics is an area in which injuries occur frequently, resulting in loss of time, money, and games. Players, as well as management, have an important stake in minimizing these losses. Injuries in all sports are increasing despite technological advances in safety equipment. No doubt this is due in part to the increasing number of participants, to a greater emphasis on athletics, and to an increasing amount of leisure time available, particularly in the Western world. It is likely that the number of participants and injuries in athletics will continue to increase. It is important, therefore, to develop and increase our knowledge of possible etiological factors in the complex injury process with hopes of reductions in personal debilitation.

In the past 20 years it has been found by several investigators (Hinkle and Wolff 1958; Rahe et al. 1964; Holmes and Rahe 1967) that onset of illness is significantly associated with an increase in the number of social events which require some adaptive or coping behavior on the part of the involved individual. These social events often are life situations which the individual has perceived as overwhelming, threatening, unsatisfying, or conflictual. It has been shown that the onset of certain diseases occurs at such times (Rahe et al. 1964). While most investigations have been concerned with various disease states, we have wondered whether acute trauma and injuries may also be associated with an increased perception of stressful events. Anyone who has experienced an accident or close miss remembers the strong emotional response following it and can appreciate the immediate effects stressful events may have on one's ability to adapt and react appropriately and safely.

This paper reports . . . on the relationship of psychosocial events to injuries in athletes [and] describes the . . . Social and Athletic Readjustment Rating Scale (SARRS) and . . . the application of the . . . SARRS to the varsity football players of a major university. . . .

Steven T. Bramwell, Minoru Masuda, Nathaniel N. Wagner, and Thomas H. Holmes. Psychosocial Factors in Athletic Injuries: Development and Application of the Social and Athletic Readjustment Rating Scale (SARRS). *Journal of Human Stress.* Volume 1, Number 2, June, 1975, pages 6-20. Copyright ©1975 Opinions Publications, Inc. The present article is an abridged version of the original.

We acknowledge with thanks the assistance of the University of Washington Department of Sports Programs and the Division of Sports Medicine of the Department of Orthopaedics.
This research was supported in part by U.S.P.H.S. Undergraduate Training in Human Behavior Grant No. 5–T2-MH-7871-06 and Undergraduate Training in Psychiatry Grant No. 5-T2-MH-5939-17 from the Institute of Mental Health; the Scottish Rite Committee for Research in Schizophrenia; and the O'Donnell Psychiatric Research Fund.

METHOD

Members of a university varsity football team which played a major college schedule were selected for study because of their availability and the frequency of occurrence of salient injuries in this sport. Practice and game injuries were well documented by the Division of Sports Medicine at the university. The judgment of injury was made independently by Sports Medicine personnel who were unaware of the life change magnitudes of the individual players.

An Athlete Schedule of Recent Experience (ASRE) was constructed to include the items scaled in the Social and Athletic Readjustment Rating Scale (SARRS) (Table 1). This paper-and-pencil test allowed the subjects to identify the occurrence of the items in specified time intervals. The two time intervals contained in the schedule were for one year and two years prior to the football season under study. A life change score was derived for each time interval by assigning the scale magnitude to the item reported by the subject and summing the numbers.

After about three months, at the completion of the playing season, the injury record for each of the players was obtained. For the purpose of analysis, the injured group was defined as those players who missed three or more practices and/or one or more games due to a specific injury. Those football players who did not meet these criteria composed the noninjured group. These criteria were accepted because they identified a major time loss injury. Injuries which did not result in a game or part of a game missed, or less than three practices missed, reflected minor though nagging injuries commonly suffered by contact sport participants. These are incurred by almost all participants at one time or another and are not of interest in this study.

RESULTS

The injured group contained 36 players. The mean one-year Life Change Units (LCU) for this group was 632 (range 142-2260) and the mean two-year LCU was 1008 (range 299-3900).

The noninjured group included 46 players. The mean one-year LCU for this group was 494 (range 150-1552) and the mean LCU for the two-year interval was 797 (range 296-1972). Comparison of scores is summarized in Table 2.

Statistical analysis was applied to the differences in mean scores for each group in each time interval. Both time interval mean differences were found to be significant at the 0.05 level.

Not all accumulations of life events are associated with football injuries. For use in prediction of injuries, players were divided into low-risk, moderate-risk, and high-risk groups on the basis of low, moderate, and high LCU (Table 3). In the low-risk group (0-400 for one year, 0-700 for two years), 30 percent of the players suffered injuries. In the moderate-risk group (400-800 for one year, 700-1200 for two years), 50 percent of the players suffered injuries. In the high-risk group (>800 for 1 year, >1200 for two years), 73 percent of the players suffered major time loss injuries.

DISCUSSION

The relationship of the perception of life events accumulation to football injuries shows a significant association. The data indicate that the risk of an injury to a football player increases in direct relationship to the accumulation of the challenging life events under study. This appears to be true

Table 1. Comparison of Ranking of 37 Like Items in the Social Readjustment Rating Scale (SRRS) and the Social and Athletic Readjustment Rating Scale (SARRS)

LIFE EVENTS	AMERICAN (N = 167) RANK	COLLEGE FOOTBALL (N = 79) RANK
Death of spouse	1	1
Divorce	2	5
Death of close family member	3	2
Marital separation	4	6
Jail term	5	12
Personal injury or illness	6	8
Marriage	7	3
Marital reconciliation	8	22
Change in health of family member	9	9
Being fired	10	7
Death of close friend	11	4
Sexual difficulties	12	16
Gaining a new family member	13	15
Business readjustment	14	26
Changing to different kind of work	15	14
Change in number of arguments with spouse	16	19
Change in financial state	17	11
Taking mortgage or loan greater than $10,000	18	20
Foreclosure on mortgage or loan	19	18
Change in responsibility at work	20	17
In-law problems	21	24
Begin or cease formal schooling	22	10
Revision of personal habits	23	27
Change in living conditions	24	23
Wife begins or stops work	25	21
Outstanding personal achievement	26	13
Change in recreation	27	37
Change in work hours or conditions	28	28
Change in residence	29	33
Change in church activities	30	36
Mortgage or loan less than $10,000	31	29
Change in social activities	32	25
Change in sleeping habits	33	31
Change in eating habits	34	30
Change in family get-togethers	35	34
Vacation	36	32
Minor violation of the law	37	35

Table 2. Mean Life Change Units (LCU) of Injured and Noninjured Groups

	1-YEAR SCORE	2-YEAR SCORE
Injured (N = 36)	632 (range 142-2260)	1,008 (range 299-3900)
Noninjured (N = 46)	494 (range 150-1552)	797 (range 296-1972)
Mean difference	138 ($p \leqslant 0.05$)*	211 ($p \leqslant 0.05$)*

*Student's t-test.

Table 3. Rate of Occurrence of Injuries (%) in Low, Moderate, and High Risk Groups Established by Magnitude of Life Change

LOW RISK		MODERATE RISK		HIGH RISK	
One Year* (N = 32) (0-400 LCU)	Two Year** (N = 34) (0-700 LCU)	One Year (N = 39) (400-800 LCU)	Two Year (N = 33) (700-1200 LCU)	One Year (N = 11) (>800 LCU)	Two Year (N = 15) (>1200 LCU)
72%	73%	44%	48%	35%	29%

*Life Change Units (LCU) for 1 year prior to athletic season.
**LCU for 2 years prior to athletic season.

regardless of whether a one- or two-year time interval prior to participation is examined. These results are similar to those summarized by Holmes and Masuda (1973) for health changes in general.

This correlational investigation represents only a starting place in the possible role of life events in sports injuries. Certainly the genesis of injury is a complex, multifactor process. A dangerous set of conditions involving high energy exchange has to be dealt with by individuals who are prepared in varying degrees physically and psychologically. Each individual then must react to the conditions in accordance with his perception of the situation and his ability to respond based on that perception. The role played in this complex interaction by the accumulation of the life change events is unclear at this time. The effect of life change may be to hinder concentration on environmental cues that are crucial (i.e., sensing the blind side block) and/or to block previously learned adaptive responses when difficult and potentially damaging situations are recognized (i.e., "freezing up").

It is with some hesitation that these data are published. This is not because of doubts about the relationship of the perception of life events to football injuries, but rather because of the possible misuses of this experimental approach to the study of injury. Individuals associated with an activity as important as major college and/or professional football have enormous concern with the subject of injuries. Often the course of a team's progress rests on the health of key personnel. The perception of life events may be seen by some as a predictive test to be used as a screening instrument so as to know what confidence may be placed in an individual's potential for injury-free competition.

To protect the athlete and to cope with the serious ethical issue involved in such screening, the practice of informed consent could be made routine. There is also the important issue of group versus individual prediction. We are dealing here with group scores and group prediction. Individual athletes with low magnitudes of life change were injured during the season. Other individual athletes with high life change scores had no injuries. The importance of understanding the complex multifactor nature of sports injuries and the incompleteness of our understanding cannot be emphasized too strongly.

SUMMARY

As a part of this investigation of the perception of life change events in athletic injuries, . . . modifications were made in the Social Readjustment Rating Scale (SRRS) developed by Holmes and Rahe, in order to measure more precisely the experiences encountered by athletes and to increase the credibility of the instrument with that population. . . . A correlation study was done with regards to life event accumulations over one- and two-year intervals and to injuries defined in college football. . . .

The Athlete Schedule of Recent Experience (ASRE) was given to 82 college football players. All life event score accumulations were obtained for each. . . . The scores of players suffering major time loss injuries were compared with scores of players not having time loss injuries. Statistical differences in mean scores over one- and two-year intervals were found between the injured and non-injured groups. Football players with low, moderate, and high life change scores could be predicted to be at proportionate risk for sustaining injuries.

REFERENCES

Hinkle, L. E., and Wolff, H. G. 1958. Ecologic investigations of the relationship between illness, life experiences and the social environment. *Ann. Intern. Med.* 49:1373-1389.

Holmes, T. H., and Masuda, M. 1973. Life change and illness susceptibility. In *Separation and depression,* ed. J. P. Scott and E. C. Senay. Publication no. 94. Washington, D.C.: American Association for the Advancement of Science.

Holmes, T. H., and Rahe, R. H. 1967. The social readjustment rating scale. *J. Psychosom. Res.* 11:213-218.

Rahe, R. H.; Meyer, M.; Smith, M.; Kjaer, G.; and Holmes, T. H. 1964. Social stress and illness onset. *J. Psychosom. Res.* 8:35-44.

EMOTIONAL STATES: AGGRESSION

Dr. Ruth E. Tandy has been chairperson of the Denton Board of Women Officials, chairperson of the college division of the Texas unit of the Division of Girls' and Women's Sports, a member of the National Association for Girls' and Women's Sports Evaluation and Rating Committee in Volleyball, state basketball sport director for the Texas Association of Intercollegiate Athletics for Women, and coordinator of officials for both the state and the regional basketball tournaments in Texas. She played collegiate field hockey and basketball; coached collegiate field hockey, basketball, and tennis; and coached and played AAU basketball. She is an associate professor in the College of Health, Physical Education and Recreation at Texas Women's University. Dr. Joyce Laflin has coached in several sports, including volleyball, basketball, and gymnastics on the secondary level and tennis on the college level. She is an assistant professor at the University of Science and Arts of Oklahoma. This article concisely expresses two theories about the effect of aggression in sports on participants. These theories are seemingly incompatible, since one suggests that aggression in sports reduces aggression in participants, while the other suggests that aggression is increased because of learning. An understanding of the theories, however, may be useful in the evaluation of other writings and research on the not easily answered question.

Coach Robert Corran has worked with the Ohio State University ice hockey team on performance testing and anxiety through his capacity as assistant hockey coach. His experience includes coaching high school football, tennis, and hockey. He is currently completing a doctoral degree at the Ohio State University, School of Health, Physical Education and Recreation. This article approaches the topic of aggression from the perspective of how a coach might actually be a contributing factor. Taking the view that aggression is a learned response, the author offers suggestions about what a coach can do to reduce the occurrence of violence among athletes, even when game conditions cause frustrations.

Dr. Robert L. Arms, Professor Gordon W. Russell, and Dr. Mark L. Sandilands are all psychologists who have become interested in what factors stimulate aggression. They are on the faculty of the Department of Psychology at the University of Lethbridge. This article extends the question from consideration of how aggressive sports affect participating athletes to how they affect spectators.

Aggression and Sport: Two Theories

Ruth E. Tandy and Joyce Laflin

Sport provides an intriguing clue to the complex American culture, and parallels the establishment of many behavior patterns within society. Three dominant forces have emerged in our culture. Individuals search for *identification,* seek emotional *stimulation,* and strive for *achievement and status.* These cultural behaviors are reflected in sport.

The need for identification is encompassed by two antithetical concepts—the driving need to identify with our "super heroes" in sport and the concern for the development of a personal sport skill. Some believe man must find action in sport which is meaningful and self-gratifying as a personal form of involvement, whereas other segments of the society find satisfaction in merely adopting a successful team in order to strengthen their superegos.

The need for stimulation is found in the obsessive attention which we devote to sports, and especially team activities. More people are watching sports events, either by means of television or by attendance at the athletic arena, than at any previous time in our history, satisfying a need for vicarious emotional pleasure.

Perhaps the most significant parallel is seen in our intense competition for achievement. The concern for money, status, "We're Number 1," and quality performance are concepts sanctioned by our society in many areas as well as in sport.

It is interesting to note that these three specific needs—identification, stimulation, and achievement—are all served by the generalized drive of aggression (Feibleman 1963, p. 16). In addition,

Which is the correct behavior model?	
Aggression Theory No. 1	**Aggression Theory No. 2**
1. Aggression is instinctive.	1. Aggression is learned.
2. Society is predisposed to aggression.	2. Sport teaches aggression.
3. Sport serves as a catharsis.	3. Sport contributes to a violent society.

Ruth E. Tandy and Joyce Laflin. Aggression and sport: Two theories. *Journal of Health, Physical Education and Recreation* 44 (June 1973):19-20.

aggression is a term frequently used in describing the American culture. The question of paramount concern is whether sport, as a subculture, serves as a positive outlet for this aggressive drive or whether sport teaches and encourages aggression.

AGGRESSION THEORY No. 1

If we consider the theoretical position that aggression is instinctive, that our society is predisposed to aggressive behaviors, then we can suggest that sport may serve as catharsis.

In the early development of animals and man, aggressive action served to supply food, shelter, protection, and reproductive needs. Survival itself depended upon the constructive function of aggression in primitive man. Guided by instinct man ate, fought, claimed space, and mated. Though modern man now offers only token protection and acceptance of the weaker person, the instinct of aggression still operates and allows the stronger to dominate. Our society accepts and encourages a more aggressive, dominant role for male children as opposed to the female. In play groups, children generally select the larger, stronger companion as their temporary leader.

The aggressive instincts are especially noticeable in the historical growth of our country. American development is founded upon aggression. History records the American people victorious over a new land, Indians, slaves, and the rule of kings. Americans have engaged in war with their original homeland, fellow countrymen, and foreign powers throughout the world. "As our nation grows more centralized and our energy more concentrated, as our inner tensions grow more desperate and our frustration in our own land and in the world more embittered, we can no longer regard hatred and violence as accidents and aberrations," says a noted American historian (Schlesinger 1968, p. 62). It appears that we are aggressive beings easily given to violence.

The aggressive instinct still exists; the need for its expression has intensified, and yet the number and availability of acceptable outlets in society has declined. This natural instinct cannot be ignored, but must be alleviated with positive methods.

Competitive games provide an unusually satisfactory outlet for the instinctive aggressive drive. A program of exercise or sport does much to ease the tensions and stress of modern life. The close identification spectators develop with a player, a team, or a sporting event allows them to vicariously receive the benefits of action. The use of play, games, and sports in the treatment of exceptional individuals leads to the assumption that such methods may well be even more valuable and effective as preventive measures than as corrective methods. To deny the opportunity of channeling the aggressive instinct into constructive, competitive games is to take away one of the methods of behavior control in our society.

If the theory that aggression is instinctive, that our society is predisposed to aggressive behavior, and that sport can serve as catharsis is accepted, then it may also be concluded that sport has a very positive influence on society. However, there is a second theory that deserves equal attention.

AGGRESSION THEORY No. 2

This theory is based upon the beliefs that aggression is a learned behavior, that sport teaches and encourages aggression, and that the intense emphasis upon sport participation and association contributes to the competitiveness and resultant violence in our society.

Investigators have studied both animals and humans in the attempt to determine whether aggression is an instinctive or a learned behavior. Puppies were denied normal satisfaction of sucking needs and the result of this frustration was not aggressive behavior but perverted sucking of their own feet and objects in the environment (Levy 1941). Mice were placed in cages with inadequate room or food but did not demonstrate destructive aggressive behavior toward other mice. Later, through laboratory conditioning, the same mice were taught to fight and transferred this training to gain dominance over other mice when food was limited (Scott 1958 p. 20). Sherif and Sherif (1969, pp. 226-227) concluded that aggression is not an invariable response to frustration, for in both animal and human studies it has produced highly different responses.

Bateson's study (1941) of the Balinese people indicated that both children and adults of this culture are willing to suffer frustration infinitely without becoming aggressive. Following his investigation of the Semai of Malaya, Alland (1972) concluded that aggression is not instinctive. The aggressive tendencies must be cultivated, for there exists no one instinct of aggression in humans or animals.

Children exposed to aggressive adult models demonstrated significantly more violent and destructive responses after their exposure than those exposed to non-aggressive models (Bandura, Ross, and Ross 1961). Punishment of aggression was successful in decreasing the amount and intensity of aggression in the particular situation in which the punishment occurred. However, the aggression seems to have been more displaced since it increased in frequency and intensity when the situations were unlike those in which the initial punishment was given (Child Welfare Research Station 1961, p. 89).

Berkowitz (1965) states, after an extensive review of the literature, that quantitative research has not consistently supported the catharsis hypothesis. Intense rivalry[1] developed by the competitive spirit can result in deterioration of character. Beisser (1967, p. 17) states that "aggression . . . may lead to success in sports, a successful business career, a one-way trip to San Quentin, or frequent trips to a psychiatrist."

Sports capitalizes on the teaching of aggressive behavior for retribution, achievement, and justice of the game. The vocabulary, which includes such phases as "beat 'em," "be tough," "fight," and "kill him," suggests that violence is sanctioned and necessary. If the aggression built into sport participation were absolved within the activity itself, there would be little need to become concerned. However, aggressive acts, rather than the catharsis effect, frequently lead to further aggression and a reduction of inhibitions on subsequent occasions.

Studies by Hammond and Goldman (1961) and Sherif (1969) seem to indicate that competition most frequently leads to an increase in aggressive behavior. These studies reveal that participating in or viewing aggressive behavior is far more likely to increase rather than reduce the probability of aggressive behavior.[2]

The participant or spectator may be unaware of the tension he has absorbed during a sporting event since these emotional states and attitudes can be transferred from person to person unconsciously. Tension developed during the game often results in displaced aggression which may produce a riot immediately following the conclusion of regulated activity, or one of a number of "after the game incidents" that plague our schools and communities. Sport, through reinforcement of aggressive responses and the lowering of inhibitions for such behavior, actually contributes largely to the aggressive and violent social patterns so prevalent today.

---

[1] See the article by Corran on pages 129-132. —Ed.
[2] See the article by Arms, Russell, and Sandilands on pages 133-142. —Ed.

THE PARADOX

The preceding discussion has produced what appear to be two incompatible theories. The issue faced by physical educators is that of reevaluation rather than acceptance or rejection of either model. It is time to reconsider sport and its role in the development of the American character, but our understanding must be broadened to accept the knowledge that sport provides a laboratory for the expression of individual and group behavior which can be positive or negative.

Have we established what are acceptable and unacceptable aggression patterns for sport events so that attainment of skill becomes the important goal? Should we apply more stringent rules to curb rampant aggression, frustration, and hostility in sport? Have we considered the effect of different types of sport upon achieved levels of aggression when planning physical education and intercollegiate programs?

Since aggression, whether instinctive or learned, is an integral part of our most popular activities, we must answer these questions because sport and games will continue to influence American society.

REFERENCES

Alland, A., Jr. 1972. *Time,* 22 May, p. 69.

Bandura, A.; Ross, D.; and Ross, S. 1961. Transmission of aggression through imitation of aggressive models. *Journal of Abnormal and Social Psychology* 63:575-582.

Bateson, G. 1941. The frustration-aggression hypothesis and culture. *Psychological Review* 48:350-355.

Beisser, A. R. 1967. *The madness in sports.* New York: Appleton-Century-Crofts.

Berkowitz, L. 1965. *Advances in experimental social psychology,* vol. 2. New York: Academic Press.

Child Welfare Research Station. 1961. Digest of studies on aggressive and hostile behavior. In *Preventive psychiatry project,* State University of Iowa.

Fiebleman, J. K. 1963. *Mankind behaving: Human needs and material culture.* Springfield, Ill.: Charles C. Thomas.

Hammond, L. K., and Goldman, M. 1961. Competition and noncompetition and its relationship to individual and group productivity. *Sociometry* 24:46-60.

Levy, D. M. 1941. The hostile act. *Psychological Review* 48:355-361.

Schlesinger, A., Jr. 1968. *Violence: America in the sixties.* New York: New American Library.

Scott, J. P. 1958. *Aggression.* Chicago: University of Chicago Press.

Sherif, M., and Sherif, C. 1969. *Social psychology.* New York: Harper and Row.

Violence and the Coach

Robert Corran

In the past few years a great deal of attention has been focused on the increasing violent be-haviour of sport participants and spectators.[1] There have been numerous accounts of fighting between players in football, basketball, and hockey games as well as rioting by spectators at various sporting events. Many people (Freud 1962; Lorenz 1966) have defended violent behaviour in a sport setting, claiming that it is natural for athletes to flare-up at times and become participants in violence. They further feel that these occasional flare-ups are beneficial to the players exhibiting this type of be-haviour and to society as well in that naturally occurring aggressive tendencies can be relieved in a controlled situation with minimal negative effects on the players involved and on the rest of society as well.

Most researchers have disclaimed this cathartic view, however, feeling that aggression is actually learned or is a response to frustration, and that sport may in fact be teaching people to be more aggressive through various forms of reinforcement of violent behaviour or by the creation of exces-sively frustrating situations (Berkowitz 1962; Martens 1975; Singer 1971; Tomkins 1962).

Assuming acceptance of this latter theory of the origin of aggression in sport, it becomes clear that those of us involved in coaching occupy a most influential position in the learning of reponses to frustration on the part of the athletes under our charge. Much of the learning of sport participants can be directed effectively by a coach away from the excessive aggression which has become so much more dominant in sport today.

A number of factors which could temporarily change the behaviour of sport participants have been studied, but much of the research has not been developed for the practitioner. This is due in part to a lack of consensus on the part of researchers regarding their findings, but there are some re-sults and theories which have gained wide acceptability and, therefore, can be applied to the field.

Winning and losing have been found to play a large part in the level of aggression exhibited by participants following athletic contests. Losers tend to have higher levels of aggression after compe-tition than do winners (Laird 1970; Ryan 1974). Coaches may be able to reduce levels of aggression in losing competitors by praising their efforts and maintaining a positive note throughout post-game

Robert Corran. Violence and the coach. *Coaching Review* 1, 4 (July 1978):40-45.

[1] See the article by Tandy and Laflin on pages 125-128 for two theories of aggression and sports. –Ed.

comments to athletes. Negative and inflammatory comments can have the effect of increasing already heightened aggressive feelings. In such a state, athletes may become involved in antisocial acts as a means of expressing their aggression. Considering this, it is important for any losing coach to develop a post-game atmosphere which will decrease or eliminate aggressive feelings in the athletes involved.

A second factor found to influence the aggressiveness of participants is the perceived intent of an opponent (Berkowitz 1962; Nickel 1974). If an opponent is perceived in a positive way, little aggression will be directed toward him or her; a negative perception of an opponent will lead to greater levels of aggression being directed at that opponent. It is frequently within the coach's ability to control this perception. Exhortation of players with references to the dirty tactics and unfair practices of an opponent will help develop a negative perception of that opponent and invites an eruption of violence during that particular contest. Some coaches feel that they must build up feelings of hostility toward an opponent in their players, using real or fabricated information to achieve this end.

Such methods of motivation may be effective in arousing emotions and may result in a victory over that opponent, but coaches who subscribe to this method of motivation must be prepared to bear the responsibility for flare-ups of violence which will inevitably occur as the result of such motivational practices.

Coaches should be attempting to direct their players toward a more positive perception of their opponents. It is not unwise to praise opponents for their respect of rules and sense of fair play before a contest. Emphasizing such positive virtues would do a great deal to reduce or eliminate the possibility of violence during athletic contests. This is not to suggest that athletes enter any contest, particularly contact games such as football or hockey, in a complacent or unmotivated state since this can often lead to injury and/or defeat. Rather, athletes should be motivated through accentuation of their own positive values and always with a sense of fair play and sportsmanship.

In addition, this positive approach toward opponents may create an environment more conducive to the development of friendships among competing athletes. We have claimed for many years, without much substantiation, that sport and competition are excellent in helping young people meet and become friends with their opponents, yet we have coached with the attitude that the opponent is the "enemy." Perhaps a more positive approach toward the opponent on the part of coaches would alter the perceptions of athletes and make it more possible for them to develop friendships with one another.

It has also been found that the expectations of athletes regarding their opponents' behaviour are important determinants of aggressive behaviour (Ryan 1974). Actions which are illegal but expected within a particular sport, such as holding in professional basketball, will not produce frustration or aggression in the participant who is being fouled. But unexpected or unacceptable actions, whether legal or illegal, will produce frustration and often subsequent aggression.

Coaches can do a great deal to prepare athletes for handling these situations during games by making the players more aware of acceptable behaviour in that sport. Often young athletes are unfamiliar with accepted tactics and become frustrated at what is actually a legitimate tactic or technique as exhibited by an opponent. This frustration can lead to aggression against the opponent. Coaches should spend time educating less experienced athletes as to what they can expect during a game, thereby dealing with the situation before it is given the chance to develop into an incident.

Coaches should also be attuned to these frustrating situations developing during a game and be prepared to take a player out of a game in order to provide him or her with the opportunity to reduce frustration levels. An awareness of a player's personal problems, which might cause excessive frustration to that player, would be of benefit to a coach in his or her attempts to reduce frustration during games. The coach can provide counsel for the athlete and present a calming influence. This will not only help avoid a possible violent incident but will also help decrease the arousal level of the athlete to a more efficient range and thereby increase motor functioning of that athlete.

The reinforcement of violent behaviour, both positively and negatively, has been found to influence athletes' learning and subsequent behaviour (Lorenz 1966; Smith 1972*a*; Smith 1972*b*). The positive reinforcement of violence can lead to more violence by an individual; negative reinforcement of violent behaviour has been found to bring about a decrease in violence. Coaches are in a position to provide both of these types of reinforcement, thereby exhibiting considerable influence over athletes' behaviour. While few coaches provide positive reinforcement of violence by praising an athlete for such behaviour, many coaches do provide a form of positive reinforcement of violent behaviour by a conspicuous absence of any negative reinforcement.

Coaches who wish to control violence in sport should provide negative reinforcement for any act of violence whether during practices or games. Such negative reinforcement will reduce the players' tendency toward aggression; the player learns, through the reinforcement applied, that aggression is not an acceptable form of behaviour.

In the same fashion, athletes can learn non-aggressive responses to competitive situations. This can be accomplished by positive reinforcement of non-aggressive responses to a particular situation, a situation which in the past might have brought about an aggressive response by that particular athlete. Reinforcement can be applied in many forms, but it is essential that it be applied in a consistent manner among all players if the appropriate learning is to take place.

Sociologists claim that the frontier attitude toward aggression is obsolete in our modern technological society and greater co-operation between people will be necessary for our civilization to survive in light of the problems which our world faces today. The development of a non-violent attitude through sport can serve mankind in a much more positive fashion than can our present belief in aggression and ultra-competitiveness as essentials in sport. We do not have to sacrifice competition to teach more appropriate non-violent responses to competitive situations. It is possible to retain our feelings for competition, yet eliminate the need for violence within that competitive environment.

It appears that competitive sports have inherent qualities that make them frustrating (winning/losing, unexpected actions by opponents) and hence are a potential source of aggression. But research also shows that individuals can learn non-aggressive responses to these situations. Learning occurs mostly by observing others and by being reinforced positively for appropriate responses and negatively for inappropriate responses. Coaches have the opportunity and the responsibility to help develop in the young athletes with whom they are working a non-violent approach toward sport and competition. Through this approach we can better serve athletes and society as a whole.

REFERENCES

Berkowitz, L. 1962. *Aggression: A social psychological analysis.* New York: McGraw-Hill.
Dollard, J.; Dobb, L. W.; Miller, M. E.; Mowrer, O. H.; and Sears, R. R. 1939. *Frustration and aggression.* New Haven: Yale University Press.
Freud, S. 1962. *The complete works of Sigmund Freud.* London: Hogarth.
Laird, E. M. 1970. Comparison of aggressive responses among and between women athletes and non-athletes at three educational levels. Unpublished doctoral dissertation, Springfield College.
Lorenz, K. 1966. *On aggression.* New York: Harcourt, Brace and World.
Martens, R. 1975. Social psychology and physical activity. New York: Harper and Row.

Nickel, T. W. 1974. The attribution of intention as a critical factor in the relation between frustration and aggression. *Journal of Personality* 42, 3 (September):482-492.

Ryan, E. D. 1974. Sport and aggression. In *The winning edge: Proceedings of the First National Sports Psychology Conference,* ed. W. C. Schwank. Washington, D.C.: AAHPER Publications.

Singer, J. L. 1971. *Personality and psychopathology.* New York: Academic Press.

Smith, M. D. 1972a. Aggression and the female athlete. In *Women and sport: A national research conference,* ed. D. Harris. Pennsylvania State University.

———. 1972b. Assaultive behavior of young hockey players as a function of socioeconomic status and significant others' influence. Unpublished doctoral dissertation, University of Wisconsin, Madison.

Tomkins, S. 1962. Imagery consciousness. New York: Springer.

Effects of Viewing Aggressive Sports on the Hostility of Spectators

Robert L. Arms, Gordon W. Russell,
and Mark L. Sandilands

Hostile outbursts occurring at a number of spectator sports have contributed to a general international concern with escalating levels of violence. While that concern has primarily dealt with illegal aggression on the field of play, attention has also been focused on those relatively rare (Zillmann and Sapolsky 1978) but newsworthy occasions in which violence has erupted among fans viewing sports contests. In noting incidents of rowdyism, the newspaper *Komsomolskaya Pravda* publicly criticized Soviet sports fans for their unruly behavior at sporting events, stating that "drunken louts, foul-mouthed boors, oleaginous scalpers and female groupies are penetrating Moscow spectator sports in disturbing numbers" (New York Times Index 1975). Spectator violence, far from being unique in history, has drawn comment at other times in this century. Writing in 1903, Patrick (1903, p. 104) cites a characterization of English soccer fans of that era: "The spectators, under the excitement of a great game, become hoodlums, exhibiting violent partisanship and gross profanity, bestowing idiotic adulation upon the victors and heaping abuse upon the referee, restrained oftentimes only by the players themselves from inflicting upon him actual bodily harm." In recent years alarm over rampant soccer hooliganism has been expressed both in Britain and on the continent (Scottish Education Department, 1977; *Time* 1978). Elsewhere, soccer fans supporting their team in a losing cause in Guatemala recently attacked fans of the winning side with machetes, hacking five people to death (*San Francisco Chronicle* 1977).

Although athletes and spectators are physically separated at sporting events, violent outbursts involving both parties have required the lines of demarcation be made more visible and, in some instances, more impenetrable. Hence, steel fencing, dogs, and dry moats have been used to defend the soccer pitch against invasions by excited fans. Controls to minimize intra-spectator conflict have

Robert L. Arms, Gordon W. Russell, and Mark L. Sandilands. Effects of viewing aggressive sports on the hostility of spectators. *Social Psychology Quarterly,* in press. Portions of this paper were presented at the Canadian Symposium for Psycho-Motor Learning and Sports Psychology, Banff, Alberta, Canada, 1977.

This project was supported by a University of Lethbridge research grant ULRF #86-1168.
The writers wish to thank Stu and Helen Hart (Foothills Wrestling Association) for their generous support of the study. We also wish to acknowledge the assistance of Andy Andrews, Keith Hart, and the Morrow Brothers, Ed and Jerry. The assistance of Dennis Kjeldgaard and Bill Burton of the Lethbridge Broncos in providing facilities and that of Jon R. Amundson and Nicholas J. Previsich in coordinating the movement of subjects is gratefully acknowledged. Lastly, Pat L. Dortsch helped with the analyses and organization of data.

included the segregation of rival elements by means of steel grilles, establishing a no man's land between home and away supporters, and the unobtrusive monitoring on television of troublesome sections by police (Marsh, Rosser, and Harré 1978). While these and similar tactics may be successful in confining people to the stands or playing field, they offer little or no resistance to an ongoing, two-way flow of influence. For example, where aggression is actively urged by spectators, the likelihood and magnitude of overt aggression is increased (e.g., Borden and Taylor 1973). Furthermore, reviews of audience effects on aggression (Baron 1977, pp. 118ff.; O'Neal and McDonald 1976, p. 188) conclude that individuals in the presence of an audience which they perceive to merely favor aggression will seek to gain their approval by behaving aggressively. However, when individuals are performing before an audience they know disapproves of aggression, aggression is not likely to be displayed (Baron, 1977, p. 124). In turn, spectators are influenced by the character of events they witness. Smith's (1978) archival study of collective violence among sport fans found that approximately 74% of hostile outbursts were preceded by extraordinary displays of violence among the players (primarily assaults on members of the opposing team).

At the level of public beliefs, the notion of a "safety valve" or catharsis enjoys widespread currency.[1] This view, as it applies to spectators viewing aggression on the field of play, predicts that such displays serve to reduce hostility and physiological arousal in the viewer. This cathartic viewpoint is bolstered by the influential writings of Freud, Lorenz, Tinbergen, and their popularizers.[2] In general the position has received little encouragement from the experimental literature (see reviews by Baron 1977; Geen and Quanty 1977; Quanty 1976). Compelling as the notion of catharsis may be, vicarious participation in aggressive displays serve generally to enhance, rather than diminish, hostility in the onlooker. While cathartic effects have been demonstrated to occur under highly specific conditions, i.e., where an angered individual sees his assailant aggressed against by a third party (Doob and Wood 1972), or where the angered party directly attacks his aggressor (Konečni and Ebbesen 1976), in this form the concept has limited application to sports spectatorship.

Generalizations from the experimental laboratory to real-life settings inevitably contain an element of risk. However, when the results of investigations conducted in the more complex naturalistic setting accord with lab findings then confidence in their applicability is greatly enhanced. Unfortunately, few such complementary investigations of spectatorship have been undertaken. Field studies investigating the effects on fans of viewing aggressive sports have produced conflicting results. Kingsmore (1970) reported professional wrestling fans showed less extrapunitive and intrapunitive aggression on the Thematic Apperception Test (TAT) and less self-reported aggression following the matches. Basketball fans also showed less extrapunitive aggression after a game. Turner (1970) reported college males showed increases in TAT aggression at basketball and football, though not at amateur wrestling.

The annual Army-Navy football game provided the setting for a field study by Goldstein and Arms (1971) whose design pitted the cathartic against the enhancement position. A sample of males leaving the stadium after the game scored significantly higher on the Buss-Durkee hostility scale (Buss 1961) than an equivalent sample entering the stadium before the game. Pre- and post-event measures for males at an equally competitive but nonaggressive control event (an intercollegiate gymnastics

---

[1] See the article by Tandy and Laflin on pages 125-128 for a statement of this theory. —Ed.
[2] It should be noted that Lorenz (Evans 1974) and Tinbergen (1968) have modified their views regarding its applicability to mass spectator sports.

meet) did not differ. The major finding was an overall increase in hostility of fans of *both* Army (winners) and Navy (losers). The results strongly supported a general disinhibition position (Bandura and Walters 1963) which predicts that the observation of aggression leads to a lessening in the strength of inhibitions against expressing hostility.

Inevitably, a number of plausible rival interpretations remained to explain the heightened postevent hostility. The authors suggested a selection bias whereby football fans might be presumed to be more volatile than those attracted to a gymnastics competition. Other potential sources of bias include individual versus team competition and different norms governing expressive behavior at the two events. Also cited (Goldstein and Arms 1971) were differences in the density, numbers, and activity levels between the football and gymnastics fans. Goldstein (1976) has suggested that the student interviewers may have gained in confidence in the pregame stage and, unwittingly, approached and been successful in interviewing more aggressive-looking fans after the game. Furthermore, the differential consumption of alcohol at the two events cannot be discounted as a contributing factor. Often cited as a cause of crowd disturbances (e.g., Scottish Education Department 1977), alcohol could be implicated in the increase in hostility among football fans. Taylor, Gammon, and Capasso (1976) have demonstrated that intoxicated subjects behave far more aggressively in threatening circumstances than they do in nonthreatening situations. Moreover, where elements of threat are not present there is little difference in the aggressive behavior of intoxicated and sober subjects. Finally, Mann (1974) suggested the overall increase in hostility may have arisen from all fans experiencing a dull, lopsided game (Army 27, Navy 0).

The present investigation was designed as a systematic replication (Sidman 1960) of the Goldstein and Arms (1971) study that would also test the merits of rival explanations advanced to account for their results. Departures from the original design were the inclusion of female spectators, the substitution of ice hockey for American football, and a provincial team swimming competition for gymnastics.

A special case for cathartic effects due to exposure to *stylized* aggression has been persuasively argued by Noble (1975). Cartoons, roller derby, or professional wrestling—displays in which interpersonal mayhem may be seen as fictional or a spoof—would qualify as stylized aggression. Thus, professional wrestling was chosen to represent stylized aggression and hockey, realistic aggression.

PROCEDURE

Students (N = 127 females; N = 87 males) were recruited from an introductory psychology subject pool at the University of Lethbridge. Subjects received a 4% research participation bonus and free admission to their sporting event. Assignment to the events and to the pre-and post-event conditions was random within the female and male categories. Departures from the random assignment procedure to events proved necessary in 5% of the cases (typically because of conflicts with examinations).

Return transportation was provided to the professional wrestling, hockey, and swimming (control) venues though most subjects made their own travel arrangements. Preevent subjects arrived 30 minutes before the event, were given their tickets, and were then escorted to a spare dressing room to complete a set of hostility measures. Before taking their seats (dispersed) these subjects were asked not to discuss the measures with others. Postevent subjects arrived 15 minutes before game time, were given their tickets, and were asked to remain momentarily seated following the event. At the conclusion of the event, they were escorted to the same room to complete the hostility scales.[3]

To ensure a more complete mapping of the multidimensional domain of hostility, the following measures of the dependent variable were administered: the Buss-Durkee (Buss 1961) subscales of *indirect hostility, resentment,* and *irritability* summed by Goldstein and Arms (1971) to provide an overall index, the aggression scale of the Nowliss (1965) Mood Adjective Check List (MACL), and a punitive measure (Goldstein et al. 1975) based on the prison sentences subjects would assign to individuals convicted of serious crimes.

The complete MACL (short version) was administered to provide the general pattern of mood changes at each event and as background against which any resulting changes in hostility could be better understood. Earlier comment (Stone 1973) and discussions with pilot study subjects suggested that a sexual component may be inherent in contests involving heavily padded athletes in one case and contestants in swimsuits at the remaining two events. Thus, while "sexy" is not a Nowliss factor, it was included along with "aroused" in the MACL format. An index of involvement was calculated for each subject by summing self-report ratings of frequency of TV viewing, actual attendance, and general interest in their assigned sport. Finally, subjects assigned to the wrestling match were asked: "What percentage of professional wrestling action do you think is 'faked' or just acting?" An 11-point percentage scale anchored by "Completely Real" and "Completely Faked" accompanied the item.

Several weeks after the study was conducted subjects were informed of details of the design and preliminary findings in a lecture to the introductory psychology sections.

RESULTS

Differences in pre- and postevent levels of spectator hostility were tested by *t* tests (two-tailed). As presented in Table 1, significant increases occurred at wrestling and hockey though no changes were observed at the control event. At wrestling the MACL aggression measure proved sensitive to stylized aggression ($p < .01$), the combined pre- to postevent increase originating principally with females. The overall increase in hostility at the hockey game was significant ($p < .05$) using the punishment index and marginally so ($p < .06$) with the Buss-Durkee scales.

Changes in other dimensions of mood assessed by the MACL are presented in Table 2. While anxiety and fatigue were unaffected by experiences at the events, *all* events produced a significant decline in feelings of Social Affection. Surgency declined significantly at hockey and swimming while feelings of sexiness dropped at the swim meet whereas arousal evidenced no change.[4]

The distributions of male and female involvement scores were strongly skewed towards the "uninvolved" end of the continuum. The same strong skewness was apparent in the authenticity ratings by subjects assigned to wrestling. Virtually all were skeptical, thus precluding any meaningful analyses of these variables.

---

[3] These procedures represent a refinement of those developed in a pilot study conducted during the preceding semester. On that occasion subjects (N = 49 females; N = 76 males) were also taken to a hockey and wrestling match with the Canadian Mixed Curling Championships (Seagram Cup) serving as the control event. Because of the unique character of each hockey game or wrestling match, it was not deemed appropriate to combine the pilot data with those reported herein.

[4] Admittedly, the single adjective rating represents a less than adequate test of this component of the concept.

Table 1. Mean Pretest and Posttest Hostility Scores by Sex at Three Events

	MACL (AGGRESSION)					BUSS-DURKEE			PUNISHMENT		
	N	Pre	N	Post	t	Pre	Post	t	Pre	Post	t
Wrestling											
Females	32	1.72	22	5.59	3.61***	13.39	14.55	.81	29.94	23.71	1.07
Males	16	3.06	20	3.80	.60	12.56	12.98	.24	18.72	34.85	1.72†
Combined	48	2.17	42	4.74	3.18**	13.11	13.80	.64	26.20	29.01	.55
Hockey											
Females	24	2.08	23	3.52	1.02	12.23	14.50	1.60	18.52	22.74	.97
Males	17	2.29	16	2.50	.22	14.06	15.81	1.06	12.41	24.19	3.03**
Combined	41	2.17	39	3.10	1.02	12.99	15.04	1.90†	15.99	23.33	2.45*
Swimming (Control)											
Females	12	3.08	14	1.36	1.24	13.00	14.86	1.05	25.17	33.82	1.05
Males	8	3.25	10	3.40	.13	11.38	13.40	.85	26.35	15.60	1.77†
Combined	20	3.15	24	2.21	.98	12.35	14.25	1.34	25.60	26.23	.11

†$p < .10$
*$p < .05$
**$p < .01$
***$p < .001$

DISCUSSION

The coordination and movement of subjects at the events was accomplished smoothly and without incident, mainly the result of improved procedures developed during the pilot stage. Near capacity crowds were in attendance at the hockey game (3,600) and swimming meet (300) whereas wrestling played to a relatively small audience (350). The local Western Canada Hockey League club (Tier 1, Junior A) badly outclassed the visiting Flin Flon Bombers, winning 11-1 in a lacklustre contest. In addition to being a rout, the game was devoid of major fights, with only the occasional flash of playmaking skill in evidence. The "good guys" also won the main tag team event on the professional wrestling card. Whereas students in the earlier pilot study remained aloof from the ring action, the present subjects entered wholeheartedly into the spirit of the evening, booing, cheering, and trading insults with the villains. Only an alert security force averted audience participation by several enthusiastic regulars at ringside. The swim meet was fiercely competitive with the spectators easily as vociferous as those at the other events.

Posttest hostility means were, almost without exception, greater than the mean pretest scores. Although aspects of the cathartic and enhancement viewpoints were conjoined in the present design, support was forthcoming for only the latter position. Subjects exposed to stylized aggression (wrestling) showed a significant increase on the MACL aggression scale, a combined effect arising principally from the female data. Furthermore, the choice of professional wrestling to represent stylized

Table 2. Mean Pretest and Postest MACL Scores by Sex at Three Events

	ANXIETY	t	SURGENCY	t	FATIGUE	t	SOCIAL AFFECTION	t	SEXY	t	AROUSED	t
Wrestling												
Combined Pre	2.06		9.40		2.65		4.85		.73		1.60	
Post	2.32	.63	8.35	1.29	3.07	.70	3.09	3.42***	.81	.37	1.76	.68
Females Pre	2.28		9.91		2.44		4.88		.56		1.56	
Post	2.64	.60	8.00	1.76†	3.09	.80	2.91	2.80**	.64	.33	1.64	.24
Males Pre	1.63		8.38		3.06		4.81		1.06		1.69	
Post	1.94	.58	8.75	.31	3.05	.01	3.30	1.94†	1.00	.15	1.90	.61
Hockey												
Combined Pre	2.12		9.38		2.23		4.71		.80		1.63	
Post	1.90	.54	6.51	3.34***	3.33	1.89†	3.26	2.58*	.62	.88	1.26	1.56
Females Pre	2.00		8.78		2.43		4.38		.54		1.58	
Post		.16		2.48*		1.23		.71		.41		1.50

Post	2.09	5.83	3.35	3.78	.65	1.13
Males Pre	2.29	10.18	1.94	5.18	1.19	1.71
	1.00	2.27*	1.40	4.15***	1.96†	.67
Post	1.63	7.50	3.31	2.50	.56	1.44
Swimming Combined Pre	1.70	9.15	2.25	5.40	1.50	1.60
	.17	2.87**	1.93†	3.67***	4.31***	1.95†
Post	1.79	5.79	3.92	3.25	.29	.96
Females Pre	1.83	8.83	1.92	5.58	1.42	1.33
	.85	2.85**	1.67	3.19**	3.02**	1.84†
Post	1.21	4.86	3.86	3.14	.29	.64
Males Pre	1.50	9.63	2.75	5.13	1.63	2.00
	1.39	1.24	.93	1.80†	2.99**	1.07
Post	2.60	7.10	4.00	3.40	.30	1.40

†$p < .10$
*$p < .05$
**$p < .01$
***$p < .001$

aggression was borne out insofar as subjects overwhelmingly saw it as a sham. Subjects at the hockey game showed increased hostility on the Buss-Durkee and punishment scales, the males in particular contributing to the latter increase. Spectators at the control event showed no significant changes in hostility on any of the three measures. The present results are consistent with the earlier Goldstein and Arms (1971) findings and provide further support for a general disinhibition position (Bandura and Walters 1963; Bandura 1973).

Although hostility increased through exposure to displays of both stylized and realistic aggression, such increases were not registered consistently on all three measures. Nevertheless, each measure was shown to be sensitive on at least one occasion. This makes it apparent that reliance on a single measure of aggression could be misleading. The use of multiple measures in the present design leads to a conclusion consistent with, but less decisive than, that reached by Goldstein and Arms (1971). That is to say, the observation of aggression on the field of play leads to an increase in hostility on the part of spectators though displays of stylized aggression may increase one type of hostility in the viewer and realistic aggression, another. The Nowliss (1965) aggression measure essentially provides the subject's perception of his current affective status whereas the widely used Buss-Durkee scale (Buss 1961) assesses the more stable, characteristic behavior of individuals over time and situations. Quite a different measure is represented by the punishment index (Goldstein et al. 1975) which is concerned more with retributive justice and is undoubtedly modified by one's beliefs about law and order and/or the effectiveness of jail sentences in deterring would-be criminals. Perhaps the MACL is more sensitive to those theatrical aspects of stylized aggression which may alter only a temporary mood state, dissipating in the short run. When aggression is realistic the observer may experience a more profound, longer lasting increase in hostility. While the question of the temporal effects of exposure to stylized and realistic displays of aggression is important, the present design did not provide for its investigation.

In comparing the present results to those few studies conducted in naturalistic field situations, general support was found for Turner's (1970) study of football and basketball fans whereas Kingsmore's (1970) finding of a reduction in the levels of several categories of aggression was not supported. The present results extend the generality of the earlier Goldstein and Arms (1971) results and largely negate the rival explanations advanced to date. Increases in spectator hostility have been demonstrated to occur in a different culture with two additional aggressive sports, one a stylized display. Furthermore, the increases in hostility found among avid Army and Navy fans seem also to be true of females and student spectators without strong sporting interests or team loyalties. The previously mentioned rival explanations of the Goldstein and Arms (1971) conclusion that aggression on the field of play leads to increased hostility on the part of observers have been tested in the present design. The likelihood of a selection factor operating to attract less volatile spectators to their control event (gymnastics) or the unwitting selection of less hostile preevent males was negated by the random assignment of subject to events and to pre-and posttest conditions. With the number and density of spectators at wrestling and the control event equal in the present study and alcohol not present at the events, it seems unlikely that differences could have arisen from these factors. The hockey game was easily as lacklustre as Army's runaway victory over Navy. However, the final wrestling bout was in doubt until the dying minutes of the match when the forces of good overcame the forces of evil. Mann's (1974) suggestion that increased hostility on the part of football fans arose from the dull, one-sided nature of the contest thereby seems less plausible. Yet a final explanation is that the males exiting from the football stadium were annoyed at being delayed in their efforts to beat the other

100,000 fans onto a crowded freeway at the conclusion of the game. Suffice it to say, sports fans in Lethbridge (population approximately 50,000) do not face problems on that scale.

In addition to hostility, changes along other dimensions of mood were explored using the remaining MACL measures. An overview of Table 2 points to a general deterioration in the quality of interpersonal relations. The most pronounced and consistent decrement occurred in Social Affection, a dimension characterized by the adjectives "affectionate," "forgiving," "kindly," and "warm-hearted." It is particularly noteworthy that diminished social affection occurred at the nonaggressive control event as well as at wrestling and hockey. Thus, the reduction in social affection cannot be attributed to aggressive content but rather arises from other features of the spectator experience. Furthermore, postevent scores on the Surgency factor ("carefree," "playful," and "witty") were lower for males viewing the hockey game and for females attending the swimming competition. Where changes in mood have occurred, such changes have consistently been towards a more negative emotional state. The most parsimonious explanation for the abrupt drop in feelings of sexiness at the swim meet is that the subjects anticipated several hours of viewing well-endowed members of the opposite sex in competition. Contrary to subjects' expectations, most of the competitors were prepubescent—the eldest perhaps 14 or 15—and still several years short of full physical maturity. The disappointment did not, however, induce an increase in aggression except for males who showed a significant increase in "irritability" on one of the Buss-Durkee subscales. Perhaps females are more philosophical about such matters!

The present results call into question an assumption that sports events are necessarily rich social occasions where goodwill and warm interpersonal relations are fostered. Mehrabian (1976, p. 284) describes the dynamics of spectatorship in the sports arena as follows: "The congregation of large numbers of highly aroused, uninhibited people who share similar interests and attitudes is also conducive to socializing; it may lead to the development of new friendships or the renewal or intensification of old ones. . . . In the generally pleasant setting, then, gregariousness is further enhanced." It appears one cannot simply equate high levels of arousal occurring in pleasant surroundings with warm social interaction without considering other elements in the situation. Because moods became more negative at all three events, the deterioration could have originated with any of the following: viewing competition, physical demands imposed on the spectators, or even the realization that the entertainment was over. For example, the steeply tiered rows, side by side seating arrangements (Sommer 1969, p. 121), and a common focus on a distant field of play could severely restrict interaction and the development of friendships.

One approach to a more comprehensive mapping of the dynamics of mood fluctuations in response to the complexities of a sporting contest would be to provide additional data points during the course of the event, perhaps at the intermission(s). Changes in spectator mood might thereby be related to the changing fortunes of a favored or disfavored team, final outcome of the contest, or environmental constraints imposed on the spectators.

Closely related to spectator mood is the question of identifying the factors involved in *enjoyment* of sport contests. Zillmann, Bryant, and Sapolsky (1978) have recently taken an important initiative in applying their dispositional theory of mirth to the enjoyment of sport contests where affective disposition or the degree of prior liking for an athlete or team emerge as important determinants. Priority in future investigations should be given to delineating the relationship between emotionality and the enjoyment of contests.

REFERENCES

Bandura, A. 1973 *Aggression: A social learning analysis.* Englewood Cliffs, N.J.: Prentice-Hall.

Bandura, A., and Walters, R. H. 1963. *Social learning and personality development.* New York: Holt, Rinehart and Winston.

Baron, R. A. 1977. *Human agression.* New York: Plenum.

Borden, R. J., and Taylor, S. P. 1973. The social instigation and control of physical aggression. *Journal of Applied Social Psychology* 3:354-361.

Buss, A. H. 1961. *The psychology of aggression.* New York: Wiley.

Doob, A. N., and Wood, L. 1972. Catharsis and aggression: The effects of annoyance and retaliation on aggressive behavior. *Journal of Personality and Social Psychology* 22:156-162.

Evans, R. I. 1974. A conversation with Konrad Lorenz about aggression, homosexuality, pornography, and the need for a new ethic. *Psychology Today,* November.

Geen, R. G., and Quanty, M. B. 1977. The catharsis of aggression: An evaluation of a hypothesis. In *Advances in experimental social psychology,* ed. L. Berkowitz, 10:1-37. New York: Academic Press.

Goldstein, H. H. 1976. Conducting field research on aggression: Notes on "Effects of observing athletic contests on hostility." In *The research experience,* ed. P. M. Golden, pp. 248-257. Itasca, Ill.: F. E. Peacock.

Goldstein, J. H., and Arms, R. L. 1971. Effects of observing athletic contests on hostility. *Sociometry* 34:83-90.

Goldstein, J. H.; Rosnow, R. L.; Raday, T.; Silverman, I.; and Gaskell, G. D. 1975. Punitiveness in response to films varying in content: A cross-national field study of aggression. *European Journal of Social Psychology* 5:149-165.

Kingsmore, J. M. 1970. The effect of a professional wrestling and a professional basketball contest upon the aggressive tendencies of spectators. In *Contemporary psychology of sport,* ed. G. S. Kenyon, pp. 311-315. Chicago: Athletic Institute.

Konečni, V. J., and Ebbesen, E. B. 1976. Disinhibition versus the cathartic effect: Artifact and substance. *Journal of Personality and Social Psychology* 34:352-365.

Mann, L. 1974. On being a sore loser: How fans react to their team's failure. *Australian Journal of Psychology* 26:37-47.

Marsh, P.; Rosser, E.; and Harré, R. 1978. *The rules of disorder.* London: Routledge & Kegan Paul.

Mehrabian, A. 1976. *Public places and private spaces: Psychology of work, play and living environments.* New York: Fitzhenry & Whiteside.

New York Times Index. 1975. Athletics and sports. 1:142.

Noble, G. 1975. *Children in front of the small screen.* Beverly Hills, Calif.: Sage Publications.

Nowlis, V. 1965. Research with the Mood Adjective Check List. In *Affect, cognition, and personality,* ed. S. S. Tompkins and C. Izard, pp. 352-389. New York: Springer.

O'Neal, E. C., and McDonald, P. J. 1976. The environmental psychology of aggression. In *Perspectives on aggression,* ed. R. G. Geen and E. C. O'Neal, pp. 169-192. New York: Academic Press.

Patrick, G. T. W. 1903. The psychology of football. *American Journal of Psychology* 14:104-117.

Quanty, M. B. 1976. Aggression catharsis: Experimental investigations and implications. In *Perspectives on aggression,* ed. R. G. Geen and E. C. O'Neal, pp. 99-132. New York: Academic Press.

San Francisco Chronicle. 1977. Five die in soccer melee. 19 February.

Scottish Education Department. 1977. *Football crowd behaviour.* Edinburgh: Her Majesty's Stationery Office.

Sidman, M. 1960. *Tactics of scientific research.* New York: Basic Books.

Smith, M. D. 1978. Precipitants of crowd violence. *Sociological Inquiry* 48:121-131.

Sommer, R. 1969. *Personal space.* Englewood Cliffs, N.J.: Prentice-Hall.

Stone, G. P. 1973. American sports: Play and display. In *Sport and society,* ed. J. T. Talamini and C. H. Page, Toronto: Little, Brown.

Taylor, S. P.; Gammon, C. B.; and Capasso, D. R. 1976. Aggression as a function of the interaction of alcohol and threat. *Journal of Personality and Social Psychology* 34:938-941.

Time. 1978. Football fanimals. 17 April.

Tinbergen, N. 1968. On war and peace in animals and man. *Science* 160:1411-1418.

Turner, E. T. 1970. The effects of viewing college football, basketball and wrestling on the elicited aggressive responses of male spectators. *Medicine and Science in Sports* 2:100-105.

Zillmann, D.; Bryant, J.; and Sapolsky, B. S. 1978. The enjoyment of watching sport contests. In *Sports, games and play,* ed. J. Goldstein. Hillsdale, N.J.: Erlbaum.

PERSONALITY
VARIABLES

A second article by Dr. William P. Morgan[1] is his review on personality. This article not only reports on particular studies of personality but also provides a discussion of methodological or research design considerations. The findings about personality and sports show what knowledge is available on the topic; at the same time, the discussion of research design serves as a basis for judgments about what conclusions seem justifiable and generalizable.

Dr. Eva K. Balazs has taught gymnastics on the college level and has taught swimming and skiing for clubs. She has completed research on the characteristics of members of the Hungarian Olympic teams and the U.S. Olympic teams. She is a psycho-movement therapist at the McLean Hospital, the psychiatric unit of Harvard Medical School. This article is the result of her study of women on the 1972 U.S. Olympic teams. The report gives the reader a first-hand account from written and in-depth interviews of the lives of world-class women athletes. Conclusions are drawn about the personality and the motivational, social, and familial backgrounds of these competitors, with some comments on their experiences as female athletes.

J. Stuart Horsfall participated in collegiate soccer, basketball, and cricket in his years in England and has coached high school basketball and high school and college soccer. A mountain climber and skier, he is a doctoral candidate at the University of Northern Colorado. Dr. A. Craig Fisher was a member of basketball, football, track, and hockey teams in high school and has coached high school basketball and track teams. He is an associate professor in the School of Health, Physical Education and Recreation and chairperson of graduate programs in physical education at Ithaca College, New York. Dr. Harold H. Morris participated in high school football, track, and basketball and was a member of track and cross-country teams in college. He has coached track and cross-country teams at both high school and collegiate levels, including a runner-up NAIA team. He was also head track coach at Northern Illinois University, where he fielded two undefeated dual meet teams. He is an associate professor of physical education at Indiana University. This article acknowledges the substantial work in the literature that aims at identifying the personality characteristics of athletes, but it suggests that future work should reexamine the basic premise used to date, viz., that personality traits that are measured will always be shown by an athlete in all situations. Instead, this article suggests the need for situation-specific testing, which would determine what behaviors an athlete will

[1] Other articles by Morgan appear on pages 4-18 and 297-303.

show under specific conditions; e.g., anxiety might occur under game conditions but not under train-ing conditions.

Dr. Rainer Martens has been a consultant to the U.S. Olympic Development Camp for track and to the U.S. nordic ski team, has conducted clinics for the U.S. Wrestling Federation, and was a mem-ber of the U.S. Olympic Committee's Sports Medicine Committee. He has coached college and high school football and wrestling teams. He is a professor in the Department of Physical Education at the University of Illinois. This article, focusing on the impact of sports on youth, is appropriate for this section because personality development forms throughout early life. The article not only examines the role of sports but also provides some insights on the influence of role-taking, psychological punishment, coaches' expectations, modeling, and implicit hypocrisy on the moral development of youth.

Personality Dynamics and Sport

William P. Morgan

Overview

As one observes sport and physical activity, whether as an athlete, coach, trainer, team physician, or spectator, it becomes quite obvious that participants from various athletic sub-groups differ in a number of respects. Indeed, there is a wealth of research literature attesting to the differences in physiologic and somatotype differences of athletes from various sub-groups. While observers of sport seem to be equally confident that such differences have psychologic correlates, there is actually little agreement as to the psychologic ways in which these same athletic sub-groups differ from each other or from nonathletes. The purpose of this section shall be to (1) review the existing literature concerning the athlete's personality, (2) attempt to explain the lack of agreement which seems to exist on this topic, and (3) offer suggestions for research strategies to be employed in the future.

Interpretation of the literature dealing with athletes' personalities might be approached from a number of perspectives. However, the author feels that it is efficacious first to examine this literature from the standpoint of the independent and dependent variables which have been used historically.

Independent Variables. First of all, numerous independent variables have been employed, and furthermore, various operational definitions have been used for the same variable by different investigators. For example, research designs have included comparisons of (1) athletes from various sub-groups, (2) athletes and nonathletes, (3) team and individual sport athletes, (4) combative and non-combative sport groups, (5) the same athletic sub-groups from different types of educational institutions, and (6) athletes of differing ability levels. Also, investigators such as Golas (1971) have compared athletes from team and individual sports and then reassigned the athletes into combative and and non-combative sport groups for comparative purposes.

[A] general problem has been that investigators have failed to employ universally acceptable definitions of group affiliation. The general practice has simply consisted of testing intact athletic sub-groups, with no attempt to differentiate between ability levels. The athlete who "rides the bench" throughout his athletic career might differ in a number of ways from the "starter." In other words, while athletes from one sub-group may not differ from those in another, it is quite possible that the "successful" and "unsuccessful" members of such groups would differ both within and between sports.

William P. Morgan. Sport psychology. In *The psychomotor domain: Movement behavior,* ed. R. N. Singer, pp. 193-228. Philadelphia: Lea & Febiger, 1972. The present article is an abridged version of the original.

In view of the fact that investigators have failed to employ adequate operational definitions of the independent variables used in this area of inquiry, it is not surprising that general confusion seems to exist. It is clear, of course, that subsequent investigations must include rigorous operational definitions of the independent variable.

Dependent Variables. The assessment of personality can be pursued with either direct or indirect methods. The majority of investigators in the field of sport psychology have elected to employ direct methods which consist of self-reports such as the Edwards Personal Preference Schedule (EPPS), Eysenck Personality Inventory (EPI), Minnesota Multiphasic Personality Inventory (MMPI), and the Sixteen Personality Factor Questionnaire (16 PF). Several investigators have employed indirect procedures which are unstructured. Examples of these projective techniques are the Rorschach Test, Figure-Drawing Test, Thematic Apperception Test (TAT), House-Tree-Person (H-T-P) Test, Sentence Completion Test (SCT), and the Rosenzweig Picture-Frustration Study.

The use of direct methods of personality assessment as compared to indirect techniques as well as the efficacy of employing a battery of both direct and indirect procedures in sport psychology have been discussed previously (Morgan 1968*a*). In view of the nosologic problems associated with projective methods, it would seem that sport psychologists have chosen the correct approach; that is, direct techniques facilitate within and between laboratory replication.

Unfortunately, investigators have employed various personality inventories such as the EPI, EPPS, MMPI, and 16 PF, and then attempted to make direct comparisons with one another's work. The traits measured by these inventories are essentially psychologic constructs that have been derived from factor analytic work. The output of such analyses is dependent in large part upon the input. Also, were factor analysts to begin with the same input, subsequent rotation and labeling might differ markedly. On the other hand, independently constructed inventories such as Cattell's 16-PF, Guilford's personality inventory, and the Eysencks' EPI measure the dimensions of extroversion-introversion and neuroticism-stability "with almost complete agreement" (Eysenck and Eysenck 1970, p. 13). At the same time, while the MMPI contains a measure of extroversion-introversion (E) it was not designed for the measurement of E in "normal groups and it is not well adapted for this purpose" (Eysenck 1967, p. 111). Also, fractionation of the MMPI is hazardous and the specific scales should be examined in light of scores on other dimensions of the MMPI. At any rate, while it is difficult to make direct comparisons of investigations which have used different inventories, this is certainly possible if the investigator has an understanding of the various instruments and the recommended procedures for their administration and interpretation.

Rather than simply review investigations which have dealt with the psychologic characteristics of the athlete, the author has elected first to comment on the methodologic problems which have historically plagued this area of inquiry. One of the more obvious problems has been the general inadequacy of operational definitions of the independent variables used in these investigations.[1] Also, while more acceptable operational definitions have been employed for the dependent variables, the variety of instruments employed does not make for ready comparisons. These points should be kept in mind when attempting to interpret the literature in this area.

---

[1] See the article by Horsfall, Fisher, and Morris on pages 163-168. —Ed.

PERSONALITY CHARACTERISTICS OF ATHLETIC GROUPS

The present review deals with investigations which have been directed toward an understanding of the personality characteristics of various athletic sub-groups. Studies have been conducted on participants in baseball, basketball, cross-country, football, golf, karate, marathon running, parachuting, swimming, scuba diving, tennis, track, weightlifting, and wrestling. Also, psychoanalytic observations of sport have been made by Adatto (1963), Beisser (1961; 1967), Deutsch (1926), Harlow (1951), and Whitman (1969).

In addition to evaluating athletes from different sub-groups, investigators have also compared athletes and nonathletes, athletes from different types of educational institutions, and athletes of differing skill levels. Also, numerous psychometric tools have been employed in these studies. Therefore, any categorization of this research for discussion purposes must obviously be arbitrary. In most instances there has not been sufficient research on specific sports to justify a review. It does seem, however, that several common research strategies have been adopted by investigators, and these have been used in developing a topical outline for this review.

Sampling

Most investigators have tested readily available, intact groups of athletes. The assumption has been that participants in a given sport in one educational institution or geographical locale are similar to those athletes in the same sports in other schools and areas. There is evidence which suggests that athletes from different sports have different somatotypes (Morehouse and Rasch 1963). Also, a gymnast or diver at one school would not be expected to be a football tackle or heavyweight wrestler at another institution. Therefore, if Sheldon's theory of personality (Hall and Lindzey 1970) were adopted, this sampling technique might not be as dangerous as it seems. At any rate, there is evidence which suggests that sampling is a very important consideration in attempting to explain the athlete's personality.

This point is well illustrated in an investigation by Morgan (1968a), who administered the Eysenck Personality Inventory to English-speaking wrestlers participating in the 1966 world championships. The group consisted of the Canadian, South African, and United States teams. When viewed collectively, this sample was stable, but somewhat more extroverted than normal. However, when the teams were evaluated independently the United States team was found to score significantly lower on the neuroticism-stability dimension than the South African team. In short, a somewhat typical profile was observed at the collective level which actually clouded the rather unique characteristics of these two sub-groups. These findings are illustrated in Figure 1.

Ability Levels

In addition to comparing athletic sub-groups, several investigators have directed their attention toward an understanding of the relationship between personality and level of performance. For example, in one of the earliest investigations Johnson, Hutton, and Johnson (1954) administered the Rorschach and House-Tree-Person Test to 12 athletes from contact and noncontact sports who were

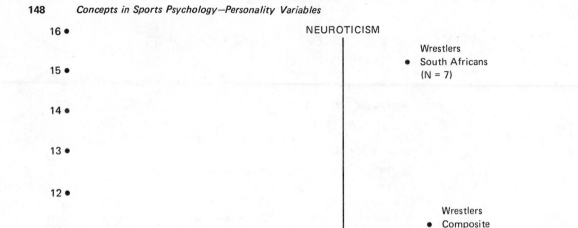

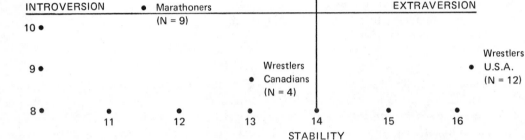

Figure 1. Extraversion-introversion and neuroticism-stability in wrestlers and marathoners. (Reprinted in part from the *Journal of Sports Medicine & Physical Fitness,* 1968, 8, 212-216.)

either of All-America or national champion caliber. These outstanding athletes were found to possess several distinguishing characteristics. These characteristics included "extreme aggressiveness, a freedom from great emotional inhibition, high and generalized anxiety, high level of intellectual aspiration, and feelings of exceptional self-assurance" (p. 547).

Another investigation of outstanding athletes was conducted by La Place (1954), who administered the MMPI to 49 major league players who served as his "successful" group and 64 minor league players who represented his "unsuccessful" group. The major league players scored significantly lower than the minor league players on the Schizophrenia and Psychopathic Deviate Scales. Both groups, however, scored within one standard deviation of the mean for the general population, and therefore, it would appear that neither group differed appreciably from the normal. This investigation revealed that the major league players were better adjusted than the minor league players. Whether these differences existed prior to each group's entrance into professional baseball and hence played a role in determining success, or whether these differences were a consequence of achievement levels cannot be inferred.

A related investigation was conducted by Singer (1969), who administered the Edwards Personal Preference Schedule (EPPS) to 69 athletes at Ohio State University. The athletes consisted of 26 varsity baseball players, 33 freshman baseball players, and 10 varsity tennis players. The ability level of each athlete was ranked by his coach. Comparisons were made between the baseball players, tennis players, and the EPPS norms. Also, comparisons were made between the highest- and lowest-ranked athletes in both sports and the EPPS norms. The baseball team scored significantly higher than the other two groups on the Abasement factor, significantly lower than the other two groups on the Intraception variable, lower than the tennis group on the Achievement variable, lower than the norm group on Autonomy, and lower than the tennis group on Dominance. Both the baseball and tennis groups scored significantly higher than the norm group on the Aggression factor. No differences were noted between high- and low-rated baseball players, and the high- and low-rated tennis players only differed on one of the 15 measures.

This investigation would be difficult to replicate since ability was not assessed with a universally recognized tool. Also, one would expect differences on numerous variables to be greater between major and minor league players (La Place 1954) than between high- and low-rated athletic groups from the same university team. Similarly, high- and low-rated baseball and tennis groups from the Big Ten Conference might differ on a number of the EPPS scales, but such differences might not necessarily exist within any given conference school. It is recommended that sport psychologists employ clear distinctions of ability in testing high- and low-performance groups.

The MMPI was administered to freshman and upper-class athletes and nonathletes by Booth (1958). Comparisons were made between (1) athletes rated as poor or good competitors, (2) athletes who participated in team, individual, or team-individual sports, and (3) freshman and upper-class athletes and nonathletes. The results revealed that the athletes and nonathletes and the athletes from the various sport groups differed significantly on several of the MMPI scales.[2] Also, an analysis of the 550 MMPI questions revealed that 22 of the items discriminated between poor and good competitors.

Kroll (1967) administered the 16 PF to 94 amateur and collegiate wrestlers consisting of 28 superior athletes who had been on the United States Olympic team or had been NCAA or NAIA champions or place winners, 33 college wrestlers who were rated as excellent by their coaches and had won at least 60 percent of their matches that year, and a group of 33 wrestlers from the same teams who were rated as average or below average. Discriminant function analyses failed to demonstrate differences for the criterion groups. Also, the wrestlers differed significantly from established norms only on the tough-mindedness factor.

On the other hand, Morgan (1968a) administered the Eysenck Personality Inventory (EPI) to English-speaking wrestlers who participated in the 1966 world tournament, and he reported that performance in the tournament was significantly correlated with the extroversion dimension. Success, however, was not related to neuroticism.

More recently, Morgan and Costill (1972) administered the EPI, the IPAT Anxiety Scale, and the Depression Adjective Check List to a group of experienced marathoners. Correlations were computed between performance in the marathon, the maximal oxygen intake of these subjects, and the psychologic variables. Marathon performance was not significantly correlated with any of the variables. This is somewhat surprising since most observers of the marathon readily agree that these runners represent a "special breed." They are, of course, quite unique from an anatomic and physiologic standpoint. This uniqueness, at least in part, explains the lack of significant correlations between

[2]It is of interest to note that the varsity athletes in the individual sports were significantly more depressed than those from the team and team-individual groups. A later report by Carmen, Zerman, and Blaine (1968) revealed that the highest incidence of depression in Harvard athletes occurred among swimmers (an individual sport).

the variables cited; that is, they are so similar that their homogeneity suppresses the likelihood of significant correlations. This group of marathoners scored much lower on the anxiety and extroversion variables than the average population; that is, they were characterized by introversion and low anxiety.

The 16 PF was administered to 246 football players from four colleges by Straub and Davis (1971). The teams were from a small private college, an Ivy League university, a Big Ten university, and a small state college. It is interesting to note that the purpose of this investigation "was to determine if there were significant differences in team personality profiles" (p. 39). ... Subsequent analysis revealed that the Big Ten team differed significantly from the other three teams. Whether this difference reflects primarily (1) recruitment, (2) gravitation, (3) mortality, (4) cause and effect, or (5) an interaction effect remains to be demonstrated.

Parsons (1963) administered the 16 PF to champion swimmers and found that they differed from the average population on 15 of the 16 factors. However, those swimmers in this champion group who were selected to participate on the 1962 Canadian team did not differ from those swimmers who were not selected. This might simply reflect the homogeneity of the group. Also, it should not be assumed that members of any country's team are necessarily the best athletes available. Indeed, it is rather clear that numerous economic, political, sociologic, and personal factors influence the composition of national teams.

The Thurstone temperament schedule was administered to 21 high school swimmers by Newman (1968). The subjects were ranked in swimming ability as measured by actual mean competitive times in dual meets. Correlations were then computed between ranks on performance and the seven Thurstone traits. Three of the correlations were statistically significant, but since approximately two would be expected due to chance alone, this suggests that there was no relationship between personality and swimming performance in the sample studied. However, as mentioned earlier in this chapter, testing such hypotheses in isolated, intact, readily available samples does not lend itself to demonstration of significant relationships. The primary reason for not observing significant correlations relates to the homogeneity of variance which often characterizes such samples.

More recently, the 16 PF was administered to 338 swimmers from two Olympic Development Swim Clinics; swim clubs from California, Indiana, and New Jersey; and five college and university teams by Rushall (1970). The swimmers were pooled from the respective teams in order to form performance and maturational categories. The data were evaluated by means of stepwise multiple discriminant function analyses. Rushall concluded that "personality appeared to have no relation to success in swimming" (p. 103).

Several years ago, Kane (1964) reviewed the literature pertaining to personality and physical ability and came to the conclusion that a positive relationship exists between "athletic ability and (1) Stability as opposed to Anxiety, and (2) Extraversion as opposed to Introversion" (p. 89). On the basis of the present review, it would be hazardous to advance any generalizations regarding the interaction of personality and physical performance. The results of investigations conducted since Kane's review (1964) have been equivocal. The equivocal nature of this research can be explained in a number of ways.

First of all, one of the most serious shortcomings of investigations in this field has been the unitary nature of inquiry; that is, attempts to understand physical performance have been limited to the personality domain. This is rather interesting since considerable evidence is available which suggests that success in sport is dependent upon certain physical capacities. In other words, sport psychologists have attempted to discriminate between high- and low-performance groups on the basis of their scores on various personality inventories. There has been a general failure to consider biologic and sociologic factors as well as additional psychologic phenomena which might contribute to high-level performance.

An exception to the preceding generalization has been the research strategy of Kane (1964), who has examined the relationships between various physical abilities, personality factors, physique, and sociometric status. His factor analytic work prompted the advancement of the following hypotheses (1964, p. 94):

> *(1) that a high level of physical ability favours extravert development; (2) that among those of high physical ability only those achieve high standards in competitive conditions who rate highly in Extraversion, and (3) that size supports stability.*[3]

Confusion regarding the relationship of personality and physical ability will persist until different research strategies are used. It is recommended that investigators concerned with this problem (1) organize multidisciplinary teams, (2) adopt theoretic models, (3) employ precise operational definitions of dependent and independent variables, and (4) use meaningful sampling procedures.

Athletes and Nonathletes

Investigations which have been concerned specifically with comparisons of athletes and non-athletes will be reviewed in this section.

Henry (1941) administered a questionnaire consisting of items from the Thurstone neurotic inventory and questions pertaining to ascendence-submission to student pilots, members of a college track team, physical education major students, and a group of students enrolled in weightlifting. The track athletes and pilots were found to be quite similar and these groups were significantly less hypochondriacal and introverted than the weightlifters. Also, they were significantly more neurasthenic than the physical education majors.

Slusher (1964) administered the MMPI to high school athletes who had won letters in baseball, basketball, football, swimming, and wrestling, and to nonathletes from the same population. The athletes and nonathletes differed on all of the MMPI scales except the M (hypomania) and K (validity). These MMPI scales are known to fluctuate with various treatments. For example, scores on the depression scale decrease following the administration of antidepressants and numerous other therapies. At any rate, since the MMPI is not comprised of *trait* measures *per se,* it cannot be inferred that the athlete and nonathlete groups differed prior to the athletes electing to participate in sport.

Schendel (1965) administered the California Psychological Inventory (CPI) to ninth-grade, twelfth-grade, and college athletes and nonparticipants in athletics. The ninth-grade athletes differed from the nonathletes on eight of the CPI scales, differences existed on 4 scales for the twelfth-grade sample, and nine differences were observed for the college *S*s. This investigation supports the view that athletes and nonathletes differ in personality structure, and while cross-sectional studies have obvious limitations, it also suggests that athletes and nonathletes differ from the outset since both the younger and older groups differed.

---

[3] Stability refers to lack of neurotic signs in this sentence.

The Gordon Personal Profile was administered to 22 Negro and 35 white athletes and 19 Negro and 35 white nonathletes by Hunt (1969). He reported that Negro and white varsity athletes had similar personality profiles as did the Negro and white nonathletes. Also, the athletes, regardless of ethnic background, tended to differ from the nonathletes.

The Edwards Personal Preference Schedule (EPPS) was administered to 950 male freshmen by Fletcher and Dowell (1971). These subjects were further divided into groups who had participated in high school athletics and those who had not. The two groups were found to differ on the Dominance, Aggression, and Order scales of the EPPS.

College wrestlers and experienced marathoners have been found to score significantly lower than the population average on anxiety (Morgan and Hammer 1971; Morgan and Costill 1972). Also, American world-class wrestlers were found to be more extroverted than the normal population and marathoners (see Figure 1), who in turn were more introverted than the normal population and most other athletic sub-groups (Morgan 1968*a*; Morgan, 1968*b*; Morgan and Costill 1972). These investigations as well as the majority of the studies reviewed in this section suggest that athletes represent a unique population. Perhaps it is inappropriate to make comparisons between athletic sub-groups and published norms for the "normal" or "average" population if, in fact, athletes represent another population; that is, extensive norming on athletes might be appropriate.

The Eysenck Personality Inventory was administered to 46 team sport and 36 individual sport athletes as well as 40 nonathletes by Golas (1971). The 82 athletes were also classified as representing either a combative (N = 41) or noncombative (N = 41) sport. Regardless of classification procedure, the athletes were found to be significantly more extroverted than the nonathletes. The sport groups did not differ on the *E* dimension, however. Also, none of the groups differed on the neuroticism-stability dimension.

One consistent finding throughout the sport psychology literature has been the observation that athletes tend to be normal on the neuroticism-stability dimension of personality. Indeed, American wrestlers were noted to be extremely stable even when tested 24 to 48 hours before competition in a world tournament (Morgan 1968*a*). It may well be that stability is a prerequisite for high-level competition. A report by Yanada and Hirata (1970) suggests that this observation may reflect selective mortality. They reported that those students who dropped out and those who continued in their athletic clubs scored within the abnormal and normal ranges respectively on the Tokyo University Personality Inventory (TUPI). Those students who continued in their sport clubs were less neurotic, less depressive, and more hypomanic than those who dropped out.

A different interpretation, however, might follow from the work of Carmen, Zerman, and Blaine (1968), who compared the use of the Harvard Psychiatric Service by athletes and nonathletes. Athletes used the service less frequently, but those athletes who requested treatment tended to have more problems than did the nonathletes. Also, Pierce (1969) reported that athletes are less likely to make use of campus psychiatric facilities than are other students. Of further interest was his observation that differences between athletes and nonathletes were "related to ability to take the role of patient than to actual degree of pathology, and the suggestion is made that ways of helping these less verbal, less intellectually oriented students be developed and used" (p. 249).

Little (1969) compared athletic and nonathletic neurotics. There has been an absence of neurotic markers in the life histories of the athletes, whereas neurotic markers were quite common in the nonathletic group. Also, the athletic group was highly extroverted and sociable while the nonathletic group was characterized by introversion and a lack of sociability. Despite histories of good mental health, "the prognosis under treatment for the athletic group was, in general, less favourable"

(p. 194). Neurotic breakdowns were associated with a threat to physical well-being (that is, illness or injury) in 73 percent of the cases for the athletic group, while the percentage was only 11 for the nonathletic group. The implication here for directors of athletic programs is that psychologic first aid is just as important as physical treatment for the injured athlete. Little's findings are essentially in agreement with those of Carmen, Zerman, and Blaine (1968), and Pierce (1969); that is, athletes display fewer neurotic symptoms than nonathletes, but prognosis for the athlete is not favorable once he is referred to a psychiatric service.

On the basis of this review as well as the material contained in the previous section, it seems reasonable to conclude that athletes have consistently been found to differ from nonathletes on a number of personality traits. The athlete tends to be stable and extroverted, with the exception of cross country runners and marathoners who are characterized by introversion. There is some evidence which suggests that even though they might be in need of such attention, athletes are less likely to seek psychiatric service than nonathletes. Once the athlete arrives at a psychiatric service, however, it appears that his prognosis is less favorable than that of the nonathlete.

The Female Athlete

There have been very few investigations directed toward an understanding of the female athlete's personality.[4] However, with increased emphasis on age group competition for the female athlete as well as national tournaments for the college-age female, it is quite likely that personality studies will become more frequent.

The 16 PF was administered to 38 female athletes who participated on the 1964 United States Olympic teams by Peterson, Wever, and Trousdale (1967). This sample consisted of individual sports participants in swimming, diving, riding, fencing, canoeing, gymnastics, and track and field. These subjects were compared to 59 team sport athletes who participated on either the 1964 Olympic Volleyball Team or one of the top ten AAU basketball teams for 1964. The two groups were found to differ on 7 of the 16 factors. The athletes from the individual sports were significantly more dominant and aggressive, adventurous, sensitive, imaginative, radical, self-sufficient, resourceful, and less sophisticated than the team sports group. The athletes from the individual sports were more introverted than the team sport athletes, and both groups were characterized by emotional stability. These female athletes were found to be more intelligent, conscientious, persevering, and aggressive than female nonathletes of similar age and educational background.

The findings of Peterson, Weber, and Trousdale (1967) were corroborated by Ogilvie (1968) in part. He compared their results with the 16 PF profiles of female swimmers from San Jose State College who were found to have profiles similar to the individual sport athletes in their study.

A related investigation was conducted by Malumphy (1968), who administered the 16 PF and a personal information questionnaire to 77 female athletes and 43 randomly selected nonathletes from five state universities. Comparisons were made between athletes in team sports, individual sports, team-individual sports, subjectively judged sports, and the nonathletes. The four groups of female athletes differed from the nonathletes on various factors, a result which is in agreement with the report of Peterson, Weber, and Trousdale (1967). Also, the participants in the various sports groups differed on a number of factors. Of major interest was the observation that athletes from individual sports were more extroverted than those athletes from team and team-individual groups. This seems

---

[4] See the article by Balazs on pages 156-162. —Ed.

to be in disagreement with the findings of Peterson, Weber, Trousdale (1967). However, they tested high-level competitors whereas Malumphy's sample only included one Olympic athlete. This might easily explain the apparent contradiction. Malumphy also found that the team sport group was less extroverted than the nonathlete. If this in fact is the case, it would represent a major distinction between the personality of male and female athletes; that is, with the exception of distance runners, male athletes tend to be extroverted.

More recently, Williams and her associates (1970) administered the 16 PF and the EPPS to 30 female fencers who participated in the 1968 national championships. Comparisons were made between high- and low-level achievers, and they were found to differ only on the measure of dominance. Since they did not differ on any of the other 38 variables, this one variation was probably due to chance. However, this group of female athletes was found to differ from national norms on a number of 16 PF factors and EPPS measures. The authors concluded that a definite fencer's personality emerged from their analysis, and this profile was different from that of participants in other sports. In this respect it was reported that "the 'sport type' to which their profile was the most related was the male and female competitive race car driver" (p. 452). In general, these athletes tended to be reserved, self-sufficient, autonomous, assertive, and aggressive, and they scored below average on affiliation and nurturance.

It has previously been demonstrated that participants in psychologic investigations differ from both nonvolunteers and pseudovolunteers (Morgan 1972). In the study by Williams and her associates (1970), 45 of the 60 participants in the tournament volunteered to complete the tests. Subsequently, 15 of the subjects failed to return the tests. Hence, there were 30 volunteers, 15 pseudovolunteers, and 15 nonvolunteers. It is quite likely that these three groups differed on certain features of the 16 PF and EPPS. Therefore, it is suggested that the "fencer's profile" identified by Williams and her associates be viewed with caution.

The female athlete, like the male athlete, tends to differ from the nonathlete on a number of personality factors. Also, female athletes from different sub-groups tend to differ on various dimensions of personality. On the other hand, we know much less about the personality of the female athlete than the male athlete. Hopefully, investigators concerned with the study of the female athlete will not commit the same methodologic errors which have characterized research with the male athlete. Specifically, it is recommended that investigations be conducted on the personality of the female athlete with the following points in mind: (1) such investigations should be pursued within the framework of a theoretic model, (2) from the very outset an attempt should be made to gather extensive normative data, (3) appropriate sampling procedures and statistical techniques should be employed, (4) rigorous definitions of the dependent and independent variables should be adopted, and (5) a longitudinal model would seem to be necessary.

REFERENCES

Adatto, C. 1963. On play and the psychopathology of golf. Paper presented at the meeting of the New Orleans Psychoanalytic Society, New Orleans, January 1963.

Beisser, A. R. 1961. Psychodynamic observations of a sport. *Psychoanalytic Review* 48:69-76.

———. 1967. *The madness in sports.* New York: Appleton-Century-Crofts.

Booth, E. G., Jr. 1958. Personality traits of athletes as measured by the MMPI. *Research Quarterly* 29:127-138.

Carmen, L. R.; Zerman, J. L.; and Blaine, G. B., Jr. 1968. Use of the Harvard psychiatric service by athletes and nonathletes, *Mental Hygiene,* 52:134-137.

Deutsch, H. 1926. A contribution to the psychology of sport. *International Journal of Psychoanalysis* 7:223-227.

Eysenck, H. J. 1967. *The biological basis of personality.* Springfield, Ill.: Charles C. Thomas.

Eysenck, S. B. G., and Eysenck, H. J. 1970. A factor-analytic study of the lie scale of the junior Eysenck personality inventory. *Personality* 1:3-10.

Fletcher, R., and Dowell, L. 1971. Selected personality characteristics of high school athletes and nonathletes. *Journal of Psychology* 77:39-41.

Golas, R. W. 1971. A comparative study of two personality dimensions in athletes and non-participants. Paper presented at the meeting of the Eastern District Association for Health, Physical Education, and Recreation, Philadelphia, April 1971.

Hall, C. S., and Lindzey, G. 1970. *Theories of personality.* (1st ed.) New York: John Wiley & Sons.

Harlow, R. G. 1951. Masculine inadequacy and compensatory development of physique. *Journal of Personality* 19:312-323.

Henry, F. M. 1941. Personality differences in athletes, physical education, and aviation students. *Psychological Bulletin* 38:745.

Hunt, D. H. 1969. A cross racial comparison of personality traits between athletes and nonathletes. *Research Quarterly* 40:704-707.

Johnson, W. R.; Hutton, D. C.; and Johnson, G. B. 1954. Personality traits of some champion athletes as measured by two projective tests: The Rorschach and H-T-P. *Research Quarterly* 25:484-485.

Kane, J. E. 1964. Psychological correlates of physique and physical abilities. In *International research in sport and physical education,* ed. E. Jokl and E. Simon, pp. 85-94. Springfield, Ill.: Charles C. Thomas.

Kroll, W. 1967. Sixteen personality factor profiles of collegiate wrestlers. *Research Quarterly* 38:49-57.

La Place, J. P. 1954. Personality and its relationship to success in professional baseball. *Research Quarterly* 25:313-319.

Little, J. C. 1969. The athlete's neurosis—a deprivation crisis. *Acta Psychiatrica Scandinavica* 45:187-197.

Malumphy, T. M. 1968. Personality of women athletes in intercollegiate competition. *Research Quarterly* 39:610-620.

Morehouse, L. E., and Rasch, P. J. 1963. *Sports medicine for trainers.* Philadelphia: Saunders.

Morgan, W. P. 1968a. Personality characteristics of wrestlers participating in the world championships. *Journal of Sports Medicine & Physical Fitness* 8:212-216.

——. 1968b. Extraversion-neuroticism and athletic performance. Symposium presented at the meeting of the American College of Sports Medicine, State College, Pennsylvania, May 1968.

Morgan, W. P., ed. 1972. Ergogenic aids and muscular performance. New York: Academic Press.

Morgan, W. P., and Costill, D. L. 1972. Psychological characteristics of the marathon runner. *Journal of Sports Medicine & Physical Fitness* 12:42-46.

Morgan, W. P., and Hammer, W. M. 1971. Psychological effect of competitive wrestling. Paper presented at the meeting of the American Association for Health, Physical Education, & Recreation, Detroit, April 1971.

Newman, E. N. 1968. Personality traits of faster and slower competitive swimmers. *Research Quarterly* 39:1049-1053.

Ogilvie, B. C. 1968. Psychological consistencies within the personality of high-level competitors. *Journal of the American Medical Association* 205:156-162.

Parsons, D. R. 1963. Personality traits of national representative swimmers—Canada. 1962. Unpublished master's thesis, University of British Columbia.

Peterson, S. L.; and Weber, J. C.; and Trousdale, W. W. 1967. Personality traits of women in team sports vs. women in individual sports. *Research Quarterly* 38:686-690.

Pierce, R. A. 1969. Athletes in psychotherapy: How many, how come? *Journal of American College Health Association* 17:244-249.

Rushall, B. S. 1970. An investigation of the relationship between personality variables and performance categories in swimmers. *International Journal of Sport Psychology* 1:93-104.

Schendel, J. 1965. Psychological differences between athletes and non-participants in athletics at three educational levels. *Research Quarterly* 36:52-67.

Singer, R. N. 1969. Personality differences between and within baseball and tennis players. *Research Quarterly* 40:582-588.

Shusher, H. S. 1964. Personality and intelligence characteristics of selected high school athletes and non-athletes. *Research Quarterly* 35:539-545.

Straub, W. F., and Davis, S. W. 1971. Personality traits of college football players who participated at different levels of competition. *Medicine and Science in Sports* 3:39-43.

Whitman, R. M. 1969. Psychoanalytic speculations about play: Tennis—the duel. *Psychoanalytic Review* 56:197-214.

Williams, J. M.; Hoepner, B. J.; Moody, D. L.; and Ogilvie, B. C. 1970. Personality traits of champion level female fencers. *Research Quarterly* 41:446-453.

Yanada, H., and Hirata, H. 1970. Personality traits of students who dropped out of their athletic clubs. *Proceedings of the College of Physical Education* no. 5. University of Tokyo.

Psycho-Social Study
of Outstanding Female Athletes

Eva K. Balazs

Psychological research on high achievement of women in sports is extremely limited.[1] The major purpose of this study was to identify variables in the psychological make-up and social development of a group of outstanding female athletes. Some of the questions asked concerned patterns of similarity in the development of the subjects' lives and differences that distinguished them from the average female population.

CONFLICT BETWEEN FEMININITY AND COMPETITION

To be successful in sports—or in any other endeavor—the person has to display competence, self-reliance, and willingness to take risks. These attributes are highly admired in American society, but seem to apply to men only. Where women are concerned the same qualities are not appreciated. Dorothy Harris (1971) describes the dilemma and deplores the fact that if a girl wants to participate in a competitive sport, she too has to display the same traits, but if she does, she risks her feminine image. Matina Horner (1968; 1971) puts the same idea into a wider perspective when she says that in our achievement-oriented society achievement, self-realization, and the development of all the potentials of the individual are rewarded and valued.

Cultural attitudes toward the male role-expectation, however, is different from that of the female. Society's inability to reconcile femininity with ambition and personal accomplishment is well-documented in Horner's research. Women worry not only about failure but also about success. The situation described is perhaps nowhere more evident than in sports. The more successful a woman becomes as an athlete, the more afraid she seems to be that she will lose the feminine image. The stereotype of female athlete: aggressive, frustrated, unfeminine, well-described by Malumphy (1971), poses a threat or a least discouragement to many girls who would like to participate in sports. The notion persists even today, that girls and sports do not go well together. Society seems to be saying that females are somehow different, even "abnormal" if they pursue excellence in athletics.

Eva K. Balazs. Psycho-social study of outstanding female athletes. *Research Quarterly* 46 (1975):267-273.

[1] See the review article by Morgan on pages 145-155. —Ed.

Research on those who do achieve eminence in sports is growing, but it is still scarce. Among the few investigators are Kane and Callaghan (1965) who focused on the personality characteristics of world-class female tennis-players. The investigators found that emotional stability, ego-strength, and low frustration characterized these top players. The authors reported no loss of the "feminine traits, valued within the culture and society." In fact there was strong evidence that this sample of women had "markedly feminine personalities in the presence of outstanding success as competitors." Ogilvie and Tutko (1967) studied the personality traits of female swimming champions. These researchers also found that "traits which our culture define as feminine, like low aggression, low dominance, and high nurturance were characteristic of the group." Ogilvie (Ogilvie 1967; Ogilvie 1968; Ogilvie et al. 1970; Ogilvie, Johnsgard, and Merritt 1973) further investigated the personality structure of top women athletes in such varied sports as fencing, parachuting, and racecar driving, but the personality development in relation to athletic achievement is still a largely unexplored area.

PROCEDURE

Twenty-four female subjects volunteered, who represented the U.S. in the 1972 Olympic games as members of the swimming, gymnastics, track-and-field, and ski teams. The subjects were contacted by letter to ask for their cooperation in the research and to establish a date and place for a meeting. In-depth interviews were then conducted with each subject at various parts of the U.S. A wide variety of topics was covered concerning the athletes' lives from early childhood to the present time (Table 1).

A tape recorder was used. Each athlete was also asked to complete a Personal Data Questionnaire (PDQ), which was a biographical inventory developed by the researcher, and a standardized psychological test, the Edwards Personal Preference Schedule (EPPS). While the clinical data represented the heart of the study, the PDQ was helpful in separating the factual material from the clinical analysis. The EPPS was selected as appropriate for this study because it provides an instrument for individual and group assessment of such normal personality traits as achievement autonomy and aggression and the scores on these personality scales can be compared with the general female population similar in age and educational background.

The organization was as follows. First the factual data, obtained from the PDQ was presented. The findings were analyzed, and frequency distribution, mean, median, and standard deviation were recorded. Then the clinical material of the interviews was analyzed. The subjects' life experiences were studied according to the life periods of childhood, adolescence, and young adulthood. It was possible to identify and report a number of development dynamics that existed and seemed to pervade through the life stages of all subjects. Finally, the scores on the EPPS were analyzed and arranged to provide a personality profile for each individual. At the end 24 profiles were averaged into a group profile which was then compared with the national norm for a female population corresponding in age and education.

RESULTS

The data on the PDQ revealed that more than half of the subjects were first born children or first born daughters. This seems to be a rather typical finding in research on outstanding women (Douvan

Table 1. Topics Raised in the Open-ended Interviews

Relationship to father, to mother.

View of yourself as a child.

Relationship to brothers and sisters.

Most pleasant childhood memory.

Performance in school. Relationship to teachers. Socialization with peers. Like or dislike of physical education.

Favorite childhood activities (intellectual, sport, manual, etc.)

Favorite companions in school and outside of school.

Nature of choice of the particular sport. Why? At what age?

Setting of goal directions. When? Why? Motivation toward Olympics as a goal.

Relationship to coach. Feelings toward the male or female dominant figure.

Early dating pattern. Adolescent relationship to boys.

Peer group influence. Pressure or recognition of adolescent society.

Current view of men. Marriage plans.

Career plans. View of future.

Hobbies. Special interest other than sports.

Factors that aid toward success (psychological, social, physical).

Hindering factors in athletics.

Reward and pleasures of a successful sportswoman.

Problems she has to face.

Persons and/or factors that contributed most to your personal development.

The most valued sports event or award achieved. Why?

Most important traits for a woman to become successful in athletics.

1966; Hennig 1971). The athletes ranged in age from 15.5-20. The majority came from four-sibling or larger families and 66% of the sisters and brothers were also engaged in various forms of competitive athletics. The data also revealed that the swimmers started earliest as competitors and made it to the top at the youngest age. One swimmer was only 5 yr old at her first competition and 15.5 when she won a Gold Medal at the Olympics. The data analysis indicated that two athletes made the Olympic team after only 2 yr of competing, while two others accomplished this in 12 yr time. It was also interesting to note that one of the skiers was 24 yr of age when she first entered competition.

The analysis of the clinical data (interviews) suggested that there were some basic, identical patterns in the developmental dynamics. All subjects had a strong and early drive to achieve, to "be the best in something," "to become somebody." They internalized this need early in childhood and set a goal for themselves to excel in a sport. The wish to perform on the highest level was intense and remained constant throughout the years, even during adolescence, when the majority of girls would abandon such wishes. The subjects found ways to cope with peer society's pressures to conform to the norms and lived up to their own aspirations rather than to peer's expectations. "Kids didn't have the feeling for what I was doing. They just couldn't understand me and frankly I didn't give a damn. . ."

It was clearly apparent from the case histories that the childhood experiences and family set-up played a crucial role in the subject's development. Fathers were described by almost all as "available."

"He was around a lot"—and they seemed to indicate the importance of this fact. Findings from other studies (Hennig 1971; Konopka 1965) also affirm the significance of the father in the lives of achieving females as an identification figure in carrying values and setting ideals. It was also apparent that the majority of subjects regarded their parents as the main motivating force in their development. "My parents belief in me was terribly important to me. Their encouragement and constant feedback motivated me more than anything else. I don't know if anybody needed it that much . . . it sure worked for me!"

The support of both father and mother was positive and consistent. "I could always count on my family, they were all behind me," "My parents helped me in everything, they never put me down." It was also clear that while supportive and understanding, the parents expected a great deal. "Only doing my very best would do in my family," "I could get away with nothing less than top performance, in schoolwork or in anything else."

The theory of expectancy seems to apply here, namely, that the expectancy of achievement by the parents has an effect of evoking achievement-behavior in the offsprings. As Gardner (1968) puts it: without the expectation of excellence there is no achievement of excellence. Another theory is also applicable here, the concept that unless the family believes in certain values and attaches importance to the activity—be it intellectual, artistic, or physical—the child is not likely to excel in that specific endeavor (McLelland 1958; Ogilvie 1968). This was certainly true with the subjects. In these families everyone believed that sports are worthwhile endeavors and being outstanding in a sport is all right for girls. Sports do not make a girl unfeminine seemed to be the message.

The same ideas were constantly reinforced by the coach,[2] who—psychologically speaking— became an extended father figure. Indeed, in some cases the coach was the father himself. The coach had a tremendous potential to mold the young girl's development. He was accepted as an authority figure and was described by many with an emotional tone of voice. "He is the best, I love him. . . ." "He was like a father, teacher, and a friend all put together." "He is a king of heart, I would do anything for him."

There was ample documentation in the reports that the parents' and coaches' positive influences provided strongly internalized feelings of self-worth and self-esteem which then had a positive effect on goal attainment. The theory appears to be correct here that there is a high positive correlation between self-esteem and achievement (Gardner 1968).

Heterosexual relations were described as satisfying and important to the subjects. As youngsters, the girls perceived themselves as tomboys, who could do "anything as well or better than the guys" and who felt very comfortable in boys company. During adolescence, however, there was a break in the relations. Many a boy, unable to handle a "girl who is more famous than they" reverted to teasing. "Wow, look at those muscles," "Hey, Baby, wanna wrestle?"—these and similar remarks were painfully remembered. As the years went by, the picture began to change.

The young male, now more secure, began to appreciate the accomplishments of these competent, confident girls. At the time of the interviews almost all of the subjects had feelings of enjoyment in dating and being regarded as attractive and desirable by the opposite sex. "Guys are fun." "I love to be in male company." Marriage was for almost all definitely part of the future. Twenty-five percent of the athletes were already married (at the average age of 21.5 yr).

[2] See the article by Singer and Hilmer on pages 56-62. —Ed.

The psychological dynamics, revealed in the case histories can be summarized as follows:

Strong drive to excel
Early goal-setting and following through the original goals
Positive self-image
Well-developed heterosexuality
Family atmosphere where support was coupled with high expectations
Main motivating force: parents and the coach

The analysis of the 15 personality traits on the EPPS revealed a distinct characteristic: the psychological group-profile was almost completely lacking in any deviant or abnormal attributes. As illustrated, the group profile was a well-balanced curve, indicating no significant deviation from the normal population, with the exception of two very high scores on achievement and autonomy (Figure 1).

The outstanding female athlete of this study may be described as a person with two important personality needs: a high need for achievement and a high need for autonomy. The needs associated with these variables suggest a person with a strong desire to do well, to get ahead, to be a success. These words are almost identical to the ones that best describe the sample group. She is nonconforming, she does things that are different and does them without regard to what others may think. This variable, too, seems to correlate well with the clinical data.

The somewhat above-average group score on aggression and succorance suggest a person with a rather positive self-concept, she tends to be self-confident, but she has a need for encouragement from those persons who are important to her (parents, coach). The group scores on the variable of heterosexuality, also somewhat above average, bespeaks of a need for social interaction and experiences with the opposite sex. The remainder of the group scores were almost identical to the average for the normative group.

The evenness of most of the EPPS group scores suggested an essentially normal personality development. The curve implied emotional stability and normal personal adjustments—which might be necessary, perhaps even imperative for females to achieve eminence in athletics or possible in other endeavors as well.

In summary, it seems reasonable to conclude that the young women of this study projected the picture of a very well put together human being. They had a value-orientation that pushed them from childhood on toward the highest level of performance in sports. Beyond motivation and talent they had a particular family dynamics that seemed to be crucial: the parents' support and encouragement was coupled with their high expectations. The subjects gave manifestation of integrity and autonomy and they appeared to hold satisfying social contacts and heterosexual relations. All and all, they had a positive attitude toward life and seemed to enjoy what they were doing.

The insights gained by this study, however, should be viewed with some caution, since only 24 athletes participated, who were not randomly picked, but who volunteered and the sports were four specific, individual sports. The findings can hardly be descriptive for all female athletes in all sports. The merits of the study lies in the fact that it presents an analysis of a particular group of outstanding sportswomen, which might contribute to the understanding of others who are striving for excellence.

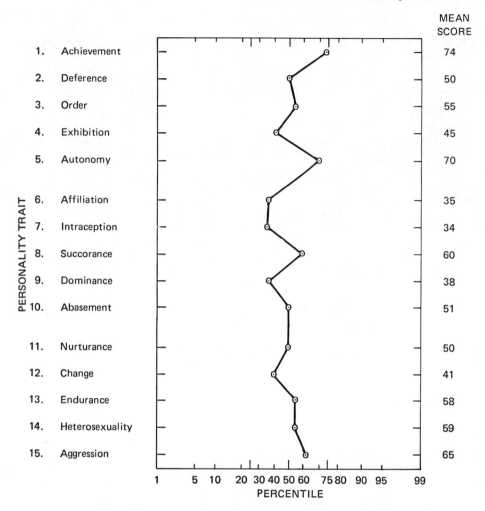

Figure 1. EPPS group profile of 24 Olympic female competitors

REFERENCES

Douvan, E. 1971. New sources of conflict at adolescence and early childhood. In *Feminine personality and conflict.* ed. J. M. Bardwick et al. Belmont, Calif.: Brooks Cole.

———. 1966. *The adolescent experience.* New York: Wiley.

Gardner, J. 1968. *Excellence.* Boston: Little, Brown.

Goerzel, V., and Goerzel, M. 1962. *Cradle of eminence.* Boston: Little, Brown.

Harris, D. V. 1971. The sportswoman in our society. In *Women in sports.* Washington: NEA Publication Sales.

Hennig, M. 1971. Career development of women executives. Unpublished doctoral dissertation, Harvard University.

Horner, M. S. 1968. Sex differences in achievement motivation and performance in competitive and non-competitive situations. Unpublished doctoral dissertation, University of Michigan.

———. 1971. Femininity and successful achievement: A basic inconsistency. In *Feminine personality and conflict.* ed. J. M. Bardwick et al. Belmont, Calif.: Brooks Cole.

Kane, J. F., and Callaghan, J. L. 1965. Personality traits in tennis players. *British Lawn Tennis* 1 (July).

Konopka, G. 1965. *The adolescent girl in conflict.* Englewood Cliffs, N.J.: Prentice-Hall.

McLelland, B. 1958. Dronfenbreumew, Stodtbeck. *Talent and society.* Princeton, N.J.: D. Van Nostrand Co.

Malumphy, T. M. 1971. Athletics and competition for girls. *Women in sports.* Washington: NEA Publication Sales.

Ogilvie, B. 1967. *The unanswered question: Competition, its effects on femininity.* Santa Barbara, Calif.: Olympic Development Committee.

———. 1968. Psychological consistency within the personality of high level competitiors. *Journal of the American Medical Association* Special Report

Ogilvie, B.; Johnsgard, K. W.; and Merritt, E. 1973. Female parachutists as contrasted with other high level competitors (pt. 3). U.S. Army Aeromedical Research Laboratory, Fort Rucker, Ala. Contract DABCOR-71-3995.

Ogilvie, B., and Tutko, T. A. 1967. *Problem athletes and how to handle them.* London: Dellissin Books.

Ogilvie, B.; William, J. M.; Hoepnew, B. J.; and Moody, D. L. 1970. Personality traits of championship level female fencers. *Research Quarterly* 41:446-453.

Roe, A. 1953. *The making of a scientist.* New York: Dodd, Mead.

Sport Personality Assessment: A Methodological Re-examination

J. Stuart Horsfall, A. Craig Fisher, and Harold H. Morris

In recent years a few psychologists and more than a few physical educators have become increasingly interested in assessing the personality of athletes. Questions have been raised concerning certain general premises which are embodied in the athletic world. It is commonly asserted that the football player is highly masculine and hyper-aggressive while athletes in other sports possess other specific personality characteristics, and moreover, that sportsmen in general are easily distinguished from the wider population. If indeed athletes can be differentiated from non-athletes and across various sports, this information would be extremely useful to coaches. Assessment techniques could be developed for the screening of athletic potential and athletes could be matched with the sport or sports with which they are most highly compatible.

The importance of this area has inspired a large number of researchers[1] to collect personality data with perhaps the rather overoptimistic hope of an instant answer. However, rather than shedding light on the matter, the answers obtained have done little more than engender uncertainty and confusion; the results have been diverse to say the least.

Many studies in this web of conflicting results can be dismissed as inconsequential for obvious reasons—their atheoretical nature, illogical premises, and methodological shortcomings—insufficient numbers of subjects and inadequate experimental designs and data analyses. These issues have been raised and discussed at length elsewhere (Fisher, Ryan, and Martens 1976; Kroll 1970) and time does not permit any detailed elaboration here.

The great majority of empirical research in sport personality has utilized assessment devices which embody the factor theory as their main premise. As expressed by Cattell (1973), the factor theory searches for consistencies in behavior. It is assumed that internal dispositions or traits are relatively stable and so enduring that they override environmental or situational influences. This infers that questions could be asked in any situation and the responses generalized to a sport situation. Take for example the broad category of anxiety. Is knowing that a person scores low on an omnibus

J. Stuart Horsfall, A. Craig Fisher, and Harold H. Morris. Sport personality assessment: A methodological re-examination. In *Psychology of sport and motor behavior*, ed. D. Landers. Proceedings of the North American Society for the Psychology of Sport and Physical Activity, Pennsylvania State University, 10 May-20 May 1975. Pennsylvania State HPER Series, no. 10. Also published in *International Journal of Sports Psychology* 8 (1977):92-102.

[1] See the review article by Morgan on pages 145-155. –Ed.

inventory of anxiety enough to conclude that he will *never* exhibit anxiety? Are there no situations in which his heart rate may increase *a little?* The situationist position as exemplified in Mischel's (1969) social learning theory, appears to go too far to the other extreme, entering into open debate with personologism. This paradigm can be regarded as the antithesis of the factor theory and maintains that behavioral variation is primarily a function of the situation in which a person is placed.

Brunswik (1956) bases his rationale for adopting the situationist construct on the assumption that it is more relevant to sample situations than subjects as "individuals are probably on the whole more alike than are situations among one another." Or are they? Intuitively, it would appear to be the other way around. However, the question becomes immaterial when the constructs are considered in total perspective.

Just as it is illogical to conceive of behavioral variation being totally attributable to traits, it is no less illogical to overemphasize situations at the expense of individual consistency. It would appear that some personality researchers have assumed the situation to be the major source of variation since trait results have been consistent in their inconsistencies. Such an assumption is untenable. To deny traits as the major source of behavioral variation is not evidence enough to accept situations as the prime locus.

While most advocates of situation specificity do not completely discount individual personality differences and most supporters of trait personology do not dismiss environmental factors entirely, some sources (Bowers 1973; Moos 1969) have indicated the mutual involvement of traits and situations in the determination of behavior. Such a paradigm was suggested by Endler and Rosenstein (1962) and has since been appropriately labelled interactionism. With the person-situation dilemma in mind, these investigators constructed an S-R inventory of anxiousness designed to partition total behavioral variance. The inventory listed a sample of general situations ranging from innocuous to potentially threatening and a selection of common physiological modes of response that were assumed to belong to the anxiety category. The numerous samples of subjects were asked to relate the extent to which they manifested each of the modes of response in each of the situations on a five-point scale. Conclusive analysis of the data was delayed until 1966 due to the lack of availability

Table 1. List of Situations Used in the S-R Inventory of Anxiousness (Form O)

SITUATIONS

1. "You are just starting off on a long automobile trip"
2. "You are going to meet a new date"
3. "You are going into a psychological experiment"
4. "You are crawling along a ledge on a mountain side"
5. "You are getting up to give a speech before a large group"
6. "You are going to a counseling bureau to seek help in solving a personal problem"
7. "You are starting out in a sail boat onto a rough sea"
8. "You are entering a competitive contest before spectators"
9. "You are alone in the woods at night"
10. "You are entering a final examination in an important course"
11. "You are going into an interview for a very important job"

Table 2. List of Modes Used in the S-R Inventory of Anxiousness (Form O)

MODES OF RESPONSE	1	5
1. Heart beats faster	Not at all	Much faster
2. Get an "uneasy feeling"	None	Very strongly
3. Emotions disrupt action	Not at all	Very disruptive
4. Feel exhilarated and thrilled	Very much	Not at all
5. Want to avoid situation	Not at all	Very much
6. Perspire	Not at all	Perspire much
7. Need to urinate frequently	Not at all	Very frequently
8. Enjoy the challenge	Enjoy much	Not at all
9. Mouth gets dry	Not at all	Very dry
10. Become immobilized	Not at all	Completely
11. Get full feeling in stomach	None	Very full
12. Seek experiences like this	Very much	Not at all
13. Have loose bowels	None	Very much
14. Experience nausea	Not at all	Much nausea

of the appropriate model. The conclusions based upon these data proved to be highly damaging to both the trait and the situation constructs.

Only approximately 7 percent of the total behavioral variation was accounted for by persons, and a similar amount (6 percent) was attributable to the specified situations. As can be seen, roughly 87 percent of behavioral variance remained unaccounted for. The modes of response, however, contributed almost 24 percent to the total variance—roughly three to four times that for either situations or persons. An interpretation of this clearly implies that it is highly important for different raters of anxiousness to consider the same indicator responses. Any discrepancy in such could obviously lead to a disagreement in results. For example, consider two studies. If in the first study the investigator nominates the subject's perception of his heart rate to be an indicator of anxiety, and in the second the subject's dryness of mouth is considered, there is no reason to believe that there will be any similarity in results between the two.

A third piece of evidence to be gleaned from the results was that the three single interactions taken together accounted for approximately 27 percent of the variance thus implying that it is not a case of either/or but rather the combination of the different factors which is important. In reality, the person versus situation dilemma is a pseudo issue (Endler 1973).

It is significant to note that of all the sources of variation, the residual or error component is by far the largest (36 percent).

Based on the model previously described, an S-R inventory of anxiousness that related specifically to situations encountered in basketball was designed. Anxiety was selected due to the fact that it is not difficult to attribute apparent construct validity to anxiety as it relates to sport. Again, three-way analysis of variance techniques were employed to isolate variance components.

It is helpful at this point to anticipate what the factor theorist and the situationist may expect from such an analysis. Trait theory would suggest that the percentage of variance due to persons would be of extreme importance, since it is asserted that behavior is primarily a function of the

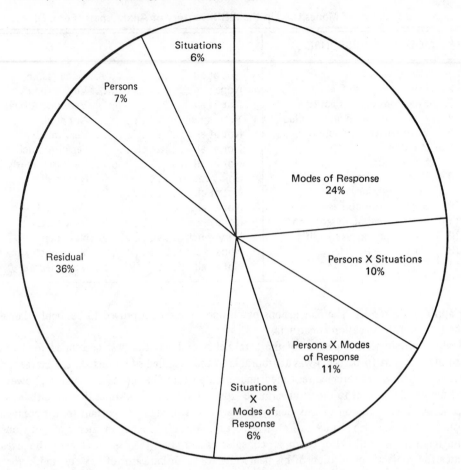

Figure 1. Partition of total behavioral variance. (Adapted from Endler, N. S., and Hunt, J. McV. 1966. Sources of behavioral variance as measured by the S-R Inventory of Anxiousness. *Psychological Bulletin* 65:336-346.)

individual's trait structure. On the other hand, the situationist would suggest that the majority of variation would be attributable to circumstances and little if any to the individual. As can be seen, neither of these proved to be the case.

Our present results closely parallel those found by Endler and Hunt (1966) with almost equal percentages attributable to persons and to situations—percentages of limited consequence. The compatibility of these two sets of data—one from the general population and one from a supposed population—reinforces an assertion made by Rushall (1971). He maintains that sport in general, the type of sport, and even a situation within a sport cannot be isolated with definable parameters. However, the modes-of-response variance in basketball situations is roughly a quarter of that in general situations. It is very plausible that the response indicators overall were more applicable to sport situations than to the general situations devised by Endler and Rosenstein (1962). Although basketball players do not digress from the general population in terms of personality, it is not too

Table 3. List of Basketball Situations

SITUATIONS

1. "Your team is already through to the divisional play-offs. One week before the first game is scheduled to be played you learn, by means of a newspaper report, who your opponents will be"
2. "You are a freshman at the varsity tryouts which are taking the form of trial games. The whole situation is new to you and you are waiting to go on court"
3. "You are on the team bus which is approaching the site of an important away game"
4. "It is the final game of the season and you have gone undefeated. You are in the locker room listening to the coach's last-minute instructions before you go out to play this all-important game"
5. "You have never had a winning season; it is the last game of the present season and you have a 1-19 record. You are in the locker room prior to the game listening to the coach telling you the same as he has told you all season"
6. "One week before an important game the coach told you that it was going to be your job to control the high scoring player of your opposition. You are now on the bench waiting for the game to begin"
7. "You enter a gymnasium where a game is to be played and there are no spectators present"
8. "You are waiting for the game to begin and there is a professional scout in the audience. He's there to watch *you*!"
9. "You are continually fouled under the boards and the referee doesn't call it"
10. "The score is tied at 80-80 with five seconds remaining. It is your first full game after recovering from severly torn knee ligaments incurred during a loose-ball situation in your last game. There is now an identical loose-ball situation and you have to get the ball"
11. "You have just committed a foul with the score tied at 90-90 and only two seconds remaining in the game. Your action may have cost your team the game"
12. "You are in the locker room after losing a game you really expected to lose"
13. "The game is over and you are in the locker room. The coach then tells you that you were fouled in the last second of the game but due to the noise of the crowd the timekeeper did not hear the referee's whistle. You are now awarded two free shots (1 and 1) which you must go back to the court to take. The score was 92-91 against you, but now, *you* have a chance to win a game you thought you had already lost"

difficult to conceive of their homogeneity in relation to their perception of physiological modes of response. Note again the greatest single source of variation—the residual component.

If we are to establish improved methods of personality assessment, what direction are we to take? The holistic view of personality presently in vogue, i.e., the proliferation of trait after trait, is obviously misaligned with reason. Surely logic tells us that it is fruitless to even attempt to relate such factors as intelligence or imagination to sport achievement. Only relevant characteristics should be assessed and the decision as to *which* characteristics ought to be derived from one's specific research questions. Conversely, the atomistic view of personality that searches for behavioral insights but only utilizes one small source of information must also be questioned. It is clear that continued employment of the factor theory will only serve to confound the problem. Are we to be satisfied with a claimed 20 percent predictive power?[2]

[2] J. E. Kane 1973; personal correspondence with A. C. Fisher.

Table 4. Behavioral Variation of General Population Samples and a Basketball Sample

ENDLER, HUNT AND ROSENSTEIN RESULTS	SOURCES OF VARIATION	HORSFALL, FISHER AND MORRIS RESULTS
7%	Persons (*P*)	9%
6%	Situations (*S*)	10%
24%	Modes of Response (*M-R*)	6%
10%	*P* X *S*	10%
11%	*P* X *M-R*	8%
6%	*S* X *M-R*	15%
36%	Residual	42%

The persepective is clear! Individual differences, situations *and* their interactions must be considered. Even in light of this, there still remains an "unknown quantity" of behaviorial variation which resided within the residual component. This magnified the difficulty of *any* possible accurate description, understanding or prediction of human behavior, whether it be sport-related or not! After all, not only do we have a personality, we also have a physiology, an anatomy, a role and a social status. Whatever made us think that personality alone would give us an index predictability. Perhaps in light of this comment and the typical results derived from the Endler et al. paradigm, it might not be truly inappropriate to advocate the residual approach to personality assessment since this is the major source of behavioral variation.

REFERENCES

Bowers, K. S. Situationism in psychology: An analysis and a critique. 1973. *Psychological Review* 80:307-336.

Brunswick, E. 1956. *Perception and the representative design of psychological experiments.* Berkeley: University of California Press.

Cattell, R. B. 1973. Personality pinned down. *Psychology Today* 7 (July): 40-46.

Endler, N. S. 1973. The person versus the situation—A pseudo-issue? A reply to Alker. *Journal of Personality* 41:287-303.

Endler, N. S., and Hunt, J. McV. 1966. Sources of behavioral variance as measured by the S-R Inventory of Anxiousness. *Psychological Bulletin* 65:336-346.

Endler, N. S., and Rosenstein, A. J. 1962. An S-R Inventory of Anxiousness. *Psychological Monographs* 76 (17, whole no. 536).

Fisher, A. C.; Ryan, E. D.; and Martens, R. 1976. Current status and future direction of personality research related to motor behavior and sport. In *Psychology of sport: Issues and insights,* ed. A. C. Fisher. Palo Alto: Mayfield.

Kroll, W. 1970. Current strategies and problems in personality assessment of athletes. In *Psychology of motor learning*, ed. L. E. Smith. Chicago: Athletic Institute.

Mischel, W. 1969. Continuity and change in personality. *American Psychologist* 24:1012-1018.

Moos, R. H. 1969. Sources of variance in responses to questionnaires and in behavior. *Journal of Abnormal Psychology* 74:405-412.

Rushall, B. S. 1971. The environment as a significant source of variance in the study of personality. Paper presented at a meeting the Third Canadian Psycho-Motor Learning Sports Psychology Symposium, University of British Columbia, October 1971.

Kid Sports: A Den of Iniquity or a Land of Promise?

Rainer Martens

Parents naturally are concerned about the well-being of their children in sports—and, in sports such as "pee wee" football and "midget" hockey, physical injury is a legitimate worry. But parents today are even more concerned about the psychological well-being of their children.

According to journalists, increasing numbers of kids are turned off, burned out, and hung up after participating in sports. Impressionable kids are learning by example how to swear, cheat and fight. Despite the criticisms, parents see a great deal of good in youth sports. Youth sports programs continue to flourish with boys and girls alike participating in greater numbers than ever. As a result concerned parents are in a dilemma: they want their kids to participate but they are uncertain as to whether youth sports create sinners or saints.

Obviously, youth sports programs can facilitate moral development when conducted correctly and also can facilitate the development of immoral or amoral behavior when conducted incorrectly. The more pregnant question is, what experiences in youth sports enhance moral development and what experiences contribute to immoral development?

MORAL DEVELOPMENT

In 1908, William McDougall wrote "the fundamental problem of social psychology is the moralization of the individual by the society." Through the process of moralization all the major phases of social development arise and are resolved. Moral development is the development of the conscience or superego. A child's conscience is developed from experiences with his environment, providing him with opportunities to internalize society's standards. Successful moralization of the child eliminates the necessity for constant surveillance and threats of punishment by society. Moral behavior within a sport context is called "sportsmanship."

Psychologist Lawrence Kohlberg demonstrates that a child may move through three distinct phases of moral development. Each phase emerges out of and subsumes its predecessor and is more cognitively complex than the one before it. *Premoral hedonism* is the first phase of moral development;

Rainer Martens. Kid sports: A den of iniquity or a land of promise? *Proceedings of the National College of Physical Education Association for Men,* conference at Hot Springs, Ark., January 1976. Extensive footnoting and the bibliography have been omitted.

the child behaves simply to avoid punishment. From premoral hedonism, the child's conscience develops into a phase where his moral behavior is guided by what he believes others will approve of and by an increasing concern for external rules and sanctions. This phase is known as the *conformity-phase*. In the final phase of moral development the individual places greater reliance on internal moral principles. A person enters what is known as the *internalization phase*. It is a morality based on the need for harmony between persons rather than inflexible conformity to rules.

SOCIALIZATION THROUGH SPORT

Philosophers, psychologists, and physical educators have eulogized play, games, and sports as a means not only for developing morality in children but socializing them to many facets of society. According to these academicians, games may act as a buffer, permitting children to learn the realities of life without sustaining the total impact of negative consequences. But do not for a moment believe that play and games are not serious business to children. Through the eyes of a young boy, failure to learn to ride a bicycle is just as serious as his father's failure in business.

Play may be a source of self-discovery, a means for learning new social roles, a medium for parent and child to communicate. Games and sports may permit a child an opportunity to learn how to cheat in the process of learning the meaning of fair play. Just as play, games, and sport have the capacity for positive socialization, they also may breed deceit, hatred, and violence. Thus it is not the game, the play or the sport that automatically determines the worth of these activities for the child; it is the nature of the experiences within these activities. It is the interactions with parents, teammates, and coaches that determine if sports help the child develop morally or immorally. Reinforcement principles[1] and modeling can be used by coaches to make sport an experience that enhances moral development.

REINFORCING MORAL BEHAVIOR

Through popular psychology it is easy to obtain the impression that the application of reinforcement principles in modifying behavior is straightforward. We simply reward moral behavior and punish immoral behavior. But the use of reinforcement principles with humans is not as easy as Skinnerians have led us to believe because people are not pigeons or rats (at least not most of them)!

Seven-year-old Billy, a goalie with the Buffalo Bombers of the midget hockey league, becomes entangled with teammates and opponents in a skirmish around his net. Billy is hit and dazed, but is uncertain by whom or what. Billy retaliates by punching out the nearest opponent. The referee throws Billy out of the game and his coach punishes him by sitting him out of the next game. As a result Billy may hesitate to hit an opponent again in a similar situation to avoid punishment, but he may not understand why he should not. If, on the other hand, the coach explains that it is wrong to hurt people, Billy may also hesitate to punch other children when he is off the ice.

The point in this example is that the things coaches say to a child are of particular importance to the internalization of moral standards because they help form thoughts that the child associates

---

[1] See the article by Rushall on pages 63-72. —Ed.

with rewards and punishments. When a coach tells a child why he is being punished, he may provide the child with a general rule that helps him control his own behavior in a variety of situations.

UNDERSTANDING THE GOLDEN RULE

In the hockey game Billy retaliated because he was hurt. He was unconcerned whether the other players intended to hurt him or if the hurt was accidental. Children younger than seven or eight years of age seldom show concern for the intent of the act. With cognitive development, occuring in part from maturation but more through learning experiences, the child becomes aware of other persons' intentions by developing the ability to place himself into the role of the other person. Role-taking, which normally develops in the 8-12 year age span, is an essential skill for the development of morality. The Golden Rule, "do unto other as you would have them do unto you," has no significance for the child unless he can take the role of others.

Youth sports provide valuable opportunities to develop the role-taking ability. Sport is a social situation and the role-taking ability can only develop in a social context. Coaches, parents, and other involved adults have unique opportunities through sport to develop children's role-taking capacity. In brief, through sport the coach with empathy strives to teach his players empathy.

UNDERMINING MORAL DEVELOPMENT

Another hazard in the use of rewards and punishments is that extrinsic rewards may undermine the development of intrinsic motives. Too often in youth sports the child's intrinsic interest in the sport is decreased by inducing him to engage in the sport as an explicit means to some extrinsic goal, such as a trophy, a trip or a state championship. When these extrinsic rewards for playing are removed the child may lose all intrinsic motivation to participate in the sport.

PSYCHOLOGICAL PUNISHMENT

Parents inevitably must decide how they will punish their children. Among the most significant findings in the child development field is the discovery that children punished psychologically, using love-withdrawl or approval-withdrawl and reasoning, develop stronger consciences and are more susceptible to guilt feelings than children punished physically. Children disciplined mostly by corporal punishment tend to display substantially more overt hostility.

Subsequent research has shown that love-withdrawl is not as critical a factor in shaping the conscience as the reasoning given to the child for the withdrawl of love. As we observed before, reasoning with a child encourages him to take the role of others and it helps the child internalize moral standards by providing him with thoughts that he associates with rewards and punishments. What is important in the moral development of the child is that he have experience with moral judgments more advanced than his own, but not so advanced that he cannot understand them.

A coach's threat to use psychological punishment obviously will not be overly upsetting to a child who has no love for his coach. Approval becomes an effective reinforcer only when the child is concerned with what the coach thinks; the child must have respect for his coach.

PYGMALION AND SPORT

My final observation about the use of rewards and punishments for moral development concerns the powerful effects that expectations can have on the behavior of young people. Popularized recently as the Pygmalion effect, but more aptly described as the self-fulfilling prophecy, social psychological research has shown that kids sometimes become what we prophesy for them. If a coach has the expectation that a child will not be a good athlete or that he is immoral (and irrevocably so), the child may sense his coach's expectation and act to fulfill it.

A coach's expectations may influence the child's learning of skills and moral standards through one of more of four factors. The coach may create a warmer social-emotional mood around his "special" athletes; he may give more feedback to these athletes about their performance and behavior; he may teach more material to these athletes; and he may give his special athletes more opportunities to participate and question events.

I suspect as kids we all have been in situations where we sensed that others felt we were inferior. Kids with self-confidence usually confront such expectations as a challenge to be proven wrong. Kids lacking self-confidence, however, may simply accept their lot and behave to fulfill their coach's negative expectations. The process, of course, may function in reverse. Coaches' positive expectations may help motivate kids to achieve what they otherwise thought could not be attained. What coaches must remember is that expectations can reinforce both positive and negative behavior and that these expectations are communicated not only knowingly but often unknowingly.

MODELING

Kids learn moral behavior not only by being rewarded and punished, but by observing other people behave morally and immorally. Learning by observing is pervasive in children. They imitate mom and dad in their games, mimic their siblings and peers in play, and model themselves after their sport heroes. But kids do not instinctively imitate everyone in their environment. Children are likely to imitate those who command resources or have access to desirable goals. The coach who controls the child's participation in sports and games often commands an important resource or goal for the child.[2] Thus it is no surprise that kids often imitate their coach.

Kids may not only imitate specific behaviors of their coach, but may strive to become exactly like him. Known as *identification*, this complete imitation of an emulated person has a profound influence on the development of the child's self-concept. To the extent the child perceives that his attributes match those with whom he identifies and that the culture regards these as good, he develops a positive self-concept.

[2] See the article by Zaremski on pages 235-246 and the article by Corran on pages 129-132. —Ed.

SUPERFICIALITY

Children show less development of strong moral standards when they grow up with adults who reinforce only the surface appearance of their behavior. Adults who serve as models for kids can create, by overly assertive and domineering behavior, the attitude that an immoral act is only immoral when it is detected and punished. Coaches in particular may easily give the impression that cheating is not really wrong unless it is detected, and then only to the extent that it hurts the chances of winning. When coaches promote immoral behavior to attain victory, youngsters may conclude that "the-end-justifies-the-means" attitude is a proper code of morality.

HYPOCRISY

One of the difficulties in working with kids is that we want them to be better than we are ourselves. Too often we preach one thing and practice something else; or one day we do one thing and the next day we do the opposite; or one parent says one thing and the other does the opposite.

These inconsistencies must be resolved by the child if he is to form a stable conscience. Does he do as we say, or as we do? Does our preaching or our practice have a greater influence on our children's moral behavior? Recent evidence showed, for example, that when generosity was modeled by adults, kids increased their own generosity, but exhortations to be generous did not prompt increased generosity. More important, hypocrisy did not affect the children's generosity; that is, kids were as generous when observing a generous model who preached avarice or stinginess as those who practiced and preached generosity. Actions speak louder than words. If we want our kids to mature morally, then bellwethers of sport must be paragons of virtue.

PUTTING IT INTO PERSPECTIVE

Although brief and oversimplified, I have discussed a few social learning principles that may help the young athlete enjoy and benefit from his experience in sports. But implementing these principles, as well as knowledge from other sport sciences, into positive coaching behaviors is impeded because of (*a*) the lack of an effective delivery system for communicating what is known to adults working with young athletes; and (*b*) inadequate means for motivating these adults to use this knowledge when coaching. The latter problem is particularly vexing. So often we know what is right for our kids, but we do something less than what is best. We know that screaming derogatory remarks at a child when he makes a mistake does not help him, but in the midst of the contest we sometimes forget. We repress the child's needs for ours. We lose our perspective. But these problems are surmountable—we can develop an effective delivery system and we can help coaches maintain their perspective.

Let's consider next some facets of youth sports that the critics say are not in perspective.

COMPETITIVE STRESS

Undeniably there is at times an over-emphasis on winning in youth sports, but no one knows for certain the magnitude of the problem. Among the major criticisms of the winning-is-everything philosophy is that it places too much stress on kids. Critics impute that the resultant fear of failure leads to competitive stress equivalent in some cases to the stress manifested by soldiers in combat. When the fear of failure outweighs the fear of detection, immoral behavior, such as cheating, is more likely to occur unless the child has a well-developed conscience. Consequently it would be helpful to know precisely how much stress kids can handle for each of the three phases of moral development.

To understand the proper dosage of competitive stress we need to examine the complexities of competitive stress. First we must consider whether the stress to excel in youth sports is unilaterally detrimental or whether there are occasions when this stress may be beneficial.[3] Some experts tell us that we should eliminate all sources of stress for our children or at least keep them to a minimum; kids will have enough stress in adult life and they do not need to be burdened with it as a child. These same experts tell us that youth sports are entirely too stressful; they should be eliminated and children should be encouraged to participate only in unstructured play.

Other experts believe kids must learn the harsh realities of the world and coping with stress is one of these realities. Learning the hard knocks of life as a youngster will prepare the child better for a successful adult life. These experts usually promote "miniaturized" big league sports programs; they encourage extremely competitive, highly organized programs because they build character.

Stress research and common sense suggest a position between these extremes. We can, no doubt, overstress our kids: we can burn them out, damage their self-concept, and retard their moral development. On the other hand, kids raised in sterile environments who have little opportunity to learn to cope with stress have significantly greater problems in adjusting to adult life. Children need opportunities to learn to cope with increasing degrees of stress.

The key to whether youth sports are opportunities for learning to cope or jungles where a high degree of coping is essential to survive is dependent upon the objectives emphasized by parents, coaches, and sport organizers. When the predominant emphasis is toward the child's physical and psychological development and not just on winning, the chances increase that competitive stress will be in perspective.

MORE ON WINNING

To discuss the issue of winning further we need to consider what the objectives are of youth sports in our society. Minimally we want youth sports to be fun without having negative consequences on the child's development. Optimally they are to be fun while contributing to the physical, psychological, and social development of the child. Most adults involved in youth sports will tell you that winning is not the important goal, but their behavior sometimes defies their words.

Critics of youth sports are the first to point out that all too often these developmental objectives conflict with adults' desire to win. Competing to win, however, is not necessarily a negative goal; striving to achieve can foster personal growth. In fact it may be that moral development is nurtured more when moral decisions come into conflict with winning. Walter Kroll, in an impressive paper on sportsmanship, made this point vividly. He writes:

> *Perhaps we need to inspect the notion that noteworthy acts of sportsmanship seem always to involve sacrifices of success strategy in favor of a decision guided by moral criteria.*

[3] See the article by Oxendine on pages 103-111, the article by Harris on pages 112-118, and the article by Bramwell et al. on pages 119-123. —Ed.

Success is not easily relinquished when it is so highly esteemed, but the conduct pre-scribed by a code of moral behavior can—and often does—compel the individual to forego the rewards of success. . . . Unless winning is important, putting success in jeopardy in favor of conduct compatible with a moral code fails to qualify as a noteworthy event. Such a proposition really needs to be considered by those harsh and outspoken critics of athletics who lambast the emphasis upon winning, who urge that cooperation replace competition.

Competition as a process of striving for a valued goal is unjustifiably maligned by critics intending to say something else. Competition is not a den of iniquity nor is cooperation utopia. Competition and cooperation are not antithetical, but complementary. What the critics intend to say when they attack competition and extoll the virtues of cooperation is that winning is over-emphasized and the cooperative emphasis will bring winning back into balance.

The crux of the problem then is knowing when winning is over-emphasized.[4] Actually it is not as difficult as it may appear to detect the win-at-all cost philosophy. We can with some accuracy infer coaches' motives by observing their behaviors. When coaches play injured youngsters, when they leave players sitting on the bench the entire season, and when they routinize practice so that it becomes a complete bore, over-emphasis is indicated. When in the frantic race to be first the develop-mental objectives blur into the background, winning is out-of-bounds.

CONCLUSION

Youth sports are not inherently evil nor are they inherently good—they are what we make them. Youth sports are more likely to build character when coaches with character have some knowledge of social learning principles and apply them. A coach cannot permit himself to repress his players' needs in order to satisfy his own need to win. A moderate degree of competitive stress, created by an environment where winning is prized and losing is not scorned, is more likely to be helpful than harmful in the moral development of the child.

To enhance the probability that youth sport participation will help the psychological and social development of our children they need an environment that is warm and friendly, where adult be-havior is firm but consistent, and where opportunities are ample to make decisions within their cog-nitive capacity. How the environment we create can influence our kids is succinctly expressed in these words:

If a child lives with criticism, he learns to condemn. If a child lives with hostility, he learns to fight. If a child lives with fear, he learns to be apprehensive. If a child lives with encouragement, he learns to be confident. If a child lives with praise, he learns to be appreciative. If a child lives with approval, he learns to like himself. If a child lives with recognition, he learns to have a goal. If a child lives with honesty, he learns trust.

[4] See the article by Zaremski on pages 238-246. —Ed.

THE PERSONAL VIEW

Part Two

Olympics—The Personal View **179**
  — *Phil Gunby*
After the Golden Moment **202**
  — *William Johnson*
What Makes a Champion? **212**
  — *Lones W. Wigger, Jr.*
    Hershel L. Anderson
    James P. Whitaker
    Bonnie D. Harmon

THE PERSONAL
VIEW

Part II offers some personal orientations to sports, viewed as athletes experience them. For the first article, Phil Gunby set about asking "How do you win in Olympic competition?" and sought out former Olympians such as Dr. Benjamin Spock and Capt. Micki King. This article also gives a sports physiologist's view on how much further future athletes can stretch human endurance for new world records, and it reports medical-psychological concerns that Olympians present to team psysicians.

For the second article, William Johnson interviewed Olympic medalists to find out the impact of their peak experiences on their later lives. The interviews give a flavor of the motives, personality styles, personal stresses, and ideologies that shaped their Olympic experiences, and they convey a unique sense of the personal meaning of athletics and the "golden moment" that separates one champion from another.

The series of articles that ends Part II represents personal replies to the U.S. Army Marksmanship Unit's request for an answer to the question "What makes a champion?" The respondents are all proven world-class champions with outstanding and continuing records. Maj. Lones W. Wigger, Jr., who has been winning since 1964, has been a member of eight major U.S. international teams, including three Olympic teams. He earned 2 Olympic gold medals and an Olympic silver medal, has won a total of 41 international medals, and has held 14 world records in riflery. SFC Hershel L. Anderson, one of only two U.S. competitors who has qualified for every U.S. international pistol team at least once, has performed with two Olympic teams and is the holder of 12 records. Capt. James P. Whitaker has held 5 national records in skeet shooting, was a member of the 1972 Olympic team, and has been state champion of two states. Whitaker discusses mental attitude in the third article in this series. SFC Bonnie D. Harmon has been U.S. national champion and a member of the U.S. team for the Pan American games, a medalist in international competitions, and state champion of three states in pistol shooting. Harmon refers to the use of visualization for mental preparation, a technique which is discussed in detail in Part III of this book.

Olympics—The Personal View

Phil Gunby

OARSMAN No. 7 RECALLS 1924 GLORY DAYS

A self-described "miserable high-jumper" who became an oarsman on an undefeated rowing crew recalls no particular personal psychological stress at the 1924 Olympics.

The jumper-turned-rower is Benjamin Spock, MD, whose book on infant and child care has sold some 25 million copies in this country alone. He was No. 7 oar in the Yale University shell that won that event on the Seine River in Paris a half-century ago.

That trip to France was the first abroad for the future physician, author, and presidential candidate, and, in his words, "everything was exciting about it." But, in retrospect, he thinks the real competitive tension came before the Yale crew even left the United States.

"The Olympic trials were on Schuylkill River in Philadelphia. That was a wildly close race. We came down the whole 2,000-meter [slightly more than a mile] course a quarter-length behind what was called the Navy officers' crew . . . the best people from some of the previous Naval Academy crews.

"They got the jump on us, and we caught them in the last 20 strokes. It was by far the closest, most tense, and most exhausting race that I ever was in, despite the short distance."

From then on, Dr Spock says, "our coach did all the worrying for most of us."

The Yale coach, Ed Leader, had come to New Haven the year before from the University of Washington in Seattle. It was because of that cross-country move, and a Yale rowing captain named Langhorn Gibson, that third-year student Spock found himself in the Olympics.

"I was a miserable high-jumper at Andover, where I went to boarding school. I'd gotten a half-point in the Andover-Exeter track meet by tying for third place in the high-jump, clearing 5′6″. That was the only athletic skill I had. When I went to Yale as a freshman, I thought: 'I'd better capitalize on what I've got, even if it isn't much.'

"So I went out for track and got my freshman numerals by, you've guessed it, getting a half-point in the Yale-Harvard meet."

Phil Gunby. Olympics—the personal view. *Journal of the American Medical Association* 236,2 (12 July 1976): 170-184.

Then, in midwinter of that year, the Yale freshman stopped on the way to indoor track practice to watch crew members work out in rowing machines.

"I happened to be standing behind Yale's varsity crew captain, Langhorn Gibson, son of Charles Dana Gibson, the artist who made the 'Gibson girl' famous. He was surely 6′3″ or 6′4″ and had a handsome imperious face. I was impressed to even be standing next to him. Here was an important person!

"He turned slowly around and looked me up and down. Then he asked: 'What sport are you out for?' In a meek voice, I said: 'High-jumping.' If it had been appropriate, I would have added, 'sir.' 'Why don't you go out for a man's sport?' he replied.

"Instead of being insulted, I was delighted. The captain of the crew thinks I could compete for a place! That same afternoon, I went over to the crew office and signed up. The rest of my freshman year, five days a week, I was at crew practice."

At the time, Dr Spock says, "Yale had been beaten by everyone but Harvard for years" in rowing. Young Spock did indeed successfully compete for a place on a Yale crew. But it was the 'M' crew—13th and lowest—of the freshman crews.

Then, as the future pediatrician began his sophomore year, Ed Leader arrived to coach Yale's oarsmen.

In his first year, Dr Spock remembered with awe, Ed Leader "turned Yale's varsity crew from the most defeated crew in the nation to 'top of the river' as English oarsmen say."

Sophomore Spock found himself on the junior varsity, and moved up to the varsity the following year. The reasons, he says, were pretty much beyond his control.

"I was able to get on the crew because of a complete switch in styles with the arrival of Ed Leader. They had been rowing the English style. It depended on a sharp body angle forward, then a sharp body angle back. On the West Coast, as Americans interested in mechanics, crew coaches found this to be terribly wasteful of energy. There is nothing harder than to lean 'way back, then jerk yourself 'way forward again.

"In Washington State and California, they realized the important thing is the leg, which has some of the strongest of human muscles. Ed Leader taught us to get the length of stroke, not by body angle but by slide. [An oarsman's seat is on rollers.] So he and the California coach didn't use anyone who was shorter than 6′, and they preferred people who were 6′2″ [Dr Spock's height is 6′4″]. A long slide by long-legged people means more oar time in the water. It looks a bit humdrum by contrast with the English stroke, but it's more effective."

The young Yale man, who already was thinking about some kind of career that would help children, had another advantage.

"Besides my height, I'd never rowed before coming to Yale. At that time, college crews mostly were made up of people who had come from the rowing boarding schools like Groton, St Mark's, St Paul's, and Choate. They were all using the English stroke. So when Ed Leader arrived with his American stroke at the beginning of my sophomore year, there was no question that you had an advantage if you were tall and never had learned any other way to row."

As No. 7 varsity oarsman in his junior year, Benjamin Spock helped row Yale through an undefeated season and the exciting Olympic trials (followed, as a kind of dessert, by the defeat of traditional rival Harvard over a four-mile course a week later).

Because of that long-scheduled race with Harvard, they sailed for France later than the other American Olympic contenders. As Dr Spock recalls it, the Yale crew—eight oarsmen, the coxswain, four substitute oarsmen, and an extra coxswain—was quite relaxed. Coach Leader was not. Nor would he be until the Olympic gold medal was theirs.

"An individual event, such as in track and field, and a team event like rowing with eight others in a racing shell are totally different," Dr Spock points out. "It isn't even possible to compare crew rowing with a team like football. On a football team, each person does an individual job that is somewhat different from the others. In a shell, everyone except the coxswain is meant to be doing the same thing in the same tenth of a second.

"So, my answer about any strain for us at the Olympics is that, if you're a group of eight people going through exactly the same motions as you have for several years, you don't really worry. Either you've learned it or you haven't. If you've 99% mastered it, you're not likely to do any better just because you're in the Olympics."

But Ed Leader, as Dr Spock recalls, did enough worrying for everyone.

His first crisis was the first breakfast for his crew in the Olympic Village in France. Dr Spock still remembers it.

"It consisted of an orange that was no bigger around than, say, a 50¢ piece. It was just dry pith inside. There was no juice to spoon out. And there was one croissant roll and a curl of butter.

"Well, American college athletes at that time were used to starting off the day with an orange or grapefruit, dry cereal or a couple of bowls of oatmeal, fried eggs and bacon, a stack of toast, and milk. Ed Leader immediately found this Olympic Village diet totally unsuitable.

"So they moved us out of the Olympic Village to a beautiful town outside Paris [St. Germain en Lage] where we occupied a small apartment house and ate at a then very famous restaurant called 'François Premier' [King Francis I]. Incredible luxury! All this was because the Yale rowing committee contained some very wealthy men. These were the same men who had stables of racing horses. We were just another stable. Money was no object."

Dr Spock, who shared the enthusiasm for oatmeal of the great Finnish runner Paavo Nurmi, recalls that the waiter in the French restaurant was at loss how to call this dish. He finally settled for *potage.*

To honor the Fourth of July, the proprietress of the restaurant (a husky woman with a black mustache), without consulting anyone, prepared a platter of lobsters. It was another crisis for the coach.

"Ed Leader considered seafood to be extremely dangerous for us. Lobsters were totally out of the question with him. Our meals were a round of steak, roast beef, chicken, lamp chops, and back to steak. The vegetables were peas and spinach, the spinach being meant to have special invigorating qualities. We were not even allowed fried potatoes for fear they'd give us indigestion and cut our wind.

"Anyway, the sight of that huge platter of lobsters absolutely terrified Ed Leader. He roared: 'What's this!' Someone explained that madame had prepared a banquet because it was the Fourth of July. Ed yelled: 'Take 'em out!' So the whole platter of 24 lobsters went back to the kitchen. We had cold sliced beef instead."

With reluctance, the coach consented to let the crew take a break and attend that famous and stylish horse race, the Grand Prix. Even then, Dr Spock says, "he was anxious that something might happen to us. He warned us: 'Don't sit on any stone walls. You'll get piles.' "

The Yale crew won its preliminary race. But in the other preliminary event, one shell fouled (locked oars with) another. Ed Leader apparently spent the night worrying that this might happen to his crew in the final event.

"When the lanes were drawn," Dr Spock says, "it turned out that an English crew would be next to us and would be the one—if there was to be any fouling—to foul us. As we put our shell into the water, our coach went over to the English coxswain. Towering over him, he bellowed: 'You stay in your lane! Do you hear? Don't you foul us!' The coxswain looked absolutely bewildered, and we looked away in shame."

The Yale crew won by several lengths.

The No. 7 oarsman rowed again in his senior year, when Yale's varsity again was unbeaten. Then he went on to two years of medical school at Yale, the final two at Columbia, internship, residency, practice, in New York City, and posts at Mayo Clinic, the University of Pittsburgh, and Case Western Reserve University, Cleveland.

He never again was involved in rowing, even as a spectator, although the youngest of his two sons (finishing his senior year of high school at Westminster in England) did row in the Henley Regatta. Nor has he followed the Olympics.

"It seems rather pathetic to try to keep this kind of glory alive," he suggests. "It's marvelous to be on an Olympic crew, and it was marvelous in those days to beat Harvard. But you have to go out the first day of college in the fall and work all year long at it. You're barked at by the coach, telling you the same thing for four years because each of you has his own special faults. And even with all the coaching and scolding, you never completely get rid of them. So it's four years of being scolded for the same thing."

Even so, Ed Leader didn't completely corner the market on concern in Paris a half-century ago, Dr Spock concedes.

"Our stroke oar, who always gave the impression of being quite bored with life, didn't sleep a wink the night before the Olympic gold medal race.

"So, after winning, we rowed past the grandstand, as was traditional, to receive the applause. Then we were supposed to row away. But our stroke was so exhausted from going without sleep and the exertion of the race that he collapsed. So we just sat there. Without him, we couldn't get going.

"The spectators politely continued to applaud. We were much relieved when the stroke finally revived and we could row away. We were afraid we were going to wear them out. It began to look as if they might have to applaud forever."

DIVER MICKI KING SEEKS "A SORT OF CALM"

Things were looking good for Micki King in the 1968 Olympics. With only two dives remaining, the recent University of Michigan graduate led in the finals of the three-meter diving competition.

Then, on her next-to-last dive, she hit the diving board on the way down.

She didn't know it then, but she had fractured the left ulna. All that she knew as she climbed from the pool was that she was in great pain, feeling faint, and had seven minutes until she must dive again.

Trainers placed ice on the forearm and gave her smelling salts. Recalling those tense seven minutes today, she says: "None of my responses to the trainers indicated the arm was broken. But even if I had known for sure, if I had seen x-rays, I doubt I would have done much different. Perhaps if we had taped the arm . . . hindsight is always 20-20, you know . . . I might have gotten a medal, maybe a third place.

"In any case, I surely wouldn't have withdrawn from the competition. One of the doctors said later: 'If I had known it was broken, I wouldn't have let you dive.' My reaction was: 'Hey, that wasn't your decision. I didn't train for eight years to drop out in the last round.'"

Despite the pain and shock, she completed her tenth dive, finishing fourth. No medal.

Gazing out at the Rampart Range of the Rocky Mountains from her office at the Air Force Academy, Capt Maxine J. (Micki, of course, is a nickname) King, BS, brings those days back to mind. "When I was flying home from Mexico City after the 1968 games, I thought to myself: 'This is my first and last Olympics. There is no way I can ever reach that peak again. I was red hot, the greatest I could ever be, and a freak accident took it away from me.'"

Her immediate reaction was anger.

"Watching my teammate receive the medal, my emotion was not sadness or feeling sorry for myself—which I've felt since, although not now—but of being so put out. I wasn't angry with her because she won but at me for blowing that dive. Diving isn't like football, where a teammate might throw me a bad pass, so I couldn't make a touchdown. When you're in an individual sport, you haven't anyone to blame but Number One."

But two things happened between that long flight home and the 1972 Olympics in Munich.

First, her concern about the five-month layoff (while her arm healed) proved to be unwarranted. "I was amazed how easy it was for me to come back. In the past, I had been off for a couple of weeks on occasion and, when I resumed diving, felt as if I was starting over. Here, it was five months. I thought everything would be rusty. If it was going to be too hard for me to get back in shape, I wondered if I was willing to pay the price. But everything came back so easily that I decided: Hey, this is the way it was meant to be!"

Second, a "little older and lot more experienced" Micki King began to realize that "I didn't need to work out my body as much as my head."

She sought the pattern of consistent successful performance. "One meet, I'd miss the swan dive. The next meet, I'd hit the swan dive for eight [out of a possible ten points]. So I asked myself: What is the pattern? Why these inconsistencies? How can I be sure to hit it every time? I put together certain things that I did before successful dives."

Today, Capt King says, "I know there is a moment when 'all systems are go.' I can feel it. Standing there, thinking over my dive, I feel my legs tingle. I take a deep breath. All that tingling goes away and a sort of calm comes over me. When that calm reaches me, I'm ready to go and I'm not going to miss."

This critical peak moment has to be re-established for each dive, she has found. "Diving is not like sports where you go all-out for a short time or pace yourself for a long time. You have to re-establish that peak when the adrenalin is shooting through you. Then, in a tenth of a second, it's over. For my next dive, I have to feel it again, to do it all over again."

She also has learned to pace herself, "to reach the peak when it's my turn to dive, not the turn of the diver before me or the diver after me."

At the 1972 Olympics, she was ready. She had put Mexico City behind her. ("I don't remember even thinking about what happened there. I was a whole new person.") She had the technique and timing for "pumping up to a peak" at exactly the right moment. ("You want to go. You really want to go. Waiting is hard. You've got to kill that waiting time between dives. People still joke with me about my twitching, tugging at my suit, wiping my hands in my hair, all the nervous-looking gestures that I used to kill time between my dives in Munich because I was not ready. I had control, and I wasn't going off that board before the moment, before the calm came over me and my adrenalin reached its peak. Otherwise, I'd be fighting it, contrary to it.")

Micki King, the only returning U.S. diver from the 1968 games, won the Olympic gold medal in 1972.

Further, her final and winning dive from the 3-meter springboard was a reverse one-and-a-half somersault with one-and-a-half twists. This was the dive that she attempted with a broken arm four years earlier.

The conscious channeling of energy that made her an Olympic champion does not suggest a lack of nervousness, Capt King feels. "Any nervousness I feel, though, is a positive nervousness. If I don't have it, I worry. When I do have it, it filters through my whole body and gives me strength. It takes me about four divers' performances to get ready. If I'm the ninth diver, I start to prepare myself about the time that the fifth diver is up there."

As diving coach at the Air Force Academy in Colorado Springs, Capt King is experiencing additional benefits from what she learned. "I find the most rewarding, self-satisfying part of my coaching today is to be able to see some of my knowledge work on somebody else, and to see them progress. I've had some divers who are very nervous. This thing about taking that deep breath and waiting for the moment to come really seems to help them. When they realize that there can be a moment of calm, they say: 'Hey, that's just what she showed me!' "

In the discipline of the academy, where Capt King has served since March 1973, cadets respond to her with a "yes, ma'am" or "no, ma'am." But it also is clear that they respond to her coaching. Her diving team calls itself "all the King's Men."

She is with them every afternoon, encouraging, demanding, counseling the young athletes from poolside with a loudspeaker system. From time to time, she takes to the board to demonstrate.

"I've been working out regularly for more than 18 years," Capt King says, in explaining the discipline that she demands. "Since I went to the University of Michigan in 1962, until my diving in Munich in 1972, I worked out at least six days a week. If I missed a workout, I felt it might mess up my chances in the next national competition. I try to instill that in my team. If I even go in a little bit late to team practice, I go in irritated, because I want to set an example of dedication. If I don't demonstrate it, too, I lose credibility."

As the first woman to teach physical education at this heretofore all-male institution (women cadets will be admitted for the first time this summer) and the first woman ever to coach at a service academy, she says: "Diving was my life. Now I have my job, my team, other things. I'm lucky to have coaching to make this transition. The best divers don't always make the best coaches, but I've had pretty good success."

Besides natural ability, hard work, and self-discipline, Capt King's career has demanded a certain amount of suffering. "I wouldn't call myself injury-prone, but I've had my share of injuries. When my foot gave 'way during a practice bounce on the springboard, it took 36 stitches to close the wound. I dived in the National Amateur Athletic Union (AAU) finals four weeks later and won [one of ten AAU titles that she earned]. And I've had broken eardrums."

Hitting the springboard on a dive is not that uncommon, she says. "It's not an everyday thing. But if it happens, it's not a big deal. I've hit my knuckles and my heels. But the Mexico City dive was a severe hit."

Recalling that ill-fated dive, she says: "Divers are phenomenal. We often talk about what goes through your mind in a split-second, the things you analyze. In literally a tenth of a second on that dive, I realized I was too far back on the board, I was going to have to turn my somersault over slower, I was going to have to come out earlier, and I was going to have to stretch sooner if I was going to save it. Because I stretched sooner, I was two feet longer . . . with my arms over my head . . . as I came down past the board. Even hitting the board as I did, I got 6½s and 7s from the judges on that dive. If I hadn't extended my arms to accommodate for the poor takeoff, I would have gotten 4s and 5s."

Now a professional diver, Capt King competes in challenge events and "superstar" contests in which female professional athletes attempt events other than their specialty. (She finished third in a field of 24 women in 1975, placing in all seven events and winning the 50-meter swim and 440-yard run.)

She is chairman of the Athletes' Advisory Council, a branch of the United States Olympic Committee. The parent committee didn't heed its newly created council at first, she concedes, "but we had no intention of existing in name only. We decided that we had been given a voice and we were going to talk. They decided it would be to their best interest to listen, and they have done quite a bit of changing to accommodate our suggestions. Unfortunately, we won't see these improvements by this year's Olympics.[1] But we're looking at the big picture and think it's encouraging."

Capt King also is one of seven athletes on the U.S. Olympic Committee's Board of Directors, and is a member of the President's Commission to Study Olympic Sports, the final report of which is due this summer.

"I'm over my head in causes," the attractive 170-cm Michigan native says. "I've had very little time to myself and with my family in Pontiac and boy friend. One cause I've ignored is the Micki King cause."

In addition to her cadet team, Capt King is coaching three Air Force officers for the forthcoming Olympic diving competition.

"We hope to be very successful," she says. "Then maybe I can sit back a little bit and be a spectator sometimes."

"FASTER, HIGHER, STRONGER"—MORE THAN A MOTTO

Picture an International Olympic Committee, far in the future, facing this situation.

The ultimate performance has been achieved in many Olympic events. Several competitors in each event are capable of achieving that ultimate performance. Instead of a single gold medalist, there are likely to be two, three, four, or more athletes tied for first place in many events.

Is this situation possible, far ahead?

"If you want to get into fantasy and speculation about the future," says Albert B. Craig, MD (who obviously does not), "it might be something like that."

At the moment, says Dr Craig, who is professor of physiology at the University of Rochester School of Medicine and Dentistry, "when you come to the Olympics, the purpose is to be world champion. Although world records may be established, performing in record time [in racing events] is secondary. Beating everyone else is the primary thing. You do what you have to in order to win, and forget the time."

How about Mark Spitz' breaking four of his own world's records during the 1972 Olympics?

Dr Craig has a theory. "I still think that when you're up on that Olympic starting block, you're not thinking 'am I going to establish a world's record?' but 'am I going to beat my competition?' It

[1]1976. —Ed.

may be necessary to establish a world's record to beat them, but I think the goal still is to beat the other people. In swimming, you usually can't see where the other competitors are. I think Mark Spitz knew the quality of the competition, couldn't see where they were, so went all-out to be sure he'd win."

As a physiologist, Dr Craig says, "I find world's athletic records to be very interesting data. They are very precisely measured." He became interested in the 1968 Olympic Games in Mexico City particularly because of the higher altitude (2,200 meters) at which they were conducted, and later studied performances in some events of the 1972 Olympics as well. However, he adds, "to do it again this year, I would have to determine a physiologic reason. I won't do it just to extend my series."

Since he does not actually go to the games, he characterizes himself as "an armchair observer," adding: "I probably can see more from my television set anyway."

As part of his 1968 study, he looked at Olympic track and swimming records back to 1900, concluding (*JAMA* 205 [1968]:740): "The most dramatic improvements (55%) have been made in the throwing events, which include shot put, hammer throw, discus, and javelin. Swimming times have decreased 24%, and field events characterized by jumping (high, long, and triple jumps) have improved about as much as long-distance running (12%). Sprinting times have decreased the least, 7%.

"Olympic performance has averaged 3% less than the listed world marks, despite the observation that 44% of those who have won gold medals held the world record at some time during their careers. Theoretical considerations indicate that involvement of more people in the sport will result in improvement of world records. Prediction of ultimate records is impossible from the information which exists at present."

However, in the same *JAMA* report, he ventured: "If in the next 50 years a much larger part of the world population is involved in competitive athletics, records will continue to improve at a very fast rate indeed. After this goal has been reached, patterns indicating the approach to the ultimate record might be discernible. The latter status might be reached by the year 3000."

In his apparatus-filled office in the old Strong Memorial Hospital building at the medical school, he enlarged a bit: "Every [speed] record has a finite point, just by definition of measuring velocity and speed. You don't get into negative speeds. No one is ever going to run 100 yards in one second. For every human activity like this, there is a finite number. What it is going to be is the question.

"The principle in physiology about such things is that you look at them as a function of time. When things increase or decrease, they do so exponentially. In other words, change is most rapid at the beginning, then by smaller and smaller increments until the ultimate is reached.

"Now, let's look at this in terms of a world's athletic record. There is an ultimate value. The way to predict that ultimate is to graph the increments of change against time. When you have enough of the curve for an equation, it is possible to extrapolate the data to a finite number."

He emphasizes, that there are insufficient data at this time to make even an educated guess about the ultimate performance in most racing events. "You have to have enough data before you can extrapolate."

As for the possibility of more than a millennium passing before some trends are discernible: "Of course that is not a statement that you can back up with hard data. It is just a feeling that I get from looking at this."

A possible exception, he suggests, is the 100-meter dash. "That is changing very little now. In this event, we've got to do what we're doing in swimming now—keep track of it in hundredths of a second instead of tenths of a second. To tie the record [set by Jim Hines of the United States at the

1968 Olympics] in the 100-meter dash, you have to run it in 9.9 seconds. At present, you would have to run a tenth of a second faster to beat it. That is slightly more than 1% faster, and in world's athletic records, that is a big break-through. Usually, world's records are broken in terms of a half-percent at most."

In the 1972 Olympics, he points out, the average winning times in swimming—men and women—improved the world records by slightly more than half a percentage point (0.55%), largely because of the performances of Mark Spitz and Shane Gould.

The swimming events were held before the terrorist killings at the Olympics in Munich. Some suggested there might have been a psychological effect on participants in the men's track events, which were held afterward. But Dr Craig notes that while men's track performances have improved steadily in this century, the Olympic times have rarely been world records. This pattern held in the 1972 Olympics.

One of the most remarkable track and field achievements in Munich, Dr Craig says, was that of Bernd Kanenberg winning the 50,000-meter walk in less than four hours—3:56:11.6. The West German's world record breaks the previous one by 3.33%, although Dr Craig notes that some allowance may have to be made for the differences in course from Olympiad to Olympiad.

Other outstanding improvements in world record performance during the 1972 Olympics included Ludmilla Bragina's 4:01.4 time in the 1,500-meter run. The Soviet athlete's winning time was 2.23% faster than any recorded previously for a woman.

There were, however, no surprises in 1972 of the magnitude of the United States' Bob Beamon, who set a long jump record of 8.87 m (29 feet, 2½ inches) in 1968—6.8% better than the previous record—which some experts thought would not be achieved for another quarter-century.

A swimmer himself at Princeton, Dr Craig had Olympic ambitions but "they weren't holding the games—World War II was in progress—so that killed that." In swimming and other sports, he sees improvements in performance up and down the line as youngsters become involved at earlier and earlier ages. Thus, he views it as not just a few trailblazers setting records, but comparably better performances at all levels.

For instance, he explains, "kids obviously are starting competitive swimming at a younger age. World records in the butterfly, using the dolphin kick—quite complicated—now are being made by kids that learned it at age 6 or 7. Before, people learned the butterfly in high school. So the record in the butterfly has zoomed in the past few years. A general principle in any physiological function, say playing the piano, is that just by doing it repeatedly you will learn to do it with a maximum efficiency. 'Practice makes perfect' is the usual way of saying it. If you have to swim 5,000 yards a day, you can't stand that program unless you can do it efficiently. So therefore, a lot of 'unconscious learning' goes on in swimming these days."

Physiologists don't completely understand what makes a person move through the water, he concedes. "If you look at improvements in the world's records in swimming compared with track, swimmers are improving much faster. You know that humans haven't improved their maximum aerobic and anaerobic capacity that much over the same 50 to 60 years. So the obvious implication is that the efficiency in swimming has improved."

Collaborative work with researchers at the State University of New York at Buffalo School of Medicine tends to bear this out, he says. "We find a direct and positive correlation between the maximum stroke length and the maximum velocity."

GYMNASTS MUST TUNE UP BODY AND MIND

"The night before, often weeks before, sometimes months before a competition like the Olympics, the gymnast mentally can picture both extremes—winning or crashing and burning."

Thus combining the terminology of two of his worlds, gymnastics and flying, Lt Col Karl Schwenzfeier sets the psychological stage of the individual on the apparatus.

"In most sports, you don't know what the precise game situation is going to be. In gymnastics, you know 90% of the factors. You can go through the routines in your mind months before the big meet toward which you are pushing."

When the actual moment comes, says the colonel, "as you warm up your body for your routine, you are warming up mentally. Then you are out there. It is time for you to raise your hand, signaling that you are going to begin the routine. The whole mental-psychological process is trying to reach a culmination so that, when you actually touch the apparatus, you are at the precise second ready to go."

And in the midst of the performance, he says, "if you are highly trained, mentally you can see everything that is going on, down to extremely small details. As you reach higher and higher pressure levels, the top athletes are able to respond very quickly mentally and physically. Gymnastics is an extremely rapid sport at times, when you must react immediately, probably in millionths of a second. You must have mental control."

Lt Col Schwenzfeier knows something about that pressure and the need to be in control psychologically. As a top gymnast with Pennsylvania State University's national championship teams, he personally won the National Collegiate Athletic Association (NCAA), Amateur Athletic Union (AAU), and Eastern all-around titles in one year (a "grand slam" yet to be repeated), was chosen for the 1956 U.S. Olympic team (only to be injured), and was an alternate on the 1960 team. He came through 622 hours of combat flying in Southeast Asia, coached the winning U.S. gymnastics team in the strife-ridden 1975 Pan American Games, and is coach of the gymnastics team in this year's Olympics. (He retired from the Air Force in June and is returning to Pennsylvania State University as gymnastics coach.)

"Gymnastics is an unusual sport," he says. "International competition requires an all-around gymnast, performing in six different events. The Olympic team is comprised of only six men, so it is extremely difficult to make the games in this sport.

"Each of the six events is designed to show a different facet of motion, testing the body in flexibility, strength, and—interestingly enough—brainpower. These involve aesthetics as well as difficult and highly technical moves. So the sport lends itself to mental activity as well as motor skills.

"The Japanese, Russians, and Europeans, who know the sport very well, consider the male who wins the gold medal in all-around individual gymnastics at the Olympic games to be probably the premier athlete there. Many Americans might consider the decathlon winner the premier athlete. But a 17-year-old has won the decathlon [Robert Mathias in 1948]. I believe, very strongly, that no 17-year-old man will ever win the individual all-around gymnastic event at the Olympics." Coach Schwenzfeier believes most male gymnasts reach their prime in the mid 20s.

Natural athletes, "those who walk into the practice room and do wonderful things the very first time, much more quickly than others," rarely reach the top gymnastic levels, he says. "Perhaps because it comes more easily to them, they often do not seem to learn the step-by-step discipline. The athlete who is not so gifted often shows greater desire, realizes what he must do, and goes through the steps of painstaking effort."

One way this discipline is manifested is in complete concentration when competing. "A loss of concentration anywhere along the way normally results in a break in the routine. The Japanese have dominated men's Olympic gymnastics since 1960. It is much too easy to write this off as a body mechanical advantage. There probably are such factors as that country pushing better athletes toward gymnastics because they can succeed there quicker than in other sports. But the Japanese people's ability to concentrate, at least what I have observed on the gymnastics floor, is also a plus.

"They are extremely happy people, a free people like us in terms of thought. But when it is time to approach the apparatus, maybe because of their Oriental background, they seem to concentrate deeply, then really lock on to what they are doing."

Such concentration is critical if the team competition is very close, he emphasizes. "Then you feel double pressure to do your routine at its utmost. Extra points are given in gymnastics for risk, originality, and virtuosity. When you consider the complexity of triple fly-aways, triple somersaults off the horizontal bar, and triple full twists in the floor exercise, these present psychological problems in themselves.

"On top of that, you may have team pressures in which you are expected to do the job for others as well as yourself. And in every meet you have crowd pressure. You are out there by yourself, the focal point of attention."

In his coaching at the Air Force Academy, for international competition (and, beginning this summer, at his alma mater, Pennsylvania State University), he considers psychological preparation vital. "I feel that, in my time as an athlete, not enough of that was done. With the U.S. team for the Pan American Games, we started months ahead of time, preparing them for the political situation that I felt we would encounter.

"Unfortunately, it did occur. The crowds in Mexico City to some extent appeared to be organized to create an impression of alliance with the Cuban athletes and non-alliance with the Americans. Although I believe the average Mexican citizen does not have that opinion, certainly the crowds were horrendous, cruel, and crude.

"Our preparation, plus the psychology of rugged individualism and competitive spirit of the American athlete, saved us. But the shock might have been too great if we hadn't prepared. Months before, we began reviewing what happened in Columbia during the previous Pan-Ams.

"Gymnastics usually is a quiet competition. Obviously, when the routine has been a beautiful one, there is applause when it is over, even an ovation at times. But crowd noise is minimized while the gymnast is performing. In Mexico, we ran into what we had prepared for psychologically—12,000 people in attendance every one of the six evenings; tremendous shouting, booing, and whistling during the routines.

"In gymnastics, the games boiled down to a dual meet between the United States and Cuba. We ended up winning. The six American men gymnasts were responsible in the team competition for 72 routines. Of those, they hit 70 without a major break. That is an extremely high output under very rough conditions."

Coach Schwenzfeier has few illusions about beating the Japanese in this year's Olympic games. But he is telling the U.S. team that "this is our time" to at least win some medals.

Men gymnasts from the United States "have not earned even a bronze medal in any event, individual or team, in the Olympics since 1932," he reminds them. "We are pointing very hard to be in the top three as a team in Montreal. We are pushing psychologically to prime our gymnasts to make a maximum, dedicated effort to be the best that the United States has been able to produce in 44 years. It is my job to represent that to them, to make it believable."

Even practice can be exciting in gymnastics, he contends. "You learn something each day. In some sports, they may not throw you the ball for a long time. In gymnastics, you have the ball all the time. We tell our gymnasts that it is a matter of their ambition, their psychological drive, whether they are going to improve and how far they go. As long as you can advance through increasingly difficult techniques and routines, this sport is rewarding—immediately, and in practice as much as in meets."

Because there will be only 12 male gymnastic teams in Montreal, Coach Schwenzfeier's first task was to qualify his U.S. team for the Olympics by scoring well in two international dual meets. (They did.) "I'll be very pleased," he remarked at the time, "once I know that I am an Olympic coach of a team that actually is going to the Olympic games."

Then, as an afterthought, he added: "In the long run, you either learn how to face up to the problems, compete, and do well, or you don't belong in the Olympic games anyway."

OLYMPICS REFLECT DIFFERENT PHILOSOPHIES

Among the psychological challenges for which American athletes should be prepared at the Olympics, suggests a three-time participant, are differing concepts of sportsmanship and the virtually inevitable political over-tones of international amateur sports competition.

"From a psychological standpoint," says former Olympian Wayne Baughman, "when you live all your life with one set of standards, then encounter a completely different set, it can really blow your psyche."

In the field of wrestling, where he is coaching the United States' freestyle team in the current Olympics, he finds it helpful that an increasing number of American wrestlers are gaining international experience before competing in the quadrennial games. Nonetheless, he notes that even when funds are raised to provide this exposure to top competition—and often different philosophies—overseas, it often is difficult for American wrestlers to take time away from their jobs and other responsibilities.

Now a major in the U.S. Air Force, coach Baughman is considered by many to be the man who has come closer than any other American to winning an Olympic medal in Greco-Roman wrestling. No American has ever earned a medal in any of the ten weight classes of this event.

As captain (for the second time) of the U.S. Olympic Greco-Roman team, he was leading in a critical final bout that would determine which wrestler received a second-place medal and who finished fifth in 1972. He lost the match and, while making no excuses, reflects on a psychological difference that may have influenced the outcome. That is, whether—when things are not going well—it is better to leave the mat and surrender points (while saving the match), or take the classic American "stand and fight" stance. He chose the latter.

Maj Baughman notes, however, that his concentration could have been better in that critical match, explaining: "Wrestling requires a high degree of concentration. In a sport where you are competing against another human who can physically and psychologically affect you, it is important to concentrate on what you are doing right now and what he is doing right now, what you have just done and what he has just done, and what you are going to do and what he is going to do. It's a strategy situation at all times—the time remaining, the score, how strong your opponent is right now, whether he is a strong starter and weak finisher, or conserving his strength for the final moments, or strong throughout the match. All these things have to be programmed in your mind, quickly computed, and an appropriate reaction brought out."

In the course of winning 14 national championships in freestyle and Greco-Roman wrestling, a gold medal in the Pan American Games, and a berth on eight World Championship and three Olympic teams, Maj Baughman was known to capitalize on his strength, technical skill, dedication to conditioning, strategic concentration, and "desire," to offset lack of quickness and a "just average" ability to maintain balance.

Some of that "desire," he concedes, stemmed from a determination to show "those who did not believe I would ever even graduate from junior high school" that he could succeed.

Ironically, the future National Collegiate Athletic Association (NCAA) champion, three-time NCAA All-America, and twice Big Eight Conference (at the University of Oklahoma) champion never intended to be a wrestler.

"I was football-oriented. The high school coach insisted that we participate in some sport all year around. When I got thrown off the basketball team for fighting, wrestling was the only other wintertime sport available at my school."

Despite the satisfaction that he has derived from it, Maj Baughman says that he does not consider wrestling an "enjoyable" sport. It is a contact, combative, individualistic competition in which the wrestler psychologically faces two opponents—the one opposite him on the mat, and himself, in terms of self-discipline.

"I've competed in a number of sports," he says, "but I think wrestling makes more demands on the total individual than the others that I've been involved in. Psychologically, it is not for everybody, even if the individual is a good athlete. There have been good, aggressive, strong, mean football players who, when put on the mat, lose their aggressiveness. I don't believe it is just because they don't have ten teammates with them. In football, they do an individual job as part of the team. There is just something in the psychology."

He admits to being "psyched out" on occasion during his competitive career. One opponent, aware that he tried to avoid meeting and talking just before a match with those he was scheduled to wrestle, made it a point to seek him out and strike up a conversation. Maj Baughman recalls with horror that this same opponent once effectively "psyched him out" (and won the match) by walking up beforehand and kissing him on the cheek!

While major injuries are rare in amateur wrestling, Maj Baughman points out that pain is a psychological tool. Inflicting temporary pain on an opponent can disrupt that opponent's concentration.

The reverse also works, as he recalls. "The first time I wrestled in international competition against the Russians, I was impressed with how little emotion they displayed. They don't seem to be that disciplined any more, perhaps evidencing a change in attitude from being more relaxed in international competition. But in those early years, they maintained a kind of poker face. When you pop a guy up 'side of the head and he doesn't even blink, it has a psychological effect—on you!"

Such minimal display of emotion, Maj Baughman says, "I quickly found to be pretty effective psychologically. As a coach, I try to teach it."

Now in his first year as head wrestling coach at the Air Force Academy, Maj Baughman has additional thoughts about psychology in wrestling, in the Olympics or anywhere else: "It is a very emotional sport. When you both step on the scales, I think in about 90% of instances your opponent looks bigger and stronger.

"So you learn not to judge by appearances. Some of the most muscular people aren't necessarily strong, and some wiry types are super-strong. You can't judge. But you always look. And that initial impression always is there.

"After several years of competition, I finally learned to exactly reverse my initial impression. If he looked super-strong, then he probably wasn't going to be. If he looked weak, I was suspicious. That can be good, because you have to fight a tendency to be overconfident when your opponent doesn't look too strong.

"There is a lot of psychology in wrestling. Some wrestlers come on very aggressively and try to impress opponents with their hostility. Others come out all meek and mild, trying to lull their opponent, then explode into action. And there are all kinds of facial expressions."

Despite the individuality of wrestling, team psychology does enter in, Maj Baughman says, drawing on his own high school and collegiate experience. "I liked the ideal of being totally responsible for my own victory or defeat, not affecting anyone else. Now, at the same time, I do think that—especially in college—I was a very loyal team man. One of my greatest satisfactions is that, during my career at the University of Oklahoma, I never lost a match that made the difference between our team's winning or losing.

"No one person ever wins or loses a meet, of course. But in the upper weight classes [he wrestled as a light heavyweight], you are always in one of the last matches. If it comes down to 'you win, we win; you lose, we lose,' the monkey is kind of on your back."

In the Olympics, Americans have fared better in the freestyle, catch-as-catch-can wrestling classes (the team that Maj Baughman is coaching this time) than in Greco-Roman competition. On that topic, he says: "These two styles of Olympic wrestling differ considerably from American collegiate wrestling. But, of the two, freestyle is more similar. It involves the entire body. Greco-Roman involves the waist up; you can't attack your opponent's legs or use your own legs in any way. When you consider that probably 95% of our collegiate freestyle wrestling holds involve the legs in some way, then Greco-Roman really limits the American wrestler."

That problem may be compounded by sambo (a Russian word translated as "defense without weapons"), a combination of judo and wrestling that is being introduced. If this form of wrestling catches on in enough countries, it may appear for the first time in the 1980 Olympics. Maj Baughman views this as an advantage for the Russians: "The Soviet Union is host for the 1980 Olympics, and the host nation has the prerogative of introducing two sports in which at least some countries are conducting tournaments and national championships. The Russians are making a concerted effort to encourage it in enough countries to justify introducing it in the 1980 Olympics. That probably would assure the Russians of another ten gold medals—eight or nine at least—because they are way ahead of any other country in sambo."

Turning to this year's Olympic games, Maj Baughman sees some other psychological distractions for his wrestlers (and other U.S. athletes). "You have to share workout facilities with teams from other countries. So you often are unable to work out at your accustomed time. Frequently, it is a different time each day, which upsets your routine. I've found that, from the psychological standpoint, this usually has more of a detrimental impact on American athletes than on those from other countries. We're a little bit spoiled, I think, because of all the advantages we have here—regular routine, ample diet, comfortable beds—things that are pretty ideal compared with other places, even the Olympic games.

"On the other hand, people from some other countries may find themselves in a better environment than they are used to. So they are going up psychologically while we have to guard against going down."

Maj Baughman has an additional voice in such things as a member of the U.S. Olympic Committee's Athletes' Advisory Council. Coaching the freestyle returns him to the kind of wrestling that he did so successfully at the University of Oklahoma. ("I didn't attempt to compete in Greco-Roman until my collegiate eligibility was over in 1963.") But he also knows the psychological challenges of coaching." As a coach, you are trying to treat everyone the same while still allowing for individual differences and the personal touch. That can be a conflict in itself."

DR LEE TYPIFIES RESPONSE TO ADVERSITY

The dean told him that he did not have a chance of finishing even his first year of medical school. The experts told him he was too old to win another gold medal in Olympic diving.

And, says Sammy Lee, MD—who earned both his medical degree and an unprecedented second Olympic gold medal—"if the Army had told me that I never could reach the rank of general, I probably would have stayed in the service to prove them wrong, too."

Psychologically, Dr Lee seems to thrive on adversity—perhaps because he has had to face so much of it.

He demands the same dedication and determination (to overcome obstacles) from all the youngsters he coaches. "If you don't have enough desire to overcome your fear, you're not on my team," he tells them.

The test usually comes when Dr Lee believes the youngster is ready and able to perform a more complicated and potentially dangerous dive than he or she has yet executed. "I never send a young diver to do anything that I wouldn't have my own son do," he emphasizes. "When I send them up there, I know they are ready and capable of doing whatever dive I'm calling for."

But if there is prolonged hesitation, Dr Lee makes his position clear. "At the end of ten minutes, if you haven't attempted the dive, I'm walking out of here. It's the last time that you'll see me as your coach."

Sometimes it comes to that. Rarely, however, are there hard feelings. He likes to tell of one young diver he encountered at a meet some time after dismissing him as a pupil. The former student had just performed very well, and Dr Lee congratulated him, adding that he was pleased to see that the young man had conquered his fear. In fact, he conceded, "your performance makes me look foolish."

"Oh no, Dr Lee," the young diver rejoined. "You aren't a fool. We respect your position. You have your standards and I didn't measure up."

Dr Lee does his coaching after office hours on Wednesdays, Saturdays, and Sundays. He usually gives this task 12 to 16 hours a week; more in an Olympic year. His practice in the Santa Ana area near Los Angeles is limited to diseases of the ear.

There is no remuneration for this. "But I feel it's my repayment for all those years that the late Jimmy Ryan coached me for no charge." Dr Lee was instrumental in having the Fred A. Cady Trophy for coaching an Olympic diving champion awarded posthumously to Mr Ryan, a former Pacific Coast diving titlist who died eight years ago. (In turn, Dr Lee received the Cady Trophy for coaching Bob Webster, who became the second American to win back-to-back Olympic gold medals in platform diving. Dr Lee still laughs when he recalls Webster's saying, after winning the second medal, that he now was too old—at 26—to try for any more Olympic titles. Dr Lee was 28 when he won his first Olympic championship!)

At the moment, the refrigerator in the Lee household comes under assault from three 16-year-olds. One is his son Sammy, "a tennis nut." The two other young men, not related, are diving hopefuls. Of one (Greg Louganis), Dr Lee unreservedly says: "I think he's going to be the greatest diver of all time." Dr Lee already has set young Mr Louganis' first major challenge: Make the Olympic team and prevent Italy's Klaus Dibiasi from winning a third straight platform diving championship. Says Dr Lee: "If anybody is going to break the record of two consecutive Olympic high diving championships, I want it to be an American."

Dr Lee was born in Fresno, Calif, Aug 1, 1920, of Korean parentage. He recalls seeing the flags for the 1932 Olympics in Los Angeles while shopping with his father, who operated a grocery. When his father explained the meaning of the event, the youngster announced that, somehow or other, in some sport, he would become an Olympic champion.

He also recalls those as the days of the so called "yellow peril," when persons of Oriental ancestry often were denied admission to many facilities. But he did get to swim in a local public pool and, while playing follow-the-leader, discovered he could do things from a diving board that other youngsters could not imitate. A black athlete, Hart Crum, became his first diving instructor.

Then, from 1938 on, young Mr Lee came under the tutelage of tough-talking Jim Ryan, who once told the great Hawaiian swimmer Duke Kahanamoku: "I'm going to make Lee the world's greatest diver, or kill him!"

Dr Lee credits Mr Ryan with bringing him "from mediocrity to the Olympic medals." Coach Ryan was a hard driver, but Dr Lee says: "He didn't have to push me. I wanted it."

Shortly before his first Olympic competition, Dr Lee met Farah Simaika, an Egyptian who narrowly missed the gold medal in a controversial judging decision of the 1928 Olympic high diving. Mr. Ryan had coached the Egyptian, who told Dr Lee: "You are the product of his frustrations. But you will be the first nonwhite diver ever to have a chance to win the gold medal. However, if you are not 15 or 20 points better than the next man—if he's white—you'll never be judged the winner."

Part of the Ryan approach to training was a one-meter springboard in his backyard over, not water, but two tons of sand. "Rain or shine, seven days a week, we would somersault into the sand. Of course we were panic-stricken. A mistake would leave you a quadriplegic. Ryan didn't want any cowards. And if you broke your neck, it was because you were stupid."

Along the way, Dr Lee developed his adrenaline theory. "When I was young, I was the greatest diver in practice. But when the competition started, I'd unleash so much adrenaline that I'd blow higher than a kite and wind up seventh or eighth. In fact, I developed a great handshake because that's the only recognition I used to get. They only gave medals for first, second, and third."

As he matured, the adrenaline helped. "It's a matter of psychology. As I got older and came to the critical meets, I might not be feeling 100% sharp, as I thought I ought to when I was younger. That no longer bothered me. I knew that, with that surge of adrenaline, I'd sharpen up. Instead of carrying me over the mark, it would carry me right up to my peak."

By this time, the young diver was in medical school, and the nation was moving into World War II. The dean was less than impressed with the new student's initial performance, however, and kindly suggested that since he had no chance of successfully completing his first year, he might wish to drop out in order not to prejudice his chances for readmission after the war.

Once again meeting a challenge head-on, young Lee decided to stick it out. Two years and nine months later he received his medical degree under the Army's Specialized Training Program.

While he was interning, the reigning national high diving champion suggested to Dr Lee that he was fortunate to have won the national diving title when he did, since he was "too muscular and lacked the gracefulness to compete with the current competitors."

That did it. Dr Lee took three days off and regained his national championship on the 10-meter tower.

The war-delayed Olympics were about to resume. Dr Lee suggested to the Army that, if he were to be stationed in California, he could train after hours and perhaps make the U.S. team. Such a suggestion from a junior officer might have resulted in his going to Alaska instead, but the Army surgeon general chanced on the scene and directed that Dr Lee be sent to his home state. He placed first from the 10-meter tower and third from the 3-meter springboard in the tryouts and went on to become the first American-born Asian to win a gold medal for the United States. He also won a bronze medal by placing third on the springboard.

"I was so nervous, I thought I was going to faint," he recalls. "I was the final diver. I knew I was leading in the ten-meter event. I was going to do the forward 3½ somersault that I put in the book back in 1939. [Up to that time, it was believed that an attempt to do this would cause a diver to lose consciousness. So Dr Lee, in a sense, advanced the cause of physiology.] I was thinking: 'You've trained for 16 years. If you blow it now, you'll be too old ever to do it again.' The year before, in the national championships, I mistook the sky for the water and pulled out of a dive too soon. In that place it would be easy to do the same thing again.

"I dove, hit the water, felt numb and then tingling and decided: 'I did a belly flop! I came thrashing out of the water to look at the scores. The first was 10—perfect! Then 9½, 9½, 9, and the British judge, who didn't like my diving, gave me a 7. It was all my imagination. I hadn't belly-flopped. I just walked on water out of that pool."

Four years later, Dr Lee says with a grin, "everyone said I was too old. Well, you know how it is when someone says you can't do something."

He again convinced the Army to station him where he could train. He went to the Olympic 10-meter diving tryouts at 3 P.M., knowing his wife already had sailed for Europe at noon. "She was ten hours at sea before she learned via ship-to-shore radio that I would be coming to Europe too."

Dr Lee won his second consecutive Olympic gold medal on his 32nd birthday in 1952. The year before, in the Pan American Games in Buenos Aires, he lost to Mexico's Joaquin Capilla when, on his final dive, "I opened up thinking I had 15 feet when actually I had 15 inches, and I belly-flopped. I wasn't going all-out on the dive and it taught me that, if you let up at any time, anyone can beat you."

A newspaper in Helsinki predicted that 'MAJ Sammy Lee will be defeated today by Joaquin Capilla." Says Dr Lee: "That was just what I needed! I showed up at that pool with the adrenaline really pumping." Leading as they went to the final dive, he did his favorite—the front 3½ somersault—everything went just right. As he went cleanly to the bottom of the pool, Dr Lee says he told himself: "Happy birthday, you so-and-so. You did it again!"

Thus he added the distinction of being the first male diver in Olympic history to win back-to-back high diving gold medals to his already long list of achievements. But, when he got out of the Army three years later, he faced another challenge before finally "breaking the color barrier" to buy a house in the area where he has practiced now for more than 20 years.

He and his Chinese-American wife still live in the area. Their other child, Pamela, 20, is a junior at the University of Southern California, where her father went to medical school.

Among Dr Lee's honors are the James E. Sullivan Award as an outstanding sportsman (he was the first nonwhite and the only male diver so far to win it), the International Swimming and Diving Hall of Fame, and appointment to the President's Council on Physical Fitness and Sports (to which he was reappointed by President Ford). He was the U.S. women's diving coach in the 1960 Olympics, coached the Korean team in 1964 and 1968, and has been an Olympic diving judge. He has toured much of the world as a sports goodwill ambassador.

If Dr Lee has his way, his students only dive "when it counts" on competition days. There is a tendency, he thinks, to worry too much about what you did right or wrong in a practice dive during a meet. As part of this psychology, he tells his students to make every dive an Olympic dive, and never to give up on a dive. He makes them practice until "no matter what kind of position they get into, it will never be foreign; they will recall once having been in that position and still salvaging the dive."

While he has never suffered a major injury, Dr Lee says he has hit the water in just about every known position, sometimes concluding: "I must be dead, it hurts so much." One time when he thought he had detached his retinas, it turned out that his upper eyelids were everted. On another occasion, he experienced hemoptysis.

These experiences remind him to encourage his young charges to have faith in their coach. "You have to have faith when you're plunging down at 35 mph and spinning, and someone orders you to arch your back and stretch for the water."

But, most of all, he tells his students: "You may never win the Olympic championship. But as long as you do the best that you possibly can do, then I'm happy."

PHYSICIAN MUST EMPATHIZE WITH ATHLETE

Winston P. Riehl, MD, a person very likely to be visited by someone under stress during the last Olympics, says most American participants seemed to handle the pressure pretty well.

"The fact that they have the capacity to handle pressure probably contributed to their getting as far as the Olympics," suggests Dr Riehl, who was chief physician for the American team.

Nonetheless, says the soft-spoken New Orleans native, "not all athletes are stoic, do-or-die types. In competition, some become more sensitive to little things that they think may affect their performance. They will come in to see a physician for seemingly trivial complaints that, at times when they are not competing, probably don't bother them at all."

Consequently, he thinks, one part of the Olympic medical support effort that perhaps could use more attention is individual counseling. "Some of the athletes just want someone to talk with."

Sometimes coaches, trainers, or teammates fill the function. But sometimes the athlete has very little time to get acquainted. While it is even less likely that he or she will have gotten to know the team physicians very well, Dr Riehl points out that "you hope to have physicians on the medical team who can relate to people and do it on fairly short acquaintance."

Further, Dr Riehl says, "the Olympic team physician has such a wide range of people to care for—athletes as young as 13 or 14 years old, who probably are in the realm of pediatrics, up to persons almost in the realm of geriatrics.

"You see, we don't just take care of the athletes. There also are coaches, officials, U.S. Olympic Committee members, and spouses.

"In essence, we take care of anyone who walks in."

Those walk-ins have totaled between 35 and 50 people a day during the 1968 and 1972 Olympics at which Dr Riehl has practiced. The International Olympic Committee provides a clinic and a medical staff to serve all participating contingents. But most large nations bring their own medical team, the size of which depends on the number of people to be served. In 1972, the United States sent three physicians, and two others were on hand in other capacities.

"No one is required to come and see us unless he or she wants to," Dr Riehl says. "We think we've had the best medical care around the Olympics. We have a lot of people from a lot of countries coming over to take advantage of our medical service."

Language has not been a barrier in such instances. "Generally speaking, English is pretty much the international language." Dr Riehl also has been pleased with the opportunity to help people from smaller national contingents which have no physicians of their own. "It's a chance to do some good."

Although the American team physicians can turn to the International Olympic Committee medical unit for unusual needs, they bring all of their own supplies (all of which are donated), "down to the last Band-Aid."

In addition, the American medical team sizes up the nearest available facilities for treating more serious problems. "Before the games, you make pretty darn sure you know what medical facilities are available, where they are, and what kind of staff they have."

Even so, people connected with the American contingent who become ill or injured are sometimes taken off in an ambulance "and we don't know where they went. We spent almost a whole day in Munich, looking for the wife of one of our administrative people because nobody knew where she had been taken."

Also, Dr Riehl notes, despite excellent facilities, some foreign hospitals do not have central admitting offices. "You have to go from ward to ward to find people."

The American physicians do no treating in such hospitals. "We could always take our people out if we didn't like what was going on. But this is very rare."

American medical teams set up practice in the facilities housing their national contingent. These, of course, vary. "In Mexico City, all the buildings were high-rises. In Munich, the buildings varied. The women were separated and even our women nurses sometimes had difficulty getting in over there."

The medical team, including two nurses, the trainers, and—in 1972—a dentist ("a couple of Russians were among those who dropped by for his services"), is available 24 hours a day. Mornings usually have been the busiest time.

One of Dr Riehl's most pleasant memories of the 1972 Olympics is the success of swimmer Steve Genter of California, who became a medalist less than a week after being hospitalized for a pneumothorax. He swam with the stitches still in his chest. (Most American swimmers prefer to be more streamlined. One item of equipment that Dr Riehl purchased abroad is a set of clippers to allow swimmers to snip off all body hair—the men sometimes even shaving their heads—to reduce friction in the water.)

One of Dr Riehl's less pleasant memories is the Rick DeMont situation. Californian DeMont, then 16, won the gold medal in the 400-meter freestyle swim, only to lose it after considerable debate among officials when urinalysis indicated a trace of ephedrine. Ephedrine is on the Olympic "forbidden" list. Swimmer DeMont is an asthmatic and long had been taking a bronchodilator mixture that includes ephedrine sulfate.

"You tell them: 'Don't take anything, anything at all. If you want any medication, come and see us first,' " Dr Riehl says. "This is what we preach. As much as we stress this, as much as we advise the athletes and coaches, people will take over-the-counter things because they don't think of them as medication. It's not something they received as a result of a doctor's writing a prescription on a piece of paper."

Some of the squads on the American Olympic team will, if they are large enough and the exposure rate to injury is high, try to have a physician on hand during the pre-Olympic training. When all the squads come into a kind of "staging area" to complete their paperwork and other details just before the games, the American medical staff gives each athlete a physical examination.

"All we're going to find at this point," Dr Riehl notes, "is some acute, relatively minor condition. If they have any major problem, it's going to show up long before they get to this level of competition."

A real problem, however, is the number of requests to involve this select group in various research projects. "These individuals are highly sought-after by every conceivable group of researchers. You have to guard against this becoming literally overpowering. You get requests for all kinds of studies, but you simply can't do it. They're under enough pressure as it is."

Some information—which Dr Riehl terms feasible and uncomplicated, such as data on biochemical functions—does result from the mandatory physical examinations, however.

Testing to determine whether certain female athletes are in fact female (as well as drug testing of all medalists and a random sampling of other participants) is done by International Olympic Committee physicians (as well as by the U.S. Olympic Committee before the athletes leave the country). "They do a good job insofar as you can police these things," says Dr Riehl, who notes that the drug tests are not only to prevent any unfair advantage but also to keep athletes from injuring themselves. He is not personally enthused about chromosome testing, emphasizing that physicians must be "extremely careful with it" because of potentially devastating psychological consequences.

While the sexual identity question has particularly potent psychological possibilities, Dr Riehl notes that psychological pressure—self-inflicted and the results of a certain amount of international psychological warfare—is always present at the games. (Sometimes, as with the tragic killings during the 1972 games, there is actual warfare. Even if there had been survivors on that occasion, Dr Riehl says, the Olympic site medical facilities are not equipped for any prolonged care of major injuries.)

In any case, there is considerable variation in reaction to the psychological stress. In his office on the edge of the Tulane University campus, where he is director of the university health service (as well as assistant professor of medicine at Tulane's medical school in another part of New Orleans), Dr Riehl finds an oft-mentioned anecdote recorded among his mementos: A female competitor finished 12th out of an Olympic field of 12. When efforts were made to console her, she chose not to look at it with disappointment: "This means I'm the 12th best in the whole world."

However the individual reacts, Dr Riehl knows that "the pressure can be very great. So it's important to have someone, perhaps in some cases the physician, with whom to relate at perhaps the most important time of their competitive lives in amateur athletics."

SKATING OR SURGERY, GOAL IS PERFECTION

When Tenley E. Albright, MD, was eight years old, her physician-father bought her first pair of ice skates. She promptly traded them in.

"They were hockey skates," she explains today with a grin. "We traded them in for figure skates."

Clearly, it was an advantageous trade. As most of the world knows, the young New Englander went on to win a host of figure skating titles and to become the first American woman to win the world amateur title and an Olympic gold medal in this event.

If father, a nonskater, was a questionable judge of ice skates in the early 1940s, he made up for it as a molder of backyard ice rinks in wintry Massachusetts. "He was wonderful," his daughter recalls. "The first couple of nights, he would get up to water the rink every couple of hours, pulling the hose back into the house so it wouldn't freeze along with the water. And he did all this in a coat thrown over his pajamas."

Fortunately for father (Hollis L. Albright, MD, a still-active surgeon), his daughter soon was practicing indoors at the Skating Club of Boston. It probably was a relief for mother, too. She was lacing and unlacing ice skates for neighborhood children; providing bathroom facilities, drinks of water, and telephone service; and trying to prevent the escape of heat from a house-turned-thoroughfare in the midst of a Boston (or, more precisely, Newton Centre) winter.

The family still is very close. Dr and Mrs Albright live across the road from "Dr Tenley" (as their office people call her to distinguish among the three surgeons in the immediate family) west of Boston. Younger brother, Nile L., a former speed skater and the third surgeon in the office, lives nearby.

(An indication of the family's closeness: Dr Nile Albright's first name is the reverse of his mother's given name, Elin. Dr Tenley Albright's daughters are Elee (5), Elin (9), and Lilla (13); the first two of course relate to the grandmother's name and the last is part of a Swedish phrase meaning "Little Friend," a term of endearment used by their great-grandmother in addressing grandmother, Elin.)

Little in Tenley's first months of skating indicated extraordinary athletic talent. Then, at age 11, she contracted poliomyelitis. Although it was nonparalytic, muscles on her right side were involved and physicians ordered prolonged bed rest.

"It was something like preparing for a skating competition," she recalls. "They told me that, on Friday, I would be asked to take a few steps. I counted the days and tried to be ready."

This experience in preparing mentally for a challenging physical task would serve her well in future figure skating. "After having polio, I really began to value skating."

In a matter of months, she won the Eastern United States Junior Ladies title, then (at 13) the U.S. Ladies Novice championship, followed a year later by the U.S. Ladies Senior medal (at 16). The following year, she claimed the triple crowns of U.S. Ladies Senior, North American, and World competition. By this time, she was attending Manter Hall School in Cambridge, Mass, and practicing on an indoor rink for up to four hours before breakfast, when she could play the music to accompany her and skate without inconveniencing others.

A considerable sacrifice for an attractive, popular young woman? The response comes in a rush: "It annoys me to death when people talk about what they gave up for sports. To begin with, they don't have to do it. It is a form of recreation. They shouldn't forget that. The other thing is, sports opens up so many opportunities. I am always surprised when people ask me how I feel about what I had to give up. Give up? My gosh! Skating has taken me around the world and opened so many advantages. I have learned things and met people I never would have known. Skating still is doing that for me."

What the successful athlete has to give up, she suggests, is inefficiency. "I think that most of us athletes feel that, if we have three hours of work, we ought to be able to do it in two, not by cutting corners, but by compressing it through efficiency and effort."

She continues to find the mental aspects of successful performance fascinating. "During the time when your concentration is most acute and you must not be disturbed by any of the things you are perceiving, you nonetheless are most aware of your timing with the music, your location in the rink, and all sorts of little things. You know that the left shoelace is tucked in a little more than usual, things like that. And later, you can recall who was sitting where in the audience. The brain is capable of handling so many inputs at once!"

As for gauging her own readiness for competition: "I always knew I was all right if I yawned. A couple of hours before going on the ice, I would really slow down. If I could drop off to sleep—it didn't matter how long—and just completely let go, then as the time to compete came, everything was sort of mobilized to release at the right moment."

In 1952, she was runner-up in women's figure skating at the Winter Olympics. During the busy 1953 year, she won or retained four titles, presented six exhibitions in Japan, traveled around the world, and entered Radcliffe College. Additional titles followed in 1954 and 1955 and then, as she prepared for the 1956 Olympics in Cortina, Italy, disaster struck. While skating backward, she noticed a photographer preparing to snap another skater. Swerving to provide him with a clear field, she hit a rut and fell, her left skate blade inflicting a severe laceration on the right leg.

Refusing to let physicians cut off her skate, she underwent treatment and returned to practice. "Athletes don't want the competition to know they are hurt. Sometimes you have to exercise mental discipline, telling yourself not to notice the pain. I knew I would finish my routine in the Olympic competition; I just didn't know how I would get off the ice afterward."

She won. And a month later, she claimed her fifth straight title in the U.S. figure skating championships, "still aware" of her wound. She bears the scar to this day.

While she concedes with a smile that the athlete sometimes thinks of the competition almost in life and death terms, Dr Albright declines to make any direct comparison with surgery. Yet she thinks some lessons learned on the ice carry over to the operating room. "Naturally, you want to do your absolute best. You should not be doing surgery or competing if you are not trying for that 100% performance. But you also can't decide: 'Well, maybe I could have done that a little bit better, so I'll start over.' You have to keep going, not dwelling on what is less than perfect, and rise to the challenge of the best total performance of which you are capable."

A firm believer that you "shouldn't beat yourself; you have to concentrate on what you are doing," Dr Albright remembers asking her father: "How did you ever dare do your first operation, to make an incision for the first time?" His reply: "By the time you have been in the operating room as a fourth assistant, then third assistant, second assistant, and finally first assistant, when you get that scalpel in your hand, you know you are ready."

By the time she was 11, she had decided to become a physician. "I didn't intend to go into surgery originally. I considered pediatrics or psychiatry. I was surprised to find that I liked surgery, and didn't even admit it to myself for a while. The first time I was in the operating room, I had to hold the retractors and couldn't even see the incision."

Medical school at Harvard brought an end to competitive skating, but she (and her daughters) go to the Skating Club of Boston as often as possible. "I still find it relaxing and, even though it hurts a little to know you can't do something as well as when you practiced it regularly, I'd love to skate for hours every day if there were time."

There may not be time for hours of daily skating in Dr Albright's life now, but she seems to be able to respond to many of the requests for her presence and services while meeting her obligations as a physician and a parent. Her honors have been many, including honorary degrees and inclusion in two figure skating halls of fame. She is active in community activities, professional organizations, on the President's Council on Physical Fitness, and with the athletes' and medical advisory committees (as well as the Executive Committee) of the U.S. Olympic Committee. Increasingly active in sports medicine, she is working with the director of the National Library of Medicine on compiling data in this area, and speaks and conducts clinics on physical fitness.

She continues to be fascinated by what can be accomplished through concentration and "really stretching yourself, trying to go all out for the maximum performance." Among athletes, she concludes, "an awful lot goes unsaid that is just understood. There is a commonality of experience. We expect more of ourselves, and we feel we should."

After the Golden Moment

William Johnson

To the world, Olympic heroes tend to endure at their moment of victory. Flushed with youth, exalted by triumph, they are crystalized in time. Perhaps that is the essence of the Olympics—a single, intense, theatrical instant shared by competitor and spectator alike. There are the gold medals—actually gilded silver—the anthems, the flags, the transcendent applause. It is so fleeting and so beautiful. But, of course, there is more. And though our memories of them may not admit it, Olympians carry no marks of identification once the victories are won, the medals given out. Nothing is predictable except that their lives are never again the same. As a group, only one thing can be said of them: their feet are made neither of gold nor of clay, but only of flesh.

PAAVO NURMI, RECLUSE

He is a legend and newspapers have his obituary on composing-room trays, waiting to be pulled out when he dies. Most have had the type set for years. But perhaps they will not know when he dies, for Paavo Nurmi is a recluse. He is 75 years old and his heart, once perhaps as steady and as strong as any on earth, is feeble. He suffered a massive coronary failure four years ago, others more recently. He cannot get about without a cane.

In Helsinki, where he lives in an apartment overlooking Sibelius Park, Nurmi is considered to be a miser, a shrewd and sour fellow who made a lot of money in real estate and with the Paavo Nurmi shop, a men's clothing store. He won nine gold medals, more than any Olympic runner in history. He also won three silver medals. He entered 12 Olympic races in 1920, 1924, and 1928.

Nurmi was born on the nails of poverty in 1897 in Turku, the old capital of Finland. His father died when he was 12 and he become an errand boy, pushing a wheelbarrow. He began running in the black-pine forests near Turku and soon became so intense about it that people avoided him; where he had been taciturn to the point of glumness, now he did nothing but talk—about nothing but running. After elementary school he became a machine-shop worker, then went into the army where he was a weapons fitter. He never stopped running, but he became more and more withdrawn. He loved classical music and attended concerts frequently, but always alone. He was married for a year,

William Johnson. After the golden moment. *Sports Illustrated* 37 (17 July 1972):28-41.

then divorced. Neither he nor his wife remarried. He has one son, Matti, whom until recently he rarely saw.

Perhaps because of his early deprivations, Paavo Nurmi was known as a pothunter. It was once said, "Nurmi has the lowest heartbeat and the highest asking price of any athlete in the world." Nonetheless, he has always been a hero in Finland, a man whose fame put his country on the map of the world. A statue of him was sculpted in 1925. It now stands outside Helsinki Stadium, and recently an old friend, discussing the life of Nurmi, shook his head and said, "Think, for years Nurmi has had to look at his own statue. What would that do to a man?"

In 1952, when the Olympic Games were held in Helsinki, Paavo Nurmi astonished everyone by appearing suddenly at the opening ceremonies to run the final lap with the Olympic torch. He had trained hard for that role and his celebrated stride was unmistakable to the crowd. When he came into view, waves of sound began to build throughout the stadium, rising to a roar, then to a thunder. When the national teams, assembled in formation on the infield, saw the flowing figure of Nurmi, they broke ranks like excited schoolchildren, dashing toward the edge of the track.

A few years ago, after his first severe heart attack, Paavo Nurmi arranged to leave his estate (valued at about $240,000) to a foundation that supports heart research. When he announced the bequest, Nurmi agreed to hold a brief conversation with reporters. One asked, "When you ran Finland onto the map of the world, did you feel you were doing it to bring fame to a nation unknown by others?"

"No," said Nurmi, "I ran for myself, not for Finland."

"Not even in the Olympics?"

"Not even then. Above all, not then. At the Olympics, Paavo Nurmi mattered more than ever."

ELEANOR HOLM, EX-DECORATOR

She is 58, saucy as ever, with that stunning, fresh, *huge* smile which captivated the world in 1936 after she was canned from the U.S. Olympic team for drinking and staying up late during the voyage to Europe. "I was drinking *champagne!*" she said. "If it had been whiskey or *gin,* well, all right."

She now lives in a penthouse apartment in a Miami Beach condominium loaded with pink French provincial furniture, carved wooden chests, bureaus and tables, and Oriental lamps. On her walls are two Dalis and a Renoir. Much of this came from her second husband, the late Billy Rose, after they were divorced in 1954.

Eleanor Holm first went to the Olympics at Amsterdam in 1928. She was 14. Her father was a New York City fire captain. She won no medals, but in Los Angeles in 1932 she won a gold in the 100-meter backstroke and she doubtlessly would have won another in Berlin if she had been allowed to compete.

"The afternoon before I was kicked off the team I won a couple of hundred dollars playing craps with the reporters in the first-class cabins," she recalled. "I didn't give it back either, and I'm sure this didn't sit too well with the officials. Of course, *they* were all in first-class cabins and they didn't like my being there. I *tried* to buy my own ticket to go first class, but they wouldn't let me. I was an *athlete!* To them athletes were *cattle* and they had to be fenced off. So they put us down in *steerage,* four to a room, way down in the *bottom* of the boat! God, everything smelled like liniment. *Yukkk!*"

Eleanor Holm speaks almost exclusively in italics and exclamation points, always with gestures and usually wielding a lighted cigarette to lend further emphasis to her remarks. "Well, it was such a *mess!* I was no baby. . . . Hell, I was married to Art Jarrett and he was the star at the Cocoanut Grove and I had been singing for his band before the '36 Games. I'd been working in *night*clubs when I made the team.

"I guess it was the second night out of New York and I was sitting around with the newspaper boys when this chaperone came up and told me it was time to go to *bed*. God, it was about nine o'clock, so I said to her, 'Oh, is it really bedtime? Did *you* make the Olympic team or did I?' I had had a few glasses of champagne. So she went to Brundage and they got together and told me I was fired. I was *heart*broken!"

Well, not *perma*nently heartbroken. In Berlin, Eleanor was the belle of the Games. "I had such *fun!* You know, athletes don't think much about politics at all. I *enjoyed* the parties, the Heil Hitlers, the uniforms, the flags and those *thousands* of cleaning ladies with their gray dresses and brooms.

"Goering was fun. He had a good personality. So did the little one with the club foot [Joseph Goebbels]. Goering gave me a sterling-silver swastika. I had a mold made of it and I put a diamond Star of David in the middle."

When she returned to the U.S., she was a celebrity. "Jarrett, my husband, was going to sue Brundage for kicking me off," she said, "but then we started getting all of these fabulous *offers* and, well, he dropped it. I did all right after the Los Angeles Games, but 1936 made me a *star*—it made me a *glamour* girl! Just another gold medal would never have done *that!*"

Eleanor Holm has lived in her Miami Beach apartment for 11 years. "I play golf," she said. "*Awful* golf. One hundred and eighteen is my *consistent* score. My *best* is 106. I made a living doing interior decorating for a while. I was pretty good, too. But, my God, going up against those rich, showy broads. They'd have all this *jewelry* dripping off them. To impress them, when I was trying to get their decorating jobs, I'd run down to my bank vault and get out this one big *rock* that Rose gave me. I'd put it on and then go talk with them and I'd sit flashing that big rock back and forth in front of my face. Oh, they'd *notice* that *rock,* all right. Then when I was done selling them, I'd run back to the bank and put my rock back in the vault. I couldn't afford to insure it."

HERB ELLIOTT, SALES MANAGER

When he was 22, Herb Elliott was the most promising runner since Paavo Nurmi. He won the gold medal in the 1,500 in Rome and he held the world record in that distance and in the mile, an event that he never lost. Then he quit.

Elliott is now 34 and it is as if he had never been anything but what he is today, an ascending and extremely ambitious sales manager for Australian Portland Cement Ltd. He lives with his wife and six children in the Melbourne suburb of Moorabbin. "I believe life falls into categories," he said. "When you are a voungish sort of bloke, as I still class myself, your career has to be developed to a level that makes you happy. I am not happy by any means. There is a family to educate and a home to build and pay off. The first 15 or 20 years of married life must be a selfish sort of existence where job and family come first."

When asked what interest he has in track now, he answered sharply, "Nil." When asked if his celebrity as a medal winner had helped his career, he said, "No."

When asked if he ever appears before athletic associations, he said, "I accept those invitations only if they are for a very close friend or if they will help me in my job or if they will pay me."

Elliott discussed his brilliant running career as if he were discussing a stranger's. "When I first started, my only ambition was to be better than I was. This gradually leads you on until you are satisfied with what you have done. I didn't realize what my goal was until I felt satisfied. I felt satisfied when I won an Olympic gold medal and broke a world record. Once that hunger had been satiated, I lost interest altogether.

"Every time I ran it was an enormous strain on me, even if it was at a little country meeting. I hate the four or five hours before a race. I was twisted up and knotted up inside. It was a ghastly feeling. The nervousness and the pressure increased as my unbeaten record got longer. The pundits, the damned journalists would say, 'Today's the day Elliott's going to be knocked off,' and in England and all over the world tens of thousands of people would turn up just to see if I would be beaten. It was a drag."

MICHELINE OSTERMEYER, PIANIST

She is 49, a graceful woman with gray hair and horn-rimmed glasses. At London she won two gold medals and a bronze for France—golds in the shotput and the discus, a bronze in the high jump. Then Micheline Ostermeyer went on to become a concert pianist, but her performance at the Olympics remains a magical event. "The Olympics were, no doubt, the biggest moment of my life," she said. "But you must not forget life is not a moment. In a way, I suppose the Olympics was a prolongation of my childhood."

Mme. Ostermeyer was born in Berck in the north of France; her mother was a piano teacher, her grandfather the composer and virtuoso Lucien Laroche. Victor Hugo was a great-uncle. She attended the Paris Conservatory of Music and practiced the piano five or six hours a day. She practiced track five or six hours a week, usually at night. She was married for many years to an Armenian-born kinestherapist, Ghazar Ghazarian, who died seven years ago. She now lives quietly with her two children in an apartment in Versailles. She teaches piano at the Claude Debussy Conservatory. She rarely gives concerts now, although last autumn she did write a note to Count Jean de Beaumont of the IOC asking to play for Olympic competitors in Munich. "I've had no reply, alas," she said.

Her own career as a pianist was not enhanced by her fame as a gold medal winner. "They thought that I was an athlete who happened to play the piano. In reality, I was a pianist who happened to compete in athletics. If I had played tennis or something mundane like that it might have been all right, but other musicians thought—track and field? There was prejudice. I had to show them my diplomas.

"For a long time I could not play Liszt, though, because he was too *sportif.* I knew what other musicians would say—'Well, *of course,* what else *would* she play?' So I had to play Debussy, Ravel, Chopin. In 1954 or 1955, I finally played Liszt at a recital and I had such a success with it that I thought, 'Oh, why didn't I play it before?' "

ALAIN MIMOUN, CIVIL SERVANT

When the mother of Alain Mimoun was carrying him in her womb, she lived in a dismal mountain village in Algeria. One night she dreamed that she was walking across a desolate, stony landscape lit only by the moon. The moon was a comfort and she stopped walking to gaze at it. It seemed to drop a little closer to her. It became brighter, more silvery, and it descended gradually toward her, until at last it loomed so close that she reached up and embraced it and held it to her bosom. In the morning she was troubled by the dream. She could not forget it because she could not understand it. She went to see a crone who interpreted dreams. The old woman said, "The child you carry will someday do a magnificent thing."

Alain Mimoun now lives in the Paris suburb of Campigny-sur-Marne. His home has a wine cave where he keeps a fine stock of Beaujolais and an excellent champagne, which he purchases from a private supplier. He is 51, a prosperous civil servant in the French national sports program and the most popular sports personality in French history—overshadowing Carpentier, Cerdan and Killy. He has named his daughter Olympe, he calls his home L'Olympe and he has a room filled with his medals, which he calls the Olympic Museum. He says, "If the Olympics is a religion, then the museum is my chapel." He entered four Olympics from 1948 through 1960. He won a silver medal in London, two more in Helsinki. In Melbourne he won the gold medal in the marathon. At Rome he was injured and won no medals.

Mimoun left Algeria when he was 18 and joined the French army. He was named a Chevalier in the Legion of Honor in World War II, but his mother did not tell him of her dream. Over the years he won a record 32 long-distance running championships. She said nothing. She remained silent when he won his silver medals. Nor was he told about the dreams after he became a physical-education teacher in France—a position of magnificence to the peasants of his village. He was 36 in Melbourne, but he was in fine condition. "I knew I was older and I was losing speed," he said. "I am a realist. But I also knew my resistance was as good as ever."

So he ran the marathon. Only his old nemesis, Emil Zatopek, who had beaten him in every Olympic race he had ever run, and a solitary journalist said that Mimoun had a chance to win. When Mimoun entered the stadium and neared the finish line he turned to see if Zatopek was gaining. There was no one in sight. Mimoun shook off the officials who crowded about to congratulate him and stood gazing at the stadium entrance. "I was sure Emil was there at my heels," he said, "I was hoping he would be second. I was waiting for him. Then I thought, well, he will be third—it will be nice to stand on the podium with him again. But Emil came in sixth, oh, very tired. He seemed in a trance, staring straight ahead. He said nothing. I said, 'Emil, why don't you congratulate me? I am an Olympic champion. It was I who won.'

"Emil turned and looked at me, as if he were waking from a dream. Then he snapped to attention. Emil took off his cap—that white painting cap he wore so much—and he saluted me. Then he embraced me."

Alain Mimoun weeps at the memory. "Oh, for me," he said, "that was better than the medal."

The gold medal won in the Melbourne marathon was what the mother of Alain Mimoun had been waiting for. "She said to me, 'That's it! That's what my dream meant!' And then she told me about embracing the moon and of the magnificent thing she had been waiting for me to do. I suffered much, but I knew the real Olympics to be religious games as the Greeks had planned them. You can't fabricate an Olympic champion. You are an Olympic champion in your mother's womb."

GISELA MAUERMAYER, LIBRARIAN

A homemade pullover sweater covers her big frame, and there is in her face a hint of haggardness of age and loneliness and the dry fatigue of a life filled with too much work. Gisela Mauermayer, 58, lives in the row house in Munich where she was born. She is a spinster. Her married sister shares the house; Gisela Mauermayer works as a librarian at the Munich Zoological Society.

Anyone who has seen photos of Berlin's Olympians will never forget Gisela—a 6-foot blonde beauty who won the discus. She was the very flower of Nazi maidenhood and she gave the Nazi salute as the swastika rose on its staff and the stadium roared.

Hitler had made it a state policy to produce gold medal winners for the Games and Gisela was discovered by the Führer's Olympic talent scouts. She spent the year before the Games in intensive training under government coaches. Despite her resolute devotion to the Führer, her gold medal brought her no great material reward. After the Games, Gisela was given the same teaching job she applied for earlier. She taught in Munich during the war. When American troops occupied the city, her home was robbed of all her medals and trophies. She was removed from her teaching job because of her Nazi party membership. "I started from scratch at the Zoological Institute of Munich University," she said, "and I earned my second doctor's degree by studying the social behavior of ants."

In her home a Bechstein grand dominates the living room; next to it is a cello. Gisela Mauermayer plays chamber music twice a week with friends. "I sorely miss the idealism which ought to be an integral part of sport," she said. "Nowadays, competitive sport has become too commercialized, too specialized and, last but not least, a hazard rather than a boon to health. As a zoologist, I can attest from my scientific experience that no animal exists which could sustain the kind of protracted effort nowadays demanded by a high-performance athlete."

EMIL ZATOPEK, A CZECH

Emil Zatopek of Czechoslovakia ran every step of every race as if there were a scorpion in each shoe. After he won a gold medal in the 10,000 and a silver in the 5,000 in London in 1948, Red Smith wrote: "Witnesses who have long since forgotten the other events still wake up screaming in the dark when Emil the Terrible goes writhing through their dreams, gasping, groaning, clawing at his abdomen in horrible extremities of pain."

In Helsinki in 1952, Emil the Terrible let his grand agonies (which were almost entirely a matter of theatrics) transport him beyond the realm of mere human endurance as he won gold medals in the 5,000, the 10,000 and the marathon. No man had ever done such a thing, and it was the more amazing because Zatopek had never run a marathon in competition before. When it was over he said, "The marathon is a very boring race."

In 1967 Emil Zatopek spoke to a reporter from the London *Times* about his appreciation of the Olympics: "For me the 1948 Olympics was a liberation of the spirit. After all those dark days of the war, the bombing, the killing, the starvation, the revival of the Olympics was as if the sun had come out. I went into the Olympic Village in 1948 and suddenly there were no more frontiers, no more barriers. Just the people meeting together. It was wonderfully warm. Men and women who had lost five years of life were back again." For many years Emil Zatopek was a colonel in the Czech army and the toast of the Communist Party. Crowds used to gather around him in the street. Then in

1968 he signed the 2,000 Words Manifesto. After Russian tanks stamped out the rebellion, he was expelled from the party, transferred to the reserves and given a pittance for a pension. He worked for a time as a well-tester, but he lost that job. He became a garbage collector, but people recognized him at his work. They helped him carry the garbage cans. This was viewed as a symbol of solidarity against the regime, so he was fired. Then last year he publicly recanted his liberal views. While this incurred the ire of the Czech public, it prompted Party Boss Gustâv Husâk to say that he held "Zatopek in esteem as a man of character." Zatopek is now working for the Czech Geological Research Institute on oil-deposit research. He says it is an outdoor occupation that allows him to go home to Prague once a fortnight.

ABEBE BIKILA, SOLDIER

He will have a seat of honor at the Munich Olympics, but it will be a sad and futile tribute of the type that healthy men pay to the cripples whose still, gleaming wheels line the sidelines at athletic contests.

Abebe Bikila of Ethiopia will be there in his chromium-plated wheelchair, a doubly painful sight because he was so graceful and so strong before he was paralyzed. Now 39, Bikila became a historic figure in Rome in 1960 when he won the marathon: it was the first gold medal for a man from black Africa. He was unforgettable when he ran through the streets of Rome that day. He was barefoot and his stride was easy, though his legs seemed far too thin to carry him over so many miles. His face was set in a gaunt, brown mask that somehow seemed beatific at the same time it was grim. When he won, the mask cracked, bursting into a radiant smile.

He made Olympic history in Tokyo when he won his second consecutive gold in the marathon: there he did a handstand just after he broke the tape. He might have won a third marathon in Mexico City except that he ran with an injured ankle. He did not finish.

Now Bikila is a paraplegic; he cannot move from the waist down. In 1969 an automobile he was driving near Addis Ababa overturned. He was flown to England for special treatment and Haile Selassie himself made a trip to visit him there. But the doctors could do nothing and they say now that his chances of ever moving his legs again are a million to one.

Though he is virtually helpless, Bikila still holds the rank of captain in the Imperial Bodyguard. He was a private in the army when he went to Rome, was promoted to corporal after the gold medal, won promotion to sergeant in the Imperial Bodyguard before Tokyo, was made a lieutenant following that triumph and became a captain after Mexico City. "My life was enriched by the Olympics in that way," said Bikila.

He lives with his wife and four children in a cottage among groves of gum and eucalyptus on the outskirts of Addis. About his house are the shabby huts of his peasant neighbors. There is a seven-foot corrugated iron fence around Bikila's property, and inside, on brilliantly green grass, half a dozen sheep graze, chickens pecking at their feet. Inside the house, the floors are polished to a fine sheen and the walls are hung with war shields. His trophies, stained and discolored by the damp mountain air, are displayed in a cupboard. The scent of incense permeates the rooms.

"Men of success meet with tragedy," said Bakila. "It was the will of God that I won the Olympics and it was the will of God that I had my accident. I was overjoyed when I won the marathon twice. But I accepted those victories as I accept this tragedy. I have no choice. I have to accept both circumstances as facts of life and live happily."

The path leading to Bikila's door is trod by dozens of Olympic aspirants who come to him for inspiration and advice. Little boys and soldiers alike arrive daily to visit him. They wish to run as he did; they wish to win as he did. It is a pilgrimage to Ethiopia's Olympic oracle. And the honor is more profound than any he will receive in Munich.

JESSE OWENS, PUBLIC IMAGE

The morning was warm and sunny in Binghamton, N.Y. On the infield, runners were warming up, the distance men floating with a long gliding gait, the sprinters chopping furiously through starts. Jesse Owens came down the stadium steps and walked out onto the infield with the short, bouncy, confident stride that appeared so often in the newsreels and movies from Berlin 1936. He was erect, square-shouldered, and all the fluid power that used to explode in his sprints still seemed to be available if he had decided to call upon it. Seemed, but only fleetingly. Jesse Owens was 58, pouched around the eyes and 25 pounds heavier than in 1936. The features of the older man scarcely resembled those of the young. But no one would *ever* be quite like the young Jesse Owens, who electrified the world by winning four gold medals in Berlin, a black man who threw the Aryan racism of Hitler back in his face.

Owens was in Binghamton for a teenage track meet sponsored by the Junior Chamber of Commerce. Besides the busy legs of competitors warming up, the infield was also alive with the grins of go-get-'em junior executives and the smiles of rising young salesmen. They moved in to shake hands with Jesse Owens and he was enormously friendly, enthusiastic, not unlike a Jaycee himself. There were only 100 or so people in the stands. *The Star-Spangled Banner* was playing through a loudspeaker from a tiny cassette recorder and a Jaycee said rather tremulously into a microphone, "I give you America's greatest Olympic hero, Jesse Owens!"

Jesse Owens spoke in a deep, impressive voice, his words wonderfully well enunciated. He was at work, of course, and he said, "On behalf of the Ford Motor Company and the Lincoln-Mercury Division of Ford, we're glad to be a part of this fine Sport Spectacular here with the Junior Chamber of Commerce of Binghamton . . . a lot of good luck to all of you and God bless."

He left the infield then, grinning, waving, signing every autograph requested, and climbed into the back seat of a Lincoln furnished by the local dealer. The president of the Binghamton Jaycees was at the wheel and he drove Jesse Owens to Schrafft's Motor Inn where he was staying. The red plastic letters on the marquee were arranged on one side to spell DINNER SPECIAL SEAFOOD PLATTER. On the other side they said WELCOME JESSE OWENS. It was time, said Jesse, to eat lunch—a ham and egg sandwich and a bottle of beer.

When Jesse Owens speaks, even with a bite of ham and egg in his mouth, grand oratorical echoes roll out. If you ask him, for example how he liked the Games in Mexico City, he will reply, "I saw 10,000 people competing there, and it was the aim of every girl and every boy to be victorious. Yet, there they were—eating together, singing together, dancing together, rapping together, and I thought, 'If this does not bring the nations of the world together, what ever will?' " Or if you ask what material advantage a gold medal may bring to a man, he will say, "Material reward is not all there is, sir. No. How many meals can a man eat? How many cars can he drive? In how many beds can he sleep? All of life's wonders are not reflected in material wealth. . . ."

This is a natural way of talking for Jesse Owens, unless he is very relaxed. He is a kind of all-round super combination of 19th-century spellbinder and 20th-century plastic P.R. man, fulltime banquet guest, eternal glad-hander, evangelistic small-talker. Muted bombast is his stock-in-trade. Jesse Owens is what you might call a professional good example.

For this he is paid upwards of $75,000 per annum. Some of the income derives from the 80 or 90 speeches he gives each year. Some is from the corporate clients he "represents"—meaning, in essence, that he sells them his celebrity and his reputation for use at public events where the client wishes to display its "Jesse Owens image," as one ad man calls it. Among his clients are the Atlantic Richfield Company, Sears, Roebuck and Company, the American League and the Ford Motor Company. In pursuit of his career, he travels 200,000 miles a year. On the average he spends four days of every week sleeping in a hotel bed and taking his meals with Jaycees, salesmen and other strangers.

Jesse Owens spoke of his growth as a public orator: "I was once a stutterer and when I was at Ohio State I took a course in phonetics from a master teacher. I've always admired the great orators of my day even more than the great athletes. Roscoe Conklin Simmons and Perry W. Howard and, of course, Martin Luther King and Adam Clayton Powell." His own style of oratory is grandiose and soaring, perhaps more notable for its delivery than its context. "Mostly, I'd say the substance is sheerly inspirational," he said. "I work for my payday like anyone else and things fall into a routine. I have a speech on motivation and values, one on religion, one on patriotism. I have one on marketing and statistics for sales conventions; pointing out that training for athletics is like training to sell. Parts of the speeches are interchangeable, but I'm talking to kids most of the time and I tell them things like this. . . ."

His voice made a slight adjustment, became deeper, a dignified holler that bounded around the restaurant. "Awards become tarnished and diplomas fade," he said. "Gold turns green and the ink turns gray and you cannot read what is upon that diploma or upon that badge. Championships are mythical things. They have no permanence. What is a gold medal? It is but a trinket, a bauble. What counts, my friends, are the *realities* of life: the fact of competition and, yes, the great and good friends you make. . . ."

He readjusted his voice to show that he was no longer orating but the timbre remained. "Grown men," he said softly, "stop me on the street now and say, 'Mr. Owens, I heard you talk 15 years ago in Minneapolis. I'll never forget that speech.' And I think to myself, that man probably has children of his own now. And, maybe, *maybe* he remembers a specific point I made, or perhaps two points I made. And maybe he is passing those points on to his own son, just as I said them. And then I think"—Owens' voice dropped near a whisper now—"then I think, that's immortality. You are immortal if your ideas are being passed on from a father to a son and to his son and to his son and on and on."

The banquet following the Jaycees' Sports Spectacular in Binghamton was held at the Harpur College Union. Jesse Owens was dressed in a beige suit of modified Edwardian cut, a muted-green shirt and a loud, wide tie. He entered the banquet room by himself while several hundred guests waited in the lobby. He stood at the head table and gazed at the sea of empty tables for a moment and said, "God, I always have these damn butterflies before I talk. Wouldn't you think I'd get over it?" Soon the crowd came in and everyone ate. Then the Jaycee who was master of ceremonies said, "I give you the greatest Olympian of them all—*Jesse Owens!*"

The crowd rose as one man to give an ovation that lasted two full minutes. Jesse Owens stood easily at the rostrum and when everyone sat down, he made his speech on motivation and values.

". . . There'll be winners and there'll be losers . . . but friendships born on the field of athletic strife are the real gold of competition . . . awards become corroded, friends gather no dust . . . youth is the greatest commodity this nation has . . . honor thyself . . . honor thy God. . . ."

After yet another meal taken among strangers, Jesse Owens and the Jesse Owens image were working nicely in tandem again.

What Makes a Champion?

Lones W. Wigger, Jr.
Hershel L. Anderson
James P. Whitaker
Bonnie D. Harmon

WHAT MAKES A CHAMPION?

Lones W. Wigger, Jr.

Shooting is a unique sport because it is not necessary to have exceptional strength, size, athletic ability or natural ability to become a champion. The learned attributes are much more important than the God given ones. Champion shooters are made up of both sexes, come in all sizes and from all walks of life. However, there are certain criteria which contribute toward the development of a shooting champion. Although these vary according to the individual I believe the most important factors are: better than average intelligence; learning to shoot at an early age; complete dedication to the sport with definite goals; an ideal environment which provides the opportunity and necessities needed for an individual to learn, progress and achieve goals; the development and training of the mental aspects needed; and the necessity of competitiveness and desire.

Intelligence is a key factor in developing a champion shooter. It is important during both the mechanical and mental learning phases of his development. During the mechanical learning phase the shooter must be able to think for himself, analyze fully the techniques involved, weigh all courses of action and make the right decisions concerning his development and training. In the mental learning phase he must train himself to exercise complete control over his mind to cope with match pressure in order to produce the results necessary to become a champion. The more intelligence an individual possesses the more quickly he will develop because he is able to utilize this intelligence more fully.

I believe an individual has a much better chance of eventually becoming a champion if he can start his learning process at an early age during his formative years. His father or first coach is also very important because he must be available to render all the physical support possible such as proper equipment and hopefully be qualified to give the needed technical assistance necessary for his development. It is very easy for the father or coach to make the mistake of pushing the young shooter or demanding too much of him rather than letting him progress at his own rate, within his own learning ability so he develops his own desire to excel rather than the desire of his father or

From *Profile of a champion*, pp. 5-7, 16-22, 53-54. Fort Bennings, Georgia: U.S. Army Marksmanship Unit, 1974.

coach.[1] Target shooting must remain personally rewarding, fun and challenging for the young shooter. Many young shooters or for that matter youngsters in all sports lose interest or become turned off by over zealous fathers.

I was introduced to the sport by my father at an early age. A good competitive shooter in his own right and a competent coach, he was able to install in me the desire to want to learn and was careful enough to not push me beyond my learning capability or to the point where I rebelled. He was very instrumental in developing in me the personal desire, will to win and competitive spirit so necessary to excel in the shooting sport.

To be a champion in any sport requires complete dedication and definite goals. The shooting sport is no exception. During my collegiate years I learned of the United States Army Marksmanship Unit and their efforts in Olympic and World Championship type shooting. Although I had harbored a secret goal since I began target shooting of someday participating in the Olympics, I never really allowed myself the illusion of accomplishing this goal until I attended a USAMU international shooting clinic conducted by known name shooters at a collegiate tournament. I was very impressed by these instructors and realized my goal might be reached if I was able to somehow locate myself with that group of shooters in Fort Benning, Georgia.

I then made the decision to completely dedicate myself to the shooting sport with the immediate goal of becoming a part of USAMU and ultimately representing the United States in international competition. In my opinion this decision played the most important role in my life and later in my success as a shooter. Dedication to a sport is the mark of a true champion although it may not require the completeness I have demonstrated, it certainly contributes to and enhances the chances of an individual. Little did I realize the hard work and sacrifice my family and I would have to make for me to realize my goals.

Environment also plays a key role in the development of a shooting champion. Intelligence, background in shooting and dedication are of little use to an aspiring young champion with the availability of equipment, facilities, atmosphere, support and time needed to develop these aspects. Although the U.S. Army did not provide me the complete sterile environment preferred, it was the best in the United States and gave me the opportunity to take advantage of the many means of support USAMU possessed.

After several learning, struggling years at AMU I came in contact with the second most influential man in my shooting career, William C. Pullum, who became head coach of the international rifle team. Although not a coach of the mechanical aspects of shooting he was very instrumental in creating a conducive atmosphere for the shooters, recognizing a shooter's performance in competition is directly related to the atmosphere provided him. He believed each shooter was an individual with individual problems that had to be treated as such. He stressed shooting as being about 90% mental and thinking, psychology and mental discipline is what really produces champions. Bill Pullum was very instrumental in instilling in me the importance of mental training and had a profound effect on my development and performance. Under his expert guidance U.S. Army trained shooters dominated international rifle shooting 1964-1970.

The performance level and rate of development of a shooter is also determined by other aspects of his environment. A shooter who has the opportunity to train with and learn from champion shooters has a distinct advantage over individuals who train by themselves. USAMU has had many

[1] See the article by Balazs on pages 156-162 and the article by Martens on pages 169-175. —Ed.

champions and I attribute part of my success to these shooters who I associated, trained and competed with while with the unit. Associating with champions makes you thank like a champion.

As individuals, most shooters recognize their problems and know how to solve them. Each shooter must determine his own training program because he is the only one who knows what he needs. For instance, running or organized physical training is detrimental to some shooters because they believe it hurts them. Others think it is very beneficial so for them it is beneficial. In my opinion organized athletics and team sports practiced in moderation are the best means of physical training because they inspire competition, aid reflexes and coordination, encourage teamwork and do not build unneeded muscles. A shooter needs muscle tone, not strength. The best exercise he can do is live fire practice on the range because only then is he using the muscles necessary for training.

Many hours of practice including dry firing and live firing on the range are necessary for a shooter to develop the techniques and correct shooting positions necessary to become proficient. However this type of training must be supplemented with match competition in order for the shooter to learn to shoot. I believe practice time is for experimentation and development of fundamentals; but you learn to shoot by competing in matches.

For the aspiring international shooting champion it is not only imperative he compete in all the local matches, but whenever possible he must compete with shooters from foreign countries as well. Part of the reason United States shooters have fared so well in Olympic and World Championship type shooting is because the U.S. Army's Marksmanship Unit provided the opportunity for them to compete against the best shooters in the world. Once we learned the best could be beat in insignificant matches we were able to beat them when it counted. Learning to shoot under match pressure can only be accomplished by competing against the best.

It is difficult for a shooter to entertain aspects of becoming a champion without the help of an environment such as provided by USAMU. It requires two-three years of daily, intense training of the most qualified collegiate shooters available to school them in the mechanical phase of shooting (techniques and fundamentals) before they reach the level of proficiency needed to compete on a world level. To effectively utilize the time, effort, training and money expended on an individual and for him to realize his potential he should have the opportunity to remain in this or a similar environment for six to eight years. Conditions which exist other than this make it extremely difficult for a shooter to become an international champion.

As stated before mental training is probably about 90% of shooting. The mechanical learning phase is important and necessary but practice scores do not win matches. Unfortunately the only score that counts is the one produced on match day. Learning to control your emotions, reactions and mind in a match is the key to combating match pressure. One way to learn this is by developing your ability to concentrate. Complete concentration or total involvement of the mind on your shooting will raise the level of your performance in matches as well as practice. Any outside distractions or problems such as financial, family or office will affect your ability to concentrate thereby hurting your performance.

A second part of developing mental training is learning to have confidence in your ability, equipment and yourself. All champions in any sport have confidence in themselves and their ability but not to the point they are overconfident. Concentration and confidence are not learned overnight.[2] They are learned through years of hard work and effort in training and through match experience. An indication of this is found by examining statistics which show the average age of Olympic shooting

---

[2] See the article by Suinn on pages 26-36. —Ed.

champions to be thirty-one. Most shooters are mechanically capable of top level performance long before they are mentally capable. They do not reach their top level mental capability performance wise until they have many years of match experience.

Desire or will to win is the last attribute I want to discuss. Some champion shooters have more desire than others but it is a necessary and imperative part of the makeup of all successful shooters. Those that lack in natural ability or the mechanical aspects have to make up for their deficiencies with desire.

I have never believed I was blessed with an exceptional amount of natural ability. In order to excel, my approach had to be different from others. My desire to win is much stronger and more hungry than most. I thrive on competitive shooting and my only feeling of satisfaction is found in winning. To me, winning fairly is not only everything, it is the only thing. In my opinion you can only finish in two places in a match, first or last. I hate to lose more than anything and losing is not in my psyche. When I lose I will not accept this as final and will work that much harder and strive to improve myself so it doesn't happen the next time. I try to be a gracious winner and although I am not a bad loser neither am I a good loser. I believe in the saying "good losers usually do."

There is one other factor that should be mentioned. Although some shooters don't necessarily believe in luck, I do. I think luck is very important. I have always considered I have had luck on my side and have been very thankful for it. Some people believe you make your own luck and there is a saying, "the more you practice the luckier you get." This may be true but however you get it, it is a necessary part of being a champion.

A potential international shooting champion must prepare himself for a lifetime of dedication to the sport. This will mean days and days of hard work, training, practice, personal sacrifice and if married, require a wife who understands and appreciates his dedication and desire. Target shooting, unfortunately, is not an accepted sport by the news media and because of its lack of spectator appeal is not a professional sport. Therefore there is little chance of notoriety, personal gain or compensation derived from it. His compensation is the personal satisfaction of winning, knowing he has beaten the world's best and perhaps the most important aspect of all, being the true master of his mind.

WHAT MAKES A CHAMPION?

Hershel L. Anderson

The method I use to shoot the free pistol is actually the same I use to shoot any weapon in competition. There are certain points of the fundamentals that are peculiar to the free pistol, but then that is true with each individual gun.

To shoot tens (10's) consistently with the free pistol I tried to analyze each of the fundamentals as it applies to international competition.

I started with the stance, trying each way I'd see other shooters use, methods taught by various instructors. Feet close together, far apart, points in between. Finally I determined that I had to find the stance that would be completely comfortable and hold my body movement to an absolute minimum. With my eyes closed, hands in pockets, I tried to relax my shoulders and concentrate on the movement. For me, the result was my feet were approximately shoulder width apart, leaning just slightly forward, leg muscles just tense enough to keep me erect, stomach muscles relaxed, no muscle strain across the shoulders, back or chest.

Once I developed my stance to my satisfaction I practiced it until it became second nature to me. I also started taking my shooting hand and arm out of my pocket and raising it as if holding the pistol, striving to work a natural position right in with my stance, still keeping uppermost in my mind that the movement *must* be held to the absolute minimum. Having a target up or picking out a point to use as a target I extend my arm in the direction of the target area still with my eyes closed, I turn my head as if to look at the sights insuring that there is no muscle strain in the neck or shooting arm. Opening my eyes I look down my arm and hand to see what relation my body has with the target area. If my body is not in proper relation I lean forward on my toes and shift my heels until I am in the proper position. I do this rather than shifting my trail foot because I feel that this method keeps my stance more stable.

I continue to mention the fact that constant effort must be made toward motionlessness, I do this because I feel that it is of the utmost importance. I knew that to shoot consistently in the ten (10) ring I had to stop as much movement as I could from the tip of my toes to the end of the barrel of my weapon.

The method I use, in addition to the fundamentals to train myself to hold the pistol as still as possible is as follows. I draw a cross on a piece of paper and hang it on a wall. I assume my stance and position not cocking the weapon or attempting to apply pressure to the trigger, and concentrate on aligning my sights and holding the weapon perfectly still. The farther away from the cross the less movement is noticed, so I stand as close to the cross as I can without touching it. Mentally I measure the amount of movement in relation to the vertical and horizontal lines, striving to reduce it. The objective is to stop all movement of the sights in relation to the cross, keeping my sights aligned all the while. I try not to accept any movement at all.

The free pistol, more so than any other pistol used in competition, has grips that hinder natural alignment of the sights and position. Each shooter must add to or take away, or both, on the grips as suits his own hand and body conformation. By assuming the proper stance, position and grip, aligning the sights and drawing a picture of the relationship between the target and sights several times, the shooter will have a pretty good idea of where some should be added or taken away to give natural alignment. Sight alignment must be natural and the pistol grip must conform to the hand to assist in achieving this. There must be no adjustment of the wrist, arm, hand or whatever to achieve alignment.

Breath control is very important to shooting the free pistol, as it is with all shooting. But with international shooting the opportunity to shoot in countries all over the world brings about various conditions. On many occasions high altitude, such as in Mexico, throws many shooters out of kilter. In high altitude I always take two or three deep breaths and then wait some ten or fifteen seconds after the last before attempting to shoot. If I tried to shoot prior to that I would feel slightly dizzy and my eyes would not be completely clear. Under normal conditions I use breath control in the following manner. I load and cock the pistol, the grip and sight alignment assumed naturally, bring the weapon up while I take a deep breath. When the sights cross the center of the target I cut the breath off and let the pistol rise to its maximum height. As the pistol comes back down on target I exhale slightly until the sights are a little below center of target. Then I inhale, bringing the pistol back up to center hold and cut the breath off. This is where I bring the fundamental of trigger control into play.

The thing about trigger control and sight alignment is that they are so closely related that they are practically impossible to separate while shooting. Naturally, they are spoken of, taught and thought of as separate items while not shooting. But when I shoot they work as one. That's the way I must explain it.

First, I want my sights sharp, even lined and the rear sight without serrations or marks. A serrated rear sight blends too much with the front sight. I like to look at straight lines when aligning my sights and not uneven rounded or rough edged lines. In a trigger I like a sharp, crisp trigger with my trigger stop set real close. In guns other than the free pistol I also want a little slack or travel in the trigger.

Sight alignment to me is the same as with any shooter; the front sight centered in the rear sight notch and level with the top of the rear sight. My point of concentration is not on a particular place on the front sight just the sight as a whole. If I have shots out that I can't call I watch the light on that side of my sight. I don't argue the point of center hold as opposed to any other holds. Center hold works best for me and when someone tries to argue the point of other holds and how well it works for them I just ask how many tens (10's). That determines how well does it work for them in comparison to mine.

I prepare myself mentally, before, during and after firing a shot or shots because this sequence makes me perform the best. As an example, the evening before I'm scheduled to shoot I make myself concentrate on a mental image of perfect sight alignment. In my mind's eye I visualize this sight alignment and my trigger finger applying pressure to the trigger making the weapon fire—hence a ten (10). On the firing line, especially if I feel that I'm not shooting the way I should, I close my eyes and concentrate until I visualize this image and make myself shoot a perfect round.[3] Mentally firing a shot is just as important as physically firing one.

When concentrating my point of focus on the front sight my trigger finger works in exact coordination. I see the sharp, even lines of the front sight in perfect alignment and my brain waves send the signal to my trigger finger to move straight to the rear evenly and firmly. If my eye does not see perfect alignment of the sights the movement of my trigger finger seems to go into slow motion. Sometimes it may even stop until I can see perfect alignment. Once seen, the finger starts to the rear once again. Of course, if it takes too long to get the shot off I bring the weapon down, go over the sequence mentally again, then start anew.

In a way it is difficult to explain to a fine point because I have worked, concentrated and trained so hard and long until it is habit. This, of course, is what is most desirous.

Some call this type of shooting precision shooting. There are few people in the shooting world who can precision shoot and it is definitely not recommended for any shooter to try to shoot this way. It is something that must come about naturally and through training. Concentrated effort and training condition the brain to accept only perfect sight alignment before allowing the trigger finger to reach the point of no return and firing the shot. Both the image of perfect alignment accepted by the brain and the signal of final movement of the trigger finger must peak simultaneously.

As can be seen from reading the preceeding information my training is a great deal mental. The physical aspects of the fundamentals are applied now through habit, primarily, because I have developed them that way. When I first began shooting it took a great deal of trial and error to get the position, stance, grip, etc. the exact way they best conformed to me. It took many hours of practice to be able to accomplish these items physically and in the proper sequence, but once I got them down they had also become a part of my mental makeup. If one of the basic fundamentals is not working as it should a mental light comes on and then I must re-examine all my fundamentals until it falls into place and I'm again at peace mentally.

The mental makeup of a shooter is going to determine just how well he will shoot. The attitude that a shooter takes toward his performance, and the performance of others, will produce championship

---

[3] See the article by Suinn on pages 306-315, the article by Lane on pages 316-320, and the article by Wenz and Strong on pages 328-333. —Ed.

scores. Worry over who you must beat at a match, your ability to compete with the guns and equipment of others or just your own ability to perform as a champion leads to a defeatist attitude.[4] There is definitely no room in the winner's circle for this type individual. The attitudes of others, your own negative past attitudes must be eliminated and a positive winning attitude must be adopted and maintained!

A winning attitude has certain goals and standards that help to simplify the positive approach or attitude. When I first started shooting I would set my goal to shoot just above the highest score I had ever fired for that course. Now my goal is to fire every gun for the maximum possible score. I know full well in my mind that I have the ability and by my mental effort I will one day realize this goal. To consider anything less is sheer nonsense.

An unprepared shooter can be found up and down any firing line. "I would have cleaned that string but, like a bombshell it hit me. I was clean up to that last shot and I told myself to settle down and not get out of the ten (10) ring. Don't goof up and drop a nine (9) and guess what my next shot was?"

There were two things that got to this shooter. Negative thinking and so-called "match pressure." I do not allow myself to think negative thoughts. I do not allow myself to be touched by this "match pressure." Let the pressure and negative thinking stay with those who doubt they can win, who doubt they can shoot a ten (10) each shot.

I concentrate all my mental and physical effort toward a positive attitude and I thereby eliminate all negative thoughts and approaches. My total concentration is geared to the mental sequence of perfect performance in each and every match. I have a great deal of mental conversation with myself, telling myself exactly how to shoot for each score and at the same time mentally picturing it actually being done. My mental guard against any type of negative thought or performance must be up at all times.

Although most of what I have related seems to be geared for individual effort this is not entirely true. Over an aggregate there is a possibility to pick up a point or two that I dropped due to some malfunction in my mental process, however, this cannot be done in team matches. After all team matches are really what it is all about, aren't they?

Knowing that team performance gives no room for picking up lost points, my mental and physical performance seems to become more finely concentrated toward the maximum goal. Knowing this I seem to perform better during a team match. One of my greatest efforts is to train myself to bring this fineness of mental attitude and physical performance of team matches to my individual effort. One day I will achieve it.

I believe that all this information boils down to one main item. Mental discipline, mental attitude, mental preparedness—whatever tag you want to put on it. There is, of course, a great deal of physical effort that must be put forth, particularly in the initial preparation of becoming a shooter. But you can stand knee deep in brass seven days a week with the best stance, position, grip, breath control and all the rest of the fundamentals and not have the proper mental control over yourself and you will not shoot consistent championship scores. It all must work together hand in glove, inseparable, to produce such scores.

Sometimes, as it seemed here for awhile, it gets extremely difficult to tell exactly what I do to shoot good scores. Then, just like the cartoon, a light appears over my head and it dawns on me. Proper positive application of each of the fundamentals and a definite, strong, positive mental attitude and discipline toward myself and performance is how it all comes about.

---

[4] See the article by Suinn on pages 26-36. —Ed.

WHAT MAKES A CHAMPION?

James P. Whitaker

The graduation process from shooter to winner and from winner to champion is one that evolves through all the subtleties of the mental aspects of shooting, ability assumed as a common factor.

Every aspiring international skeet shooter is continually searching for that secret formula of instant success—that short cut to stardom, particularly when he transfers to the international circuit from the domestic one after having enjoyed winning scores. Basically, we are too impatient!

Many champions have expressed their criteria for success within the shooting community, and invariably the key factor or underlying theme revolves around concentration, or control of the mental faculties. If there does exist an instant success package marketable for immediate consumption, it has to be concentration. As the ability to "tune out and turn on" is such a personal one, and is equally as diversified as our individual personalities, the secret of *how* to accomplish the task is a quest each shooter must resolve for himself. I have found it just as impossible to learn the how from them as you, the reader, will learn from me, for I can't relate to the how as expressed by them. I obviously have not perfected my own omnipotent control as I do not hold the title of The World Champion. I will attempt to describe my observations and reflections in retrospect during those instances when I have been successful.

Every time the opportunity arises to practice under less than ideal conditions, do so. Obviously a shooter must apply himself in practice just as he would under match conditions, yet the ability to learn how to concentrate is better accomplished when the mental exertion is required due to real or imagined conditions. That perfect round in practice is much more significant when you had to force your attention from other mental distractions, than the one you enjoyed when you were one bundle of shooting enthusiasm.

Establish definite goals in practice—have a purpose when you walk out on the practice field. If your objective that particular day is to concentrate on station practice, or problem birds, do so, and don't be influenced into shooting a round "with the fellows." Similarly, there exists a point in time when you must strive for aggregate score to reinforce a mental relationship in a match. If you have never compiled four perfect rounds in succession in practice, and the requirement exists to do under competitive conditions, a situation exists which you can't relate to, and mentally you are defeated because of an inability to associate with a significant learning experience.

Concentrate on one bird at a time. This simple mental fundamental can't be overemphasized. Don't think aggregate, standing within the field of competition, or the bird you just missed. Concentrate on each target in succession. I have found that when I'm shooting my best, I'm all but oblivious as to what particular station I'm on. I've actually experienced mental blanks as to whether or not I've shot all the required targets from one particular station, and done so in proper sequence. I would like to expand the opening sentence of this paragraph to read *don't think!* I'm convinced that the perfect skeet shooter would be the one who could turn the mental toggle switch to the "off" position, and walk out on the field a complete void.[5] My personal experience is that if I mentally remind myself of a particular performance on a given station it has a negative effect, i.e., "be sure and follow through at high 4 . . . lost!"

[5] See the article by Suinn on pages 26-36. —Ed.

Be hungrily aggressive; there is a certain degree of reckless abandon that is a manifestation of a positive attitude. So many times I've watched shooters who radiated or telegraphed a miss prior to calling for the bird—a visible effect of a mental uncertainty they experienced at that time.

Don't be influenced by the presence or absence of the "heavy-holders" at any given match. You are the shooter against whom you are competing—there exists no one-on-one physical confrontation with your competition in skeet shooting. If you shoot the best score, you are the champion; similarly, if you are complacent in the fact that you can defeat any of the shooters present, your concentration is broken by a relaxed mental attitude. Strive for a record breaking score, if necessary, to fabricate your own competitive environment.

Don't psych yourself out by the importance of the shoot. It's another skeet field, and the rounds are shot in the same sequence in accordance with ISU rules . . . just another two or three hundred bird match.

I think it is worth looking at the Russian shooters with respect to their attitude towards the game. The only time you are aware of their presence is at the range, be it practice or match day. You don't see them involved with any of the potential social distractions that invariably surround a shooting trip away from home. All sight-seeing, shopping, socializing and celebrating is done after the competition. They are present to win! This is the type of dedication that all of us must submit ourselves to if we are truly striving to be world champions.

I would like to relate an experience I witnessed by The World Champion, Egenev Petrov of the Soviet Union. The shooting conditions in Moscow were perfectly horrible with respect to target irregularity. Petrov was working on a perfect score for the day, and was shooting doubles at station seven. The low house bird jumped straight up approximately a foot and half just as he shot, in an obvious irregular attitude not attributed to wind conditions. All of us on the squad were outraged at the referees ruling of lost and felt the bird should have been repeated; at the end of the round I told him I felt he had been cheated, and fully expected him to protest the ruling. He merely shrugged his shoulders, as though nothing had transpired, and proceeded to apologize to us for the quality of the referees. The man's emotional stability and obvious mental prowess characterize that necessary to win consistently at the world level.

WHAT MAKES A CHAMPION?

Bonnie D. Harmon

Why do I shoot the way I do? When I am asked this question, I find it not easy to answer in one sentence of 25 words or less because many physical and mental factors contribute to my ability to shoot rather well.

In 1962 I was introduced to competitive pistol shooting, green, no experience, and didn't know what to expect. In 1963, I was a new shooter all the way and that year I was awarded the gold Distinguished Pistol Shot Badge. In retrospect, more emphasis was on service pistol than any other pistol, but now I realize it takes strong emphasis with each pistol in today's type of competition.

In my tyro years, a pistol match didn't excite me like it does now. In my younger years, a pistol match was somewhat considered just another military duty with no significance. This was a result of inexperience, youth, and attitude. But with seniority comes experience, and with experience comes wisdom (hopefully).

Climbing the ladder to reach the elite 2650 group, periodically I would shoot a single gun aggregate that was considered excellent. I found it difficult to mass all three gun aggregates that represented any degree of winning. I would either shoot a winning score with the .22 Caliber or .38 Caliber and fall flat with the .45 Caliber or I would shoot a mediocre score with the .22 and .38 and shoot a hot score with the .45 Caliber.

I am convinced that the problem was that if I shot a winning score with the .22 or .38 I was overjoyed, overwhelmed (not having won too often), and I oversimplified the remainder of the shooting match, settling for just one gun aggregate. However, if I won only the .45 Caliber, I believe it was because my attitude changed to a more aggressive form of determination.

The longer I shoot the more I realize I must set my goal high and be determined to reach that goal. That's how records are broken. My technique of reaching this goal is to shoot just one point higher than the best score I ever fired with that particular gun.

Attaining these standards for myself I find it necessary to know each and every one of the basic fundamentals, how each works, and why. I must have confidence in my weapons. I feel more comfortable if I can handle my weapons the night before a match to reaffirm that certain feel, because each weapon fits differently in my hand. I like to feel and dry fire my guns the night before a match. I feel more close and intimate; I call it shooter and weapon relationship. The two are inseparable.

When I train, I need or would like to train as close as possible to actual match conditions. This method eliminates major changes in physical or thought processes. I also need to train sufficiently with a gun until I'm having no problems with the trigger or grip, to a point where I am confident. On the other side of the coin, I can reach a saturation point because of too much practice beyond that point of confidence. When time permits, I prefer to practice three days before a pistol match, having a day off prior to the match for weapons cleaning, reaffirming my zero, and working on any shooting problem that might have developed during practice.

When I know the exact date of a match, my preparation starts then and slowly builds up as the match date advances. I also like to know the level of competition, so I can adjust my psychic preparation. Knowing who I must beat helps me to develop a proper attitude toward winning.

I try not to change my regular daily routine. I try to get 6-8 hours sleep prior to a match when possible. I always eat a hearty breakfast 1½ to 2 hours before the match starts. I take natural vitamins each morning and at evening meals. I eat a light lunch and what I want at the evening meal. I never drink alcohol to the point of being intoxicated at least 3 days prior to a match.

Experience has taught me. The most damaging and detrimental state of being for me is the loss of sleep. I find the loss of sleep causes a feeling of fatigue, with reaction time slowed down and an unstable feeling.

I would advise any new or young upcoming shooter that it isn't the act itself but rather it's the pursuit of fulfillment that will agitate and lessen your ability to win and think clearly.

I find experience in shooting NRA and international events helps a great deal. In general, 9 times out of 10 an individual firing for the first time in an important match will find himself rather nervous and tense.

I remember my own experience in the 1967 Pan American Games (first big international match). I was nervous and even scared because people were watching, pictures were being taken, and because of lack of experience, I paid more attention to my surroundings. I now know I should have envisioned the small details pertaining to shooting. Match pressure never really leaves me completely, but experience helps to ease anxieties.

I try to create a state of tranquility in my domestic affairs. Observation and personal experience proves to me a shooter can't put all his effort into competitive shooting if his wife is constantly nagging. . . . My wife encourages me to win and is happy as I am when I do win. . . .

After having learned how to use the basic tools for shooting and having won a victory, I find it similar to a child's first taste of ice cream; they like it. I too like to win because it gives me a feeling of accomplishment. One victory creates a desire in me to win again and/or be a part of a winning team. The prestige and recognition further stimulates my attitude toward achievement.

Travel to foreign countries is another incentive for me to shoot well. The thought of competing against another country always stimulates my psychic circuit to the point where I want to try a little harder.

The many contributing factors that enable me to shoot the way I do are:

1. Understanding the basic fundamentals.
2. Good training habits.
3. Taste of victory developing the proper approach to attitude.
4. With a positive attitude a desire to win is developed.
5. The incentive of winning is a large motivating factor.

It is my conviction that, if I know how to apply the fundamentals, have a positive attitude, and high spirits, I have more time to devote to the small, delicate, and perplexing details of shooting one shot or 5 shots.

My mental preparation consists primarily of a technique I call "visualization" combined with know-how, experience, and confidence. The visualization technique consists of formulating a mental picture of what you want to accomplish, whether it be one single shot or a 5 shot string, it can be used to train yourself to stand still and hold still, to see your score in increments of 100 or 300, or to visualize your entire aggregate.[6] This is not a new technique, but it is not really used too often in shooting. However, I do believe it's used more often than the shooter realizes.

Some days this technique works better than other days with due respect to your physical and psychological well-being and attitude.

Mental discipline, I believe, is developed in the process of good sound training techniques. Also paying particular attention to small details, such as small errors and not accepting these errors when it's possible to correct them.

Recognizing an error can be corrected only if I am aware of the mistake, if I am aware of the error, I can either stop—correct—or shoot the shot. If I shoot a shot while being aware of an error, I have either lost concentration, patience, or mental control—generally the latter. Prior to shooting a shot or a series of shots I try to hold a vivid picture of the preconceived mental picture of the end result desired, which is, of course, a 10, 50, or 100, after each shot or series. I must reaffirm this mental picture each time. Having faith in my own abilities is derived from having fired good scores in practice for the last match.

This technique of visualization is always accompanied with confidence, desire, mental discipline, and faith in my convictions. I suppose I could base my philosophy of thought on an age-old cliché, "The end result desired is equivalent to the degree of faith you have in your thoughts," and "that which cannot be conceived in the mind's eye first will have much difficulty in materializing."

---

[6] See the article by Suinn on pages 306-315, the article by Lane on pages 316-320, and the article by Wenz and Strong on pages 328-333. —Ed.

In conclusion, the tools I find necessary for shooting good scores are: Sufficient practice with each weapon I will fire in the match, test-proved equipment, mentally preparing myself by keeping my goal in mind, developing positive attitude toward these standards and formulating a mental picture of what I want to shoot, which is one point higher than I've ever fired. And keeping my mind, body and psychic spirit on the infinite details of shooting one shot or five shots.

APPLICATIONS

Part Three

COACHING VARIABLES 227

The Gymnast's Perception of the Coach: Performance Competence and Coaching Style **229**
— *Joe Massimo*

Hurting, Winning, and Preparing **238**
— *Barbara Zaremski*

How to Ruin an Athlete **247**
— *Byron Richardson*

Use of Groups to Improve Athletic Performance **250**
— *David Nesvig*

Psychology of Coaching **261**
— *Cal Botterill*

Goal Setting and Performance **269**
— *James D. McClements and Cal Botterill*

MENTAL STATES 280

Attentional Focus—Self-Assessment **281**
— *Robert M. Nideffer*

Psychological Techniques for the Advancement of Sports Potential **291**
— *Maurie D. Pressman*

The Mind of the Marathoner **297**
— *William P. Morgan*

BEHAVIORAL STRATEGIES 304

Body Thinking: Psychology for Olympic Champs **306**
Appendix A: Muscle Relaxation Exercise **310**
Appendix B: Psychological Preparation on Competition Day **313**
— *Richard M. Suinn*

Improving Athletic Performance through Visuo-Motor Behavior Rehearsal **316**
— *John F. Lane*

The Loneliness of a Long-Distance Kicker   **321**
— *Robert W. Titley*

An Application of Biofeedback and Self-regulation Procedures with Superior Athletes: The Fine Tuning Effect   **328**
— *Betty J. Wenz and Donald J. Strong*

Cognitive-Behavioral Skills in Golf: Brain Power Golf   **334**
— *Daniel S. Kirschenbaum and Ronald M. Bale*

Psyching the College Athlete: A Comprehensive Sports Psychology Training Package   **344**
Appendix: Mahoney-Avener Gymnast Questionnaire   **351**
— *Philip R. Spinelli and Billy A. Barrios*

ISSUES IN SPORTS PSYCHOLOGY   356

Ethics in a Highly Visible Environment: Consultation and Intervention with Athletes and Athletic Teams   **357**
— *Robert W. Titley*

Applied Psychology in Major College Athletics   **362**
— *Wayne Lanning*

COACHING
VARIABLES

Dr. Joseph Massimo has been team psychologist to the U.S. national gymnastics coaching staff, has consulted with the U.S. Gymnastics Federation, and was coach-psychologist with the 1971 U.S. national gymnastics team in Europe. He has been involved with psychological testing and training of U.S. Olympic gymnastics team members. Dr. Massimo is chief psychologist for public schools in Newton, Massachusetts. This article points out that, for more highly skilled athletes, coaching style is a more crucial factor than technical competence. Specific coaching styles are discussed, with some recommendations about the need for adjusting them according to levels of skill. The questionnaire used by Massimo is included at the end of the article.

Coach Barbara Zaremski is the 1978 Masters AAU swimming champion in three distances, the 2-mile, the 200-meter freestyle, and the 50-yard freestyle; she is an all-American in the 2-mile distance and holds two championships from the First International Masters Competition. She is a member of the National AAU Sports Medicine Committee, has coached widely in swimming, and has been a consultant on biofeedback to various competitive teams. She is director of the Biofeedback Center in Prairie Village, Kansas, where she coached the Prairie Village swim team. She is a licensed social worker and is completing a degree in coaching at the University of Oklahoma. This article offers advice to coaches from a coach-athlete who demands the maximum from herself in competing. The author covers the role of winning in competition, the relation between coaches' expectations about winning and athletes' confidence, and a possible approach towards fostering maximal performance while promoting personal growth in an athlete.

Byron Richardson's article is a brief one, with a humorous vein. However, it suggests a crucial point, that is, that performance can be disrupted if the personal-psychological aspects of athletics are ignored. Through his "recommendations," Richardson applies principles of psychology related to massed practice effects, the influence of negative approaches to reinforcement, cue conditions that precipitate stress, and issues related to self-concept and self-esteem.

Dr. David Nesvig has been a consultant to the AAU Athlete Development Program at the Squaw Valley Olympic Training Center and has worked with athletes on swimming and synchronized swimming teams. He lettered in tennis in high school and college. He is associate director of the San Diego State University Counseling Service. This article provides information on how coaches can help athletes achieve performance goals through the use of group discussions of common issues. With illustrations from swimming teams, the article gives the format and the approach that can make group meetings productive for decision making, training programs, and motivational and performance goals.

Dr. Cal Botterill was a member of the Canadian national hockey team and has coached varsity hockey at St. John's Ravenscourt High School. He has been associate physical education director at the Winnipeg YMCA and recreational director for the government of Manitoba. As assistant technical coordinator for the Coaching Association of Canada, he is involved with sports science, coaching certification, and coaching apprenticeships. This article also addresses the use of group meetings and goal setting, but with an emphasis on particular methods of behavioral goal setting. While the article by Nesvig offers group meetings as a way of increasing a sense of mutual under-standing through discussions of personal perceptions, motives, and so forth, Botterill points to the importance of direct discussion of goals and concrete plans and definitions.[1]

Dr. James D. McClements has been assistant coach for the track and the cross-country teams at the University of Saskatchewan and has served on the Officials Development Committee and the Coaching Development Committee for the Canadian Amateur Speedskating Association. He is an associate professor in the College of Physical Education, University of Saskatchewan. He and Dr. Cal Botterill[2] worked together on a study reported in this article, which adds another dimension to coaching approaches to goal setting. The authors show how, by use of a mathematical formula, individual performance goals can be set by an athlete and coach so as to train at a pace that should lead to an end goal. Thus, using times recorded at the Olympic games, the authors show what pace a skater must reach each year to meet the goal of succeeding at the next Olympics.

[1]*Another article by Botterill, in collaboration with James D. McClements, appears on pages 269-279.*
[2]*Another article by Botterill appears on pages 261-268.*

The Gymnast's Perception of the Coach: Performance Competence and Coaching Style

Joe Massimo

One of the various techniques utilized in the data collection phase of current work was that of a questionnaire specifically developed for competitive gymnasts.[1] This 6-page instrument (now expanded to 10 pages) is quite detailed and covers a wide range of information about the individual and his or her gymnastics. The questionnaire has been slightly modified to accommodate the particular experience of European gymnasts and to facilitate translation in the future. Basically, however, the questionnaire seeks the same material wherever it would be administered. Participation in filling it out was voluntary, as were all aspects of the work, and the gymnasts were told either in a covering letter or in person that they could ignore items they did not wish to answer. As one can imagine, there is an enormous wealth of material that has resulted to date from this one approach, but in this article we will deal with one particular question and an analysis of the answers received.

Near the end of the questionnaire the following inquiry is made with slight modification depending on the proposed respondent:

> *In the space below would you please list (briefly describe) the qualities you feel (look for) are important in a coach (trainer). Include style of teaching (training, coaching), personal characteristics, etc.*

The athlete was encouraged to use a separate page if necessary, and many did. A careful analysis of the responses to this item revealed some remarkable findings, which even our statistician found striking.

First of all, the qualities specified by responding gymnasts were given in two ways. Some athletes answered in a prose form, and it was necessary to translate this into a list. This was accomplished by simply taking the characteristics as they were given and assigning a number to them, e.g., 1, 2, 3, etc. as they appeared in the answer. The majority of responses gave the qualities in a numbered (list) order, and it was assumed this indicated a descending measure of importance so far as the individual gymnast was concerned. We have also made the assumption that the coaching characteristics given reflected a deeply felt need in the gymnast and indicated his or her feelings about the importance of certain attributes in the coach.

---

[1] The questionnaire is included at the end of this article. —Ed.

The overall pattern that emerged in response to this question clearly showed a trend suggesting that the gymnasts' view of what was important in a coach bore a close relationship to their own level of performance competence.[2] It was evident that the more competent gymnasts were naming (seeking) a somewhat different set of qualities in their trainer than were their less successful colleagues. (Competence in this report was determined by regional, national, and/or international performance records.) The further down the success ladder, the more scattered the expressed attributes became, except that in the less proficient athletes technical knowledge was almost always identified as very critical. Technical knowledge was also given a relatively high priority by top performers, not for its own sake, but always in terms of an ability to communicate to the gymnast information of a technical nature. It was rarely the most important characteristic identified by them, in contrast to the less competent performers, for whom it was a key ingredient sought.[2] There appeared to be an inverse relationship in this regard, that is, the less successful the performer, the higher significance the coach's pure technical ability became, and the more successful the competitor, the less crucial that quality was based on its placement and description in the list of trainer characteristics. For the top performers the major characteristics listed were in the general area of psychological motivation and support. The higher skilled the individual gymnast, the more important were these kinds of elusive characteristics in the coach. The more skilled and successful gymnasts appear to psychologically need and seek greater personal interactive closeness and motivational incentive based on an emotionally supportive relationship. Although the less competent gymnasts also need "motivation," it was not specified in incorporated terms but in very task-oriented, concrete language, such as "a coach who wants me to do well," or "who wants to win" versus "a coach who will help me realize my potential."

Variation was present in the lists compiled for both highly successful and less successful gymnasts. However, the degree of variation was considerably higher in the athletes whose actual performance record was not indicative of current competence. Further data analysis revealed the fact that for the most part the better athletes always listed the same specific qualities among the top characteristics named. Although they varied in placement, they were always present near the head of the lists. As previously indicated, in the vast majority of cases the number one characteristic sought by top performers was the coach's willingness and desire to get to know the gymnast as an individual and in a way that suggested care and emotional support. The verbal expression of this quality varied in construction, for example, "a coach interested in me as a person," "a trainer who would respect and know me as an individual," "a person I could trust and who cared about me," but the characteristics all suggested the same general theme. This kind of coach-quality was rarely indicated as of highest significance in the lists of less successful gymnasts. For that group, as discussed earlier, the major quality sought and identified was technical knowledge. This was indicated in such phrases as "a coach who knows how to teach difficult skills," "a person with knowledge of the mechanics of tricks," "an individual who is able to show me how to do various moves." Other high-regard characteristics named by the more competent gymnasts were the ability to motivate and maintain motivation, the ability to manage the sociology of a team, the ability to develop meaningful interpersonal relationships on a one-to-one basis as well as a group basis. In the less successful gymnasts more concrete attributes such as physical strength, skilled spotting, and the provision of discipline were seen as more critical and most often mentioned. It is interesting to note that two characteristics having high valence for all gymnasts were the ability to organize training efforts (time management) and a clearly shown love for the sport.

[2] See the article by Butt on pages 78-85. —Ed.

It may be of interest to our readers to know what some of the other characteristics were that were identified by gymnasts. Although some of these qualities might appear as behavior objectives many thoughtful coaches strive to develop, it is encouraging to find them confirmed by the athletes themselves. These are given with no attention to order of importance as they appeared on the gymnasts' lists, but they do represent the most frequently mentioned attributes identified by the most successful youngsters. In addition to the emotional-social factors, the capacity to communicate technical knowledge on an individual basis, a genuine dedication to gymnastics, and organizational ability, the primary qualities discussed were: the ability to get a concept across with an appreciation for the individual gymnast's learning style; a minimum of excess verbiage (talking); consistent limit setting and the firm establishment of authority; an applied sense of humor while still taking gymnastics seriously; the absence of sarcasm and negativism as a general mode of response; hard work and enthusiasm on the part of the trainer; personal predictability; fairness in dealings with gymnasts; mature way of relating (not as a peer); good control of individuals and team at competitions; the ability to translate theory into action; honest critique of work being done and not being afraid to say the truth about one's performance; the ability to make a firm decision without dwelling on it; exemplary behavior (practice what you preach); the ability to stay calm under stress (be cool); capacity to allow others to take responsibility; the ability to direct the spirit, not break it; openness to suggestions and willingness to admit error; willingness to provide the opportunity for gymnasts to socialize with one another and to listen to the gymnast's concerns and problems; reliable attention to safety factors; and an overall positive attitude about training and competition. The above listing is not exhaustive, and there were others, including some totally unpredictable and even bizarre notions, but the characteristics given represent a reasonable summation of the majority of responses.

There are several rather interesting issues raised by the material reported herein. It would be most enlightening to see if the task-oriented characteristics identified by less successful gymnasts at a given point in their careers shift to the more emotional-caring ones as their own level of ability improves. Another related intriguing inquiry would be to follow the less successful gymnasts who, at the time the questionnaire was completed, did not fit the pattern associated with their level but in fact named characteristics more in harmony with those expressed by better gymnasts, to see whether they would become more successful themselves over time. In essence, which comes first, the chicken or the egg, the success or the particular coaching approach associated with it? What is really going on here? Is there some specific psychological cluster reflected in a deeply held conviction and statement concerning the nature of the teaching-learning relationship which is predetermined in the personalities of successful athletes? If this is so, and if it isn't present in a particular gymnast, can it be acquired or developed? This is not just a matter of intellectual curiosity, for it has implications concerning the training of gymnasts.

The material reported in this article strongly suggests that homogeneous ability grouping of gymnasts is a wise way to construct programs. Although it is true that some positive benefits from the performance of more skilled gymnasts might "rub off" on less competent members of a group, our results suggest that the more highly functioning youngsters need a different type of coaching style and approach which warrants segregation.[3] Unless the coach is a Renaissance man or woman

---

[3] An independent piece of research conducted by Dr. Anne Bird of the University of California, entitled "Leadership and cohesion within successful and unsuccessful teams: Perceptions of coaches and players," yielded findings strikingly similar to those referred to in this article among members of winning and losing volleyball teams. One of her findings was that it appeared that coaching styles require modification according to level of skill or competition in such team sports.

who can easily shift technique moment-to-moment depending on whom he or she is working with, it is far more efficient to form groups whose members are very close to one another in ability. This may appear like an obvious fact which anyone could figure out without much fanfare. Experience suggests, however, that when such grouping does occur it is haphazard or done for overtly valid but not thoroughly understood reasons, such as "They are easier to work with" or "They require less spotting." The essential question is, Why is this the case and what does it say about the kind of training interaction needed? Our gymnastics history is replete with examples of how we do the correct thing but for a less than informed reason. It may seem to some that it is a subtle difference indeed between a coaching approach to a group or individual that says, "All right, I want you to do 20 compulsories each and watch execution on the cartwheel" and the coach who says, "Let's see where we need to look in this exercise for perfection; what would you say we have to focus on at this point?" But, as a matter of fact, these represent one hell of a difference in both mentality and approach.

It is important to note that many of the better performers come from well-established programs where several coaches and combinations of coaches are employed. Very often the coaching responsibilities are divided along performance level lines, one coach responsible for beginners, another for intermediates, etc. Obviously, from material reported here and elsewhere, such training organization makes eminent sense. Coach selection, however, should not be random or simply based on seniority but should be made on the basis of who can provide the kind and quality of input and leadership needed at a specific point in the gymnast's development. In most cases, the more experienced coach ends up working with the top youngsters. As has been pointed out, it is not only experience that is important, although it often accompanies the ability to motivate, but what is needed is a special personality and instruction style as well.

The relationship sought by top performers is sometimes already present, particularly if the coach and athlete have been together a number of developmental years during which time this interaction has emerged quite naturally. Many top youngsters were reporting on the kind of coaching they were receiving already, but this was not the case in all situations, and from comments made on questionnaires it was apparent that sometimes the characteristics mentioned were those desired but not necessarily present in their current training experience. It is at these junctions that progress may come to a standstill. This is the time when "driving" is still needed, but to a substantially lesser degree than an empathetic, personalized system of motivation and communication. Some coaches simply don't have the skill. They continue to rely on the old, faithful, standby techniques, tried and true, that worked at a prior time, failing to recognize that their gymnasts have grown and that the older methodology is no longer appropriate or effective. At that level of competence much support is gained from comparable peers, and the depth of talent and self-determination is such that it wins out over a less than ideal coaching situation. Loyal gymnasts "hang in," but their gymnastics becomes a maintenance operation at best, rather than a creative, forward surge at a time which often coincides with the peak learning and performance years. How much better the athlete could do should the coaching conditions be more favorable to the development of excellence remains an unknown. Perhaps this is one reason we see a considerable amount of team changing at the higher levels in this country.

If we accept the hypothesis that the more skilled gymnasts need a different applied coaching style, one which is more highly personalized and motivational in nature, as suggested by this paper, it follows that we need to pay careful attention to the background, level, and kind of expertise brought to our training camps at the national level. Coaching staffs that work at this level should be well balanced. Not only is it important to have our most technically competent coaches present, but equally, if not more critically, it is important to have coaches with a demonstrated capacity to relate to and motivate gymnasts in an emotionally supportive and psychologically caring manner. The coaches must be able to do this with gymnasts other than their own.

It would seem appropriate to consider the development of a master blueprint for the training and evaluation of coaches on a national level along the lines suggested by our observations. Currently, time in the sport is often a major criterion for selecting training camp personnel. Although this factor may be correlated with coaching ability, longevity does not necessarily ensure the presence of the specific characteristics named in this research. Another common, and perhaps more reliable criterion, is to nominate the coaching staff from among those coaches who have the top gymnasts, the assumption being that if they have the best youngsters they must be the best coaches. Again, this may be a very erroneous assumption. There may well be some coaches working in our programs today who have no top competitor in the current gymnastic ranks but who nevertheless are superb trainers with excellent style-shifting and relationship-building ability. Conversely, it is quite possible that some coaches with current top gymnasts may not be as sensitive and appropriate at a more finely tuned level as it may appear on the surface. Giftedness along the dimensions suggested in this report is not as mysterious as it may seem; the desired characteristics can be identified and should be prerequisites for selection. Some individuals will resist this notion, perhaps for selfish reasons, but somewhere along the line soon priority will have to be given to the overall welfare of the gymnasts above any other factors or adult motivations.

In this same regard it is interesting to contemplate what would happen if we asked our top performers, all of whom know most of the coaches working on the national scene, whom they would like to see at the training camp. If this were done anonymously there is considerable evidence that some gymnasts would not endorse their own current coach. Without recourse to a secret ballot this could be accomplished by asking each gymnast to nominate two coaches, one from their own gym and one from another. Although this might result in some painful ego blows, it would assist in the process of weaning from the single-coach model and would help our top athletes to get the type of assistance they felt was important from coaches whom they felt could deliver it at a crucial time.

Some additional comments are appropriate at this time. The gymnasts responding to the questionnaire were all 12 years of age or older. What about the highly talented 6- or 7-year-old? What kind of interaction is most effective here, what are the motivation issues, and what about the parent-coach-child relationship as it relates to the evaluation and development of talent in a democracy? Child development theory tells us much, as does the literature from the movement education field, but there is more to learn about this all-important age and the promotion of gymnastics.

Our readers will note I have made no differentiation in this article along sex lines. The explanation is simple and somewhat surprising considering that the personality configurations of male and female gymnasts are different. Although further analysis is necessary, there appeared to be little difference between the identified characteristics sought in a trainer by female gymnasts and those sought by male gymnasts. Small variances can have large implications, but our first inspection suggests that what differences did exist were primarily a matter of emphasis rather than content.

ELITE GYMNAST QUESTIONNAIRE

(Short Version)

Dr. J. Massimo

(Please type or print.) (Use the back of page whenever necessary.)

Name _____ Date of Birth _____

Home Address (Street) _____ (City) _____

(State) _____ (Zip) _____ Home Phone _____

School Address _____ School Phone _____

College _____ Year _____ Degree Program _____

Grade Point Average _____ Marital Status _____

Father's Occupation _____

Mother's Occupation _____

Religious Affiliation _____

Siblings (Please give their names, age, present location, and occupation if appropriate.)

(List others on back.)

Gymnastic Coach (current) _____

Competitive Experience (national or international meets only) _____

(Use back if necessary.)

Special Training Experience (camps, etc.) _____

COLOR OF EYES _____

HANDEDNESS—Rt./Lft. _____

Is weight a problem for you? _____ Are you on a special diet? _____

Your weight _____ Your height _____

Elite Gymnast Questionnaire (Continued)

Event Rating—Please rate 1 (strongest) . . . 6 (weakest).
Men: FX_____   SH_____   SR_____   LHV_____   PB_____   HB_____
Women: FX_____   SHV_____   BB_____   UPB_____

Hobbies and Sports (other than gymnastics)_____
_____

GENERAL (Yes, No, Brief Description)

1.   Do you enjoy extracurriculum reading?_____   Kind of material: _____
     Fiction_____   Biography_____   Autobiography_____
     Nonfiction_____   Newspapers_____   Magazines_____
     Other_____

2.   Have you taken a high school or college level course in: Physics?_____   Anatomy and
     physiology?_____   Kinesiology?_____   Psychology?_____   (If yes, what
     areas of psychology have you studied?)_____

3.   Do you have a favorite academic subject?_____   What?_____

4.   Do you smoke?_____   What?_____   How many?_____
     Do you drink?_____   What?_____   How much?_____

5.   If single, do you have a relatively steady boy or girlfriend?_____
     If yes, is he or she in gymnastics?_____

6.   Women: Has your menstrual cycle begun?_____   When you have your period does it
     create any difficulties for you in workouts or meets?_____

7.   Have you had any dance training? _____   How many years?_____   What
     type of dance?_____

8.   Have you done any extensive travelling other than gymnastics?_____   Where?_____

9.   Have you ever held a full- or part-time job? _____   What and how long?_____

10. What has been your greatest personal disappointment to date?_____

     What accomplishment or experience are you most proud of to date?_____

11. What are your future educational and vocational plans?_____
     _____

Elite Gymnast Questionnaire (Continued)

12. How much time do you spend working out a week? (average hours/day)_____

13. Do you enjoy working compulsories?_____

14. Do you like to teach skills to other gymnasts?_____

15. Do you prefer to work: (rank 1, 2, 3, 4)
    alone_____   small group_____   large group_____   any setting_____

16. What do you enjoy about the competitive (meet) situation?_____
    _____

17. How anxious do you get before a competition? (very—1 to not at all—5)_____
    Comment if appropriate. _____
    _____

18. How do you relax before a meet?_____
    _____

19. Do you have any techniques to "peak" yourself before a meet?_____What are they?
    _____
    _____

20. Do you find it relatively easy to go to sleep the night before a competition?_____

21. Do you like to watch the performance and see the score of the competitor who precedes you in
    an event?_____

22. Do you have any specific habits or particular difficulties that you are aware of pertaining to the
    gymnastic experience? (rituals, order of working events in practice, hand trouble, cold/warm
    gym, etc.)_____   Can you briefly describe these?_____
    _____ (Use back.)

23. Have you had any serious injuries in gymnastics?_____   What?_____
    _____(Use back.)

24. Are you currently able to execute the skill(s) that you were performing when you received the
    injury(ies) described above?_____
    _____

25. What most frightens you (if anything) concerning this sport?_____
    _____

26. In designing your optional exercise do you prefer to:_____
    Construct it yourself?_____   Have the coach develop it?_____   Work with the
    coach on the routine?_____

27. Are the majority of your associates gymnasts?_____

Elite Gymnast Questionnaire (Continued)

28. How did you first become interested in gymnastics?_____
_____

29. What has been your chief motivation for continuing in this sport?_____
_____

30. In the space below would you please briefly describe the qualities you look for in a coach. (Include style of teaching, personal characteristics, etc. Use the back if necessary.)

    [About half a page is left blank here for athletes' comments.]

31. How many coaches have you had?_____
Please briefly state your reasons for leaving one coach for another. _____
_____

32. Do you and your coach have any kind of contact outside of the gym?_____   If yes, what activities do you share?_____
_____

33. Is your coach married?_____   Do you know how old he or she is?_____
Please give age._____

34. Do you have a special school schedule that has been arranged by your coach?_____
What is that schedule?_____
_____

35. Do you, your coach, and teammates view films?_____   Discuss mechanics of skills?
_____

36. Would you be willing to take some tests to help me better understand you as an individual? _____

COMMENTS: Feel free to comment below on any aspect of this questionnaire.

Hurting, Winning, and Preparing

Barbara Zaremski

As we look at the vast amount of time swimming athletes spend in the water and doing dry land exercises and the tremendous amounts of energy required to do that work, we may well wonder what it is that makes a swimmer swim and just exactly what it is that puts a tiny percentage at the top. Certainly dedication and discipline have their effects before any youngster makes the decision that it is worth reaching toward membership in the top 1 percent of athletes in the country or in the world. One might say that someone who succeeds at that is a gifted athlete and would have made it to the top anyway, but, unfortunately, this view no longer appears true. Athletes who make it to the top are not only gifted and not only have put in the necessary hard work but also appear to have a little something extra.

Richard M. Suinn (1977) of Colorado State University calls this something extra a *quiet confidence*, as in "facing the Olympics intending to win instead of hoping to win," the ability to concentrate completely on performance in situations in which physical skills are so closely matched that the competitors' "psychological approach to competition" becomes the critical factor that determines who wins.

From my discussion with Eastern Europeans[1] who have been working with learning enhancement techniques to train athletes, it appears that Nadia Comaneci's 10 scores were definitely not accidental: included in her training were techniques that promoted her self-confidence and her concentration on gymnastics. Most swimming coaches have known some athlete who forgot how many laps had been completed and lost the race because of "just not being with it," even though the contest mattered a great deal. We might identify the minutiae that affected that swimmer in that event, but the fact remains that an athlete who "has it all together" on a regular basis, under any circumstance, is really something special. A close scrutiny of the differences between these two competitors might reveal that the first lost place by allowing other mental processes to enter the arena, while the latter had learned to exclude any and all distractions, both mental and physical, from the competitive scene.

Since there is always something that demands attention or that becomes a distraction from the task at hand, we may ask, How can we facilitate the learning of this ability in the first athlete? If it is possible to build this concentration into one's competition, then perhaps we need a new

[1] Ivan Barzakov (now of San Francisco) 1978: personal communication.

paradigm for training athletes. One step is to reappraise the premises from which coaching derives. Do we have notions that preclude new thought-processes simply because they are unfamiliar and because we cannot see their application or their effect on the outcome of competition? To risk taking an alternate approach to training, which might not only work but actually be of great benefit in training, is a big step but is quite a possible one.

Critical factors for us, coaches, are

1. How do we handle ourselves with regard to the training of athletes and with regard to competitive situations?
2. How do we handle ourselves with regard to the athletes' perceptions of us?
3. Do we help athletes grow with competitive situations?
4. What can we do to improve and add that extra something to bring an athlete to the top?

Rushall (1970) feels that there is a need for "consistency of the sport system. The training and competitive regime, coaching behaviors, expectations and consequences of behavior, if consistent, will lead to reliable and systematic responses from athletes." Training is individual; each athlete needs his or her own system, consistently applied, throughout all phases of a sport.

The old approach to coaching has been one of "fight" and pain and agony. We mentally "rev up" for competition, weeks in advance, and build to a peak that finally brings coach, competitor, and family to the verge of hysteria. Couldn't the goal be achieved in a different way? Why not a smaller expenditure of energy and, instead, a greater concentration of energy through centering and visualizing?

Consider these familiar phrases: "You don't have what it takes," "Don't let that person get away with treating you like that," "If I fail in this, I'll be discredited," "This effort won't count," "The reward won't be worth the effort," "Do it later," "Hide your deficiency" (Bassett 1975, pp. 20-23). In situations that elicit any of these responses, one's self-esteem is threatened, anger and frustration lead to aggression towards oneself and others, and the scene is set for failure. Competitive sports involve primarily instrumental aggression—one tries to defeat an opponent to experience the satisfaction of proving one's competence—but, for some athletes, aggression is linked with anger directed at the opponent. Layman (1970, p. 27) pointed out that, since winning always involves physical or psychological injury to one's rival,

> there are some athletes who cannot force themselves to win unless they perceive the opponent as the enemy and . . . become angry. . . . We should note that both frustration and anger can lead to behavior other than aggression. They can lead to fear, flight, or withdrawal.

In this way, again, athletes expend energy that could better be utilized in performance. Is it possible to look at competition in a different light? Why has it been necessary to have aggression towards the person in the other lane or the other heat? What possibilities of action would be opened by a change in our concept of competition? A national team is comprised of members from a number of different teams from various parts of the country; the psychological adjustment that such athletes need to make to view a former opponent as a teammate, possibly as a roommate, precipitates unnecessary stress. It diverts considerable energy from the actual competition, instead of heightening the energy that is available to the athletes.

What makes a winning athlete? Each of us has definite ideas about who has the potential to become a winner and who will actually make it to the top. If we were asked to specify the qualities that we look for in a champion, we would probably be hard pressed to come up with any particulars. We are aware that a champion, like Mark Spitz or John Nabor, has something extra. This same phenomenon is observed with actors and singers, too. Perhaps, by momentarily removing ourselves from sports, we can bring this intangible quality into clearer focus. Singer Leontyne Price, a consummate performer, by her poise and her manner of moving conveys to us a sureness of person and knowledge of her art. Nothing surprises her. These are the same qualities that we should promote in athletes. A person who conveys this sureness has learned to take all the areas of performance into consideration and feels mastery of them all. An athlete who presents sureness of self is a consistent performer and has had support in personal growth to accomplish this. Development in this direction must be promoted by a coach who takes time and makes time to give all possible information and feedback whenever it is needed or required. The coach must also give the athlete sufficient leeway to experiment with new thought-processes about the sport and about body movement.[2]

Recently there has been an interest in athletes who "almost make it" to the top. It is generally assumed that each athlete focuses mainly on being number one. What does an athlete stand to gain or lose by being number one? How many secondary gains are lost because of efforts to attain that position? Is the athlete psychologically ready to take the responsibility of being tops?[3] The anxiety an athlete feels and the frustration coaches feel may stand in direct relation to the responsibilities that they expect will be placed on them by winning.

To explore an athlete's fears in an open, understanding way sometimes is the key to a blossoming, not only in competitive life, but also in all other areas of life.

All superior athletes have the ability to survive disappointment and defeat. The responsibility for what an athlete does, good or bad, can be attributed to others, but, in the final analysis, it rests with the individual athlete. A top performer might sometimes lose some self-confidence but never loses faith in his or her powers and abilities.[4] The question is, Can we help athletes become more responsible for their own behavior, which in turn determines what athletes can perform at consistently high levels?

The use of projective tests, such as the Tutko Motivational Rating Scale, permits the construction of ongoing profiles for each athlete and for the coach. These profiles can be used to activate more positive behaviors and thought-processes in athletes. Pain-and-agony coaching has seen its day. Some athletes have enough personal drive but need help to see themselves as being tops and to counteract negative input from school, peers, and family. We can help them grow more capable and more confident if we recognize that they want to have a knowledgeable voice in their own training.[5]

What makes a successful coach? As athletes, we have particular ideas of what a coach should be and of what is needed to bring out a peak performance. As coaches, we take on a different set of ideas about what is necessary for the best performance. We define and redefine the role continuously, and, as with our attempt to describe the profile of a top athlete, we have trouble in describing what a coach really is, for coaching is mostly an art.

[2] See the article by Martens on pages 169-175. —Ed.
[3] See the article by Ogilvie on pages 86-89. —Ed.
[4] See the article by Gunby on pages 179-201 and the article by Johnson on pages 202-211. —Ed.
[5] See the article by Nesvig on pages 250-260. —Ed.

Little is known about successful coaches who are more than authority figures. I believe that coaching techniques can be made much more consistent if we attune ourselves to the needs of athletes and learn to keep our own egos out of the situation.

In preparing for a competitive event, coaches are generally so involved in the sport and in their athletes' problems that they have no time to reflect on their own general actions or language. Only after the event is over is there occasion for reflection on what has transpired during the day, and sometimes, when the press of training becomes intense, we don't find time for even this much review. But isn't it a disservice, to the coach as well as the athletes, not to take time to go over the day's interactions? Is it possible that, not only are there athletes who dare not win, but also coaches who are afraid to have a winner? We need to take time to look clearly at the processes in coaching and at the physical and emotional feelings that arise as we reflect. If we are not afraid of our own honesty, we might find that the difficulties of coaches in reaching their potentials are the same as the difficulties of athletes. Do we fear the image we present to others? In our own anxiety, do we lack the mental clarity to recognize our behaviors and those of athletes for what they really are? For example, do we unconsciously structure anxiety by the promotion of situations in which athletes have little chance of winning or are so physically and emotionally pushed that they become depressed? Spino (1978, p. 45) calls for

> *coaches who have intentions for our larger personality ... new ways of fitness that are easier, techniques with connotations for the whole person. In the new framework the coach is a "spirit guide" who can interpret experiences and put them in perspective. The coach is no longer just a stopwatch guide. It's a paradigm change, a switch from competitive-oriented, time-result, physical rewards to the satisfaction that comes from an integration between your spiritual side and your physical possibilities. ... The new ethic takes the pressure off winning. It gets to be more and more fun to run.*

We can lessen our own anxiety by being honest with ourselves—not a vindictive, destructive honesty, but honesty whose clarity separates fact from rationalization and gets to the core of truth. There is less feeling of anxiety if there is little discrepancy between the real and the ideal. Coaching can lead to this awareness and growth. Guidance of an athlete toward this new self requires skill. How well do we really know the operational patterns of athletes? Can we work within the framework of these patterns to limit the threat to self that looking at oneself brings forth? And can we change this looking from one that provokes anxiety and fear to one of adventure and expansion? Some may say that that is a job for a psychologist, but I remind them that this introspection is the very psychology that makes or breaks both athlete and coaches. Levitt (1974) believes that

> *the main responsibility of our coaches is to provide something in athletics that is more fulfilling to the athlete than merely a medium for approval and ego support. ... It seems that if mastery and knowledge of oneself is approached, winning will be incidental. ... The more successful athletes tend to be higher in realistic appraisal of themselves and lower in resting anxiety than the less successful.*

Others take different views of what is involved with new coaching methods. These are no longer based on "try harder" but emphasize *being* or *is*ness and a feeling of new vitality. Gallwey and Kriegel (1978) note that *anyone who has ever been involved in any sports or games will know the infuriating gap that occurs between what you are supposed to do and what actually happens. This gap is a separation between body and mind, or between the outer and inner game. Since all physical activities have some kind of a goal and they present obstacles between you and the goal. To get over the obstacles and reach the goal is what sport is about on one level. Within oneself there are other difficulties—anxiety, fear, self-doubt, lack of confidence. All these things arise from inside us and make it difficult for us to perform according to our true potential.*

According to Ronan (1977),

Concentration is one of the keys to athletic excellence. It is the ability to put all and every part of your powers of thought and desire on one point. . . . Concentration implies an effort to tune out all stimuli that can distract you from your goal. Concentration requires you to focus on one thing at a time and it takes effort and practice to develop it.

Probably the most striking characteristic of a performance that happens without obstacles is the feeling of exhilaration that accompanies it. Gallwey calls this *confidence*—confidence in yourself, confidence in your ability to do whatever you truly want to do, confidence that you can and will accomplish your goals through the power of your own mind and body.

Suinn (1976)[6] suggests that if we keep a positive goal in mind, picture it so vividly as to make it real, and think of it in terms of an accomplished fact, we will also experience winning feelings—self-confidence, courage, faith that the outcome is attainable.

Schwarzenegger (Dychtwald 1978, p. 42) describes this confidence as beginning with a "wanting power":

As long as the mind can envision the fact that you can do something, you can do it, as long as you really believe 100 percent. It's all mind over matter. . . .

  You fool your mind in order to do certain things. Thinking . . . that my biceps are enormous mountains gets my body to respond. And as your body changes, even in small ways, you gain self-confidence; you see that things are possible. Self-confidence is one of the big secrets for success. . . . You begin to realize you have an enormous command over your body. Just imagine, you get so you can move each individual muscle—you gain a lot of self-confidence by having so much command over yourself, over your body, and that, again, is a reflection of your mind.

The uncomfortable fact is that we ourselves interfere with our ability to demonstrate our potential; we often prefer to attribute breakthrough to luck or good conditions instead of rewarding ourselves for our own good performances. Schwarzenegger (*ibid.*, p. 90) states,

---

[6]This article by Suinn appears on pages 306-315. —Ed.

Physical follows mental, to win, to achieve, to change, you must expand the mental scope of your vision. . . . The body will follow through, it happens every time I close my eyes before I lift a heavy weight. I imagine it, I do it.

Want power, thought power, do power.

The process of achieving this command of performance has been carefully noted by a number of coaches. I want to share some of their practical ideas, focusing on readiness, centering, and inner feelings.

Readiness can be broken into three areas: physiological, mental, and the cooperation between the two. Physiological readiness appears necessary to prime the body's energy system to activate the best performance. Mental readiness is quite different. It is the process by which an athlete brings an event into focus, runs it through mentally, and allows the body to prepare to respond to the mental image. The third level of readiness involves cooperation between mind and body without anxiety; at this level, the athlete sees the top performance as an accomplished fact. This sounds like a combination of Zen centering and biofeedback.

Centering is being in a balanced position within oneself and having immediate awareness, a quality analogous to the "controlled spontaneity" of highly trained musicians, dancers, and actors.

Biofeedback is information from the bio-individual gained by noninvasive means, channeled into a selective information translation system, and presented in a readily understandable form to the individual. It rests on two basic principles. First,

every change in the physiological state is accompanied by an appropriate change in the mental-emotional state, conscious or unconscious, and conversely, every change in the mental-emotional state, conscious or unconscious, is accompanied by an appropriate change in the physiological state (Green, Green, and Walters 1969)*

and, second,

any physiological process that can be monitored, amplified, and made visible to an individual can be voluntarily controlled by that individual. By detecting and amplifying these signals, the instruments allow an individual to be aware immediately of the subtle shifts in his physical state. In a brief time, individuals are capable of noting correlations between these physiological fluctuations and the accompanying psychological states, which are usually in the form of specific images or fantasies. Then, it becomes possible to use the mental image to produce the physiological change at will, and the success or failure of that attempt is immediately registered by the physiological monitoring device . . . . The individual becomes involved in a "closed biofeedback loop" (Gattozzi 1971). Thus the link between psychological and physiological processes is made quite explicit.*

Another system, biofeedback without instrumentation, is one in which the art of visualization has its roots. It involves training an individual to no longer negate the body he or she lives in, to be minutely aware of its processes, and, with coaching, to discover that one is able to know oneself and can minutely control one's body. Visualization is the ability to see an object or an activity clearly in one's mind, as though looking at a TV screen. This is most easily achieved with brain wave

---

*As cited in Pelletier and Garfield, 1976.

frequencies in the low alpha and high theta ranges and with a fairly high amplitude of the waves. Information gained in this way makes it possible to use correlations between the physiological feedback of specific images to produce physiological changes at will. An athlete is his or her own closed biofeedback loop, and the link between the psychological and the physiological is made quite explicit. The goal is to achieve a mental image to produce change in an athlete in a centered way and thereby to activate the potential for superiority. Readers who are familiar with body movement systems will recognize that the imaging process activated by the Feldenkreiz system is a prime example of the activation of potential. In 1977, Betty Wenz[7] suggested that to achieve this sort of control produces important differences in a superior athlete's performance. Research conducted by Shaw and Kolb has shown significantly faster reaction times (30 percent faster) for those who have learned to center and quiet themselves.

It is important to give athletes the verbal power to help themselves through the use of this kind of a system. One must be able to describe accurately all the processes of action in a sport. A sport-specific language in combination with an athlete's home language is the working ground for making changes in physical and psychological behavior. Are you and your athlete really communicating—speaking the same language? Do athletes really understand your descriptions of the process of action? Can they verbally, accurately, and with a minimum of gestures describe what they do and what other athletes do? Once accurate language is learned, a scrupulous honesty must enter into the thought-process. As a person visualizes, there is a gradual discovery that all attempts at self-concealment, blocking, and passing the buck are futile and that the only way out is to recognize what one truly is. Such honesty is the measure of an athlete's commitment to a goal. It is necessary to take the time to teach these skills, as it appears that the ability to accurately describe and discuss one's movements is one of the keys for the fine tuning that makes the difference between the top performers and also-rans. The steps of language power, kinetic sense, and the ability to be relaxed, centered, and alert are difficult, and athletes' attempts at growth must reach coaches' awareness and must be encouraged. Ferrer-Hombravella (1970, pp. 295-296) suggests that

> *psychological training should be prescribed before an athlete competes; and the young man should not compete until he has acquired sufficient resistance to the frustrations and acquires a necessary stable emotional equilibrium, the facility of adaptation to new situations, the ability to have self-control, etc. It is only at this stage that one can receive maximum value from competition.*

On the practical side of all this are relaxation and visualization techniques. Relaxation will increase an athlete's ability to cope with the stress of competition and begin to reach his competitive potential. Many systems are available, some applicable to athletics, and some not. The set that I use for basic stress reduction and centering has its origins in Jacobson's (1938) progressive relaxation exercises.[8] I have radically changed these over the years. They allow an athlete to have greater awareness of bodily tension and physiological processes, and they identify the language of the body, which then can be carried over into training and competitive situations. Nonjudgmental observational skill is needed to evaluate the total performance. Most important is the process by which one can change oneself to become aware of one's idiosyncracies. It makes the difference between the champion and the also-rans.

---

[7]See the article by Wenz and Strong on pages 328-333. —Ed.
[8]See the article by Suinn on pages 306-315. —Ed.

Superficial attention will not stand up to the stress of competition. Athletes must be given the apparatus to carry over into practice and then into competition what they learn about themselves. They must know what it is like to have a knowledgeable feeling of one's anatomy. One must be able to relax and concentrate fully on a small part of the body. The keys are in one's being alert, centered, and relaxed. One must know that human perception can be regulated in much the same way that a knowledgeable technician can manipulate the content of the images shown on a television screen.

My system of relaxation and centering is the following. First, find a good, comfortable position that you can keep for approximately 20 minutes. When you are learning these exercises it is a good idea to lie on the floor or on a bed or to use a recliner chair. Close your eyes. Take a few long, slow, deep breaths and then view and feel your feet. Tighten the muscles of your feet as you take in a long, slow breath. Hold it for a moment, and, as you exhale, relax those muscles. Continue up your body with the muscles of your calves, the muscles around your knees, and then the muscles of your thighs, hands, forearms, and upper arms. Move on to the muscles of your abdomen, lower chest, upper chest, head, face, and neck and shoulders. Stay comfortable for a while, keep your breathing long and slow, and allow yourself to become quieter and quieter with each long, slow breath. When you feel quiet and mentally intense, visualize a part of the process of motion of your sport. Just watch completely and make no judgments on what you feel and see in yourself. Any correction should be worked on while you are engaged in the sport; in other words, allow the visualization process to carry over into your training and competition.

Centering of attention is also the gateway to the flow experiences alluded to by Gallwey, Spino, and others. Furlong (1976) observed that

> *people in Flow undergo an intense centering of attention on the activity. They do not try to concentrate harder. . . . The concentration comes automatically. Your body feels good and is awake all over, your energy is flowing very smoothly, you feel relaxed. In Flow there is a sense of being lost in the action. Flow is a floating action in which the individual is aware of his actions but not aware of his awareness. . . . Another factor in Flow is the clarity of response that the individual gets from the activity . . . being in complete control of his world.*

Ask an athlete what it feels like to flow. The experience is usually strong enough that one can give a good description of it. Give permission during practice to enjoy and work in the experience if it happens during workouts—and watch your athlete move ahead.

REFERENCES

Bassett, R. 1975. *Zen karate*. New York: Warner.
Dychtwald, K. 1978. Interview with Arnold Schwarzenegger. *New Age* 3, 8 (January):38-52.
Ferrer-Hombravella, H. 1970. Psychic and somatic pathological effects of precocious competition. In *Contemporary psychology of sport: Proceedings of the Second International Congress of Sport Psychology*, ed. G. Kenyon, pp. 295-296. Chicago: The Athletic Institute.
Furlong, W. B. 1976. The fun in fun. *Psychology Today* 10, 1 (June):35, 38, 80.
Gallwey, W. T., and Kriegel, B. 1978. Tame the mind, trust the body. *New Age* 3, 8 (January):42, 46-69.
Jacobson, E. 1938. *Progressive relaxation*. Chicago: University of Chicago Press.

Layman, E. 1970. Aggression in relation to play and sports. In *Contemporary psychology of sport: Proceedings of the Second International Congress of Sport Psychology*, ed. G. Kenyon, pp. 25-34. Chicago: The Athletic Institute.

Levitt, S. 1974. Anxiety and the athlete: Some considerations for coaches. *Track and Field Quarterly Review*, 74, 3 (September):180-182.

Pelletier, K., and Garfield, C. 1976. *Consciousness: East and west*. New York: Harper.

Ronan, D. 1977. *The swimmers memorandum on mental training*. West Islip, N.Y.: Durite Printing.

Rushall, B. 1970. Some practical applications of personality information. In *Contemporary psychology of sport: Proceedings of the Second International Congress of Sport Psychology*, ed. G. Kenyon, pp. 167-173. Chicago: The Athletic Institute.

Spino, M. 1978. Marathon man. *New Age* 3, 8 (January):45.

Suinn, R. M. 1976. Body thinking: Psychology for Olympic champs. *Psychology Today* 10, 2 (July):38-43.

———. 1977. Easing athletes' anxiety at the winter Olympics. *The Physician and Sportsmedicine* 5 (March):88-93.

How to Ruin an Athlete

Byron Richardson

This information is not intended for the half-hearted coach. It is purely for the dyed-in-the-wool, true-blue, totally conscientious coach who wants to insure that his athletes never run again when they finish school. For simplicity's sake, I have broken the program down into three areas: the workouts, the races and the social life of the athletes. All three can be manipulated in such a manner as to quickly end an athlete's career.[1]

THE WORKOUTS

1. Keep as little variety as possible in the workouts. Do all training on the track during track season. During cross-country season, use the same course day after day. If meets are on Saturdays have one stock workout for Mondays and Wednesdays, and another for Tuesdays and Thursdays.

2. Make sure your athletes are overtrained. The best way to check on training load is to compare meet times with practice session times. If meet times are slower than times projected from practice sessions, the athlete is overtrained. To accomplish this goal, make sure you don't give trivial workouts such as 10 X 440. Do at least 20 for starters, and increase to 30 or more after the first week of practice.

3. Make sure it hurts. After all, train without pain is train without gain. Establish a point system, with a trophy awarded to the most fragile individual.

For instance, the point scale may be: doesn't complete workout—10 points; throws up on field—10 points; has to be carried off field—25 points; needs hospital treatment—50 points; needs hospitalization—100 points per day; crippled for life—500 points; dies—750 points; dies on field—1000 points.

4. Keep individual attention to an absolute minimum. Assign all athletes numbers at the first practice. Always call them by number rather than name. Never give individual instruction or

Byron Richardson. How to ruin an athlete. *Runner's World Magazine* 2 (February 1976):76. Reprinted with permission from *Runner's World Magazine*, P.O. Box 366, Mountain View, Calif. 94042.

[1] See the article by Singer on pages 40-55 for some principles concerning how *not* to ruin an athlete's motivation. —Ed.

constructive criticism. If office hours are mandatory, make them midnight Saturday to 4 A.M. Sunday and go to sleep in the back room. Simply materialize on the track on practice days, read times off the stopwatch, and go home immediately.

5. Keep the pressure on. Every practice is life-or-death, every meet a war. There is no room on the competitive boat for fun-runners. Every runner has to improve by a certain amount every day. . . . Always bark or snarl; never speak softly. When you bawl out a runner (and you must do this often), do it in front of the whole team. Make sure everyone knows what hopeless cases they are.

THE MEETS

Meets are of course an extension of practice sessions, and the rules outlined above can apply to meets as well as to practice sessions. There are a few additional pointers the coach will find useful, though.

1. Chew everyone out royally after their races. These are but a few of the sarcastic gems available: "Number 31, you look like (*a*) Wilt Chamberlain on a 20-inch bicycle; (*b*) A 500-pound woman on a pegleg; (*c*) The tin man in *The Wizard of Oz*—before he oiled himself; (*d*) An elephant with gout; (*e*) A Nazi soldier marching through a mud puddle."

2. Schedule only "away" meets. The athletes are too crummy to merit a chance to perform in front of the home crowd. Never leave the night before a meet and stay over. Leave at 4 A.M. the day of the meet. Or drive all night if it is a long distance. Never use a bus for transportation. Volkswagens are ideal, but station wagons will do if there is a minimum of 10 passengers per car.

3. After making sure your runners are overtrained, insist that they perform up to practice levels. For instance, after overtraining ex-4:30 miler Joe Smith to 5:00, insist that he do at least 4:30, preferably 4:15.

SOCIAL AND ACADEMIC LIFE

This should pretty well take care of itself. A four-hour workout daily should insure that your runners will not have time either for homework or for any kind of social life. If this doesn't prove effective, an additional 6 A.M. workout should help. Stretch the afternoon practice out by delivering an inane one-hour lecture about how great Filbert Bayi, John Walker, Frank Shorter, etc., looked in their last race.

1. Homework. Homework is irrelevant and unimportant. Runners are supposed to run, not dink around with a pencil and paper. Assign 10 demerits each time a runner is caught with a pencil, paper or notebook; 25 for a textbook; 50 if he is caught doing homework; 100 for taking study hall.

2. Dating. A 9 P.M. curfew will probably be unnecessary, as your runners will collapse the minute they get home. However, a few pointers about dating may be necessary for a particularly stubborn runner. The opposite sex ranks somewhere in the area of bubonic plague, cancer and cyanide as a threat to a runner's career. Assign at least 100 demerits to a runner who is caught with anyone of the opposite sex, family excluded.

Above all, make sure your runners know the price of success. Emphasize that the road to the Olympics is paved with blood, sweat and broken bones. To destroy an athlete, particularly a highly motivated one, requires patience, perseverance, and a total lack of understanding.

Use of Groups
to Improve Athletic Performance

David Nesvig

INTRODUCTION

As part of the Athlete Development Workshop program for AAU synchronized swimming teams sponsored by the Sports Medicine Committee, groups were introduced to discuss coach-athlete and athlete-athlete relationships.[1] It was one component of a psychologically-based regimen designed to assist athletes in coping with the results of stress in high level competition. Other modules include application of biofeedback, use of relaxation techniques[2] and autogenic procedures to improve performance levels. . . . Conducted in 1977 and 1978, these groups have been utilized with the top 25 United States AAU synchronized swimming teams during the week-long workshops conducted at the Olympic Training Center, Squaw Valley, California, as well as with a speed swimming team in a large metropolitan area.

Each group consisted of the coach and, in some cases, an assistant and his or her swimmers meeting with the facilitator (the author) to discuss concerns about competition practice, performance, team goals, and mutual expectations. Usually there were 8 or 10 swimmers in each group plus the coach.

PURPOSE

Four primary goals and one secondary goal were determined for the groups as subgoals of the more global one of improving performance levels for all participants:

1.   To explore the working relationship between coaches and athletes and of athletes to one another in terms of improving the collaboration in both directions.

   In terms of the group experience, the process could range from simple self-disclosure to develop a higher level of trust, to contracting for actual behavioral changes or other concrete agreements regarding practice routines.

---

[1] See the article by Wenz and Strong on pages 328-333. —Ed.
[2] See the article by Suinn on pages 306-315. —Ed.

2.   To effect a better understanding for coaches and swimmers of the similarities and differences of their goals and operations in relation to role distinction and clarification.

> In the group this would necessitate discussion of commitment to the sport, rewards and payoffs, the decision-making process, how conflicts are resolved, etc.

3.   To bring hidden feelings, misunderstandings, and personal agendas into the open.

> As the group discussion progresses these issues normally unfold as mutual collaboration is encouraged by the group facilitator.

4.   To integrate learnings from the other psychological components of the workshop program (relaxation, autogenic techniques, biofeedback procedures) in relation to improved performance levels.

> Particularly when the focus is on collaboration of swimmers with one another and coaches, an attempt is made to bridge the application and utilization of techniques learned in other components. The emphasis is once again on improving practices and competitive performances through lowering stress levels.

5.   To provide data for improving the psychological components of the program is a secondary goal of the groups.

> These data are collected informally by observation of the facilitator and through direct and indirect feedback of group participants. Since a formal, written evaluation is done at the end of the workshop, no attempt is made formally to structure this in the group.

For the purpose of this article, the discussion will center on the first four goals, which are primary. . . . A significant section will be devoted to swimmers' motivation and their reasons for making a long-term commitment to the sport. This will be based on actual responses by the athletes to questions concerning their level of commitment, the pay-offs and rewards for them as swimmers.

GROUP STRUCTURE AND PROCESS

During the late 60s and early 70s when the encounter group movement flourished, the typical social entree was not "What astrological sign are you?" but more relevantly then "What group are you in now?" Psychologically and growth oriented groups were given a great deal of bad press, much of it deserved.

Anyone who lived through that era is likely to have a wide range of reactions and images when presented with the generic term *group*. Unfortunately many of the images may be negative, may trigger off memories of less than positive experiences with a group led by an unprofessional, poorly trained or unethical group facilitator. The term may elicit associations like: therapy group, encounter group, confrontation group, rap group, support group, experimental group, wide-open group, counseling group, "touchy-feelie," or sensitivity training. On the other hand, the word may have a positive valence, connoting pleasant memories of a fruitful group experience resulting in growth or change. Such reactions, whether negative or pleasant, can result in a perception about groups which has the potential to significantly alter any future group experience. Our expectations are powerful determinants in influencing subsequent exposure to a perceived similar experience. Because of this, . . . I made a deliberate attempt to demystify these perceptions about groups in advance at a general meeting of coaches.[3] A brief introduction was given at the initial orientation meeting for athletes as well. Heavy emphasis was given to the central purpose of the group—an opportunity to discuss common concerns, goals, worries, and experiences related to high-level competition. Here was a chance also for the team to meet under more relaxed conditions without the usual time pressures of a tight weekly schedule.

Following this description, they were told what the groups are *not*. They are not counseling, therapy, or encounter groups. All participants were reassured that embarrassing personal questions would not be asked, their family history would not be probed, and that all questions would be answered as directly and honestly as possible by me. Informal follow-up at meals and during breaks gave me the opportunity to answer further questions of the coaches and athletes. These contacts resulted in stronger rapport and served to lower any further resistance to group participation.

At the beginning of each group discussion, the purpose and goals of the group were once again repeated, the structure explained, and the demystification process gone through. Feedback from coaches and swimmers indicated that this was not redundant or overemphasized, rather it was seen as valuable and, in some cases, essential to the group's direction and success. The next step in beginning the group was for me to make a personal statement which led into the first phase of discussion. Following is an approximation of it:

> *I've been a sports nut most of my life, as a competitive tennis player, sportswriter, and fan, and I have to tell you how impressed I am with the level of commitment I've observed in you synchro swimmers and coaches. I don't know of a sport with any higher level of commitment from its athletes, practicing five or six days a week, seven before meets, 11 months out of the year. I've heard also that it means often two practices a day, many times standing around shivering by the pool or rehearsing in chilly water. So, I'm really curious to hear from you what it is about this sport that makes you willing to go through this.*

The responses were informative and enlightening to me and often were revealing to the swimmers and coaches. Many themes developed which were common to every group, while others were idiosyncratic. In analyzing the answers given to this global question, 27 themes developed. Due to the overlap it might be more accurate to say there were consistently a dozen themes which seemed to arise in each group. Some of the most often mentioned reasons included:

> It's an opportunity to travel around the state, the U.S., and other countries.
> I've made a lot of new friends, many very close and important to me.
> It feels good to excel in something.
> I've developed self-esteem and confidence I didn't have before joining the team.
> It's fun performing for an audience.
> It keeps me in shape and slim.
> I enjoy the challenge of competition.

. . . After this opening discussion other predetermined questions were introduced by the leader to direct the flow of discussion. The questions were developed to provide a clear focus for the group

---

[3]See the article by Lanning on pages 362-367. —Ed.

and avoid meaningless meandering. In my experience many of the issues the questions were formulated to elicit, for example, contracting and conflict resolution, arose naturally from group members, requiring no prompting by me.

If the discussion on level of commitment was slow in beginning, related questions were introduced, such as "What are the rewards and payoffs for you in synchro swimming?" and "Why are you willing to sacrifice precious time you could spend studying or on other pleasures?"

DEVELOPING GROUND RULES FOR ASSISTING ONE ANOTHER

Depending on the issues raised spontaneously in discussion, this topic would be approached next. The stimulus question would be similar to this:

How do you help out one another in practice or before a meet? How about in-practice or before a meet? How about during and after competition? What have you found helpful to you and in assisting a teammate?

What is universally generated in discussion of this topic is an awareness of strong individual preferences for giving and receiving feedback on performance. It was my observation that this was concrete and specific enough, as well as universal to all participants' experience, that many areas were tapped. In fact, if there were no time constraints, this subject could be explored for the full two hours. Specific examples of ground rules will be given later. More attention will also be given to what swimmers say coaches do or say that is helpful to them.

CONTRACTING BETWEEN COACHES AND ATHLETES AND ATHLETE-TO-ATHLETE

Contracting was a topic that did not normally arise directly, but more often indirectly during group interaction. Since it is a term not usually used in verbal interactions, it was introduced when participants were talking about how discussions are made. Once the subject was broached, the leader would follow up with,

How are those decisions made? What chance are you given to provide input? Is your voice considered or heard when decisions are made that affect you?

These and similar leading questions are used by the facilitator to lead into an exploration of contracting. Principles of contracting and anecdotes illustrating them will be offered later.

CONFLICT RESOLUTION

This can be potentially the most explosive subject of all those mentioned. Likewise it can result in healing wounds which have severely obstructed communication for an entire team.

Many times current unresolved conflicts are alluded to indirectly or are raised directly by coach or athlete in another context, such as decision-making. Other times past misunderstandings which still are simmering are brought into the open. Again, if the subject is not brought up, the leader will refer to some other reference with a statement like "When you referred to your difference of opinion with [name] I wondered how you handle disagreements and conflicts on the team."

As the facilitator response indicates, the attempt is to depersonalize the conflict, that is, treat it as a normal, inevitable occurrence on any team. The message is that it is a predictable event and there are effective ways to handle disagreements. If it is clear that an unresolved conflict exists that is having a present negative effect on the team or individual, it may be briefly dealt with as an example of a conflict and how it might be dealt with. In at least three instances, it was my judgment that more time was necessary than was available to sufficiently explore the issue. In those cases a second session was arranged for another time during the workshop.

Each of the preceding sections which have been introduced will be given more detailed attention at another point in this article along with examples and anecdotes.

SWIMMERS' AND COACHES' MOTIVATION

Previously, an introduction was made to this topic detailing swimmer's responses. Not included in that section were coaches' answers to the question of their willingness to make such a significant contribution of their energy time and resources to the sport. On the one hand, their reasons were frequently similar to the swimmers, like the opportunity for travel, making friends, and the sense of excelling in an activity. On the other hand, their role as coach clearly dictates other sources of payoff and rewards for them.

As one might expect there was seldom one compelling reason expressed as the major determinant apparent in staying with the sport. Responses unique to coaches were:

The chance to work with good athletes who are also nice kids. In my experience these girls are the "cream of the crop."
I enjoy the teaching aspect of coaching.
It's an opportunity to develop my teaching ability.
Developing a team from a group of basically raw, inexperienced swimmers is a personal challenge.
To continue the tradition of excellence and winning that the [team] have established.
I can see instant results from my coaching and teaching.

Coaches in particular seemed to welcome the permission given by the group structure to be more personal in revealing the complex motivators which keep them involved despite very low pay and demanding schedules which complicate their lives. Almost without exception, the team members were hearing some of these reasons declared for the first time by the coach herself or himself. The impact was sometimes startling, not only on the athletes, but on the coaches, too.

For the coach, answering the question led sometimes to clarification of priorities, as in, "You know I realize now that I probably would have quit before now if it weren't for my compelling desire to see syncho swimming become an Olympic sport." For the swimmer, listening to her coach reveal highly personal revelations led to seeing her coach as a real person, not in a narrowly defined role of the coach. "Wow!" one girl exclaimed after her coach opened up, "I didn't know that before about you. I'm glad to know that." Here was the beginning of the breakdown of the stereotypes of coach as disciplinarian, administrator, slave driver, teacher.

Some coaches engaged in a deep level of personal disclosure as they talked. They talked poignantly of coaching filling a void in their lives left by retirement, relocation, or the death of a loved one. They spoke of coaching as a release or outlet for frustration in their professional careers apart from coaching as a source of recognition. Others spoke of the importance to them of the swimmers as their "children."

As the coaches displayed varying levels of self-disclosure and risk-taking, the seeds of collaboration were sown. This modeling by the coaches encouraged the athletes to do the same. It also was the beginning of a new perception of the coach which made him or her more approachable, less formidable or distant. Other personal agendas were now more likely to be brought into the open. A major goal of the groups was now being addressed.

Coaches are certainly not immune to personal ambition. One coach mused about her desire to crack the top five nationally and make her team eligible for a seeded position and international competition. At the same time, as she talked about her affection for the girls, she displayed her caring nature in a direct way never made clear or experienced by athletes in practice. Again, the group process became a vehicle for a previously unattained level of mutual understanding.

Other coaches shared the complex demands on a coach. Swimmers heard about their coach as a diplomat and politician who must deal with angry or pushy parents and boards. They heard about the demands of fund raising and endless details of planning and coordinating meets thrust upon the coach and assistants. They learned of coaches' own ego needs, that, to coin a pun, "Coaches need strokes too."

This knowledge was beneficial in relation to the discipline of practice; knowing in more detail the demands placed on the coach made it easier for athletes to accept demands placed upon them by the coach. They now knew on a more conscious, practical level that they were not being singled out for extra work.

Returning to the reward system operating for swimmers, coaches listening to their protégés discuss reasons for commitment similarly resulted in the coaches acquiring a deeper level of understanding and a more tolerant approach to their athletes' needs as non-swimmers. The factors which contributed to a swimmer's desire to stay involved ranged from such personal ones as family expectations ("We're all swimmers in our family") to prosaic and almost negative factors ("It beats watching TV and being bored").[4]

Of special interest to me was what girls had to say who had been competitors in other sports. Some were concurrently competing in other sports at school, including speed swimming, gymnastics, diving. For several of them, the attraction of synchro swimming was an integration of the elements of ballet, gymnastics, swimming, diving in one unique, esthetically pleasing activity.

Without attempting to organize them by category, other statements of motives for competing ran the gamut of personal recognition, group support, achievement needs, peer recognition, team loyalty, and the development of personal effectiveness. Further specific examples are:

I need the discipline of daily workouts and routines.
Being on the team is like being in a family. As a matter of fact, I spend more time with them than with my own family.

[4] See the article by Youngblood and Suinn on pages 73-77. –Ed.

I want to make the "A" team.

I want to stay on the "A" team.

I like the appeal of the form and beauty of synchro. Swimming to beautiful music inspires my creativity.

Performing in front of the public is really neat, having my friends and family see me.

I want to see our team make the top 10.

What's really important to me in staying with the team another year is beating [a particular rival].

Synchro is a special sport that a lot of girls in other sports could never be a part of—you have to be able to swim, dive, be a gymnast.

I get to travel all over. Most girls my age haven't traveled like I have.

I don't have to go home to my bad family situation after school.

It's really neat to be a [team member] and hear other kids and swimmers say, "Gee, are you a [team name]?"

I've learned a lot about getting along with people.

I feel much more confident than I ever did before I was a competitor. It's really helped me at school getting along with others.

I used to be really shy and down on myself, but not anymore. It's easier for me to make friends away from the pool, too.

I understand myself much better than before. . . . Being under the pressure of competition, having to organize my time better, working closely with others, developing a sense of loyalty, learning discipline have been incredibly valuable to me.

This last statement was not an isolated statement, but rather one that emerged in similar words from several members of each team. So much has been written and said about personal development in athletics that it has become a cliché that we have come to mistrust. Without any behavioral follow-up as documentation, it can be said that at least the self-report of these athletes is a strong indicator of a carry-over effect from participation in a sport to life situations. Their reports indicate that learning which occurs as a result of the rigors of practice and competition generalizes to their daily life problems. Personal and interpersonal effectiveness is enhanced as well as self-esteem, in many cases. Given the limitations of self-report and all of the biases inherent in this method, nevertheless, for this group of athletes, there is a trend which supports the view that sports activity can be positively correlated with behavioral changes which effect non-sports segments of their lives. In turn, these data are linked to continuation in the sport by the swimmers.

DEVELOPING GROUND RULES FOR ASSISTANCE

Following the discussion of commitment and motivation the subject of how athletes helped one another was introduced; this included practice, competition, and post-competition situations. Conversation centered around giving feedback in a helpful way as well as on the receiving of feedback from fellow swimmers and coaches. This subject area, in my observation, seems to set the stage for the next area of contracting. There appears to be a normal flow to asking for feedback to be given in a different manner or at a particular time.

In the introduction, examples of stimulus questions were mentioned. Once the group begins talking about techniques and methods they find helpful, the leader utilizes this to generate ground rules for giving assistance.

A universal ground rule was *Be specific in describing what you observed, either positive or negative.*[5] (Here a note should be made that while these principles may be well understood and effectively applied by the coaches and many swimmers, they are not equally so for all team members, and therefore worthy of repetition.) It is not of much help, as many persons noted, to say something vague, like "You didn't seem to have much crispness in your turns. You seemed kind of lazy and lackadaisical that time." The words *lazy, lackadaisical,* and *crispness* are subjective and may have a specific meaning to the observer, but to the swimmer being corrected, they may be too vague to be of assistance.

A more concrete specific rephrasing of the example might substitute "It would be better if you would turn more quickly by pushing off with more thrust from the edge of the pool." This example likewise illustrates a second principle: *Be constructive in offering criticism.*

Members of the groups consistently were critical of statements prefaced with zingers like "Well you really blew that one!" or "You certainly have a lousy attitude today." They were all more receptive to opening comments like "You might try . . ." or "It might be better if . . ." or "How about next time. . . ." These beginnings make the listener much more open to the concrete correction which follows.

Another ground rule growing out of the first two is *If possible, demonstrate the change desired.* Many movements in synchro swimming are extremely complex and difficult to describe, even for the most articulate observer. Because of individual learning patterns, modeling the correct technique may be essential. One person may be able to translate the words to the concrete physical movement designated, while another may need a demonstration to make it clear.

The next ground rule related to a frequent complaint voiced by swimmers toward their own peers and coaches as well. That complaint concerned lack of positive reinforcement or praise.[6] Swimmers groused that "you always tell me when I screw up but you never say anything when I've done well." The ground rule became *Give verbal praise when earned or deserved.* The qualifiers earned or deserved were added because the athletes wished it to be sincere, not used in a phony way to give false encouragement.

These ground rules have dealt with giving feedback but do not directly address the reciprocal nature of feedback. The same principles apply to the receiver of the feedback in acknowledging or hearing the corrections or praise. If the feedback is not understood, then the listener needs to be specific and constructive in requesting clarification. Conversely, if the feedback has been useful, it assists the person to know that it was. This knowledge makes it easier for the person to know if his or her feedback is on target.

If the observer hears "That really helped me to improve that dive. I've been having trouble with that for weeks, and I couldn't get the entry just the way I wanted it," it also makes it more likely the feedback given will risk such an observation in the future.

This latter point was reinforced through a quick exercise introduced by the leader. Each person was asked to think of a person who, in his or her estimation, gives clear, direct, useful feedback—in

---

[5] See the article by Botterill on pages 261-268. —Ed.
[6] See the article by Rushall on pages 63-72 and the article by Massimo on pages 229-237. —Ed.

short, someone who applies the principles just developed. A reporting out of these, with examples, served as illustrations. It also provided an effective summary of the ground rules for giving assistance.

CONTRACTING

The summary also led naturally into an exploration of contracting. Although seldom referred to as contracting, the notion was frequently raised in the context of decision-making. The principles of giving and receiving feedback were then broadened to encompass team issues such as practice times, planning routines, determining A and B team members, solo and duet partners, and the selecting of travel squads.

Principles of contracting are an extension of those laid down on giving assistance and feedback. An interesting array of issues was typically raised for potential contracts, from such seemingly picky items as how soon before a competitive meet costumes should be worn, to more fundamental matters of how music for a routine will be chosen. Before getting into making actual verbal contracts, group members were reminded that the goal of contracts is to improve team and individual performances. An extension of the feedback guidelines applied to contracts would specify the contingencies each person should consider:

> concrete, observable behavior (actions or words)
> the specific behavior to be changed
> state constructively and positively the conditions
> if possible or appropriate, indicate the time element involved

One of the first contracts worked out in the group dealt with what to a non-swimmer might seem an inconsequential problem; yet, to the swimmer competing on a highly ranked team, was cause for consistent pre-competition tension on the team. The tension often resulted in the flaring of tempers and distraction which, for some, led to a lower level of performance than the individual might attain under calmer conditions.

The source of irritation was a habit one team member had of not getting her hat and combs in place until a few moments before the team formally began competition. For the rest of the team the norm was to have this taken care of 15 or 30 minutes beforehand. Nagging by other team mates or coaches resulted only in more attention being paid to this annoying habit and less to essential last-minute preparations. A standoff had resulted which was the source of much unproductive gossip, name-calling, and accusations. After both the identified norm-breaker and the team discussed the reasons for their positions, a contract was decided upon, basically a compromise which satisfied both sides in the issue. The contract specified:

1. The recalcitrant swimmer agreed to have her hat and combs in place no later than 10 minutes before a meet.
2. Team members agreed in turn to make no mention of the costuming until the 10-minute deadline.
3. If the deadline was not observed, other team members would be allowed to point out her unreadiness until she complied.
4. If the deadline was met, team members would thank her for her compliance.

This example illustrates the principles. It deals with concrete, observable behavior (placing cap and combs on head), specifies the behavior to be changed (observe the 10-minute deadline), indicates what must be done in a positive statement (have hat and combs on head) rather than what must *not* be done, and, finally, makes the time element clear (10 minutes before each competitive meet, not practice).

A more complex analysis of contracting, including other principles, conditions, and follow-up, did not seem appropriate for the group. Given the shortness of time and other priorities for attention it was kept at this level.

Due to the uniformly positive evaluation of the groups, almost every team agreed to continue with follow-up meetings after leaving camp. The only exceptions were those few teams of the 25 that already had regularly scheduled team meetings. Final negotiations took the form of a contract which included time, location, who shall attend (e.g., coaches, A team, B team, volunteer assistants), frequency and length of meetings, agenda, and designated leader. This settlement was similarly used as an illustration of contracting.

CONFLICT RESOLUTION

It is inevitable on any athletic team during the course of a season that varying degrees of conflict will arise among its team members, coaches, board members, and volunteers. Based upon this premise, the topic of conflict resolution is undertaken in the group. From this stance, that conflict is normal and unavoidable, it is hoped that a dispassionate view of conflict resolution can be reached.

If a conflict, either current or past, is not raised by a group member, the facilitator will simply initiate the subject through questions or reminders or other allusion to conflict or potential areas of conflict. Occasionally a present or impending conflict on a team was immediately focused upon, as in the previous illustration of contracting (placing hats and combs before a meet).

Before zeroing in on particular conflicts, a more wide-open conversation was encouraged on the negative effects of unresolved conflicts. It was my observation that every team was aware of the consequence in terms of morale and performance. What they were unaware of was how to begin to resolve the conflict. In those instances, assistance was provided in identifying and breaking down the sources of conflict.

Once the sources of irritation were identified, they could then be approached. If the irritant was a particularly offensive rule or policy, the coach or a senior member of the team was asked to provide an understanding of the rationale behind it. Frequently the providing of information was sufficient to either resolve the individual's conflict or reduce it to the point of making it livable or acceptable.

If the conflict was interpersonal, however, it often required more time than could be justified to devote to it in the initial group. If so, a follow-up session was scheduled to continue the attempt at resolution. This was amicably accepted in three instances and a private meeting was arranged for the group.

No reason was seen as too trivial for consideration as long as it had consequences for any member of the team. Rules and policies concerning practice, travel, dress codes, room assignments on the road, free-time dating, curfew, eating restrictions, horseplay, access to the pool, and post-competition parties all were problem areas for some.

THE COACH—WHOEVER THAT IS

Ask 20 athletes and you're likely to get 20 different responses to the queries "What do you want most from a coach?" or "What do you find most helpful in a coach?" After meeting with 25 teams I have found that at least synchronized swimmers are expecting a new breed of coach. Their expectations are complex and not easy to categorize.

Consistent with a more traditional view of the coach's role, they want an organizer, a motivator, a disciplinarian, a teacher. Swimmers in the 70s and 80s, while still valuing those multiple roles, expect and sometimes demand more. They are looking for a technician, a trainer, a collaborator, a problem-solver, perhaps a personal mentor.

Psychology of Coaching

Cal Botterill

There are two major areas in which psychology can make a significant contribution to coaching and sport:

1. maximizing the athlete's performance
2. maximizing the athlete's personal growth and development

It is, however, becoming increasingly apparent that there is an extremely important relation-ship between the two areas. In order to make significant and consistent progress in maximizing performance plenty of attention must be paid to the athlete's personal growth and development. The psychological stresses that athletes have to contend with today (whether it be "pee wee" house leagues or the Olympics) are often tremendous and the vast majority of athletes who consistently perform well are those that "have their head together." They are the ones who are psychologically mature, have stable personalities, and whose personal growth and development have not been neglected.[1] They are the ones who keep things in perspective and cope well with difficult (and sometimes inappropriate) situations because they are "cool," adaptable, independent, self-confident, and self-disciplined as well as committed.

It is important to think about how kids get that way[2] and whether there are things you can do to help develop these kind of characteristics. They certainly don't happen automatically and the practical suggestions presented later in this paper can be a big help. In the end it is the athletes (not the coach) who have to be able to cope, react, and perform *on their own*. In order for them to effectively do so (and enjoy it) it is critical that the coach pay particular attention to the personal growth and development of his/her athletes.

Cal Botterill. Psychology of coaching. *Coaching Review* 1, 4 (July 1978):46-55. Also published in *Proceedings, National Coaches Certification Program, Level 5 seminar, 1978,* Canadian Amateur Hockey Association.

[1] See the review article by Morgan on pages 145-155. —Ed.
[2] See the article by Martens on pages 169-175. —Ed.

LIMITATIONS OF EXTERNAL MANIPULATION

Many of the early efforts in the area of psychology called "Behavior Modification" were made in an attempt to improve behavior without particular concern for personal growth and development. This of course led to a great deal of "external manipulation" by behavior therapists in order to motivate clients and improve behavior. This approach often led to limited and rather inconsistent results mainly because of client dependency on the external manipulation. Whenever the client moved into an environment where the possibility for external control was limited the improved behavior would often disappear.

Recent developments in this field,[3] however, have resulted in a greater emphasis on self-control and the personal growth and development of the client. By actively involving the client from the start in planning a behavior change, by discussing why certain behavior improvements are important, and by discussing detailed plans and strategies on how to improve behavior and develop *internal* capabilities, therapists have produced more effective and consistent behavior improvement and much more mature, independent, and confident clients.

Developments in the psychology of coaching have not been dissimilar. Early efforts in the field were aimed at maximizing or improving athletic performance without much concern for the athlete's personal growth and development. Results were, to say the least, inconsistent.

An example might be the topic of arousal level and the attempts by coaches to achieve an optimal arousal level for performance via dramatic pep-talks, prescribed pre-game routines, etc. Ironically though, even if the coach has control over things in the dressing room and is able to achieve a *temporary* optimal arousal level for performance (which is virtually impossible with groups of different individuals), he/she usually has virtually no control over what happens as soon as the team heads for the ice, field, gym, or whatever. The coach really has no control over spectators, the opposition, or the officials and how they might affect the athlete's motivation and state of arousal. Because there is such a limited amount that can be done by external manipulation, the only sensible thing to do is try to develop the athlete's personal capacity to cope, keep things in perspective, and regulate his/her own arousal level.

It is important to remember that the preparation of an athlete is complete when the coach isn't needed! The world of sport (at all levels) is full of examples of coaches frantically trying to manipulate things or give last second directions in a futile attempt to assist athletes in performing in situations for which they haven't been prepared as individuals. The problem often originates with coaches whose very preoccupation with physical performance results in oversights in the athlete's psychological preparation and personal growth and development. This author would suggest from experience that with the right kind of attention and preparation it is simply amazing how much psychological maturity and capacity for self-direction that can be developed in even very young kids Along with these developments athletic performance simply soars.

THE ROLE OF PSYCHOLOGY IN COACHING

Dr. Miroslav Vanek (who is probably the dean of all practicing sport psychologists) suggested at the 1976 Post Olympic Games Symposium that the role of psychology and the psychologist in sport has really been misunderstood. The perception of psychologists as "shrinks" for psychic and

[3] See the article by Suinn on pages 26-36. —Ed.

problem athletes, or magical "hypnotists" with instant psychological preparations and crisis remedies has been a deceiving and inappropriate one.

Just like physical preparation, the psychological preparation of an athlete is not an instant thing. The most important implications of sport psychology lie in long term planning and development and the prevention of crises and psychic or problem athletes. Vanek points out that he now plays a much more significant role in the long range planning and preparation of athletes and finds one of his most important roles is preventing foolish mistakes by coaches and administrators which could severely hinder personal development and performance. *An ounce (gram) of prevention is worth a pound (kilogram) of cure* and the psychology of coaching is certainly no exception!

The author would suggest from experience that if our knowledge in the psychology of coaching was applied primarily towards maximizing the personal growth and development of athletes the inevitable result would be the maximization of athletic performance. Planning for and pursuing the *total* development of young athletes is not only morally the correct thing to do but likely the only way to truly maximize their potential.

In a world where athletes need to be able to cope with pressures, adapt to circumstances, keep things in perspective, exhibit discipline, and maintain concentration in order to perform well, coaches cannot afford to shortsell the development of psychological maturity and personal confidence and stability. Most people however only pay lip service to topics like the personal growth and development of athletes and seldom offer specific suggestions to facilitate the process. The remainder of this paper is aimed at providing practical leadership ideas which can assist in maximizing the personal growth and development of athletes as well as their performances.

SEASONAL PLANNING FROM A PSYCHOLOGICAL PERSPECTIVE

If you don't know where you are going (and how to get there) you are bound to end up someplace else!

This premise not only succinctly suggests a solid rationale for the topic of detailed seasonal planning but probably also explains the majority of problems (usually unintentional) that exist in sport today.

From a psychological perspective detailed seasonal planning has incredible implications for both the coach and the athletes. However, despite the fact that it is probably the most important function in coaching, it is without doubt the most neglected. The number of problems that can be avoided or overcome, and the kind of progress and satisfaction that can be assured by doing some detailed planning and communicating with young athletes is simply amazing. All too often though, the first practice is called, the equipment is out, and the season is underway without anyone really understanding:

what the season or activity is all about?
what the coach's goals, priorities, and expectations are?
what the player's goals, priorities, and expectations are?
what the team's goals, priorities and strategies should be?

Phase I: Planning by the Coach

The coach should start by simply thinking about what the season or activity is all about and what his/her goals, priorities, and expectations are for the group. It then might be beneficial to start thinking about the upcoming season in three ways. First, what are the possible *areas of concern* for the group this year. Secondly, what are some of the *specific goals* that can be set in each of the areas. And thirdly, what might the *strategies* be in pursuing these goals.

The coach should also start to think about how the athletes can be involved in this goal setting and planning activity. It is important to find out why the athletes came out and what they are expecting as soon as possible. If the coach's goals, priorities and expectations are incompatible with those of the athletes (or vice versa) the preseason is the time to find out so that both sides can find an acceptable solution while options still exist.

There are also other reasons for involving the athletes in preseason goal setting and planning. Psychologists have gathered evidence to suggest that involving the group in discussion and decisions can increase the awareness of and the commitment to group goals. Involving the group in goal setting also results in a form of "psychological contracting"[4] which can be an extremely effective motivational and leadership technique.

At any rate it is advisable to plan and conduct a number of group planning sessions at the beginning of the year for the purpose of involving the athletes in creating and compiling a comprehensive list of goals and intentions.

Phase II: Planning with the Athletes

Prior to conducting the planning sessions with the athletes the coach should have done considerable preparation and homework. A fairly *comprehensive* list of areas of concern should have been developed along with examples of specific goals and possible strategies. (See Table 1.)

The coach also should have listed any *limitations* within which the group has to operate that season. The group should be made aware of limited practice time, required dress code or any other organizational, institutional, or economic limitations, prior to any goal setting or detailed planning. Clarifying these issues early results in more realistic goal setting and avoids the frustration of these things coming up later and disrupting the group process.

The group planning sessions should revolve around the same questions the coach has been considering:

1.   What is the season or activity really all about?
2.   What are "areas of concern" for the team?
3.   What are some "specific goals" to be strived for in each area?
4.   What are some plans or "strategies" to achieve those goals?

Many athletes have never been asked to contribute to a process like this before (some kids may not even know why they came out for the team!) and the homework the coach has done is a big help in stimulating discussion and getting everyone contributing. It may be necessary to ask questions of different individuals and suggest possible areas of concern. It may be necessary to give

---

[4] See the article by Nesvig on pages 250-260. —Ed.

Table 1. Seasonal Planning Worksheet

Team:

Age Group:

Calibre:

AREAS OF CONCERN	SPECIFIC GOALS	STRATEGIES
1. Behavior with officials.	—No arguing with officials. —No misconduct penalties.	—Loss of playing time by violators. —Only designated captains able to ask for clarification on rulings.
2. Behavior with coach.	—Share concerns with coach at earliest convenience.	—Coach to be available for consultation before and after practices and games.
3. Behavior with team mates.	—No "bitching" or destructive criticism of team mates.	—Loss of playing time by violators.
4. Behavior as a team member.	—Be on time for all team functions.	—Violators asked to do extra conditioning drills to compensate team for disruption.
5. Enjoyment and socialization.	—Enjoyable practices. —Get to know each other well.	—Work hard and play hard. —Designated "fun" games or activities in every practice. —Organize team social activities.
6. Team Tactics	—Be able to effectively execute a forechecking system.	—Presentation and demonstration of system by coach (in dressing room and on ice). —Regular drills in practices.
7. Team skills.	—Be able to skate well.	—Regular drills, games, and activities which develop agility, speed, power and endurance. —Go free skating whenever possible. —Organize and participate in shinny or scrub games on outdoor rinks.

Other Possible Areas
—Behavior towards opponents.   —Fitness.
—Behavior with parents.   —Playing time.
—Behavior with fans and the public. —Practices.
—Individual skills.   —Etc.

examples of specific goals and possible strategies. It may be necessary to give goal setting and planning "homework" exercises to designated group members or simply allow time between sessions for thought about the topics.

It is however important to set a co-operative motivational *climate* at this stage and have as many ideas as possible originate from the group. The more the group contributes to the plan the more likely they are to feel committed to it.

The coach is being democratic at this stage but not *"laissez-faire"* and it is important to be organized and appear confident, goal-oriented, and committed. The athletes should feel free and functional in contributing to the discussion but recognize the rights of majority or consensus and be aware of the commitment necessary to achieve goals.

Although some coaches seem to fear the consequences of letting athletes contribute to goal setting and planning, this author found in a variety of settings that groups consistently set tougher more desirable goals than one might have thought. The coach's biggest task is usually keeping the goals and plans realistic, specific and achievable.

It is important whenever possible to state goals or objectives in *specific, measurable, behavioral* terms. Push for specificity in goal setting sessions—it results in more meaningful, realistic, achievable goals. When statements of intent are *specific,* and *explicit,* the correlation with eventual behavior is much higher because people have a better understanding, feel more responsible, and can be held more accountable.

The following dialogue illustrates the refining of a general goal into a more manageable specific goal.

> Player: —I want to win!
> Coach: —So do I . . . but what do we have to do to win?
> Player: —er . . . well, I guess we have to play better.
> Coach: —What specific things do we have to do better?
> Player: —For one thing we have to know our positions better.
> Coach: —Right! We want to know where to position ourselves in our own end and in our opponents' end.

Similarly rather than stating a nebulous general goal like "sportsmanship," specify the *target behaviors* whenever possible.

> e.g. —shake hands with opponents after every game
> —absolutely no "mouthing-off" at officials

Clear specific behavioral and skill goals are inevitably more meaningful and achievable.

It is important especially with team sports to push for a *consensus* on goals or strategies. Discussion usually results in an acceptable compromise for all. People tend to be idealistic optimistic and co-operative at the start of the year and quickly recognize the utility of coming to an agreement or consensus. If, however, someone's goals are completely incompatible with the group goals and strategies, the beginning of the year is the time to find out. This gives these individuals an opportunity to adapt or find a group whose objectives are more compatible with their own. For example, a team may agree to approximately equal playing time during playoffs. A player who has difficulty accepting this goal should find a solution before problems develop.

Discussion of *"strategies"* to achieve goals inevitably leads to a consideration of the effort and discipline that is required. If people have been involved in setting goals and discussing the rationale behind them, they are usually much more eager to accept the kinds of behavioral controls that might be necessary to attain them. After discussing strategies and control, some groups may go so far as setting up punishments for behavior inconsistent with group goals!

> e.g. 1st offense—sit out next shift
>   2nd offense—sit out remainder of game
>   3rd offense—sit out remainder of game and following game (Return to play subject to group approval.)

Interestingly enough coercive control often becomes unnecessary as group members soon learn to recognize what is consistent or inconsistent with group goals and are able to monitor and control their own behavior. Obviously whenever possible the group should be encouraged to set up rewards for positive behavior as well as or instead of punishments for negative behavior.

During all this group planning the coach or someone he designates should jot down or *record* any specific goals or strategies about which there is a consensus. A list can be compiled and developed into a comprehensive seasonal plan which can be reviewed and distributed for final approval so that everyone is clear about group expectations and the commitment required.

Phase III: Making the Plans Work

The coach's role obviously is to encourage behavior which is consistent with group goals and discourage that which isn't. However, as mentioned earlier, if goals and strategies are clear individuals soon start to monitor their own behavior and that of their team mates in a very consistent way.

In the early stages if leader behavior is not completely self-evident, the coach should explain his/her actions and rationally tie them in with stated goals and strategies. Whenever possible the coach should concentrate on recognizing behavior which is desirable and consistent with group plans and praise it openly while explaining why. Also do not restrict praise to certain individuals—find something positive in everyone's behavior and let them know about it!

It is extremely critical that a coach's behavior is consistent with the stated goals and strategies. Youngsters particularly will usually model what adults do rather than what they say. Therefore, it is ridiculous to demand sportsmanship, poise and discipline, etc., from one's players yet regularly get overexcited, abuse officials, etc. It is important to be aware of one's own behavior and its effect on others. If coaches are to expect commitment from their players they must display that commitment and dedication themselves!

One of the best ways to reinforce commitment is to involve all group members in forms of leadership. Contributing to leadership produces a *"vested interest"* or increased identity with the group as well as an increased appreciation of the leadership role and group plans.

With a little guidance and ingenuity group members can become a terrific source of helpful ideas and leadership. When goals and strategies are clear athletes can easily be asked to create and conduct drills, "fun" games, and activities. This provides the coach with the opportunity to give special attention to individuals or subgroups. Different members can be asked to act as subgroup leaders or captains for each game, practice, or team activity. *Participant Leadership* can be a great source of enthusiasm and group morale!

A periodical *review* of stated goals and strategies serves as a reminder or restatement of intentions and commitment. In addition it provides measurable and observable feedback to the group. Areas of success become sources of pride, reinforcement, and inspiration. Areas of failure become the focal point for effort and concentration. A review also provides an opportunity to reassess goals and intentions and modify or adjust them if deemed necessary. Intermediate goals can be developed in areas of difficulty and extended goals in areas of success. It might be pointed out that when detailed group planning has been done the coach usually makes fairly regular reference to stated goals and strategies in the everyday justifying, reinforcing, or criticizing of behaviors in the group.

The coach can also do a number of things to try and insure that other factors in the athlete's environment encourage commitment to the group plan. For example copies of stated goals, intentions, and priorities can be made available to "significant others" in the social world of the group (teachers, parents, etc.). This will often increase the commitment of group members as a result of the sincere public display of intentions. It also usually produces considerable moral support and helps educate parents and supporters.

The coach can also try to insure that the total competition or participation structure encourages the kinds of behavior being strived for. This may be difficult and frustrating if the existing league or competitive structure as a whole contains behavioral problems!

CONCLUSION

These planning and leadership techniques usually result in tremendous personal growth and development in young athletes. In addition, the much more complete preparation inevitably produces dramatic improvement in physical performances. Specifically, the following things tend to happen:

Clarified goals and priorities—everyone has a better idea as to what the season or activity is all about and why it is important.

Increased commitment and motivation towards group goals.

Fairly immediate success because many specific achievable goals (other than just winning games) have been identified.

Improvement in the athletes' self-confidence and in group morale.

The development of psychological maturity in athletes which is reflected in self-discipline and skills in self-control and self-management.

Increased poise and improved abilities to adapt, cope, "keep things in perspective," and concentrate on the right things.

The elimination and prevention of problem behaviors.

Leadership usually becomes less autocratic and much more enjoyable and effective.

Increased appreciation of the importance of planning and goal setting in any activity.

Increased empathy and respect for the rights and feelings of others.

Improved communication and understanding among all parties concerned and control over "unintentional" problem behavior.

Happier athletes, better performance, and much more fun.

Maximizing the personal growth and development of young athletes is not only compatible with pursuing excellence in sports; it is usually a necessary prerequisite!

Goal Setting and Performance

James D. McClements and Cal Botterill

The basic idea behind this paper is that children and athletes are opting out of physical activity and sport because they are not getting enough from their participation. That is to say, sport and physical activity are not rewarding or self-reinforcing enough to maintain involvement. If there is one concept that we know about human behavior, it is that we participate in what we like (approach) and stay away from what we don't like (avoidance). For most of us who are committed to sport and physical activity it is difficult to accept the idea that kids don't get enough out of sport, especially when we believe that sport and competition have positive values. It is too easy to rationalize that the athlete just wasn't "tough enough" or "wasn't a winner" or "didn't have enough jam" to "stay at it" or "be a winner" or "be aggressive." Instead, our feelings are that the athlete may not have had the ability to achieve the goal of winning, but perhaps given his or her limits, they were a success.

GOAL SETTING, PLANNING, AND EVALUATION

If sport and competition has social values, then *each individual has the right to be successful.* Proper setting of goals and evaluation of this attainment can facilitate this right. Each human involved with sport has the responsibility to promote the right to be successful. In order to insure the opportunity for success, the planning process should include the goal setting and evaluation as equal partners with the skill learning, physical training, and teamwork (see Figure 1).

Certain factors interact to improve performance. (1) The program is planned so that the current level advances to the terminal level defined by the goal; therefore the program is a product of the individual's own goal. (2) Evaluation is part of the planning process in that each of the goals must be evaluatable. Evaluation is not something done as hindsight at the end of a season, but built into the entire season.

What Dimensions Should Be Considered in Goal Setting?

The goals must be more than just a wish or a dream; they must be realistic. Specific factors must be considered in setting goals.

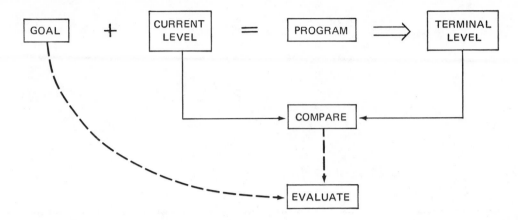

Figure 1. Interaction goal setting program development and evaluation

1. Performance. The basic factors used in setting performance goals are the individual's long-term goal, the individual's current level, and the number of seasons available to achieve the long-term goal. These are used to set a reasonable season or short-term goal as the intermediary step to achieving a long-term goal.

2. Commitment of the Individual. A less obvious but crucial factor in planning goals is the commitment of the individual. This relates to the amount of time and the degree of effort that the individual is willing to dedicate to achieving his goals.

3. Opportunity. It is also important to consider the effective opportunity that the individual has to achieve his goals. The types of opportunities that should be considered are: (*a*) practice time and facilities available, (*b*) the limits of coaches, (*c*) competitions available, (*d*) funds, and (*e*) climatic conditions.

4. Potential. The last factor—the individual's potential—is the most difficult to assess. Coaches sometimes think that they "know" their athlete's potential; however, the certainty of this subjective evaluation is at best suspect. One clue to an athlete's potential may come from a review of the individuals rate of improvement, allowing for opportunity and effort. This necessitates that progress, opportunity, and effort be regularly recorded and evaluated.

If the short-term goal appears to be unreasonable when the coach and athlete are planning the season plan, it is important to consider the feasibility of the long-term goal.

What Do You Evaluate First—Effort or Performance?

Basically, a program plan should be based on a seasonal goal which is set by considering the athlete's long-term goal, commitment, potential, and opportunity.[1] It is assumed that the athlete uses the program plan to train, practice, and compete (see Figure 2). There are two major categories of success: *effort* and *performance*. Every coach is aware of athletes who have fallen short of their potential. Sometimes this occurs because of unreasonable goal setting (athletes want too much too

---

[1] See the article by Botterill on pages 261-268. —Ed.

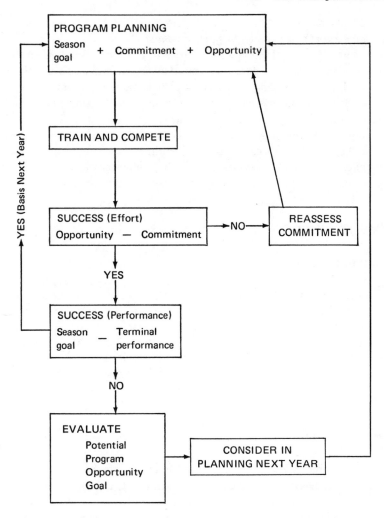

Figure 2. Programming degree of success and evaluation

fast). Adequate planning of a series of goals and evaluations should offset this problem. Setting and achieving short-term or seasonal goals should be reinforcing and this reinforcement should encourage effort. Coaches should not assume that athletes are capable of evaluating success on their own, because athletes often have inadequate reference points and cannot be objective about themselves. Other times athletes fall short of their goals because they either did not realize and put out the effort necessary to achieve their goals or they were unwilling to do whatever is required to achieve their goals. Setting readily measurable goals for effort should help reduce this problem. Planning for commitment as a method of overcoming the lack of effort will be discussed later. The main point at this time is that *if the athlete makes the effort, he or she has achieved success.*[2] The evaluation of

---

[2] See the article by Zaremski on pages 238-246. —Ed.

performance is only meaningful if the athlete has made the effort to complete the program. *It is crucial to evaluate effort before evaluating performance!*

Let us assume that an athlete has made the effort. Then and only then, the *degree of performance success* can be considered. It is very important in performance evaluation to avoid the *either-or thinking* that leads to labelling success/failure. It is more important to determine the *degree of success* and to identify the cause, i.e., program, commitment, opportunity, long-term goal, or individual potential. Again, it is vital that we as coaches assist the athletes with the evaluation because they are usually too emotionally involved to be objective. Once the degree of success has been established and the causes have been identified, then these causes can be used to plan for the upcoming season or perhaps to reconsider long-term goals. It is important to note that this process does not evaluate the person per se but rather evaluates the total program which includes the individual.

COMMITMENT AND GOALS

Why Is Commitment Important?

Perhaps the most frustrating problem for coaches concerned about athletes is the lack of commitment. How does commitment relate to performance? Commitment is the starting point for adequate preparation (see Figure 3). The preparation includes physical training (strength, cardiovascular, flexibility, etc.), learning of basic skills, plays and strategies, mental preparation for optimal arousal and concentration, and finally developing a life-style that complements rather than opposes the goal. This type of preparation cannot be legislated by rules or supervised by coaches. This preparation is the individual athlete's responsibility. Adequate preparation is the key to developing confidence which is crucial for optimal performance.

Can You Plan for Commitment?

Commitment sometimes comes prepackaged in the athlete; however, this is not always so. Commitment can also be developed through careful planning. It is not something that an athlete either does or does not have. There are three steps recommended to develop commitment.

1. Setting Reasonable Goals. These goals must relate both to performance and to preparation. (These are discussed later.)

2. Writing Contracts. Commitment is defined by writing contracts. Research suggests that there is more goal acceptance and, therefore, more improvement if the contracts are written using certain restrictions: (*a*) the goals and the contract must be determined by the athlete, (*b*) the contract must be clear and explicit, (*c*) the contract must make reasonably difficult and challenging demands,

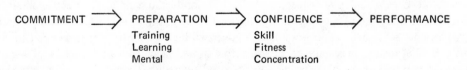

Figure 3. Products of commitment

and (*d*) the contract must be public at least among the athlete's peers and others who are significant to the athlete.

    3. Management by Objectives. Commitment is maintained by a process labelled management by objectives. Chronological records should be maintained of training programs, health, and life style. This requires that diaries refer to the athlete's goals of effort and performance. It is crucial that coaches check an athlete's diary regularly and assist the athletes to objectively evaluate their relative successes and failures.

What Are Goals? What Function Do They Have?

    It is very important that goals be set that are both difficult enough to challenge, yet realistic enough to achieve (see Figure 4). Evaluation of these goals certainly becomes a form of *feedback*. This feedback serves the function of *reinforcement*. Success becomes the positive reinforcement which is the basic unit of all learning and behavior modification. If an athlete is successful, this should enhance the will to become even better. On the other hand, if the athlete is not successful, the process of evaluation should pinpoint the cause of his falling short of the goal. The identification of the cause and effect should provide a basis for planning success. In either case, the results should produce more effective program planning.

How Do You Set Goals That Are Difficult Yet Realistic?

    Goals have been divided into three categories (see Figure 5). The first two categories, general subjective and general objective, have some basic evaluation problems. The general subjective analysis by coaches and others who are significant which says "You tried your best" is usually used after the fact as a consolation prize or a form of condolence for athletes who did not win. These comments are always well meant; however, they are not always based on fact. Unfortunately, they convey the message "You were not good enough."

    Better coaches have recognized the problem of subjective analysis and have also tried to avoid evaluating success on a win-loss basis. The issue of win-loss evaluation is linked to the dual problems of probability of success and the quality of competition. It is quite possible for two or more individuals to be progressing rapidly towards international level performance and become discouraged because they compete against each other with at best a 50% chance of success. On the other hand, victories are often meaningless and hollow if the competition is weak. Each athlete in a competition should have the potential for personal success. One popular way of avoiding this issue is the concept of personal bests. This technique is reasonably good; however, it does beg the question: how much is

GOALS	EVALUATION	PRODUCT
Difficult Enough to Challenge	Feedback	Commitment
Realistic Enough to Achieve	Reinforcement	Program Planning

Figure 4. Goal evaluation

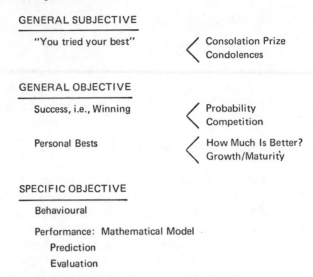

GENERAL SUBJECTIVE

"You tried your best"   Consolation Prize
       Condolences

GENERAL OBJECTIVE

Success, i.e., Winning   Probability
       Competition

Personal Bests   How Much Is Better?
       Growth/Maturity

SPECIFIC OBJECTIVE

Behavioural

Performance: Mathematical Model
    Prediction
    Evaluation

Figure 5. What types of goals?

better? It is often difficult not to improve as one grows older and gains maturity. Is a teenage 800-meter runner who improves from 1:52.0 to 1:51.9 seconds over a season of training a success? Sure he improved, but was this enough improvement to be called success? How much improvement is necessary for it to be meaningful?

Research outside sport recommends that behavior is readily changed by setting *measurable objective goals* and evaluating these goals. In sport, these goals could be concerned with: life-style, practice, physical training, and performance. Specific *life-style* goals could be food, including type, amount and calories; rest patterns (specifically hours of sleep); work habits in sport, school, or work; and recreation patterns. *Practice goals* would be related to skill learning and could include amount of time on each skill and the degree of concentration while practicing as well as actual improvement of specific skills. Physical *training goals* could specify the amount of time and intensity for each component of a physical training program, e.g., strength, flexibility, warm-up, warm-down, cardiovascular, etc. *Performance goals* should be specific, difficult yet achievable and not merely wishful thinking. It appears that if these are stated, recorded, and checked using the model of *management by objectives,* athletes are more likely to behave (living and training) in a pattern that optimizes their probability of success. Ideally, the process becomes a self-fulfilling prophecy in that proper training and living patterns lead to changes in performance that reinforce the training and living patterns.

A MATHEMATICAL MODEL

The evaluation of success of course must include performance in a competitive environment. Setting demanding yet reasonable performance goals requires good predictors, not only for the individual athlete, but also for the future competitions. In order to have good predictors for the timed and measured sports of speedskating, track and field, and swimming, a mathematical model of improvement has been developed.[3] The basic concept in predicting future performance is the principle of diminishing returns. This states that it is more difficult to achieve a unit of performance improvement as this performance approaches the theoretical limits. Simply stated, it is easier to improve from 13.0 seconds in the 100-meter dash to 12.9 seconds (a 0.1-second improvement), than it is to improve from 10.0 seconds to 9.9 seconds (also a 0.1-second improvement). In the mathematical model, recent performance trends in individual events were used to represent the difficulty of improvement. The general form of the equation is:

$$\hat{Y} = ae^{bx} + c$$

$\hat{Y}$ = predicted performance
b = rate of change
a = a constant
c = theoretical limit of man

A typical curve, men's 1500-meter speedskating, is presented in Figure 6.

Applications

There are essentially four applications of the mathematical model.

1. Prediction of Future Performance. The model allows a prediction of world-class performance in each of the measured and timed events which can be used to set long-term goals.

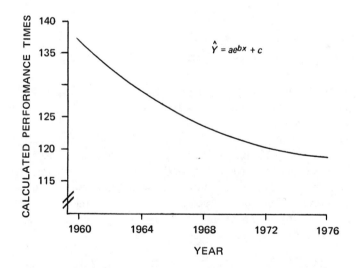

Figure 6. Speedskating winning times by year of competition

---

[3]The logic and method of developing this model can be found in J. D. McClements and W. M. Laverty, A mathematical model of speedskating performance improvement for goal setting and program evaluation, *Canadian Journal of Applied Sport Sciences*, in press.

2. Individual Goal Setting. The curves were developed to facilitate the setting of objective short-term goals that are demanding yet reasonable. It is assumed that an athlete can state a long-term goal. In this example, an athlete has a long-term goal of competing internationally by 1984 in the men's 1500-meter speedskating (see Figure 7). The index units associated with his long-term goal equal 28 ($\hat{Y}$ = 28 in Figure 7). His current level of performance is 2 minutes 35 seconds or 155 seconds. The index units associated with his current level equal 0 (x = 0 in Figure 7). In this example, it is assumed that the current year is 1976. In order to determine a one-year goal, one must calculate the index units from the goal,

$$\text{index units from goal} = \hat{Y} - x$$
$$= 28 - 0 = 28 \text{ units}$$

and the number of years available.

$$\text{years available} = 1984 - 1976$$
$$= 8 \text{ years}$$

The one-year goal is

$$\frac{\hat{Y} - x}{\text{years available}} = \frac{28}{8} = 3.5 \text{ units}$$

His next year's goal in index units is his current level in index units plus his one-year goal in index units.

$$\text{next year's goal} = x + \text{one-year goal}$$
$$= 0 + 3.5 = 3.5 \text{ units}$$

These index units are used to determine the performance goal for the upcoming season (see Figure 8). In this example, the performance goal would be 141.5 seconds or a 13.4-second improvement.[4] Assuming the athlete maintained a perfect critical path over the eight years, the *equal units of improvement* would yield progressively smaller absolute performance improvements for each successive year. In the above example the absolute performance improvement required each year would be 13.4 seconds in the first year, 8.6 seconds in the second year, 5.9 seconds in the third year, and so forth up to 0.7 seconds in the eighth year. These performance goals would be reconsidered and revised if necessary for each season. However, if the one-year goal is achieved, then the athlete is on target for this long-term goal. It is important to remember that this evaluation process is only part of the interaction of goal setting, program planning, and performance.[5]

---

[4]While graphs have been used in this paper, it is recommended that for actual use, detailed tables or computer calculations be applied. The tables and the computer services for speedskating, swimming, and track and field are available at cost from Dr. Jim McClements, College of Physical Education, University of Saskatchewan, Saskatoon, Saskatchewan, S7N 0W0.

[5]The model has been developed to facilitate planning for international level competition. It is possible to use the same model to plan for other long-term goals such as national level, intercollegiate, club, etc. Application methods for these long-term goals are also available as per the preceding note.

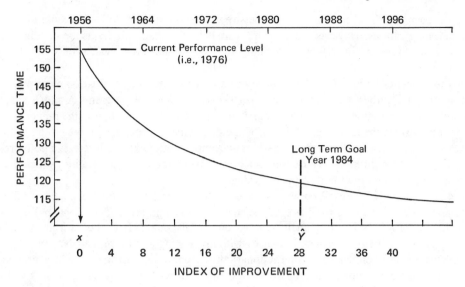

Figure 7. Use of knowledge of prior winning times to predict time needed to win in the future

Figure 8. Use of current level in index units to determine performance goal for upcoming season

3. Evaluation of Training Programs. The classical problems in evaluating programs involving behavioral change are who to place in which training program, the effect of different coaches or the bias of a coach to the method, and the specificity of the training program. The research design using the same coach and the same athletes in successive years has not been utilized because of the principle of diminishing returns. However, in real life, this is how training programs are conducted. In fact, most coaches evaluate the effect of training by using a subjective evaluation of performance or ranking.

The concept of the *index of improvement* will likely make this evaluation more objective. This is illustrated in Figure 9. Quite simply, the performance change of programs A and B are converted into index units and these units are placed in a ratio; if the ratio is less than 1, the numerator program is more effective; if the ratio is greater than 1, the denominator program is more effective. For this to be true, one must assume that there was the same amount of talent and interest in both programs or years. Perhaps it would be better to consider each individual on the two training programs and base the general decision on the trend of the individual change.

4. Evaluation of Total Program. Another possible application of the index of improvement concerns the evaluation of a total program such as a national program. Traditional political and press evaluation of programs is unfortunately based on medal counts. It is theoretically possible to be effecting dramatic national program changes without reaping any more medals. If a program curve was calculated and compared to international curves, one could estimate when a program would become internationally competitive. This same method of evaluation by using the index of improvement might be used to direct emphasis in funding, coaching, and promotion.

SUMMARY

The focus of this paper is the prediction and shaping of future behavior of athletes. An inter-relating model of goal setting, contracts, management by objectives, and evaluation is presented. It is recommended that two categories of goals be set. The first category relates to the commitment of

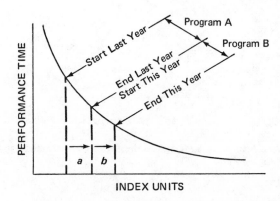

Figure 9. Relating training programs to goals

the individual to the training program, and the second category demands that difficult but reasonable goals be set on an objective performance basis. The central concept of the paper is that evaluation be a rational study of the program, tempered by logic and common sense, and not an emotional evaluation of the individual.

REFERENCES

Botterill, C. B. 1976. How to improve commitment: A theory on motivation. *Coaching Association of Canada Bulletin,* no. 15.
——. 1977. Goal setting and performance on an endurance task. Unpublished Ph.D. thesis, University of Alberta.
——. 1978. Psychology of coaching. *Coaching Review* 1 (4):46-55.

MENTAL STATES

Dr. Robert M. Nideffer has been involved in testing and research with professional and collegiate athletes in football, tennis, swimming, skeet shooting, bowling, diving, and track as well as with World Cup team wrestlers. He has been a consultant to the Buffalo Bills professional football team, was Pacific Northwest Conference diving champion, has coached AAU age-group diving, and holds a black belt in aikido. He is president of Enhanced Performance Associates and a member of the faculty of the California School of Professional Psychology. This article is a new approach to the topic of concentration, considered so important to performance. Concentration is understood as attention, and several attentional styles are identified. Additionally, the author relates the different styles to expected differences in performance, such as choking, and provides recommendations on what might be done.

Dr. Maurie D. Pressman has been a consultant to the U.S. Figure Skating Association and to the White Face Mountain Ski and Training Center at Lake Placid, was a staff member of the North American Training Center at Lake Placid, and has worked individually with Olympic figure skaters and professional bowlers, tennis players, and skiers. He is founder and president of the American Association for the Advancement of Sports Potential. Currently, he is chairperson of the Division of Psychiatry of Albert Einstein Medical Center and clinical professor of psychiatry, Temple University Health Sciences Center. This article deals with mental states that can be explored via hypnosis and with the use of hypnosis as a training device for relaxation. Some facts and fallacies are discussed concerning the limitations of hypnosis.

Dr. William P. Morgan's work appears again in this book,[1] this time in his study of marathon runners. Pain and distress in the body can be handled by some runners who attempt to reach a certain state, such as dissociation, through mental strategies. This article gives examples of dissociative and associative strategies and indicates that the latter is more characteristic of elite runners.

[1] Other articles by Morgan appear on pages 4-18 and 145-155.

Attentional Focus—Self-Assessment

Robert M. Nideffer

For me to be able to predict how you will perform in a competitive situation, I must first know if you can develop the type of attention required *under nonstress conditions* (relaxed practice sessions). Can you broaden and narrow attention and can you direct it internally and externally? Next I need to know how you react physically and attentionally under conditions of stress. Finally I need to know if you are capable of shifting from one focus to another whenever you want to.

At the University of Rochester we have been developing a paper and pencil test that attempts to provide us with this information. By your answering a number of questions about how you have functioned in the past, it's possible for us to conclude to some degree of accuracy what your attentional strengths and weaknesses are. For example, if you say that it's easy for you to shut out everything and concentrate on a book, you're telling me that you can effectively narrow your attention. If, on a question about athletics, you indicate that you make mistakes because you concentrate on one player and forget about what other players are doing, I know that you can narrow attention, but you are unable to broaden it, and when a broad focus is demanded, you have difficulty. With this kind of information, plus additional knowledge about your level of anxiety, I can suggest procedures for you to use to learn to broaden your attention.

One simple way for you to begin to learn about your attentional processes is to answer the questions in Table 1. After you've finished with the questions, total up your answers by assigning a value from 0 to 4 to each response, as indicated below. Next total your score for each of the two-item subscales (e.g., BET, OET, OIT) and then plot them on Figure 1.

0 = Never
1 = Rarely
2 = Sometimes
3 = Frequently
4 = All the time

Table 2 presents a brief definition of each of the attentional subscales. Don't become too concerned with the high or low position of your score on a particular scale. Since individuals perceive themselves and their worlds differently, it makes little sense to compare your scores with those of another person. The height of your scale score would have some relevance only if it were compared

Table 1. Attentional Assessment

Never
Rarely
Sometimes
Frequently
All the time

BET (Broad-External)

1. I am good at quickly analyzing a complex situation such as how a play is developing in football or which of four or five kids started a fight.
2. In a room filled with children or on a playing field I know what everyone is doing.

BET Total

OET (External Overload)

1. When people talk to me, I find myself distracted by the sights and sounds around me.
2. I get confused trying to watch activities such as a football game or circus where many things are happening at the same time.

OET Total

BIT (Broad-Internal)

1. All I need is a little information and I can come up with a large number of ideas.
2. It is easy for me to bring together ideas from a number of different areas.

BIT Total

OIT (Internal Overload)

1. When people talk to me, I find myself distracted by my own thoughts and ideas.
2. I have so many things on my mind that I become confused and forgetful.

OIT Total

NAR (Narrow Effective Focus)

1. It is easy for me to keep thoughts from interfering with something I am watching or listening to.
2. It is easy for me to keep sights and sounds from interfering with my thoughts.

NAR Total

RED (Errors of Underinclusion)

1. I have difficulty clearing my mind of a single thought or idea.
2. In games I make mistakes because I am watching what one person does and I forget about the others.

RED Total

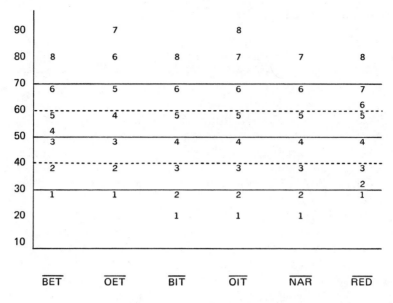

Figure 1. Attentional profile

Table 2. Attentional Subscale Definitions

BET (Broad-External)

The higher the score, the more the individual's answers indicate that he deals effectively with a large number of external stimuli. He has a broad-external focus that is effective.

OET (External Overload)

The higher the score, the more the individual's answers indicate that he makes mistakes because he is overloaded and distracted by external stimuli. He has difficulty narrowing attention when he needs to.

BIT (Broad-Internal)

The higher the score, the more the individual indicates that he is able to think about several things at once when it is appropriate to do so. He has a broad-internal focus.

OIT (Internal Overload)

The higher the score, the more the individual indicates that he makes mistakes because he thinks about too many things at once. He is interfered with by his own thoughts and feelings.

NAR (Narrow Effective Focus)

High scorers indicate that they are able to narrow attention effectively when the situation calls for it.

RED (Errors of Underinclusion)

High scorers have chronically narrowed attention. They make mistakes because they cannot broaden attention when they need to.

with the scores of a large group of individuals participating in the same sport. Of much more importance than the elevation of a particular scale is the *profile configuration*, the elevation of one scale relative to the scores you make on other scales. It's critical how you describe your own strengths and weaknesses—in other words, how you compare your ability to make effective use of a broad attention focus with your tendency to make errors because your focus is too broad. Thus, look at the position of the Broad-External scale (BET) in comparison to the External Overload (OET); the Broad-Internal (BIT) in comparison to the Internal Overload (OIT); the Narrow Effective Focus (NAR) relative to the tendency to make Errors of Underinclusion (RED). The average person scores equally high on both scales once they are plotted on the profile. Good attenders score higher on the scales indicating effective functioning (BET, BIT, NAR) than they do on scales indicating ineffective functioning (OET, OIT, RED).

The complete version of the test you just took is called the Test of Attentional and Interpersonal Style (TAIS) (Nideffer 1976). It is much longer, containing 144 items, and thus the results or scores on the complete test are far more reliable indicators of attention than scores on this brief test. By administering the complete TAIS to a large number of athletes and then analyzing their answers, it was possible to identify several major attentional styles. Some of these styles are presented, beginning with the one in Figure 2.

The athlete whose profile appears in Figure 2 differs from an optimal performer in two very important ways. First, high scores on the OET and OIT scales indicate that he cannot deal with a large number of stimuli without becoming overloaded and confused. His low score on the NAR indicates that he cannot narrow attention in order to avoid becoming overloaded. Secondly, he is unable to shift attention from an internal focus to an external one when the situation requires it. For example, let's look at some of the difficulties a hitter with this profile has. First, he has great difficulty narrowing attention and focusing on the ball. Instead, when focused externally, he is aware

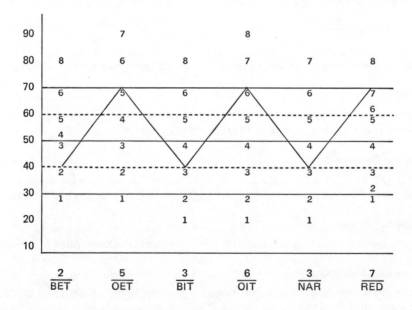

Figure 2. Ineffective attentional profile

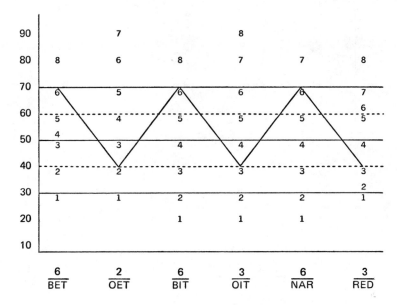

Figure 3. Effective attentional profile

of everything from the crowd noises to the movement of players on the field. Such a broad focus makes it difficult to concentrate on hitting the ball. Another problem occurs because he doesn't balance his internal and external attention. Instead he becomes trapped in his thoughts and responds to what is going on around him without thinking. In this case he may be so busy trying to analyze the situation, in an attempt to predict the next pitch, that he doesn't realize that the pitcher is already in his windup. The result is that he isn't ready when the ball arrives. He fails to shift to an external focus when he needs that kind of focus.

Athletes with this profile can learn to improve their performance by learning to narrow their attention and by learning to shift the direction of their focus. One procedure which would be helpful in accomplishing these goals is meditation. . . . In addition to meditation, athletes with this attentional style would benefit from learning how to mentally rehearse their performance.[1] . . . Mental rehearsal procedures combined with meditation can be used to teach these athletes to distinguish between the relevant cues (the baseball) and the irrelevant ones (crowd noises).

Athletes with profile configurations like the one in Figure 3, provided they have responded honestly to the test, are optimal performers as far as attentional processes are concerned. Of course profiles like this one *can be faked* if the person is trying to look good or if he has an unrealistically high opinion of himself, but since the person taking the test usually wants help, cheating is rarely a problem. If the profile is an *accurate* one, it usually belongs to a superior athlete.

The profile presented in Figure 4 is that of a theoretical average athlete. The flat line indicates that he is average with respect to his ability to narrow or broaden attention and with respect to his tendency to make errors. There is no single outstanding strength or weakness here. Since no particular

[1] See the article by Suinn on pages 26-36, the article by Lane on pages 316-320, and the article by Kirschenbaum and Bale on pages 334-343. —Ed.

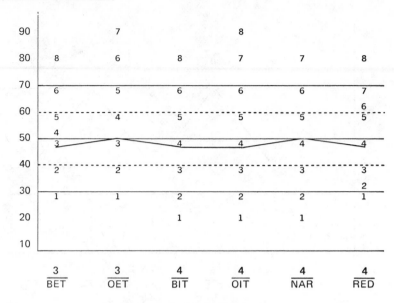

Figure 4. "Average" profile

type of problem predominates, any adjustments the athlete might want to make in his performance, theoretically speaking, would be based on his coach's preference for a particular method or because of a desire to develop a particular skill due to its relevance to a sport. For example, a quarterback might wish to improve his ability to broaden attention because he hasn't been spotting all the open receivers.

In point of fact, however, profiles like that presented in Figure 4 do not occur very often. Most of us have a particular style and tend to make specific types of errors. An important point to keep in mind, therefore, is that this average profile in no way implies that the individual shouldn't be working to improve his attentional processes. Unlike those super individuals who describe themselves as effective and as not making attentional errors, the average individual does make mistakes.

Figure 5 is associated with athletes who have a narrowed attentional focus and who have a tendency to "choke." They make mistakes in complex, rapidly changing situations because they fail to react quickly enough. In basketball they have difficulty finding the open man, or deciding if they should drive or take a jump shot. In football they don't adjust to shifts by the opposing team. Individuals with this profile would have difficulty trying to function as a wishbone quarterback—*especially* in the complex wishbone formations of today—or as the playmaker on a basketball or hockey team.

Happily there are two procedures which can help these athletes broaden their attention. First the individuals must be taught to relax. Arousal narrows an individual's attentional focus, but relaxation broadens it, and biofeedback training, progressive relaxation, hypnosis[2] . . . can be used for this purpose. In addition, mental rehearsal procedures are helpful because they can be used to teach an athlete to make more effective use of his narrowed focus. By learning to rapidly shift and direct a

[2]See the article by Suinn on pages 306-315, the article by Wenz and Strong on pages 328-333, the article by Pressman on pages 291-296, and the article by Titley on pages 321-327. —Ed.

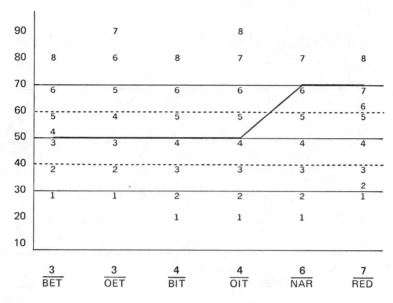

Figure 5. "Choking" profile

narrowed attentional focus to many different cues, a broad focus can be simulated. The trick, as we will see later on, is to be able to select the important cues to focus on and to ignore the others.

If you have a profile like the one presented in Figure 6, your major attentional strength is that you are able to analyze competitive situations and can plan out moves in advance. This strength, however, is also a weakness because you tend to make mistakes by becoming caught up in your own thoughts and lose awareness of what is going on around you. Your broad internal focus keeps you so involved in analyzing that you fail to respond to your environment. In effect you overanalyze and are still planning what to do when it's time to do it.

The best remedy here is to teach the athlete to be more aware of—and responsive to—external cues. As an example, baseball is a game in which there are many opportunities for players to drift away mentally from the game because they spend so much time standing around waiting for something to happen. Partially in response to this, players have developed ways to help keep their thoughts on the ball game. First of all they are constantly talking to the pitcher and to the batter, depending on which side is batting. Their chatter is designed to keep them and the other ball players alert. The custom of running out to your position on the field and then back to the dugout also helps because it keeps the player physically active, increases arousal slightly (unless the game is terribly one-sided), and helps concentration. Players also develop their own behavior patterns designed to get them to keep their thoughts from drifting away. Some players continually pound at their glove with their fist, others kick the ground, still others chew gum or tobacco. All of these, if used properly, can serve to break that internal focus and get the player's mind back on the game.

If you have a profile like that in Figure 7, you tend to be reactive rather than reflective—that is, you respond almost instinctively to changes in your environment. However, if your response is incorrect, you may fail to learn from it. When the same situation presents itself again, you then respond without reflection—as though you have never been in the situation before. Biofeedback

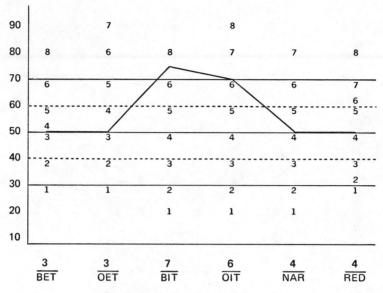

Figure 6. Internal overload profile

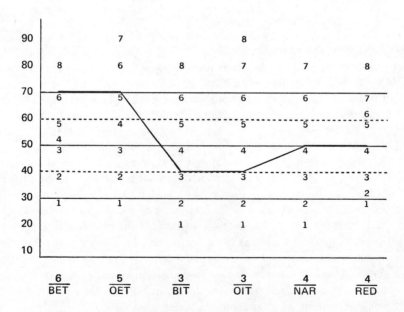

Figure 7. External distractibility profile

procedures and rehearsal techniques can be used to train you to develop more of an internal (reflective) focus. Finally, athletes with profiles like the one in Figure 7 are more susceptible to being psyched out than those with a reflective style like the one in Figure 6 because they act on impulse to each new situation.

The final profile to be discussed is the one presented in Figure 8. If this is your profile, then you have a tendency to be your own worst enemy. You're likely to become upset by your mistakes and to think about little else, forgetting about the things which are going on around you. This overly internalized focus results in what is commonly called "choking." In psychological terms, by narrowing attention to your errors and by continuing to focus internally while the game is still going on, you're a sure bet to commit an ever increasing number of errors in the game. For this individual, timeouts may offer some relief, but the real blessing is when the game ends.

At the University of Rochester we examined the attentional styles of a considerable number of athletes. We then went to their various coaches and asked them (without their having any knowledge whatsoever of the test results) to rate the athletes' ability to perform under a variety of conditions. Dramatically enough, what we found was that those athletes with an attentional profile like the one presented in Figure 8 were described by the coaches as follows: " 'choking,' inconsistent, falling apart under pressure, and unable to overcome early mistakes." To take up an earlier point, the athletes just described probably suffer from high levels of both state and trait anxiety. In other words, they are anxious human beings, and it has been our experience that through reducing the athletes' level of arousal, we can modify their attentional processes.

More specifically, many times athletes who "choke" would benefit from some external stimulus that would countermand their negative internal focus. Because these individuals are highly anxious, their attention is locked in on inappropriate things, and procedures such as hypnosis and biofeedback—which make few demands on them for implementation and which continually direct their attention externally—are most helpful.

Once the negative (anxiety equals "choking") set is broken, the athlete can regain some control over his attentional process and can then *begin* to assume more responsibility for directing the course

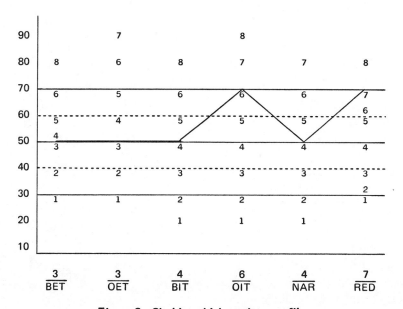

Figure 8. Choking—high anxiety profile

of his training. It may take some time for this training to produce results. Accordingly, if you find you have this type of profile, learn how to practice some relaxation and reflective or meditative procedures in order to prevent additional problems from developing. The importance of this is not to be underestimated. You *can* maintain attentional control so long as you control arousal. It isn't simple, of course, since to do this you must learn to recognize and offset anxiety before it gets out of hand.

REFERENCE

Nideffer, R. 1976. Test of attentional and interpersonal style. *Journal of Personality and Social Psychology* 34:394-404.

Psychological Techniques for the Advancement of Sports Potential

Maurie D. Pressman

In the past five years in Delaware Valley, U.S.A., a group of physicians and coaches, the Association for the Advancement of Sports Potential, was formed with the goal of advancing the cause of figure skating and other sports. Surrounding Olympic and national coaches, they were prepared to answer the questions brought to them relating to many topics including those relating to: Optimal times for warmup; minimizing injuries; nutritional regimes for a particular sport; ideologies for a sport; and psychological factors which impair or improve performance. In the course of time, more and more the interest was focused on psychological factors. We were able to create a better fit between coach and athlete. We were able to facilitate communication between coach and athlete (a situation not unlike marriage). We discovered that any sustained impairment in communication could destroy the effectiveness of the pair. For example, in the case of one talented national skater, who had idealized her coach for many years and had worked well with him, there came a period of rambunctiousness which interfered with their effective functioning. The more she became rebellious, the more he became resistant and, in the midst of his puzzlement, tightened up on her—in turn making her rebellion all the more necessary and intense. At this point, in some degree of frustration, he turned to me for advice. We were quickly able to see that this talented skater was now coming into adolescence; she was beginning to bud and show signs of sexual development; she was, in short, entering into a *necessary period* of rebellion toward a loved and admired figure, behavior that was entirely appropriate to adolescence. Therefore, it was not dislike of the coach nor disrespect which made her rebel—but rather her need to quell, to quiet her overly great attachment to him. Learning that this would be a passing phase, the coach was able to reduce his resistance and thus to calm what otherwise might have become a stormy and destructive relationship.

We searched for psychological aids to help meet the stress of competition and came to lean more and more upon relaxation and the simultaneous visualized rehearsal of performance. We turned more and more to hypnosis as the method of choice for relaxation and visual rehearsal,[1] and we did so for several reasons. First, hypnosis was dramatic and therefore well and quickly accepted by many athletes and parents. Undoubtedly too, much of the early acceptance was assisted by the endorsement of prestigious coaches; perhaps even greater acceptance, however, was achieved through the rapid spread by word of mouth of the effectiveness of the procedure. Hypnosis seemed to have a quick and at times startlingly positive effect on our athletes.

[1] See the article by Suinn on pages 306-315 and the article by Lane on pages 316-320. —Ed.

Our procedure was to put the athlete into a state of trance and to suggest that he visualize his performance. Positive suggestions were given, as well as the injunction to perform autohypnosis several times a day. Those athletes who practiced autohypnosis benefited greatly and their experience in turn had a positive effect on others who then wished to follow suit. Later, at the North American Training Center, the effort was much enlarged. The author was invited as a psychiatrist to develop psychological assists directed toward improving performance. Additionally, other groups grew interested in learning about mental functioning and the release from problems, these groups comprising coaches, parents, and judges. It was a moving experience to see the motivation within these groups. Judges, for example, seemed often to struggle with such problems as, "How shall I treat this 8-year-old child? If I advance her falsely, will I be untrue to my profession? If I tell her that she can't pass, or if she must fail this particular competition badly, am I doing her harm or irreparably hurting her personality?" This kind of poignant questioning filled with good intentions, when addressed to a sports psychiatrist, can lead to relief through knowledge, for the child who is helped to face reality is also helped to achieve maturity and personality potential.

At the North American Training Center, the value of hypnosis and visual rehearsal was quickly validated—and its reputation spread rapidly. Individual athletes were taught autohypnotic techniques and rehearsed. Their performances were benefited almost immediately, and almost universally. This quick and heady success came as quite a surprise to several of us who had been trained to remain scientifically reserved and doubtful about the results. Yet the overwhelming evidence seemed to point toward the use of this very effective instrument, so much so that the question had to be pointed towards other well-known authorities from whom we were able to evolve tentative answers relating to the effectiveness of hypnosis in advancing the athlete toward the achievement of excellence and the achievement of potential.

Our work in hypnosis included groups of all ages and groups of all sizes, from 2 to 30 members—occasionally even more.

None of this is intended to indicate irrelevance of, or the overlooking of, the individual personality factors, for they are omnipresent. How do these personal factors show their influence? In several ways. Firstly, whereas hypnosis is a universal human phenomenon, in fact biologically determined (animals are hypnotizable), there are nevertheless impediments to the use of hypnosis arising most often from some form of personal anxiety. Taking the psychodynamic view, one sees that resistances to hypnosis arise from the idiosyncratic personality. For example, one coach wanted to be hypnotized but began to giggle as he began to relax and fall into an inward state of focus; as he giggled, he began to wake up. At this point I enjoined him to ignore his giggling, for, by focusing upon it, he was purposefully waking himself up. He thereupon let himself slip past and went into the inner state of focus and achieved his hypnotic trance, as well as his desired goal to stop smoking. Reinforcement later enabled him to stop smoking for progressively longer periods of time. Another example: A well-known skier was very desirous of being hypnotized but couldn't achieve trance. Every time he allowed himself to relax and fall inward, he developed a sensation of dangerous falling. He coupled this sensation with several experiences in which he sustained severe injuries, when he did, in fact, fall during skiing accidents. An even greater deterrent, however, arose from his fear of falling into the control of anyone who reminded him of his very severe and overcontrolling father, who had dominated his life. Enabling him to have these insights and to look past his anxiety, he began to get into a deeper state although the result was never fully satisfactory.

The principle which is being described is that hypnosis does not stand alone but always conjoins with personality factors. The more one is at peace with his personality, the more one can achieve success in producing the hypnotic trance; and the more one can achieve success in the use of hypnosis, the more one can improve performance.

Much of our experience indicates that the visually rehearsed performance reproduces, not only the performance itself, but also the mistakes which result from personality factors. For example, an athlete who has a predilection toward failure will find the mistakes in his skating repeating in his visualized, rehearsed performance. In visualizing his mistakes, the athlete may rationalize that he is trying to overcome the mistakes—but, by trying to overcome them visually, he repeats them, grooves them, increases them, rewards them, and nourishes them. By advising him to repeat his performance visually, in a more and more positive way, we achieve a more positive effect and a result which then becomes generalized.

Whereas psychoanalysis teaches us that it is necessary to uncover these negative attitudes and their origins in order to correct them, there seems to be growing evidence that the teachings of Coué (popular at the beginning of this century) are being validated by experiences in positive thinking. This certainly parallels our experience with skaters, skiers, bowlers, and others, including professional musicians. This can be related also to the rehearsal of positive attitudes which are an inherent part of behavior modification (Wolpe 1973) akin, too, to the development of positive assertion through the rehearsal of assertive attitudes.

We remain clear, however, that some personality factors (emanating from unconscious sources) *will not* yield to hypnosis. It should be noted too that hypnosis is not magically lasting but must be reinforced periodically by the athlete as well as by the hypnotist. (Incidentally, I believe it is possible for a coach to invoke rehearsal of performance and rehearsal of positive attitudes through the use of progressive relaxation, focused consciousness, and image rehearsal—without necessarily waiting for the assistance of the psychologist or psychiatrist.) Criticism may weigh in on us for this advice, but it is my belief that the advanced athlete is a person who has a strong ego and therefore is not susceptible to the dangers of hypnosis. Furthermore, I believe that the dangers of hypnosis are much overstated, and, while real enough for patients who are either paranoid psychotics or borderline psychotics, these categories do not appear in athletes who have advanced to any state of competitive achievement.

There are examples, however, in which the hypnosis cannot be effective in managing major personality disorders which often are behind failures of sports excellence or the achievement of potential. I would like to detail a few examples in which the special skills of the psychiatrist become necessary in order to deal with them. The practical point of advice would be to note when the athlete is having trouble with his performance—is not achieving his potential, is not yielding to the rehearsal techniques of hypnosis—then there is reason to call for a psychiatric consultation. Similarly, where there is a real difficulty in the working of an athletic pair or an athletic team, each with the other, and the difficulty will not yield to the usual techniques of hypnosis and rehearsal, then, again, the psychological specialist should be called in. Most especially, when there are difficulties in the fit between coach and athlete, one should consult a specialist to ameliorate the strain and to correct the miscommunication.

An 18-year-old skater, a world-level competitor, consistently prejudiced his career by clowning exhibitionistically and crudely. He is a phenomenally talented athlete, and I have had the opportunity to learn quite a bit about him. He achieved prominence on a national level at age 12. He regretted this, however, feeling that it deprived him of his chance to be a child. Compounding this was the fact that his parents separated that very year. Thereafter he missed his father terribly. He combatted his anguish, loneliness and insecurity by becoming a clown—as if to convince the world as well as himself that he didn't really care very much. But of course he cared a very great deal. He seemed unaware of the fact that his clowning got him into trouble with his peers, with his coach, and with important people in the judging world. Probably all of us have seen otherwise talented athletes destroy a promising career by displaying irritating and obnoxious attitudes. In the case of the athlete described above, we had a chance to work through his clowning compulsion quickly, to make him aware of his attitudes and their impact, and later to acquaint him with the fact that he *had* to show off in order to conceal his underlying loneliness and craving for childish dependence. There still remained the misunderstanding between him and his coach. He had been skating in Canada (where he had offended an important official in the skating association) and then arrived at the North American Training Center preceded by a bad reputation. He continued to clown and goof off—to the detriment of his own reputation and to that of his very prominent coach. We thereupon arranged for a conjoint interview between skater and coach. I acted as mediator and interpreter of sorts. A great deal of ventilation took place. The skater was first made aware of the fact that he *was* acting obnoxiously; secondly, of the fact that his behavior was a threat to him and his career; thirdly, in this way he was demeaning his coach who had put a great deal of his own reputation on the line for him. I knew that this skater was very fond of his coach, in fact, almost worshipped him, and that the last thing he would want to do would be to hurt him. Therefore, when the conversation turned to the point where it was revealed that by his clowning behavior he was destroying the camp, or at least threatening to, and in this way hurting his coach, a great deal of insight and guilt was provoked and purposely maintained. He became eager to take himself in hand both for his own sake and for the sake of the teacher. He changed quickly, much to the satisfaction of all, including the judge who had been critical. In this way we not only produced insight into destructive behavior and its origins, but also invoked guilt toward an admired and idealized object in order to produce the desired change.

Another illustrative case has to do with a famous dance pair, Andy Strouckoff and Susie Kelly. They are extraordinarily artistic, have skated on Olympic and world levels, but had been confronted with the following problem. At the crucial moment, an argument would often erupt between them, destroying performance potential and shattering the opinion of the skating world. I had the opportunity to work intensively with Andy and learned that he was a man who felt that, if he let himself go a jot, he would deteriorate uncontrollably—if he admitted to his partner his admiration for her, he would be denigrated in her eyes. If he admitted that he thought that she was a better skater than he, he would be smashed. This kind of misconception, plus his misreading of reality, was related to the fact that he had a father who was very demeaning and very autocratic—and who gave Andy the idea, therefore, that he must be tough, demeaning, and disciplined at all times; that if, in fact, he let down a jot or expressed admiration, nothing but scorn would follow. After being raised to consciousness, this idea was corrected; he was able to tell his partner, in my presence, of his admiration for her. A great deal of the strain was relieved. He was also able to notice that, every time he felt inferior or threatened in any way, he would flash anger and begin to strike out. Andy had in fact almost destroyed his career by striking his partner at Olympic warmups in 1976. As time went on, we were able to see other hidden mechanisms at work; Susie, for example, was a girl who was quite afraid of closeness and could deftly stick the needle in the right place to evoke anger and criticism and thus abolish uncomfortable closeness. When this was straightened out, the skating pair were able to perform quite smoothly. They achieved national prominence, wearing the national crown in ice dance. This kind of insight could only be produced by someone who was trained and able to search out the hidden factors at work in the individuals and in the pair. It should also be noted that this work did not take very long, and that it was not only effective but, in the sense of sport career, also lifesaving.

Let us return to hypnosis. A number of indications point to the presence of a basic, even biologic, principle at work behind the effectiveness of hypnosis:

1.   The ability to be hypnotized seems to be present in a number of species of the animal kingdom.
2.   The probable ubiquity of hypnotic states during such acts as driving on the highway, during focused attention, and in meditative states.
3.   The beginning concurrence between the phenomenon of hypnosis and recent split brain studies.
4.   The surprisingly uniform and widespread improvement among the hundreds of athletes following the use of hypnosis and visualization exercises.

There is reason to believe that part of the success of hypnosis lies in the fact that optimal effort is achieved when one is in a state of relaxed energy. Dr. Arnold Gessell, psychiatrist at the University of Pennsylvania, who specializes in the function of the skeletal muscular system, pointed out that all thinking is, in fact, accompanied by motor movements, albeit movements at subliminal levels. In this he follows the work of Jacobson dating back as far as 1932. Dr. Gessell[2] pointed out that hypnosis and visual rehearsal would therefore have a training effect upon the musculature and furthermore would optimize coordination of the muscles insofar as the antagonist muscles would learn to be released at a more nearly optimal moment. The more one practiced visually, the more one was in a state of relaxed attentiveness and the more efficient would the movements become.

The practice of positive attitudes is very likely significant and related to the behavior modification and learning theories as in the work of Wolpe (1973), Brady (1976), Feather and Rhoades (1972), and Birk and Brinkley-Birk (1974). The recent split brain studies are very fascinating and are very well summarized (as they pertain to the functioning of the nondominant side of the brain) by a man prominent in the field of communications theory, Paul Watzlawick (1978). Let me elaborate this. Recently, we have come to understand much more about the difference in the functioning of the two sides of the brain. These studies have been advanced by neurosurgical procedures which split the corpus callosum, the connecting body between the right and left hemispheres of the brain, in order to control otherwise uncontrollable epileptic seizures. While at first blush it appeared that there was not that much, if any, impairment of function, more recent and more detailed studies found that, in fact, the two hemispheres function very differently. The dominant side of the brain (the left side in right-handed people) is given to thinking, to language, to details, and to building up small efforts and small details into a larger picture, a larger gestalt. The nondominant side of the brain (the right side of the brain in right-handed people), on the other hand, is very much given to the perception of whole movements, whole ideas, gestalts; it is very much given to pictures rather than words, very much given to music rather than ideas. Therefore, inhibiting or suspending the function of the left side brain, the dominant brain, frees the right side to take over. In recognizing this, we enunciate one reason for the effectiveness of hypnosis. There is reason to believe that hypnosis appeals directly to, and releases, the functioning of the nondominant brain. In a state of focused consciousness, therefore, imagery is more vivid, rehearsal of programs is more effective, and the cultivation of positive attitudes is also much more assured. Therefore, we believe we have stumbled upon a mechanism which has a basic appeal to a basic functioning of the mind. Additionally, by

[2] Arnold Gessell 1978: personal communication.

diminishing the extra edge of tension (through hypnosis and the rehearsal of relaxed attitudes) we essentially unbind the muscles, allowing the performance to flow more freely. We believe that insofar as we suspend the functions of the left side of the brain, we release the personality to flow into its activity, unselfconsciously and with smoother coordination.

REFERENCES

Birk, L., and Brinkley-Birk, A. W. 1974. Psychoanalysis and behavior therapy. *American Journal of Psychiatry* 131:499–509.

Brady, J. P. 1976. Behavioral therapy. *American Journal of Psychoanalysis* 133:896–899.

Feather, B. W., and Rhoades, J. M. 1972. Psychodynamic behavior therapy. *Archives of General Psychiatry* 26: 496–510.

Jacobson, E. 1964. *The self and object world.* New York: International University Press.

Kroger, W. S. 1977. *Clinical and experimental hypnosis.* 2d ed. Philadelphia: J. B. Lippincott.

Kroger, W. S., and Fezler, W. D. 1976. *Hypnosis and behavior modification: Imagery conditioning.* Philadelphia: J. B. Lippincott.

Suinn, R. M. 1976. Body thinking: Psychology for Olympic champs. *Psychology Today* 10,2 (July):38–43.

Watzlawick, P. 1978. *The language of change.* New York: Basic Books.

Wolpe, J. 1973. *The practice of behavior therapy.* New York: Pergamon Press.

The Mind of the Marathoner

William P. Morgan

One long-distance runner I know performs complex mathematical computations in his head during a race. Another imagines placing a stack of records on a turntable and "grooves on Beethoven." One woman visualizes on the blacktop the faces of two coworkers whom she detests and proceeds to step on one face and then the other for the entire 26 miles of a marathon! Still another runner relives his entire educational career, from the first grade through postdoctoral study; he looks forward to these recall sessions, in which he remembers favorite teachers, friends, and his own achievements. Still another enters a trance state by repeating a mantra over and over in synchrony with his respiration and leg movements. Another stares at his shadow and watches in fascination as his body "leaves" and enters the shadow from time to time, then returns to him.

All of these runners adopt the same cognitive strategy for coping with the pain and discomfort of a long, competitive race. It is a kind of self-hypnosis called dissociation, and it carries with it a variety of risks and dangers. The runner who dissociates purposely cuts himself off from the sensory feedback he normally receives from his body. He may thus expose himself to bone fractures, heat stroke and heat exhaustion, and even mental disorientation, including hallucinations.

Although occasional dissociation can enhance a runner's performance in a race, it can also ruin his "game plan." When he is out of touch with his body, he may overextend himself too early and have nothing left for the finish of the race. Or he may hold back too much, only to discover at the end that he has energy in reserve that he might have expended earlier.

The best marathoners, according to recent studies, attempt to *associate* with the pain and discomfort. The elite, or world-class, runners constantly monitor bodily signals of respiration, temperature, heaviness in the calves and thighs, abdominal sensations, and the like. Instead of diverting the mind with mantras or mathematics, they keep reminding themselves to "stay loose," to "relax and not tie up." This may be the reason that laboratory studies show they use significantly less oxygen at the same running speed than other, nonelite runners.[1]

In January 1975, the 24 runners in the United States who were considered elite, or world-class, were invited to take part in a study at the Institute for Aerobics Research, in Dallas, Texas. I was on a

William P. Morgan. The mind of the marathoner. *Psychology Today* 11, 11 (April 1978):38-49. Reprinted from *Psychology Today* magazine. Copyright© 1978 Ziff-Davis Publishing Company.

[1] See the article by Suinn on pages 26-36. —Ed.

team of doctors, psychologists, and other specialists in fields ranging from physiology to biomechanics that tested the 20 who eventually accepted. Several findings of the Dallas study suggested that elite distance runners differ from non-world-class, mentally and physically, in significant ways, and I have since confirmed those results in other laboratory work. For me, the biggest surprise of the Dallas study was the predominantly associative cognitive strategy of the elite runners, which evidently enabled them to evade what in the marathoners' subculture is known as "the wall."

"The 20-mile mark is where the marathon begins—there at the wall," according to George Sheehan, a cardiologist from Red Bank, New Jersey, who also happens to be a distance runner. Many runners agree that the last six miles are just as difficult as the preceding 20. It is at this point that a runner's homeostasis, or internal function, begins to break down. The breakdown is associated with depletion of glycogen supplies in the working muscles, there is a loss of blood volume; core or rectal temperatures sometimes rise to 106 or 107 degrees, and the body starts to become dehydrated. The runner often develops what is known as paresthesia: his fingers and toes begin to tingle, a sort of queasy feeling overcomes him, and this is followed by muscle tetany or paralysis. He may also become dizzy or light-headed, and may even faint.

I first learned of the wall in my early work with runners in the Boston Marathon, who confront, at about the same time the symptoms normally appear, the added challenge of "Heartbreak Hill," a long, gradual, and excruciating climb a few miles from the finish line. One of the questions I asked these runners was: "Do you ever enter a pain zone while competing, and, if so, how do you transcend it?"

All those I interviewed reported experiencing pain zones, and then, typically, many would add something like: "Oh, you mean the wall. Sure, I come up against the wall around 18 to 20 miles into every marathon." Once it became clear that almost everyone was familiar with the phenomenon, I asked in subsequent interviews, "How do you handle the wall—what do you think of when you come up against it?" One major theme became apparent. When confronted with the pain, they would characteristically begin thinking about something else, in an attempt to distract themselves from the sensory input. It became clear to me that what enabled most people to run a marathon was, at least in part, their ability to dissociate.

Soon after the Boston interviews, I came across an anthropological report describing some Tibetan monks who were reported to run long distances, at high, very cold altitudes, over rough terrain. The monks, or *Mahetangs,* who were specially trained in "swiftness of foot" (for the purpose of carrying messages from the monasteries, according to the one report), make our best runners of today look mediocre by comparison: they were said to have run up to 300 miles in 30 hours, or 10 miles per hour. What evidently enabled them to do so was a kind of dissociative cognitive strategy. They would gaze at a distant object, perhaps a peak 30 miles away, and repeat their sacred mantra in synchrony with their respiration and locomotion. (We don't know whether the *Mahetangs* have continued to run in recent times, since the Chinese Communists have evidently destroyed monastery records.)

Since contemporary marathoners seemed to adopt a similar strategy, I decided with some colleagues to try to replicate such dissociation in a laboratory setting, as means of measuring its performance benefits. We tested 30 young men on their ability to walk on a motor-driven treadmill until they were completely exhausted. The speed of the treadmill was 3.5 miles an hour, and the grade, or slope, was adjusted for each subject so that he had to work at 80 percent of his aerobic power (the maximum amount or volume of oxygen he can consume in one minute). In this initial test, the 30 men lasted, on the average, about 15 minutes before having to quit. Then, all were divided into two groups, dissociators and controls. We induced dissociation in one group by asking them to (1) stare at a specific object in front of them, (2) repeat the word "down" (a pseudomantra) with each leg movement, and (3) synchronize the repetition of the mantra and leg movements with their respiration.

The performance of the control group on the treadmill remained essentially the same in this retest, while the dissociators lasted an additional five minutes—a substantial gain. A second trial confirmed the performance gain of 30 percent. Not only were the dissociators superior to the controls in performance, but they also were significantly more effective than a third group, who were given a lactose capsule that was supposed to improve endurance but was really a placebo.

When the Dallas study presented the opportunity to test world-class runners, I was quite excited. I expected these elite marathoners to be dissociators; perhaps, even, in some unforeseeable way, "exotic dissociators." While discussing their thought processes with them, I would stop and ask casually, about midway through the interview, "Oh, by the way, what do you do when you come up against the wall?"

Much to my amazement, they consistently dismissed the wall as unimportant. Indeed, much of their conscious effort was devoted to avoiding the wall. "The wall is a myth," one runner told me. "The key is to read your body, adjust your pace, and avoid getting into trouble." Another said, "I don't worry about pain zones or the wall. I try not to overextend myself. There really isn't pain for me—at least not until it's over. Sometimes the aches and pains exist for days following a marathon— but not during."

"Yes, I occasionally feel that I might be experiencing the wall, as people call it, but I don't pay a great deal of attention to it," a third runner reported. "As a matter of fact, any time I begin to hurt I automatically pick up the pace. I know if I am beginning to hurt, the runners around me must really be in trouble, and so I just turn it on."

"There's no wall," a fourth runner stated categorically. "The wall exists for runners who monitor their watches instead of their bodies. I have run many marathons and I only got into trouble once. I don't know what happened to me that day—maybe it was too hot."

The Dallas study also found that elite runners differed in personality structure from other, less capable marathoners. Previous studies had demonstrated that long-distance runners were generally introverted.[2] Some of the best of the elite runners were quite extroverted, but an equal number were introverted. As a group, their overall rating was about average for the population on the introversion-extroversion scale of the Eysenck Personality Inventory.

Whether introverted individuals gravitate toward running, or are introverted because they choose to run, is not clear. However, the elite marathoner should be introverted, according to Sheldon's theory of somatotypes. The average height and weight of the winner of the Boston Marathon over the years is five feet seven inches and 135 pounds for male runners. The gold-medal winner in the 1976 Olympic Marathon, Waldemar Cierpinski of East Germany, was the same in stature. Sheldon's theory predicted that people of this body build would tend toward introversion, which would reflect genetic as opposed to environmental influences. But while there were exceptions to the rule among world-class runners, the theory may accurately describe marathoners in general.

The elite also proved, in general, to be looser and happier than other people. Like Olympic rowers and wrestlers, they scored substantially "below the surface" on the tension, depression,

[2] See the review article by Morgan on pages 145-155. —Ed.

fatigue, and confusion factors of the Profile of Mood States (POMS), but were significantly "above the surface" on vigor. Not surprisingly, this pattern of scores has been called the iceberg profile in sports-medicine circles.

One team physician has reported that the unsuccessful or stale athlete usually has a flat profile on the POMS tests: this athlete is above average on such negative factors as tension and depression, but below the surface on vigor.

The elite runners also differed appreciably from non-world-class runners in amount of effort expended in running. We asked both elite and nonelite to run on a treadmill at speads of first 10 and then 12 miles an hour, while we measured various physiological functions. We found that when running at 10 miles an hour, the elite runners were performing at 70 percent of their aerobic power, whereas the others were at 80 percent of their maximum. Also, the heart rate of the nonelite was 17 beats per minute higher (172 versus 155 bpm); their breathing volume was 20 quarts of air higher per minute, and they were producing significantly more lactic acid, an exercise metabolite that, when it builds up in the muscles, eventually makes the runner stop.

In other words, the physiological cost for the elite runners was significantly less no matter which variable was used. However, the elite runners and the less capable runners perceived the exercise intensity to be identical! As they ran on the treadmill, we asked each of the runners to estimate how hard they were working on a scale that ranged from six (extremely light) to 20 (extremely hard). It was only when the speed of the treadmill was increased to 12 miles an hour that the non-world-class runners rated the exercise intensity as more severe.

The world-class runners clearly have phenomenal physical structures. They are probably an elite not because they have learned to associate, but because they can afford to associate; that is, their lung, heart, and muscle power is such that they suffer less during a race.

For other runners, dissociation can have powerful advantages when applied thoughtfully and sparingly. One runner in the Boston Marathon, for instance, associates until he reaches the base of Heartbreak Hill. Then he regresses to a time in childhood when he would join his father in the cab of his locomotive. He imagines himself looking out the window at the pistons driving the wheels in concert with the steam being blown out into tracks, and his body is then transformed into the engine. His legs become the powerful pistons and his exhalations the steam, and he negotiates the hill with relative ease. (Incidentally, most runners, elite as well as nonelite, spend a good deal of time during training runs in the dissociative state. It makes little difference in training because of the slower pace.)

Some runners have accomplished feats while in the dissociative state, far outdoing their previous times and even setting records. One case was that of a college distance runner who encountered intolerable pain about two-thirds of the way in a three-mile race. The young man became totally incoherent and began to experience visual hallucinations. He saw two television sets on the horizon: he could vividly see himself running on one of the screens, while his parents watched him on the other. Then his body "left" him and entered the television set. He inadvertently lost all sensory input. He could not feel his feet hitting the ground; he could not feel the wind against his chest; he was unaware of his breathing, and he had the sensation of being "the mainsail on a Yankee clipper flying across the sea as if in a vacuum."

Rather than stopping, this runner went into a powerful kick and set a school and conference record that day. But he was never able to perform even near this level for the rest of his career. Nor did he appear to want to. He had repressed his hallucinatory visions, and we found out about them only by hypnotizing him later and asking him to relive the championship race. So painful was the experience, that after he relived it under hypnosis he may have made a conscious decision never to run at the same intensity again.

Books such as George Leonard's *The Ultimate Athlete* describe the experience of long-distance running in mystical, almost religious, terms. We do not know whether the high in running somehow arises from the dissociative state; we have barely scratched the surface in exploring the effects of cognitive strategies. But we do know that along with the "trip" that comes from high-intensity running, marathoners frequently become incoherent and actively hallucinate during and after runs. This is not surprising in view of the chemical and temperature changes that are taking place in the body—the loss of glycogen, the rising rectal temperatures, the dehydration.

One distance runner dissociated to the point where he collapsed. He was rushed to the hospital, cooled down, and given an intravenous solution to restore his body fluids. When the attending physician asked him what happened, he replied, "I was hit by a car in Bowling Green [Ohio]." He had actually been running in another city!"

The benefits of running, from both a physiological and psychological standpoint, have been well documented. Like most "wonder drugs," however, there is the potential for abuse. Many runners describe what best can be termed an exercise "high" that occurs during their training runs; this high is usually followed by a state of total relaxation and quiescence that may last for hours. Only those who are running long distances (for example, 10 to 15 miles), at a high intensity (70 to 90 percent of aerobic maximum), seven days per week, are likely to experience this altered state of consciousness. As with most drugs, the running-induced high can only be maintained by increasing dosage—which means more miles, higher intensity, or two- and three-a-day runs. And this is precisely what occurs in the hard-core addict.

I define the exercise addict[3] as a person who cannot exist without exercise, whatever the cost. Initially, the addict may withdraw from friends, spouse, children, and other loved ones. Then, his performance at work begins to suffer. One might argue that drinking on company time is a negative addiction, whereas running on company time represents a positive addiction. In either case, it is the company that is shortchanged.

During the final stages of the addiction, the runner begins to ignore his body. In the most serious cases, he may continue to run despite a health problem. The physician who advises a patient to stop running until a tendon inflammation subsides fails to understand that a methadone-like substitute is needed. Otherwise, the patient may end up in the orthopedic surgeon's office because he can no longer walk.

One physician I know simply places the patient's leg in a cast if he is convinced there is an addiction problem. In his view, there is no other way to stop him from running. It does seem, however, that other aerobic activities, such as swimming or bicycling, might be recommended in some cases.

Distance running is associated with lowered levels of anxiety and depression, two major problems of modern society; many psychiatrists and psychologists have recently described the efficacy of managing anxiety states and depression by means of jogging programs. Both the beginning and established runner must decide, however, on the best method of processing sensory input from the working muscles, joints, lungs, and heart. The runner may choose to associate, or pay attention to such information, dissociate or ignore it, or perhaps shift back and forth between the two as the situation dictates.

---

[3]See the article by Pargman on pages 90-98. —Ed.

Dissociation appears to be far more pleasant, since it reduces anxiety, effort sense, and general discomfort. On the other hand, the jogger who adopts it is more likely to suffer serious injury. The increased likelihood of stress fractures to the bones of the feet and lower leg cannot be ignored. The very real potential for heat stroke or heat exhaustion can lead to death or permanent impairment unless medical assistance is readily available. Finally, the beginning jogger should be warned that the quest for a "breakthrough" or "transcendent experience" can produce addiction and psychological trauma.

The choice between an associative or dissociative strategy poses a classic risk/benefit trade-off. The advantages of associating are obvious: it permits the runner to maintain a physiological steady state during a race that helps to preserve fuel and to avoid injury. But only the anatomically and physiologically well-endowed can benefit from such a strategy in a competitive race. To switch back and forth between manual pilot (association) and automatic pilot (dissociation), moreover, calls for a finely tuned "perceptostat" that takes years of training to develop.

The average jogger would do well to employ dissociation to negotiate a temporary pain zone such as the wall. But he would be well advised, whenever he can, to imitate the elite runner's associative strategy. In so doing, he might improve his competitive performance, but, more likely, he will spare himself injury, prolong his running career, and enhance the enjoyment that comes with any therapeutic procedure.

ELITE AND NONELITE: SEE HOW THEY THINK

What goes through the mind of a runner in a long-distance race can be as important as what is happening to his body. Here, in portions of taped interviews, are two runners talking about their thought processes during a race.

The first is a 35-year-old man who had been running marathons for five years and whose cognitive strategy was dissociative. His best performance in a marathon was a time of two hours and 45 minutes.

The second is a world-class runner, about the same age, who had been competing for eight years and whose thinking during a race was associative. At the time, this man was consistently finishing marathons in less than two hours and 20 minutes. (The fastest marathon to date was run by the Australian Derek Clayton, who set a record time in 1969 of two hours, eight minutes, and 33.6 seconds.)

Dissociative Narrative

"As I run the marathon I think about many different things. At the beginning, I simply look around and get into my environment. You know—the other runners, the spectators, the course, the scenery, how the temperature and wind feel, and so on. Sometimes, in the early part of the race, I strike up a conversation with another runner. In other words, I think about a lot of different things during the first five to 10 miles. It depends on what is going on around me. As the race progresses, however, I know that I will eventually come against the wall. The pain will become unbearable, and I need to prepare myself. . . ."

Interviewer: "How do you do that?"

"Mainly I try to think about other things. I try to get my mind away from the pain. I try to fight through the wall. I know if I can't break through the wall, however, I will usually drop out somewhere around the 21st or 23rd mile. In other words, the pain becomes unbearable.

"Once I get out around 15 miles I begin to imagine that I am in my study. I design a house. Sometimes it is a Cape Cod, other times a Victorian, and sometimes a way-out contemporary . . . but I always design a house. Once the blueprints are completed, I dig a footing with a pick and shovel, pour the concrete, lay the blocks, put up the frame, then the roof . . . and I nail each shingle on separately. Then I wire the house, plumb it, plaster the walls, paint it inside and out, or sometimes I brick the outside, then I do the interior decorating, furnish the house, and so on. Usually, I will then landscape the yard, walk out onto the road, and inspect my masterpiece.

"If there is a good distance to go at this point, I will usually sit down in my new den and design a room to be added or a dormer; then I proceed to build it. This usually gets me through the wall and on my way, but sometimes the pain becomes so great I just have to stop."

Associative Narrative

"At the beginning of a marathon, about the only thing I think about is position. I want to break away from the mass of humanity, get out in front early, and run *my* race. I will sometimes, depending upon who the other top runners are, keep an eye on certain runners and stay with them. However, I never let anyone set the pace. I always set my own pace, although I would prefer to run in a pack with two, or three, or four other guys.

"As the run progresses, I remind myself to drink a lot of fluid. That is hard to do because it seems to slow you down. You can learn to drink on the run without stopping, but it's inconvenient. Therefore, I need to keep reminding myself to drink. I overheat very easily, and the only way for me to do well is to drink plenty of fluids during the run. I accept drinks and wet sponges from the crowd to squeeze on my head, but I also arrange water stations with friends in advance. I also pay a lot of attention to my feet as I run. I used to get blisters a lot, and I think you can prevent that by paying attention—maybe removing your socks if you're wearing them. Also, I *read* my calves and thighs, and I pay a lot of attention to my breathing . . . you can't 'suck air' early and hope to finish. When I start sucking air—"

Interviewer: "What do you mean by that?"

"Oh, that's an expression for breathing hard. Anyway, if I start to have trouble breathing, I simply adjust my pace. I'm not worried . . . if I'm having trouble breathing, anyone near me will, too. Of course, I don't worry about sucking air on steep grades—that's natural. But when I hit the top of a steep grade, I sort of get a reward because the breathing is easier again. The only time I ever suck air on the flat is at the end, where a sort of 'modified kick' might make the difference between winning or losing.

"You might also be interested in this. I not only pay attention to my body as I run, but I also constantly remind myself to relax, hang loose, not tie up . . . that can be disastrous. A lot of good runners will tie up; you can't be tight, however, you have to be loose."

Interviewer: "How about the wall?"

"There is no wall for me . . . that's what I have been talking about. I stay away from the wall. I think a lot of guys are so concerned about the wall that they psych themselves out."

BEHAVIORAL STRATEGIES

Dr. Richard M. Suinn,[1] in this article, describes his behavior modification work with athletes and presents a sample of different behaviorial strategies for enhancing performance, including his approach visuo-motor behavior rehearsal. The field testing of such methods during the 1976 Winter Olympics shows some applications of psychological training derived from behaviorial principles.

John F. Lane has coached high school ski teams, both alpine and nordic, and studies the uses of visuo-motor behavior rehearsal. He has applied this technique to collegiate varsity baseball teams, recreational tennis programs, and high school teams in football, soccer, field hockey, basketball, and cross-country running. He is completing a doctoral degree at the State University of New York, Albany. This article identifies the applications of visuo-motor behavior rehearsal as anxiety reduction, error correction, concentration, and skill development. Illustrations of each application are given from actual interviews, which confirm these uses, along with some statistical results.

Dr. Robert W. Titley has been the team psychologist for the Colorado State University football program and is involved with visuo-motor behavior rehearsal and stress management for collegiate and professional tennis players, trapshooters, swimmers, wrestlers, and runners. He is associate professor of psychology at Colorado State University. This article gives a case history, showing an athlete's performance record before and after psychological training, and hence offers a data-based field test. While the article by Lane illustrates various applications through excerpts from transcripts, this article presents the steps taken in the design and the assessment of a single program.[2]

Dr. Betty J. Wenz has been a consultant to the AAU Women's Track and Field Olympic Development Committee, national vice-chairperson and chairperson of the Sports Medicine Subcommittee, and an international judge, all for AAU synchronized swimming. She is director of counseling services and adjunct professor of kinesiology and physical education at California State University, Hayward. Dr. Donald J. Strong, who also has been a consultant to the AAU Women's Track and Field Olympic Development Committee, has collaborated with Dr. Wenz in providing relaxation and stress management training to athletes in distance running, pole vaulting, high jumping, figure skating, swimming, and synchronized swimming. He is professor of counseling and psychology at California State University, Hayward. This article reviews a program offered in workshop format

[1]Other articles by Suinn appear on pages 26-36 and 73-77 (in collaboration with David Youngblood).
[2]Another article by Titley appears on pages 357-361.

for athletes and coaches.[3] *The authors discuss relaxation training, autogenic phrases, visualization, and biofeedback (for relaxation), with some illustrative results. This article and the next two are examples of training organized as a multimedia program, to achieve a variety of goals.*

Dr. Daniel S. Kirschenbaum has played competitive golf and tennis and has been a consultant to a collegiate golf team and to members of a company golf league. He was an assistant professor of psychology at the University of Rochester and is now on the faculty of the University of Wisconsin. Dr. Ronald M. Bale, who was a member of his high school varsity baseball team and a military golf team, competes in amateur golf tournaments (with a six handicap) and has consulted with the University of Cincinnati golf team. He is director of the Day Treatment Program, Ventura County (California) Mental Health Center. This article describes a systematic program for golf that uses relaxation, self-monitoring, imagery, and positive self-instruction. Unlike the programs described in other articles in this section, the technique presented here emphasizes a cognitive, self-instructional approach to performance—thinking through steps to remember by a checklist, deciding to review one's actions when a shot was considered good, and using self-statements to maintain a positive and relaxed approach.

Dr. Philip R. Spinelli has consulted with members of collegiate baseball, track, and basketball teams. He is coordinator of the Sports Psychology Outreach Program described in this article and is a counseling psychologist at the University of Utah's Counseling Center. Billy A. Barrios has conducted assessments of cognitive coping strategies of athletes in baseball, football, volleyball, diving, and gymnastics. He is completing a doctoral degree in the Department of Psychology at the University of Utah. This article describes an outreach program offered to athletes and coaches and outlines what happens in assessment, relaxation training, stress management, thought control, and skill training. Case reports show the procedures followed and provide data on the effects of the program.

[3] *See also the article by Nesvig on pages 250-260.*

Body Thinking:
Psychology for Olympic Champs

Richard M. Suinn

At the Winter Olympics at Innsbruck, Austria, last February, Lyle Nelson of the U.S. stunned experts with his personal performance in the Biathlon event. This event, obscure in the U.S. and normally dominated by teams from Russia and Finland, combines the endurance of cross-country skiing with rifle marksmanship. Nelson, a strong skier, had relative difficulty in shooting accurately. This time he fired two perfect rounds, shattering five targets each time, and put the U.S. in second place at the end of his tour over the Biathlon course. He far exceeded his own previous performances, at least in part because of his preparation in a unique psychological training program.

Nelson is not alone. Neil Glenesk is pointing to represent the U.S. in the Pentathlon this summer at the Olympics in Montreal. The Pentathlon requires performance in fencing, horseback riding, pistol shooting, a two-and-a-half-mile run, and a 300-meter swim. To ready himself psychologically for a grueling series of fencing matches, Glenesk sits alone, head down, eyes closed, building aggression and a feeling of hatred for the next opponent.

Other athletes use other methods to improve their fencing. Paul Pesthy, a veteran of several world and Olympic Pentathlons and a particularly outstanding fencer, uses the time between matches to reduce the tension of the previous match. "You must be able to stop thinking of the last match," Pesthy says, "and clear your head before meeting the next one." Staying quick and alert for hours on end creates the kind of tension that can drain an athlete's physical and mental energy.[1]

Pesthy's method is to retreat under a blanket or towel, close his eyes, and imagine that he is drawing a large circle. He places the number 10 inside the circle. Then he draws a smaller circle inside the first circle, moves the 10 into the new circle, and adds a nine inside the outer circle. Next he draws another circle inside the last one, moves the 10 into this new circle, transfers the nine to where the 10 was, and adds an eight inside the outer circle. This demanding sequence, as if he were building a dart board in the most difficult way possible, shifts his attention from the previous match and focuses it on a neutral activity.[2]

Richard M. Suinn. Body thinking: Psychology for Olympic champs. *Psychology Today* 10, 2 (July 1976):38-43. Reprinted from *Psychology Today* magazine. Copyright © 1976 Ziff-Davis Publishing Company.

[1] See the article by Nideffer on pages 281-290. —Ed.
[2] See the article by Morgan on pages 297-303. —Ed.

The First Psychologist

Psychological techniques for improving athletic performance are not new. Olympic and world-class athletes of several European nations rely routinely on sports psychology. It is no surprise that Russia has so dominated the Winter Olympic Games; their athletes make a career out of competition. Yet the Soviets also recognize that the mind helps determine athletic success. East Germany, a relatively recent entry into the Olympic arena, has introduced rigorous psychological training for its athletes. In the 1976 Winter Games, they carried away the second highest number of medals. Norway offers academic-degree programs in sports psychology. Austria has sent its ski jumpers to an institute for "will-power training." The Czechoslovakians, though modest about their commitment to psychology, nevertheless have a psychologist who travels with the team. In contrast, my presence at the 1976 Winter Olympics marked the first time that the U.S. provided on-site psychological services for our athletes.

My behavior-modification work with athletes began by accident about four years ago. At the time, I was adapting behavioral therapies for use with nonpathological clients. One such client was an executive who found himself unable to speak before a group. I taught him an "imagery-rehearsal" technique to be used in conjunction with relaxation as a method of reducing stress. Following progressive relaxation, he pictured himself making a presentation to an audience of supervisors in such detail that he had to formulate the exact words in his speech. The approach was so successful that I began to wonder how it might be applied to developing or strengthening other skills in normal individuals.

Coincidentally, a ski coach at Colorado State University asked me if I would help his skiers manage their competition tensions. I agreed, and received the chance at the same time to do a small study of imagery rehearsal. I divided the team into two groups, matched equally for ski-racing ability. One group would receive imagery training while the other would act as the control group. If all went well, we would soon know whether the imagery-rehearsal techniques worked or not.

I call my method "visuo-motor behavior rehearsal," or VMBR. The method can be divided simply into three steps: relaxation, the practice of imagery, and the use of imagery for strengthening psychological or motor skills.

For the first stage of the training for the ski team, I used a brief version of Edmund Jacobson's progressive relaxation,[3] which many physical educators have found effective in the past. For about 20 minutes the athlete tenses and then relaxes muscle groups. This training continues for one more session, during which the trainee tries first to eliminate the need for tensing and later shortens the time span of the whole procedure. Eventually, the athlete can become physically and mentally relaxed within seconds.

At the end of the first relaxation exercise, I instructed the skiers to practice their athletic skills by using mental imagery. The technique has been used before. Jean-Claude Killy, a three-gold-medal skier, has reported that his only preparation for one race was to ski it mentally. He was recovering from an injury at the time and couldn't practice on the slopes. Killy says the race turned out to be one of his best.

[3]Instructions for muscle relaxation are included as an appendix to this article. —Ed.

From Black and White to Color

The trick for other athletes is to discover similar techniques of mental imagery that will work for them. In my work with relaxation and stress management, I have been extremely impressed by the quality of imagery that is possible after deep muscle relaxation. This imagery is more than visual. It is also tactile, auditory, emotional and muscular. One swimmer reported that the scene in her mind changed from black and white to color as soon as she dove mentally into a pool, and she could feel the coldness of the water. A skier who qualified for the former U.S. Alpine ski team experienced the same "irritability" that she felt during actual races, when she mentally practiced being in the starting gate. Without fail, athletes feel their muscles in action as they rehearse their sport. One professional racer who took the training actually moved his boots when skiing a slalom course in his mind.

The imagery of visuo-motor behavior rehearsal apparently is more than sheer imagination. It is a well-controlled copy of experience, a sort of body-thinking similar to the powerful illusion of certain dreams at night. Perhaps the major difference between such dreams and VMBR is that the imagery rehearsal is subject to conscious control.

The final step is to use imagery to practice a specific skill. What makes this type of practice so useful is its similarity to an actual competitive event. There is little doubt that actual physical practice makes perfect, but practice under practice conditions is an imperfect way of preparing for performance under game conditions. Many coaches acknowledge this fact when they contrast a good performance in practice with a poor one in competition. According to a well-established psychological principle, a skill learned or practiced in one situation will transfer to a new situation in direct proportion to the extent that the new situation resembles the one in which the practice took place.[4] Applying this to athletics, the more an athlete practices this sport under gamelike conditions (such as a contact scrimmage in full uniform on the football field), the more likely the performance will be repeated during the game.

Using VMBR, the Colorado State skiers practiced racing techniques, course concentration, and improving their memorization of courses. They cut down on skiing errors by repeating the correct actions, and they became more aggressive. The method worked. In fact, it seems to have worked so well that the research study itself flopped. The team's head coach, impressed by the improvement in the VMBR groups, raced them but not the skiers from the matched control group. I was therefore unable to show as conclusively as I would have liked that the imagery-rehearsal technique was more effective than customary training. I can say, however, that the coach was highly impressed, and that the team won the league's overall trophy as well as the men's and women's trophies. By the standards of common sense and observation, at least, the three-stage technique worked wonders.

Three Key Rules

Thus tested on the ski team at Colorado State, the technique caught the attention of Jim Balfanz, then director of the U.S. Nordic Ski Team program. Having returned from disappointing Winter Games in Sapporo in 1972, Balfanz was putting together a sports-medicine unit that would include a psychologist. I became that psychologist.

John Bower, Balfanz's successor, and Peter Karns, coach of the U.S. Biathlon team, made it possible for me to live and work with the Olympic athletes at the recent Winter Olympiad. While

[4]See the article by Cratty on pages 19-25. –Ed.

there, I applied three key rules from behavioral psychology. First, all my recommendations were couched in terms of specific actions. Second, recommendations had to be stated in ways that could be used immediately, since we were in the middle of the Olympics and the events could not wait. Third, the recommendations had to involve known principles systematically related to behavioral change. I could not count on any personal influence I might have or on the development of special insights about the athletes.

A few examples will convey the flavor of behavioral psychology at the Olympics. Tim Caldwell, a cross-country skier, was performing inconsistently as the Games approached. The harder he tried, the worse he performed. I analyzed the event into a chain of skills and activities, and hence planned a chain of training. First, I had Caldwell ski an easy part of the course, using smooth, free movements to regain the rhythm he had lost. Once he had accomplished this, I had him ski the easy part again and then continue on through a difficult stretch, up a hill for instance, still using the same rhythm. Next, he had to ski the whole course and exert the kind of effort he would if he were racing. The final link of the training chain was to have him race—in his imagination—against Olympic competitors.

Soon after this simple regimen, Caldwell skied the relay event in the third fastest time for his lap of the relay, thereby moving the U.S. team from 12th to eighth place. The team eventually finished sixth, the best performance in the history of U.S. Nordic cross-country relay teams.

To combat those negative, doubting thoughts that sometimes lower an athlete's confidence and interfere with performance, I have introduced various thought-stopping techniques. For example, I had one skier practice to a melody with a strong driving beat. Whenever a negative thought appeared, the skier thought, "Stop!" to prevent a repetition of the thought; he then immedaitely recalled the music and focused his attention on skiing to the beat.

Brief Intervention: Successful

With the acceptance of psychological methods at the Winter Olympics, more and more athletes are likely to add mental training to their programs.[5] My work at Innsbruck demonstrated the effectiveness of even the briefest psychological intervention. Skier Tim Caldwell's chain-training program, for example, was designed and completed in three meetings of 30 to 40 minutes each. I spent only 20 minutes in a refresher course for Lyle Nelson on the morning of the Biathlon relay event. Bill Koch visualized his forthcoming race in less than a minute, while waiting near the starting gate.

The success of psychological methods at the Winter Olympics is causing other athletes and coaches to test ideas they once ignored.[6] We do not know, as of this writing, which Americans may offset the advantages the Russians and other teams already enjoy. The Biathlon and cross-country team members seem likely to extend the advantages they gained from their experiences of last winter.

The Olympic Games this summer will probably see U.S. Pentathlon-team members using some of the new psychological and behavioral methods. Pistol shooting, for example, depends almost entirely on psychological discipline. The target is so large, the distance so short, and the pistols so accurate that the U.S. Pistol coach told me he could teach even me to shoot as well as his team—in

[5]Psychological preparation should be included on the day of competition as well. Some recommendations for on-site preparation are included at the end of this article. –Ed.

[6]See the article by Lane on pages 316-320, the article by Titley on pages 321-327, and the article by Spinelli and Barrios on pages 344-355. –Ed.

practice, that is. In actual competition the stress becomes so extreme that it can cause unforgivable errors, such as missing the target completely. Several Olympic aspirants, including Neil Glenesk, used the VMBR approach during a recent international meet. It included Pentathlon competitors from Mexico, Canada and the U.S., and a former bronze medalist from Great Britain. Glenesk asked for individual sessions of visuo-motor behavior rehearsal to reduce and manage his tension. The result? He won.

Case histories like these need experimental support, and it may not be long in coming. During one recent experiment in sports psychology, I recorded the electromyograph responses of an Alpine ski racer as he summoned up the moment-by-moment imagery of a downhill race.[7] Almost instantly, the recording needles stirred into action. Two muscle bursts appeared as the skier hit jumps. Further muscle bursts duplicated the effort of a rough section of the course, and the needles settled during the easy sections. By the time he finished this psychological rehearsal of the downhill race, his EMG recordings almost mirrored the course itself. There was even a final burst of muscle activity after he had passed the finish line, a mystery to me until I remembered how hard it is to come to a skidding stop after racing downhill at more than 40 miles an hour.

APPENDIX A
MUSCLE RELAXATION EXERCISE

Muscle relaxation is sought by coaches and athletes since coordination and sustained performance are hindered by muscle tenseness. Relaxation is desirable in nonphysical activities, e.g., mental concentration, since it aids in avoiding distractions to such effort, thus the technique has been used by executives as well.

The directions in the next section are used in a relaxation exercise. As with all physical exercises, the end product is the control by the athlete of muscle groups. In this case the end product is the ability to relax completely within a short time span. With three or four practice sessions, many persons are able to achieve muscle relaxation within 5 minutes. At this point the muscle tension component of the directions can be omitted.

Relaxation Directions

The primary purpose of the procedure is to aid in focusing attention on how it feels to have muscles truly tense and, in contrast, how it feels to be relaxed (or not tense). In each step you will be asked first to tense a muscle group, then to relax. Always pay close attention to the feeling within the muscles. Tense each muscle group only as long as is required for you to attend to the tension generated. For most, this takes about 5 seconds or a count of 5. Relaxation of the muscle groups take about the same amount of time. These times are approximate—do not distract yourself by paying too much attention to counting or timing. Tense the muscles until you can really feel the tension, and then relax.

This set of directions was developed by Richard M. Suinn, Ph.D., Sports Medicine Team, for use by Nordic coaching staff and athletes. Duplication or other use is possible only through direct release from Dr. Suinn, Professor and Head, Dept. of Psychology, Colorado State University, Fort Collins, Colorado 80523.

[7]See the article by Suinn on pages 26-36. –Ed.

The exercise follows a systematic pattern: right hand (or dominant hand), left hand, right bicep, left bicep, forehead, eyes, facial area, chest, abdomen, and both legs and feet. At the start, repeat the exercise for each group twice before going to the next group. Later, omit the tension and the repetition. After completing each muscle group, permit the area to remain relaxed by not moving that area. As a start, someone should read the directions to you.

Hands. First get into a comfortable position, preferably lying down on your back. You may use a small pillow for your head. Choose a time of day when you will not be disturbed for an hour. Many practice in the evening just before falling asleep. The relaxation achieved is an especially good way of going to sleep at night.

Close your eyes so as not to be distracted by your surroundings. Now, tense your right hand into a fist . . . *as tight as you can get it* . . . so that you can feel the tension . . . really tight, the tighter the better, so that you can really feel the tension. . . . Now relax the hand, let the tension remove itself . . . feel the muscles become loose . . . and notice the contrast between the tension a moment ago and the relaxation, the absence of tension. . . . Allowing the fingers to relax . . . and then the entire right hand.

Repeat the exercise for the right hand once.

Now we'll leave the right hand relaxed and focus on the left hand. Tense the left hand by making it into a fist . . . very tight . . . and again notice how that tension feels . . . focus your attention on the muscles as they are tense. . . . All right, now relax the hand, and notice the contrast between the tension of a moment ago and the relaxation. . . . Continue to be aware of the relaxation of the muscles . . . in the fingers . . . and throughout the entire hand.

Repeat the exercise for the left hand once.

Arms (Biceps). We'll leave the hands and the fingers relaxed and move to the biceps. In order to tense the biceps, you will be bending the arm at the elbow and tightening the biceps by moving your hand towards your shoulder. Let's start with the right arm.

Bend your right arm at the elbow so that your hand moves toward your shoulder . . . tight. . . . Keep tightening the biceps as hard as you can . . . focusing your attention on the muscle tension. . . . Really notice how that feels. . . . Now relax . . . letting the arm and hand drop back down . . . and noticing the relaxation, the absence of tension. . . . Feel the relaxation as it takes over the upper arm. . . . Notice the feeling of relaxation in the lower arm, the hand, and the fingers.

Repeat the exercise for the right arm once.

Now leave the right arm relaxed and move to the left arm. Tense up the left arm by bending it at the elbow . . . really tense, as tense as you can get it . . . and focus your attention on the feelings of tension. . . . Now relax, letting your arm drop back down. . . . Notice the difference in feeling between the tension and the relaxation. . . . Permit the relaxation to take over the entire left arm . . . the upper arm . . . the forearm . . . the hands . . . and fingers.

Repeat the exercise for the left arm once.

Forehead. We'll leave the hand and the arms comfortably relaxed and move to the forehead. In order to tense up the forehead, you will frown.

All right, I want you to tense the forehead by frowning. . . . Wrinkle up the forehead area . . . very tight . . . and notice how the tension feels. . . . Now relax. . . . Let the wrinkles smooth themselves out. . . . Allow the relaxation to proceed on its own . . . making the forehead smooth and tension-free, as though you were passing your hand over a sheet to smooth it out.

Repeat the exercise for the forehead once.

Eyes. We'll leave the forehead relaxed and move to the eyes. What I want you to do is close your eyes tighter than they are . . . tighter . . . feeling the tension. . . . (Use less time for tension here so as to avoid after-images.) . . . Now relax . . . keeping the eyes comfortably closed . . . noticing the contrast between the tension and the relaxation now.

Repeat the exercise for the eyes once.

Facial Area. We'll leave the eyes relaxed and go on to the facial area. To tense up the facial area, I want you to clench your jaws. . . . Bite down on your teeth hard now. . . . Really pay attention to the tension in the facial area and jaws. . . . (Use less time for tension here.) . . . Now relax. . . . Let the muscles of the jaws become relaxed. . . . Notice the feeling of relaxation across the lips, the jaws, the entire facial area. . . . Just allow the relaxation to take over.

Repeat the exercise for the facial area once.

All right, notice the relaxation in the right hand and the fingers . . . and the feeling of relaxation in the forearm and the upper arms. . . . Notice the relaxation that is present in the left hand and the fingers . . . in the forearm and the upper arm. . . . Let the relaxation take over and include the forehead . . . smooth and without tension . . . the eyes . . . the facial area . . . and the lips and the jaws.

Chest. All right, we'll now proceed to help the relaxation across the chest. I want you to tense up the chest muscles by taking a deep breath and holding it for a moment. . . . Notice the tension. . . . Now slowly exhale, breathing normally again . . . and notice the chest muscles as they become more and more relaxed.

Repeat the exercise for the chest once.

Abdomen. Now we'll move to the stomach. I want you to tense your stomach right now . . . very tight. . . . Pay attention to the tension. . . . Now relax . . letting the feeling of relaxation take over. . . . Notice the difference in the feeling of tension a moment before and the relaxation.

Repeat the exercise for the abdomen once.

Legs and Feet. Now we'll proceed with the relaxation. To tense your legs and feet, I want you to point your toes downward until you can feel the muscles of your leg tense. . . . Notice the tension. . . . (Use tension for about 3 seconds; avoid cramping of the toes or feet.) . . . Now relax. . . . Let the relaxation take over. . . . Feel the comfort.

Repeat the exercise for the legs and the feet once.

All right, simply enjoy the sense of relaxation and comfort across your body . . . feeling loose and relaxed in the hands and fingers . . . comfortable in the forearms and upper arms . . . noticing the relaxed feeling as it includes the forehead . . . the eyes . . . the facial area . . . the lips and the jaws . . . letting the relaxation include the chest . . . the abdomen . . . and both legs and both feet.

Now, to further increase the relaxation, I want you to take a deep breath and slowly exhale . . . using your rhythmical deep breathing to deepen the relaxation and to permit you to become as relaxed as you want . . . breathing slowly in and out . . . using your rhythm to achieve whatever level of relaxation you want . . . and in the future you can use this deep breathing technique to initiate or to deepen the relaxation whenever you want.

All right, that's fine. . . . Now let your breathing continue normally.

Termination of Exercise. In a moment, I'll count backward from 3 to 1. When I get to 1, you'll feel alert and refreshed . . . no aches or pains. . . . You can retain the relaxed feeling as long as you wish. . . . All right, 3 . . . more and more alert . . . 2 . . . no aches or pains . . . and 1 . . . you can open your eyes.

General Instructions

1. If the relaxation exercise is being used for the first time, I recommend that someone reads the instructions aloud for another to follow.

2. Whoever reads the instructions should do so in a normal voice, pacing the speed by doing the tension exercises. The aim is to tense the muscle group long enough to be noticeable but not long enough to be painful, to lead to cramps, or to lead to fatigue.

3. Some muscle groups, e.g., the eyes, the jaws, and the feet, should be tensed for a shorter span, about 3 seconds, to avoid painful or cramping results.

4. Once an athlete has used the exercise once upon the direction of someone else (as indicated above), he or she can practice the exercise alone by simply tensing and relaxing each muscle group in sequence.

5. After three or four practice sessions, one can omit the tension part and concentrate on simply having each muscle group become relaxed or limp, again in sequence. With training, a person can develop the relaxation within 5 minutes; with more practice, individuals have been able to initiate relaxation control within 1 minute. Such individuals are able to use the relaxation sitting in chairs or riding in vehicles and can practice it prior to contests. Control in relaxing specific muscle groups is possible with repetition.

6. Repetition of the deep breath technique can be a useful signal for initiation of relaxation on a quick reflex basis.

7. Although the relaxation exercise can be used for other forms of training, the directions here are aimed at teaching an individual how to control muscle groups to achieve *relaxation*. As with any other physical exercise, the success of the exercise requires practice and adherence to the exercise steps. Once a day, five out of every seven days, is a normal routine. More frequent use, such as once daily, speeds up training.

8. For those who wish to speed up the training and who are at training camps with USSA Nordic coaching staff, tape recordings can be made available upon prior arrangement. Contact your coach.

APPENDIX B
PSYCHOLOGICAL PREPARATION ON COMPETITION DAY

In preparing for the competition event, two aspects of psychological activities might be planned systematically, attention to activation level and use of VMBR.

As discussed earlier, activation level can be the important variable associated with "readiness to perform." Too high a level is experienced as stress or anxiety and leads to disruption of smooth coordination, muscle tightness, poorer efficiency, impaired attentional focus, and even gastrointestinal symptoms. With too low an activation level, performances are described as "flat," uninspired, at low effort or low energy, and unmotivated, and errors are often made. The optimal level of arousal varies

---

These recommendations were presented in part at clinics held by the author at the Squaw Valley and Colorado Springs Olympic training centers.

with each individual athlete, and the signs that such a level has been reached vary as well. Sometimes it is a tingling in the fingertips or simply a subjective feeling that "this is my day." The competitor should be encouraged to pay attention to such cues in order to identify those that were present on peak performance days. Similarly, the competitor should identify the cues that signal a poor performance day. Keeping a brief log on competition days, similar to a training log, can be most helpful. The athlete should also develop a program of psychological techniques to initiate depending upon activation level. A typical example are the steps taken by a professional alpine skier:

1.   The morning of the race, he first immediately pays attention to how "ready" he feels upon wakening, but does nothing immediately to change this feeling state. He allows time for a sound breakfast, eaten without a sense of rush, and leaves for the race site. The time allowed for travel has been predetermined by a previous day's trip, including extra time for traffic and parking problems. This prevents the frustration of delays.

2.   Physical warm-up exercises are done, and a few practice runs are taken. If the activation level is low (this competitor makes it a point to do a self-analysis to find out what the level is), then extra physical action is added to increase heart rate, circulation, feeling of warmth, etc. If the activation level is perceived to be too high, then this athlete removes himself from the area, finds a quiet place, and uses deep breathing and meditation.

3.   Regardless of activation level, this skier always relies upon a VMBR or a mental rehearsal technique. The scenes used are dependent upon the specific needs he feels for a particular race on a particular day. On one race day, he might feel the need to recover a sense of self-confidence because of a poor showing in the last event. For this, he uses the imagery of a previous successful race, and he adds racing the oncoming course with a stress on correct moves. If the objective, instead, is practicing to be mentally and physically ready for a difficult part of the race course, then his scene involves making that turn over and over until it seems second nature.

4.   Once this has been completed, the athlete then forgets completely about further practice, either mentally or physically. This routine has "programmed" him to perform, in the same way that Nicklaus programs himself by using imagery of the swing, the flight of the golf ball, and even the bounce and the roll, before he actually hits the ball.

On-site preparation can involve dealing with serious tensions or anxieties. These can result from a conditioned response to the presence of another competitor, from anxiety aroused by the importance of the meet or event, or from environmental presses. I suggest the following:

1.   An athlete should first identify his or her "muscle stress profile." This is the set of muscles or reactions that seem to characterize the athlete when stress is present. To identify one's profiles, a competitor takes a quick body inventory the next time he or she is under stress, e.g., checking whether the stress is felt at tightening of the shoulder or neck muscles, unconscious clenching of hands, dryness of throat, increasing heart rate, a feeling of loss of range of motion in the upper body, cold hands, stomach "butterflies" or other signs. Individuals tend to experience stress in fairly consistent ways, and these signs can be used as early signals that stress is building.

2.   Once the early signs of stress are known, then, every 45 minutes or so on the site, an athlete should take a moment to do a body inventory, to check whether the stress profile

is beginning to show. If signs of stress are present (e.g., if your sign is a tightening in the shoulders and you notice this happening), then a relaxation exercise should be initiated to regain control and to abort the anxiety buildup. The relaxation can be any one of a variety of short methods—using a deep breath cue, tensing and relaxing each muscle group, visualizing a controlled relaxation scene, and so forth.

3. If the tension is too great for self-control, i.e., self-relaxing, two athletes can work together. One should put his or her hands on the shoulders of the stressed competitor, who remains standing with eyes closed. The non-stressed helper then instructs the stressed athlete to feel the weight of the hands on the shoulders and to let the shoulders lower to a more relaxed level. This instruction is repeated (as the helper actually notices a further lowering of the shoulders). After about three instructions, the helper should then instruct the other athlete to further relax the body by breathing with slow, deep breaths and using each breath to further loosen and lower each muscle group. About two minutes of this focusing on the voice and the instructions of a helper can do much for stress reduction.

4. On some occasions, the source of the stress is environmental. Watching others perform, seeing and hearing a fidgety coach, being a part of an excited crowd might all contribute to stress activation. In such cases, withdrawal from these environmental conditions helps. Of course, for some athletes, such environmental cues serve as activation cues that enable attainment of the optimal level of arousal; this once again points out the importance of individualizing programs.

As mentioned, the use of VMBR has helped many in programming the body on competition days and immediately before performances. My recommendations are as follows:

1. On the night before meet, do not use VMBR. If you wish, use relaxation to help you get to sleep.
2. Four or five hours before the event,
    a. list your objective, e.g., you want to emphasize a fast start, confidence, aggressiveness, or how to handle the other competitors strategically, and
    b. determine how to achieve this objective, e.g., plan to take a moment to visualize a fast start to the gun immediately before getting into the starting blocks.
3. On the site, put the plan to work. As Ralph Boston said on another topic, "Plan the work, and work the plans."
4. Immediately prior to event (before stepping into the blocks, before being called into the ring,
    a. for a second or so, visualize your complete event as you would actually perform; see it happen; make this vivid visualizing include the way your body is to feel as it performs (Dwight Stones seems to do this, and Jack Nicklaus writes about it);
    b. use an inner frame of reference—you are doing it in the scene, not watching yourself do it; and
    c. clear your mind after you have programmed your body by visualization.
5. Now let your body take off and do its job at the starting gun.

Improving Athletic Performance through Visuo-Motor Behavior Rehearsal

John F. Lane

One afternoon, as I arrived at the high school where I was studying the use of visuo-motor behavior rehearsal (VMBR) with basketball players, one of the forwards met me. "Did you hear what happened yesterday?" he asked. My heart sank. Since VMBR was still a relatively unstudied technique, I had been expecting, almost daily, to encounter a clear case of its having failed. In two years of work I had obtained, with many athletes in various sports, nothing but promising results. Nevertheless, I thought: "Here it comes." The player grinned. He told me that the day before, the coach had brought to the foul line the three players with whom I had been working most consistently; the rest of the team had closed in around these three and had yelled, waved, and otherwise tried to distract them. It had not worked; the three sank basket after basket without a miss.

VMBR was developed by Suinn[1] as a combination of relaxation plus the use of imagery for practicing athletic skills. I was studying its application to basketball, and a number of other sports. By the end of the basketball season, the effectiveness of VMBR was evident. Two of the three starting players who had consistently worked with me improved their foul shooting 11% over the previous year; one improved 15%. Two of the three were seniors. Over all of the games of the season, both home and away, while the percentage of foul shots made by three starters who had not used VMBR actually decreased, there was a 12% increase for those who had used the technique; this increase was statistically significant at the .02 level.

Since two of the most important effects of VMBR training are the ability to relax more and to concentrate better, it was interesting that most of the team's increased ability to shoot fouls was demonstrated at away games rather than home games. The players who were trained in VMBR sank 10% more foul shots during home games, and 15% more during away games; both differences from the previous year were significant at the .05 level. The team as a whole made 14% more foul shots at away games than during the previous year; this difference was statistically significant at the .001 level. The increase for the team as a whole during home games, 2%, was not statistically significant. These results indicate an important point concerning the value of VMBR for athletes: it is under the most extreme conditions of competition, in this case games played away rather than in the more comfortable environment of the home court, that the advantages of VMBR training become most clearly evident.

---

[1] See the article by Suinn on pages 306-315. –Ed.

Regarding the imagery rehearsal part of VMBR, it is helpful for the athlete to feel fully "in" the situation forming the content of the behavior rehearsal. To achieve this it is often necessary for the VMBR conductor to draw the athlete's attention to the same sorts of perceptions to which he had accustomed himself during imagery conditioning. For example, with skiers I have emphasized being aware of how their feet felt in their skis, the texture of the snow under the skis, the cold, the clouds of breath coming from their mouths. A figure skater's perceptions were of the sound of her skates, the temperature in the rink, the feelings in the muscles of her body as she skated. Baseball pitchers and basketball players have concentrated on the solidity or flexibility of the mound or court under their feet, the noises of the crowds, the colors and textures of the particular target—basket rim or catcher's glove—to which their concentration would later shift.

It is important that the athlete feel fully involved in the behavior which is being rehearsed. "Spectator" imagery should be avoided: the athlete should be engaging fully in the behavior rather than "standing outside" himself and merely "watching" himself perform. In order to keep the athlete aware of the need to use "involvement" imagery, during behavior rehearsal sessions I have asked athletes to rate the vividness of their imagery on a scale of 1 through 10. If the athlete reported imagery of a vividness lower than 7 or 8, returning to the "comfortable place" of relaxation or focusing more sharply on specific elements of the situation has usually been effective in increasing the quality of the imagery.

There appear to be four benefits which can be obtained, singly or in combination according to the needs of the particular athlete, from VMBR training: relaxation and anxiety reduction, error correction, concentration, and skill development. Increased ability to relax, and increased ability to concentrate on the goal to be attained or the skill to be performed, are both the most general benefits and those most often reported by athletes who have undergone VMBR training. The correction of errors in performance is a close third. In fact, the ability to relax and concentrate is prerequisite to the productive analysis and subsequent correction of such errors.

The ability to relax under pressure, which VMBR fosters, in itself justifies including VMBR in an athletic training program. The following discussion between a college baseball pitcher (TD) and me following TD's VMBR session, illustrates the association of VMBR and relaxation.

Lane: What were you rehearsing?

TD: The slider.

Lane: Did it seem to have an effect on your pitching?

TD: When I got out here [on the field] I was throwing it good. Whether it had any effect on it I don't know. I was throwing it better.

Lane: Could relaxation have had an effect?

TD: Yes, I think that might have helped, because I was throwing a lot harder today. Yesterday I threw a lot of pitches, and I didn't think I'd be throwing that hard today, because my arm wasn't that strong. But I was throwing good. . . .

Lane: Is it all right to rehearse just before you pitch, rather than earlier?

TD: Maybe even better, because I was relaxed. Because when I do pitch, I do tense up a lot, and so maybe this helps getting me relaxed. . . . I was pretty loose, really. When I got on the mound I was really loose, in terms of tension.

VMBR can also be used to identify errors in motor performance to practice corrections. This is illustrated with an athlete, SH, who was the best hitter on the baseball team of a small New Jersey college. A senior, he was looking forward to being signed by a major league team. He had entered a slump just at the time that there was the most likelihood of scouts being in the stands. In a game the day before his first VMBR session, SH had popped up twice and struck out twice. The following are excerpts from the first VMBR session:

Lane: Now in your mind re-create the situation you were in yesterday. . . . Exactly what did you do? Tell me step by step what happened.

SH: Took the first two pitches, balls. One was outside, one was inside. Third pitch was a fast ball. It was up and in. I thought it was a ball, it was called a strike. Fourth pitch was a curve ball, it was high. I swung at it, fouled it off, it wasn't a very good swing. The last was another fast ball, up and in, which I fielded out to left field. . . . I was upset with myself because . . . I'm not really sure whether it would have been called a strike or not. It was a high curve ball, it didn't break very much, and my weight was out in front of me and I had kind of a feeble swing at it, didn't get everything into the swing.

Lane: Let's go back to the same pitch we've been working on and do it from the time when the pitcher makes his windup to the time you hit the ball. Try and look at it in slow motion. . . . There's some point at which the problem's beginning. See if you can find that and tell me about it. . . . [SH visualizes being at bat.]

SH: I can feel what I did wrong.

Lane: What did you do wrong?

SH: I was out in front of the pitch. My weight was on my front foot. And my hands were moving forward at the time, too, like I wasn't still cocked.

Lane: Does it sound, at least it sounds to me, as if you're trying too hard? Does that make any sense to you?

SH: Yes, well I don't know if it would go with trying too hard. I'm reacting too soon. . . . I'm starting too early, or I'm committing myself too early. . . .

Lane: What was the next good pitch that you got?

SH: A fast ball.

Lane: OK, try now to visualize that and try to consciously hold back on your timing. Consciously not lunge forward. . . . The muscles of your body are very deeply relaxed. Try to get that feeling into your swing. And see if you can change it a little bit and get your timing right. Try the same pitch between three and five times. . . . [SH visualizes correcting error.]

SH ended the season by tying the school's home run record.

SH's protocol provides a good example of the non-directive role which can often be taken by the VMBR conductor, especially if he is not expert in the technical aspects of the athlete's sport. SH analyzed his problem himself; the conductor's function was to help him focus on crucial aspects of the problem, to maintain his involvement in rehearsal of the correct behavior, and to suggest scenes to rehearse based on SH's own analysis.

Increased ability to concentrate[2] is probably the single most important benefit which I think athletes derive from VMBR training. The following excerpt from two sessions with a pitcher illustrates this development of greater concentration. Notice that RN picks up an idea from WC; both are participating in the session and are deeply relaxed.

---

[2] See the article by Nideffer on pages 281-290. —Ed.

RN: I wasn't concentrating too well today.

Lane: What exactly do you mean?

RN: I was just thinking about where my arm should be and I shouldn't really be thinking about that.

Lane: What should you be thinking about?

RN: Just the target . . .

Lane: Exactly what are you trying to do?

RN: Trying to concentrate on the glove.

Lane: What do you have to do at the same time?

RN: Trying to get my motion together, throw the ball. I'm having trouble with my windup and throwing the ball together. . . . From something WC said, about not picking up the glove until halfway through the windup. I tried that and it seems to work.

Lane: You pick up the glove now halfway through the windup?

RN: I look at the batter and then about halfway through I pick up the glove. I can't lose it if I pick it up then.

Lane: Very good. How many pitches have you thrown doing that?

RN: About a dozen.

Lane: Does it seem to work each time?

RN: It has worked, yes.

Specific behavior rehearsal scenes can be created to aid the development of concentration. Two basketball players were distracted, while rehearsing, by images of spectators or other players. They found that imagining the existence of high walls lining the key as they attempted to make foul shots eliminated these distractions.

Of the four benefits which can accrue to athletes from VMBR training, the initial development of skills is the most problematic. This is probably due, at least in part, to the lack of knowledge which beginning athletes have of the technical aspects of the undeveloped skill.

With athletes at lower levels of skill development, it may be best for imagery to be triggered by specific instructions which emphasize basic elements of the skill. The following instructions were developed by the basketball coach of the team mentioned earlier, for use in VMBR training in foul shooting. As sessions continued, the athletes became thoroughly familiar with these basic moves, which allowed individual problems to be addressed. During visualizing, the athletes are then instructed,

> *Go to the foul line. Place your feet and balance your body. Bounce the ball until you feel that your hands are in complete control of it. Focus your attention over the center hook of the basket. Your head is still. When you are ready, bend your knees and allow both your body and your arm to move the ball toward the target, which is just over the center hook. Your hand follows through. Be aware of the target.*

Athletes at higher levels of skill may be able themselves to indicate which elements of the skill are most important, and thus be able to create for themselves the appropriate imagery. In these cases, the VMBR conductor's role is to make sure that the athlete maintains his focus on the appropriate elements, and to suggest shifts in focus, or changes in imagery, if they appear necessary.

There is a lack of formal research on the effects of VMBR training, although positive results have been gained from whatever research has thus far been done. To my knowledge, the only full-scale study was conducted by Barbara Kolonay (1977) on the effects of VMBR on foul shooting among college basketball players. She found that teams which had VMBR training improved significantly more over the season than did teams which had either relaxation training alone, imagery alone, or no VMBR-related training at all. Suinn (1972) reported that a group of college ski team members who used VMBR were thought by their coach to have become better than the group which had not had such training—enough better that he raced the VMBR group in preference to the other. However, due to the lack of experimental control, Suinn does not consider these results to be conclusive. In a study with recreational tennis players under relatively controlled conditions, I found that the VMBR group showed a tendency to become better than a relaxation-only group (Lane 1977). The results were not, however, statistically significant. The results of a study with high school basketball players (Lane 1978) were reported at the beginning of this article. Although somewhat impressive, from an experimental point of view, this study suffered from having a small number of athletes involved as well as from the lack of proper controls. In a related study under pre-competition conditions (*ibid.*), I found the same trend with this team as had been found with the tennis players. Again, the results, while suggestive, were not statistically significant.

Suinn[3] has suggested, and I agree, that to become thoroughly evaluated, VMBR must be subjected to further large-scale testing under controlled experimental conditions. However, from a purely practical point of view, there is little doubt that the technique, properly used, results in increasingly effective performances by athletes trained in its use. Suinn has used it at the Olympic and college levels. I have used it at college, high school, and even elementary school levels. High school students have been able to be trained, if only rudimentarily, as VMBR conductors. I have trained at least one coach (as has Suinn)—a figure skater—in its use in one session. The use of VMBR requires the ability to accept a rather non-traditional aspect of sport—the salience of the mind (or mind-body) rather than of the body alone. But the technique is available. It can be used, under the proper conditions, by coaches and athletes in probably any sport, and at almost any level.

[3]Richard M. Suinn 1978: personal communication.

REFERENCES

Kolonay, B. J. 1977. The effects of visuo-motor behavior rehearsal on athletic performance. Master's thesis, Hunter College, The City University of New York. 1977.
Lane, J. F. 1977. Effects of visuo-motor behavior rehearsal on the performance of recreational tennis players. Unpublished manuscript.
——. 1978. Four studies of visuo-motor behavior rehearsal. Unpublished manuscript.
Suinn, R. M. 1972. Behavior rehearsal training for ski racers. *Behavior Therapy* 3:519-520.
——. 1976a. Body thinking: Psychology for Olympic champs. *Psychology Today* 10, 2 (July):38-43.
——. 1976b. Visual motor behavior rehearsal for adaptive behavior. In *Counseling Methods,* ed. J. Krumboltz and C. Thoresen. New York: Holt.

The Loneliness of a Long-Distance Kicker

Robert W. Titley

A student-athlete at Colorado State University, Clark Kemble, holds the all-time NCAA major college football record for the longest field goal. His 63-yard kick occurred during the second quarter of the Colorado State University versus the University of Arizona game played in Fort Collins, Colorado on November 15, 1975. This article about the kick and the kicker is published with the permission of Clark Kemble and his coach, Sarkis Arslanian. The article also includes a case description of the application of a psychological technique known as *visuo-motor behavioral rehearsal.* Further, it is an example of a coordinated and cooperative effort among a psychologist, a coach, and an athlete.

The lot of the placekick specialist on any football team can be a lonely one. Unlike the player who is a member of the regular offensive or defensive units, the placekicker seldom experiences being part of a larger unit with broader participation and extended playing time. If he is a specialist lacking the physique, background or skill to play another position, or if his coach prefers that he restrict his contribution to kicking, he does not participate in the several drills or scrimmages which build team unity. If he is an import from another sport, e.g., soccer, he may not even be considered by some a full-fledged football player.

The kicker usually practices on a separate field away from the rest of the team, in the company of a manager or an injured player who acts as his snapper or holder. Sometimes his only company is another kicker who is trying to get his job away from him. Sometimes he practices alone, kicking and retrieving a number of footballs in a tiresome and potentially boring sequence, over and over. Under game conditions, he walks the sideline until called upon to kick. When in the game, he stands alone behind the other ten players on his team, in plain view of everyone, the visual object of thousands of eyes. His seemingly solitary existence consists of a relationship between himself and the ball and the distant, unforgiving goal posts. The result of his effort is immediately known to everyone. After the kick, he picks up his tee and returns to the sideline to stand alone and wait again. If a missed kick is the margin of a team loss, the unconsolable quiet of the locker room folds in on him. The lot of the placekick specialist on a football team can be a lonely one.

During the fall season of 1973, the Colorado State football team found itself with neither a skilled nor a potential placekicker. The situation was so desperate that Coach Arslanian made an

Robert W. Titley. The loneliness of a long-distance kicker. *The Athletic Journal* 57 (September 1976):74-80.

unusual gesture. He advertised in the student newspaper, inviting any and all comers to try out for the position. He had asked an established, well-known professional placekicker from the NFL to aid in the selection of a kicker from among the number of hopefuls who appeared. Among the candidates was one Clark Kemble, a sophomore from Fort Worth, Texas, who had played only a little football but a great deal of soccer in his high school days. He appeared more or less as a lark, interested as much in seeing a famous professional player as in making the team. At the conclusion of the try-outs, Coach Arslanian and the professional kicker agreed that the sandy-haired, quiet, pleasant young man—the soccer sidewinder named Kemble—possessed a potential and a powerful leg, the likes of which they had never seen before. In subsequent months, Arslanian was to predict flatly that some day Kemble would break the NCAA record for distance.

By the seventh game in 1973, and after weeks of careful and effective instruction by Arslanian, who personally coaches the kickers, Clark Kemble became Colorado State's regular specialist. Clark's performance was adequate, but not outstanding over the remainder of the season. Arslanian, an experienced coach of many kickers, had noticed a tendency in the young kicker to rush his kicks, to be a bit tight, and very excitable under game conditions.

Arslanian's concerns became a reality in the third game of 1974, when Clark missed a field goal in the closing minutes of the Memphis State game. Colorado State lost 20 to 18. The following week the team played the eventual Western Athletic Conference champion, Brigham Young. A courageous and dramatic comeback resulted in a tying touchdown scored on a desperation pass play as the clock ran out. What would have been a routine conversion became, by circumstances of a 15-yard penalty, a 35-yard attempt for the winning point. Kemble's kick sailed slightly wide to the left and the game ended in a 33-33 tie. The following Saturday, Clark kicked three field goals against Utah State, but missed a fourth try of 29 yards. The game ended in a 24 to 23 victory for Utah State. Although Clark's private thoughts must remain known only to Clark, he must have had a somewhat lonely feeling at that stage of the season.

Since Arslanian came to Colorado State University, we have been involved in psychological consultation with the football coaching staff. Arslanian, an excellent coach and a great motivator of young athletes, is psychologically-minded. We had recently learned the theory and practice of a new *behavior modification* technique known as *visuo-motor behavioral rehearsal* (VMBR)[1] from its psychologist originator, our departmental colleague, Dr. Richard Suinn. In a conversation with Arslanian, we mentioned that the method might facilitate his placekicker's performance under a wider range of conditions. Dr. Suinn and I interviewed Kemble at length and we concurred that VMBR was appropriate. With the permission of both the athlete and his head coach, we undertook to train Kemble with the method on a week to week basis.

No other form of psychological intervention was deemed necessary. Clark Kemble was and is a stable and well-adjusted young man. He comes from a good background, from a pleasant and supportive family, and was a well-functioning individual in his day to day campus, academic, and social life. His aspiration levels were and are realistic and he has a positive self-concept and outlook. He has a set of well-thought-out religious convictions and is a clean-living individual who trains and works hard. We found him to be team-oriented and unselfish in his attitudes. He appeared motivated toward, but not overly or unrealistically obsessed with doing well—not only for himself, but for his team and his school. Kemble is a rather gentle, gentlemanly type young man, described sometimes as modest. Although he is actually likeable, friendly, and outgoing with those who know him, he might be viewed by a new acquaintance as shy and unassuming.

---

[1] See the article by Suinn on pages 306-315. —Ed.

Handsome and well-groomed, his body type is mesomorphic, but he is not of the hard, coarse muscular type. At 5 feet, 10 inches and 170 pounds, he has somewhat heavy thighs, but overall he has more the build of a powerful swimmer than a powerful football player. A tough, swaggering bearing is not part of his makeup, nor does he ever exhibit aggressiveness toward anybody or anything, except a football on a kicking tee. Clark described himself as being somewhat *hyper* and as becoming excited when it is time to kick. We did not consider this, however, by any stretching of psychological concepts, as a personality problem. He was considered a normal young man with a healthy personality.

Like any mentally healthy person who participates in athletics would be, he was, after his costly missed kicks, down-in-the-mouth. But like any mentally healthy athlete who tries and fails, he did not need psychotherapy, or any form of restructuring of his basic motivations, attitudes, personality, cognitions, values or life-style. He needed only three things: an expression of faith from his coach, a re-examination of his skill techniques, and the acquisition of a cool-headed, loose, and eventually self-controlled mental and physical state which would allow his strength and skill to become manifest under a wider range of conditions—including game pressure. Arslanian provided the first two needs; I agreed to attempt to provide him the latter—with VMBR.

Developed by Dr. Suinn, and used most recently by Suinn with members of the U.S. Olympic Nordic and Biathlon ski teams in the 1976 Winter Olympics in Innsbruck, VMBR involves two stages. First, the athlete is trained in deep muscle relaxation. While prostrate in a large reclining chair, he is taught to achieve a relaxed state by tensing his muscle groups in sequential progressions. Muscle group tensing in sequence, followed by muscle relaxation allows the subject to focus on the contrast between tension and relaxation. Attention to the contrast results in a recognition of the proprioceptive cues of relaxation and thus an acquisition of a conscious awareness and control of the state of his muscles. The relaxed state is cued to deep breathing, with the eventual result that a more relaxed body state can be achieved at will by taking a deep breath and letting it out slowly. The subject chooses a relaxation scene, e.g., a walk in the woods or relaxing on a blanket in the warm sun, imaging himself as actually existing in this scene—not watching himself as in a picture, but as actually *there*—while he is in the induced relaxed state. He is asked to feel in the relaxation scene as he feels in the reclining chair. Once this is mastered, the subject is able to acquire the relaxed state without tensing his muscles, but by simply placing himself on the chair, concentrating on becoming relaxed, and taking intermittent deep breaths. A relaxed state can also be achieved in any tension-producing situation by using the deep breath, a phenomenon which is often attempted or acquired naturally. Notice how many people, when feeling tension build, will inhale deeply in order to relax.

The second phase of VMBR consists of imaging actual practice, pre-game or game condition scenes. With Kemble, kicking in practice, actually being in pre-game situations, on the sidelines, and in the game were visually rehearsed by the athlete in imagery while he was relaxed on the chair. The images and the concurrent stimulus cues become associated with the relaxed state and also to an *inattention* to distracting, interfering, and irrelevant cues. Imagery can include a tuning out of factors such as crowd noise, the thought of possibly missing, the present game score, the time factor, and suddenly occurring events which could preclude an effective execution of the well-learned skill. The athlete is instructed to image himself performing, again not in the manner of watching himself perform, but as actually experiencing the motor acts of his event, feeling his body perform and letting his head go along for the ride. Thus, the actual performance should become more controlled by cerebellar functions rather than by cerebral influences, i.e., muscle memory should become predominant when the actual motor behavior is performed. Rather than thinking too much, he thinks less when executing, much as one does not need to think about walking while walking.

So-called concentration becomes, then, as much an inattention to interfering thoughts as a focus on the automatic performance of the motor skill. The various components of the skilled technique and the sequence itself, as learned through coaching and practice, and including basics such as head down, follow through, etc., become virtually automatic. . . .

It is also possible to induce or suggest to the athlete, during VMBR, pre-performance motor patterns which might be additionally conducive to a calm mental and physical state before performing such as walking more slowly when he knows he is about to perform. Words such as *poise, confident, calm, feeling good, if you miss you miss,* can be used in speaking to the subject during his imagery.[2] In early VMBR, the psychologist trainer may guide the athlete in his imagery by describing the sequences; later, the athlete may merely be told to go ahead and thus be allowed to experience in imagery the execution himself, signalling when it is over by raising a finger on one hand. The kicker can also be instructed during his imagery of, say sideline situations, to notice the presence of his teammates, thus cuing stimuli in his environment to the relaxed state; or he may be instructed to visualize himself sauntering onto the field slowly and calmly placing the tee.

The ultimate goal of the psychologist administering VMBR is *not* to improve techniques; that is the coach's and athlete's responsibility—but simply to increase the probability of a well-learned skill to come through in full strength and power, in full control, and in smooth execution, whenever and wherever the motor behavior is to be peformed.

Kemble was a good subject. His ability to relax was so complete that during one session I thought he had died on me right in the chair. He never fell asleep, as do some subjects. His imagery was excellent. If a naive observer had watched our sessions, he might have received the impression that I had him hypnotized. It may be noticed that the technique and goals of VMBR may have parallels with what some athletes have tried to achieve with hypnosis or with meditation. We believe that the method was successful with Kemble, that it desensitized him to distracting cues, increased his mental coolness, increased his concentration, and that his performance became eventually more automatic and consistent. In Kemble's words, it helped him overcome mental blocks.

In the game following the first three treatment sessions, which were conducted the week following the three previously mentioned disaster games, he kicked 9 out of 9 extra points and one out of one field goal attempts. We went to a once a week session. The next Saturday, he provided the margin of victory in an 11-6 battle with Wyoming. Kemble kicked three goals, all over 40 yards, on a field made slippery by a steady drizzle. More of his kickoffs were flying higher and longer, into the end zone and beyond, and while still having some ups and downs from game to game, it was felt that some consistency was developing. By the end of the season he led the WAC in kick-scoring and set or tied several school records.

But he was not there yet. During the 1974 season Kemble had continued to mention to me factors which he felt affected his kicking, e.g., the relative heaviness of the air and stripes on the ball used in night games—stripes, he thought, made the ball seem heavier. He did not have a good spring intra-squad game, in spite of the relatively low-pressure situation and a VMBR session the morning of the game. He seemed bothered by having to adjust to a new center and holder. Kickers are notorious for being fussy about the style of the snapper and holder—sometimes independent of how good the snapper and holder might actually be. In the 1.3 second sequence from snap to kick, the smoothness of the total execution is critical, but attending to or worrying about the snap and hold may be as devastating to the kick performance as a poor snap or hold in and of themselves.

[2]See the article by Kirschenbaum and Bale on pages 334-343. —Ed.

Kemble practiced hard on his own all summer, alone with a tee, sometimes kicking 100 times a day. Come fall and we decided to leave him alone and see how he would do in practice and in the first couple of games. His practice kicking was excellent but some inconsistency between practice and game conditions seemed apparent. A skilled junior college transfer was also kicking very well in practice and was waiting in the wings to take over. Believing that Kemble's potential had not yet become fully manifest, it was decided, with the concurrence of Coach Arslanian and Kemble, to reinstate the VMBR training and also to put Clark under competitive conditions with the other kicker on practice days. We felt that having Clark under competition in practice, specifically, one or two kick-for-kick matches per week, might duplicate to some degree the competitive pressure felt under game conditions. It also meant, in a seeming paradox, that I needed to desensitize him with VMBR to the practice competition so that he could keep his cool in these weekday matches.

He kicked well in the next game, a high pressure defensive struggle in which Kemble's 26-yarder provided the margin of a 3-0 victory. But he had a bad day the following Saturday. More discussions took place with Coach Arslanian and Clark. I was convinced that Clark's head was okay; Arslanian considered the possibility that a mechanics problem might have been the culprit. Films had revealed some possible hold problems. On a seeming hunch that only good coaches have, Arslanian decided to give Clark a new holder, a quarterback with sure hands—a holder in which Clark expressed immediate confidence—he did not even think he needed to adjust.

We now felt that all skill, technique, mechanical, and psychological factors were as well under control as we could get them. We waited for undefeated Arizona State, the eventual second-ranked team in the nation. Team feelings were running high, and we wanted to win, but Arizona was too much for Colorado State. The only points scored by Colorado State were on a 21-yard field goal by Kemble.

Came the interstate rivalry game with the Air Force Academy. Kemble's confidence in himself was running quite high that week in practice. In a brief chat before being put through relaxation and imagery he revealed to me that he felt *really psyched up*, because he was going head to head against Dave Lawson, the superb AFA kicker and holder of the NCAA major college distance record of 62 yards. I was rather surprised that such a strong desire to beat another kicker in a duel of the best had emerged—previously he had never commented to me about the other teams' kickers. I wondered if the competition in practice, his ultimate success against his teammate, and his awareness of the fact that he could now remain cool, calm, and effective under competitive pressure were related to the, *I want to do better than Lawson* attitude. I became very nervous, because it was nearing the time I had to wean him away from reliance on me and allow him to become fully self-controlled, by using the breathing and self-induced imagery. Would he blow the whistle by getting overly tight for the intense, built-in emotion of the Air Force game?

In our regular Wednesday session, I had him tune out the presence of Lawson in his imagery. I also increased the emphasis on feeling good as he imaged himself on the sidelines and in the game. In previous sessions a directed emphasis on walking slowly out onto the field had been discarded because although Clark had recently been doing that very thing in the live situation, he felt that he was now thinking too much about walking slowly and this distracted him. I had also shifted, at his suggestion, to fewer imaged kicks per session. Further, rather than verbalizing his kicks for him during the training sessions, I had begun to allow him to develop his own kicking images totally, while I remained silent during his rehearsal kicks. This was partly by design, but also at Clark's request. He thought this might work even better, because his timing of the sequence in imagery was better than mine. His confidence was running so high he was even telling me how to run the psychological training session.

He won the duel against Lawson that Saturday, with 9 kickoffs into or beyond the end zone, 5 of 5 extra points, and 4 field goals of 26, 29, 40, and 53 yards. A fifth field goal attempt was straight on line, but fell about 5 yards short. It was a 67-yard attempt. His comment: *You can't make 'em all Dr. T.*

It had occurred to me, in hearing and reading his comments to reporters after successful game performances, that Clark was often repeating phrases or paraphrasing statements I used during the training sessions, e.g., *If you miss, you miss,* and *I felt good today.* Also, in spite of his not wanting to think in imagery any more about walking slowly, he told me after the Air Force game that he just sort of sauntered out onto the field, as though it was completely his own idea to do so. Although the VMBR is different from hypnosis both theoretically and in method, another of my colleagues, an expert in hypnosis, believes that a phenomenon at least parallel to post-hypnotic suggestion may be operative in the method, and that this might account partly for the positive subjective feeling and perceived physical state that VMBR apparently induces or enhances. I know of no way to verify this, but some psychologists would explain it in terms of stimulus-response learning theory, namely in the stimulus generalization effects of imagery to the real life situation. In either case, if the athlete feels good during games, is calmer, is not bothered by misses, and kicks better, so be it.

Clark's performance against Air Force was impressive. But his finest moment was yet to come—against Arizona. The entire team, including Kemble, seemed intent on upsetting Arizona, who was favored. I always ride the Colorado State bench, but this particular week I happened to be with the team and coaching staff at the Friday evening meal, and at the pre-game meal Saturday morning. The players were quiet, introspective, and in apparent deep concentration yet not overanxious. The injury situation had decimated the Colorado State defense and Arizona's balance and power proved to be more than we could handle. But early in the game, Kemble trotted onto the field and kicked a pretty 47-yarder, giving Colorado State a 3-0 lead. It split the posts, sailing 10 yards beyond. Near the middle of the second quarter Colorado State, trailing 7-3, drove to the Arizona 46, but was stalled by an incomplete third down pass. The pressure was intense—the noisy crowd seemed to be depending on Clark's foot to keep us in the game and they remembered his booming 47-yarder. A crescendo of crowd noise ushered him onto the field and he set his tee on the Colorado State 47-yard line. Then came the snap, the hold, the kick . . . a kick to remember.

It was a beautiful and awesome thing to see—63 yards and picture perfect, a new NCAA major college record. As the referee raised his arms, Kemble gleefully jumped four feet into the air and was swarmed over by teammates; on the sidelines I was, due to age and physique, able to leap only about 10 inches, but my glee was equal to Clark's. Arslanian set a new record for the widest grin—he had seen his meticulous coaching efforts, his prediction, and his faith in the boy fulfilled. The well-coached, well-learned skill, in full strength and controlled power, had come through. As though to confirm for himself that it was no fluke, Clark put the ensuing kickoff through the goal posts above the crossbar and later kicked a short chip shot field goal of 54 yards.

We lost 31-9, and after the game Kemble's feelings were mixed. I do not need to describe how hard it must have been for him to accept the praises of the reporters, when in another part of his brain and another part of his heart, he hurt because his team had lost. But such is the game of football.

Professionally, I will always remember the coordinated and cooperative effort of psychologist, coach, and player. Personally, I will always remember Clark. Delayed by nearly an hour by reporters, he was the last to dress. All the other players had gone and I saw him sitting alone in the locker room, struggling with a stubborn sweat sock, and probably still struggling with his mixed feelings. We talked a bit, stepped over towels and tape, and walked through the now dark stadium tunnel, each to go our separate ways. We will always be friends, but our professional relationship is over—he does not need my help any more. Clark moves on to professional football, having signed with the New Orleans Saints. I will be doing VMBR in consultation with Coach Arslanian, and with other athletes in future seasons. Neither Arslanian nor I will forget the sandy-haired sidewinder who answered an ad in the student newspaper.

I do not know how Clark spent that evening or the next day after the record kick. He may have been with friends, with his fiancee or he may have spent some time alone, modestly trying to savor what he had accomplished. The lot of the football placekicker is a lonely one. But Clark Kemble can now experience a certain singular good lonely feeling, an emotion only few athletes have ever known, or will ever know. He is Colorado State's all-time kick scoring leader holding 14 school kicking records. He now stands alone with an NCAA field goal distance record, above all the nation's major college football placekickers, past and present. And he deserves it. It must be a good lonely feeling for a long-distance kicker. Clark Kemble is alone at the top. He is the champion.

An Application of Biofeedback and Self-Regulation Procedures with Superior Athletes: The Fine Tuning Effect

Betty J. Wenz and Donald J. Strong

Biofeedback and relaxation procedures have emerged in recent years as being potentially useful for a variety of individuals in coping more effectively with personal stress and its resultant behaviors. The clinical use of biofeedback with certain psychosomatic disorders is becoming well known, but biofeedback and self-regulatory methods have yet to be broadly applied in nonclinical settings where individual performance might be greatly influenced in a desirable manner (Blanchard and Young 1974). Superior athletes as a group are constantly seeking to improve performance levels and could possibly benefit from biofeedback and psychological self-regulation.

Recent performances in international competitions have pointed up the need for greater attention to the psychological aspects of the competitive situation. Mental preparation is seen as essential for success at the highest levels of athletic endeavor. Psychological readiness techniques have already been used by certain European sports teams for many years and apparently contributed to the success of many athletes during the most recent Olympic games (Brown 1976).

The differences in performance among athletes of relatively equivalent skills appear to rest on a person's ability to cope with the perceived stress of the competitive situation. The stress reaction produces an anxiety syndrome that has specific physiological as well as psychological components that inhibit performance. A multifaceted and integrated approach utilizing self-regulation techniques, biofeedback, relaxation, and other psychological approaches can be viewed as an appropriate way of overcoming individualized performance stress responses. This view draws together knowledge of skill development and psychological learning from the fields of sports psychology and physiology, psychophysiology, and clinical psychology. Motivation, psychological self-awareness, and an internal sense of physiological responsiveness underlie much of the effectiveness in obtaining self-regulation. Biofeedback offers an immediate way of determining levels of physiological arousal that can be identified, monitored, changed, and psychologically reinforced (Brown 1977). These physiological states and their psychological components appear to be directly related to a person's capability to cope with stress.

RATIONALE

In order to assist superior athletes and their coaches to cope successfully with the results of stress under highly competitive conditions, a self-regulation program was designed by the authors, who are licensed psychologists. The purpose of this program is to present an understanding of the role of stress and anxiety and to provide the athlete with a number of self-regulatory techniques for coping directly with the behaviors that often detract from optimal performance.[1] The tools include some methods for relaxation, the introduction and use of biofeedback procedures, the use of autogenic phrases, and some imaging techniques.

There are several reasons for including coaches together with the athletes in such a program. One reason is to de-mystify the whole learning experience for coaches so they can then continue to reinforce the athlete's different and individualized pattern for handling stress. Also, it is beneficial for the coach to have a personal experience in the process of self-regulation. The coaches' involvement gives support to the program and to the athletes who are participating. The relationship aspect of joint involvement is of particular importance to each athlete.

There appears to be little variability in physical capabilities among superior athletes, and differences that do exist are sometimes not effectively utilized. Often it is the psychological responses of the athlete that make the real difference between success and failure in competition. The concept of "fine tuning" is used here to represent the control and sharpening of those psychological processes that enable the physical skills to be expressed in a maximum fashion. Although psychological aspects have long been seen as important, emphasis remains focused on physical training and the development of the special body skills necessary for a given athletic event. Skill development usually begins with trial and error learning and the use of external feedback from results of the activity. As coaching takes place, feedback on how to use the body becomes more refined and precise. The use of visual feedback (film or tape) clarifies more directly and specifically to the athlete what he/she is actually doing biomechanically and then what needs to be changed. At this point, the relationship between coach and athlete shifts from almost sole reliance on the coach to a collaborative process where both participate to bring about change in an athlete's physical behavior. The concepts of physical awareness, external feedback, and physical self-regulation appear to underlie most coaching and training programs.

These same concepts can also be applied from a psychological framework to further increase athletic performance through additional fine tuning. This assumes that superior athletic performance is an integrated psychophysiological process, using both internal and external awareness. Feedback and self-regulation result in an athlete's psychology and physiology working together.

PROCEDURE

A psychologically-based training program was designed by the authors to complement the physical training of athletes and to integrate psychological and physiological processes into a more consistent level of high performance. This approach appears to be particularly helpful to those who experience a level of tension and anxiety that interferes with maximum performance in competitive situations. The focus is to alter an athlete's overanxious and externally distractive response to competition through the use of several techniques which can be tailored to individual needs and psychological capability. The underlying process is to move the athlete from an external locus of control to an internal one. Self-regulation is viewed here as a basic shift of responsibility back to the individual resulting in a psychophysiological "freeing" effect that allows the person to increase relevant performance responses. An increase in self-esteem is one highly desirable result.

---

[1]See the article by Suinn on pages 26-36 and the article by Spinelli and Barrios on pages 344-355. —Ed.

An individually designed and integrated self-regulation program can be drawn from the following kinds of procedures:

Relaxation Training. Jacobson's progressive muscle relaxation is considered basic for both psychological and physiological effects. Specific muscle tension-relaxation training is followed by a combination of muscle relaxation, deep-regular-smooth breathing, the use of stimulus words, and imagery. Athletes are asked to identify points of muscle tension, extent of mind wandering, and responsiveness to stimulus words and imagery.

Autogenic Phrases. Athletes are asked to concentrate on certain words or phrases by repeating them silently or visually to themselves. Words such as *warm, serene, calm,* and *confident* are used to achieve the desired psychophysiological state. A three-stage format has been developed which ranges from feeling tense and constricted to feeling deeply relaxed, and finally to feeling competitively ready.

Imaging. Several forms of imagery are used. The first activity is visually to recall a recent important national/international championship situation including all the steps from the last practice session to leaving the competition. The athletes are then asked to fill out a perceived competition stress inventory developed by the authors. Although individual differences are apparent, critical points of stress appear in sleeping patterns, watching rivals, hearing results of various performances, waiting periods, and the use of personal rituals. The intent is to have each athlete identify points of high and low stress and the accompanying behaviors.

Specific forms of imagery training include pleasant images to facilitate the generalized relaxation response. An imaging exercise of a physical activity is used to illustrate the technique of mental rehearsal of specific behavioral skills (Suinn 1972). The focus is on the internal awareness of muscle flexion-extension patterns and weight shifts occurring as the body moves, as well as visualizing the environmental setting, such as colors and the use of physical cues. A third imaging technique was designed for achieving feelings of confidence and competence. The mental rehearsals are practiced both in slow motion and at normal or slightly accelerated speed. Athletes are finally asked to image a fully integrated top-level performance in competition with accompanying feelings of confidence.

Another exercise is a modified rehearsal of the same anxiety-arousing competition used earlier. Participants are asked to stop at each point of anxiety and apply the learned self-regulation techniques until feelings of confidence and control return. They are then asked to return to visualizing the competition, up to the next point of stress, and repeat these steps until the rehearsal is completed. Participants then fill out the competition stress check list the second time. Although self-reports are sometimes unreliable, most profiles show a clear drop in perceived stress. Generalized high perceived stress patterns for some participants typically become more localized and specific. In a few instances, perceived stress may be higher but is usually more controllable.

Biofeedback. Biofeedback training is introduced as a method of external verification of the extent of muscle activity through electromyograph (EMG) readings or extent of blood flow in the extremities by measuring finger temperature (thermal), both being measures of physiological components of stress. The underlying principle in this form of tension reduction is that a more relaxed response allows greater blood flow to the extremities and muscle tension becomes lessened. The instruments are used to demonstrate that muscle and blood flow responses are amenable to individual control. Each athlete and coach spends at least 20 minutes on both the thermal and EMG. In virtually all instances EMG readings are lowered, and in most cases hand temperature is raised. Each participant is then given a small inexpensive hand-held thermometer to practice hand warming at home.

Individualized Home Practice. An individualized home practice program is developed for each person. Several general formats are offered with variations in frequency and time spent on each activity. These options include progressive muscle relaxation; modified relaxation techniques combined with either internal muscle scan, breathing exercises, autogenic phrases, imagery for general relaxation, or mental rehearsal; and hand warming training. Each participant commits himself/herself to a specific home practice program and a schedule which is periodically reviewed.

Other Psychological Issues. Discussions and presentations of other important psychological dimensions related to athletic success are also included. Each coach and his/her athletes meet as a small group with an experienced and qualified leader to discuss coach-athlete and athlete-athlete relationships.[2] The discussion includes feelings and attitudes about the particular sport, competition behaviors and worries, and ways of working with each other to reduce psychological pressure during competition. All of the participants meet together for a discussion on levels of aspiration, goal setting,[3] and goal achievement. A modified ring-toss game is presented so that participants predict what scores or changes they would try to attain after an initial performance level. Most set moderate and sequential performance goals. Other patterns include a desire to leap immediately to the highest possible goal (perfection) or reach for an almost perfect performance while mentioning an extremely low goal in the same statement (ambivalence). This leads to a discussion of success-failure avoidant strategies used by athletes. Included in the same session is a presentation and discussion of psychological needs for achievement, power, and affiliation. Finally, the importance of moving from an external locus of control to an internal one is presented and discussed, especially as it pertains to self-regulated performance.

Follow-up. All participants are invited and encouraged to maintain contact with the psychologists. Such follow-up may include further mental rehearsal exercises for a specific activity, evaluation of home practice programs, helping coaches and athletes work more effectively together, and an analysis and resolution of individual problems encountered. Additional mini-workshops, although not as comprehensive, may be held for sports with a strong teamwork emphasis or uniform performance emphasis. In addition, assistance can be given toward applying the techniques under practive and/or actual competitive conditions. Stimulus words and phrases, such as *stretch and smooth, lateral back stretch,* and *high and smooth* can also be developed for individual athletes to help integrate their performances. In some instances the biofeedback equipment can be made available at competitions and used by athletes as a check on their level of physiological arousal and control.

OBSERVATIONAL RESULTS

Some definite results are often manifested early. The authors have worked with groups of track and field athletes as well as synchronized swimmers. Within a week, one track coach changed the starting technique of his sprinters from a tight, explosive kind of start to a muscularly relaxed but more responsive style. One of the sprinters who participated in an intercollegiate meet not only won but also showed some interesting changes in doing so. Whereas he had had a tendency to be a slow starter and also to slow down near the tape, films of the meet revealed a dramatic change in his

---

[2] See the article by Nesvig on pages 250-260. —Ed.
[3] See the article by Botterill on pages 261-268. —Ed.

getting off the blocks and actual increase in acceleration at the end. This feat was done in competition with top-level athletes from other university track teams. It was also found that the synchronized swimming athletes were using mental rehearsal well in practice and were beginning to show clear improvement in demonstrated control techniques for their required school figures. It was clear that the coaches as a group were impressed with the potential of the techniques, both in actual practice and in performance levels, and desired more of their athletes to be involved in using them.

Another example was observed during a Far Western U.S. synchronized swimming championship. One solo performer had been inconsistent and shaky in her performance to music in the preliminaries. A brief training session just before the finals included a review of the stimulus words, *stretch and smooth,* controlled breathing, muscle relaxation, and mental rehearsal which led to a significantly better performance and winning of the championship. Interestingly enough, a rival coach later described this athlete's stunning performance in exactly the same stimulus words without realizing it.

When the senior national championship for synchronized swimming was held, all the athletes who had used biofeedback and the other techniques either in the workshop or mini-programs did better than expected for that time of the season. The use of relaxation procedures clearly improved sleep patterns for nearly everyone. All of the solo finalists (the top seven) and the duet finalists (six out of the top seven) had been involved in one of these programs. First and second place winners in the team event were also participants. In one case, a duet moved from fifth to fourth place between semifinals and finals as a result of one of the swimmers using thermal feedback while the other incorporated some EMG training together with imagery. All of these performances occurred despite some inconsistent application of the recently learned techniques.

Outcomes. Various requests have come via referrals to use this multifaceted approach with other individual athletes. Two of the swim clubs asked for additional mini-workshops in order to include previous nonparticipants in the use of these techniques so they could function better as a unit in their team routine. Requests also have come from track coaches to involve other athletes showing great individual promise. As a result, the authors recently conducted a workshop for long distance women runners and coaches at the new Olympic Training Center in Squaw Valley, California. Other sport groups have indicated interest in including such a program in their national athlete development and training activities.

In general, there has been strong interest on the part of the coaches and most of the athletes who were involved in the program to continue using the model. The coaches, in reporting increased performance records among many of their athletes, have generally become firm believers in the validity of the approach used.

Limitations. There may be sporadic application by some athletes in terms of home practice and the use of the techniques in training. There may also be difficulty at times in transferring the techniques learned to actual competitive conditions. In terms of motivation, ambivalence about one's basic ability and the desire to win occasionally surfaces as a problem. The usefulness of autogenic phrases varies from person to person, and certain stimulus words may not always work as well as expected because they tend to hold different meanings for different athletes. However, the model appears to have far more positive benefits than the few limitations that have become evident to date. The next step is to make further application of these techniques with other athletes selected from a wider range of sports. It is suggested that the program be used for one sport group at a time. Commonality of training, sport language, and competitive setting appear to be important. It is also desirable to work with an individual team or club where members must function together as a group.

CONCLUSIONS

Psychophysiological fine tuning results in a greater psychological internal locus of control that produces important performance differences among superior athletes who are relatively similar in capability. Despite some limitations, the multifaceted format described above shows strong promise when applied to well-motivated athletes. A collaborative relationship between the athlete and coach, the use of self-regulation techniques, and understanding the psychological impact of competition all aid in the development of positive self-esteem and more effective performances. The use of biofeedback is an especially powerful technique to demonstrate the extent of self-regulation that can be achieved. In addition, athletes with special difficulties can be identified and, if necessary, referred for further individualized assistance. Follow-up contact with the participants is invaluable for revision and refinement of techniques, their application in athletic practice and competition, and, for some, application to life situations beyond competition. All coaches and most athletes report that training in fine tuning produces a higher degree of self-regulation, and there is often a strong desire for further training.

REFERENCES

Blanchard, E. B., and Young, L. D. 1974. Clinical applications of biofeedback training: A review of evidence. In *Biofeedback and Self-Control*, pp. 3-39. Chicago: Aldine.

Brown, B. B. 1977. *Stress and the art of biofeedback*. New York: Harper and Row.

Brown, C. H. 1976. Technical report to the United States Olympic Committee, September 1976.

Suinn, R. M. 1972. Removing emotional obstacles to learning and performance by visuo-motor behavior rehearsal. *Behavior Therapy* 3:308-310.

Cognitive-Behavioral Skills in Golf: Brain Power Golf

Daniel S. Kirschenbaum and Ronald M. Bale

Anyone who has hit a golf ball or watched someone else play golf must recognize how deceptively simple the game appears. Golfers need only to make contact with a small stationary ball. There are no coaches to monitor, no wildly screaming fans to ignore (usually), and no teammates to attend to or ignore. Yet, many complex cognitive and behavioral skills are required for effective execution of this sport as in all others (Mahoney 1977). Golfers often use imagery to focus their attention; they develop methods to relax themselves; they encourage themselves and build their self-efficacy by reviewing their previous successes and through their self-persuasions (cf. Bandura 1977); they set standards for their performance and self-reinforce accordingly (cf. Kanfer 1975).

The present paper elaborates upon the cognitive-behavioral skills that should facilitate golf performance. This is accomplished first by describing a review of the writings and recommendations provided by golf professionals. Secondly, a cognitive-behavioral skills training program, affectionally named *brain power golf,* is presented. Finally, research concerning the efficacy of brain power golf and a related investigation of attentional styles in golfers is reviewed.

GOLF PRO LITERATURE REVIEW

Since the authors are both golfers and cognitive-behavior therapists, we decided that golf pros must know something about cognitive skills in sports that we don't. After all, we reasoned, how else could they do so much better than us Ph.Ds in a game that is supposedly played on a six-inch course— the space between one's ears? So, we conducted a content analysis on what the pros said about the "mental side" of golf in a sample of 68 instructional golf books and the last two years of *Golf Digest* and *Golf Magazine.*

The book sample was obtained by reviewing all instructional books on golf in a large urban public library (Cincinnati's). The findings are presented in Table 1. Nearly one-third of the pros suggested self-regulatory strategies that were not categorizable ("Non-specific Techniques" in Table 1)

A version of this paper was presented as an invited address at the First International Symposium on Sports Psychology, University of Nuevo Leon, Monterrey, Mexico, 27 July 1978.

We extend our sincerest appreciation to William D. Bauer for his assistance in data gathering and analysis.

**Table 1. A Summary of Types of Golfing Self-management
Techniques Suggested by Golf Professionals**

POPULARITY BANKING	SELF-MANAGEMENT TECHNIQUE	1948-1976 BOOKS (N = 68)		1975-1976 MAGAZINE ARTICLES (N = 30)	
		Frequency	% of Total	Frequency	% of Total
1	Cognitive	60	30.0	31	32
2	Imaginal	25	12.5	21	22
3	Overt behavioral	23	11.5	14	15
4	Self-instructional	14	7.0	6	6
5	Attributional	9	4.5	1	1
6	Sensate focusing	6	3.0	0	0
7	Affective	1	0.5	0	0
	Sub-totals	138	69	73	76
	Non-specific techniques	62	31	23	24
	Grand totals	200	100	96	100

because of their vagueness, e.g., "get cool-mad," "develop a get-tough attitude." But, most suggestions could be tallied as evidenced in the tables. The two most frequent or popular types of suggestions in both books and magazines were:

1. cognitive techniques
   standard setting (e.g., expect to make some errors; play within capabilities)
   planning (check grip, wind, etc. before hitting; play safest shot)
2. imaginal techniques
   covert modeling (imagine yourself hitting the perfect shot)
   environmental imagining (picture the fairway as a bowling alley)

Perhaps self-regulation researchers should take a hint from the pros. Increased research attention could be directed toward standard setting, planning, and imagery procedures more so than on self-monitoring and self-reward. Also, these ideas may serve as effective bases for cognitive skills training programs for athletes.

BRAIN POWER GOLF

Based on this review and on some educated guesses, we devised a five-component self-regulation training program for golfers. The program included training in: deep muscle relaxation, planning, imagery, positive self-monitoring, and positive self-statements. More specifically, during one two-hour small group session (from two to four golfers) we instructed golfers in the following procedures. Also, from one to three additional follow-up meetings were held with all golfers to assist them with implementation of these techniques.

Deep Muscle Relaxation

We used a one-hour version of Bernstein and Borkovec's (1973) modification of Jacobson's (1938) progressive deep muscle relaxation procedure.[1] Golfers were taught how to progressively tense and relax 12 muscle groups. They were further instructed to practice this procedure two or three times per day. In reference to golfing per se, golfers employed deep muscle relaxation: (*a*) once within a few minutes prior to the first tee shot in competition, and (*b*) whenever they felt tension in specific muscles while playing—to relax those muscles.

Planning Checklist

Once on the course the first step to be taken before each shot should be to review a plan for that shot (cf. Greiner and Karoly 1976). Accordingly, each player developed a planning checklist. The checklist was kept in a small notebook that the player stored in his golf bag. Thus, before each shot the golfers either looked at the list or reviewed the list from memory. Each list was individually modified based on the following standard items:

review for *each* shot
1. distance
2. lie
3. turf condition
4. target
5. "trouble" (potential hazards)
6. wind
7. club selection

review for *each* putt
1. distance
2. break
3. condition of green

Imagery

We used a version of an imagery technique suggested by Jack Nicklaus (1974) (cf. Kazdin 1974*a*; Kazdin 1974*b*; Suinn 1972). Golfers were instructed to imagine the shot they wanted to

---

[1] See the article by Suinn on pages 306-315, the article by Zaremski on pages 238-246, and the article by Wenz and Strong on pages 328-333. —Ed.

hit after they selected their club via the planning checklist. With club in hand they learned to:

before *each* shot (including putts)
1.   picture the ball resting on the target spot.
2.   picture the ball landing in the target area.
3.   picture the flight of the ball.
4.   picture themselves executing the necessary swing.
5.   imagine the feel of the shot.

These directions were also included in the notebooks they carried in their golf bags.

Positive Self-monitoring

Within their notebooks, each golfer kept a supply of blank positive self-monitoring sheets (cf. Kazdin 1974c; Kirschenbaum and Karoly 1977). They were instructed to complete these sheets after completing each hole.

Golfers completed one positive self-monitoring sheet for each round of 18 holes. The sheets included the number or name of each club and a blank line next to each club. For example:

```
        driver _____
  fairway wood _____
        2-iron _____
        3-iron _____
```

After finishing a given hole, golfers recorded the number of that hole next to the designation of the club(s) used effectively on that hole. For example, John reviewed his drive as a good shot, as well as his 3-iron shot on hole number 7. Therefore, he entered a *7* next to *driver* and *3-iron*. As he did so, he recalled everything he could about those shots. He remembered how he positioned his feet, the feel of the swing, the target selection, and so on.

In addition to focusing on the good shots when positively self-monitoring, the golfers learned to postpone reviewing their bad shots. They were instructed to "file away the poor shots in their memories" and "recall them after the game."

Positive Instructional Self-statements

Each golfer developed a list of between three and seven statements that served as self-instructions (cf. Meichenbaum 1977). The statements directed the golfers to recall the positive aspects of their game. They served as anxiety management devices. When feeling especially anxious (or under pressure) they were instructed to refer to this list of statements that they kept in their notebooks. Examples of their statements included: "play your own game at your own pace;" "You've made great shots with this club before;" "Your competence as a golfer does not depend on your performance in any particular game."

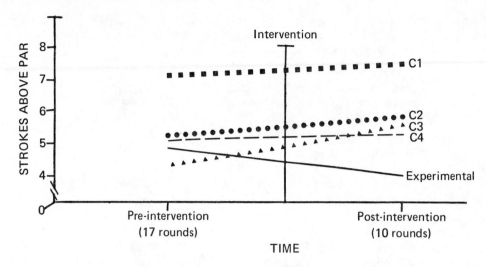

Figure 1. Mean strokes above par, pre-intervention to post-intervention

1977 STUDY

Four University of Cincinnati freshman members of the golf team volunteered to try out this brain power golf (BPG) program. The golf coach enthusiastically supported the program and helped arrange meetings and gather the necessary data.[2]

Unfortunately, only one of the four volunteers was a regular player (or "starter") on the team. Thus we were able to gather adequate performance data only on him and the other four starters. The other starters had not volunteered nor participated in BPG. As shown in Figure 1, the man who participated in BPG, labeled *Experimental,* was the only starter to improve his mean performance pre- to post-intervention. In fact, this player became the low scorer on the team following BPG intervention. He later went on to win several tournaments, including the Greater Cincinnati City Championship.

This participant's relative success following BPG may be scoffed at by those noting he improved by only one stroke—from five to four over par. Those scoffers may be interested to note that a one-stroke differential in mean 18-hole performance separated Jack Nicklaus from a player who earned $100,000 less than Nicklaus in 1976.

Of course, the fact that our subject was the only one to improve of the five starters is hardly proof of the efficacy of BPG. Great variance existed in round-by-round scores that is not apparent in Figure 1 (i.e., Figure 1 shows the change only from the mean pre-intervention to the mean post-intervention score). Also, our participant volunteered for BPG whereas the other starters did not.

[2]The authors gratefully acknowledge the help and advice of Coach Bill Schwarberg of the University of Cincinnati.

Perhaps differences in post-intervention scores reflect the expenditure of greater efforts by our participant due to a higher level of commitment. Placebo and non-specific treatment effects could also account for the observed changes (cf. Kazdin 1973).

The strength of the data for the 1977 study is boosted somewhat, albeit only in a suggestive—not a definitive—sense, by the reactions of the 4 BPG participants to the program. Table 2 presents a summary of their ratings and comments. They apparently viewed the program very favorably. In fact, on their questionnaires, these 4 players reported recommending some or all of BPG to a total of 16 other players! Since these university-level golfers had all been playing golf since they were young children, we find their enthusiasm for BPG quite encouraging.

1978 STUDY

The first year we offered BPG to the University of Cincinnati golf team (1977), only 4 of the 10 team members volunteered. After their glowing evaluation spread to their coach and teammates, the following year the coach and all of the players requested it. In 1978 recruitment, the coach had actually used access to BPG as an inducement to selected high school golfers who showed exceptional promise.

As gratified as we were by these responses, we discovered that three of the four golfers who received BPG the previous year had become starters. Thus, only three starters remained as potential subjects. One of these players could not spare the time required for training. Therefore, we conducted a multiple baseline across subjects experiment and included the third player as a nontreated control (cf. Hersen and Barlow 1976).

The first four competitive rounds (18 holes each) served as a baseline for all three subjects (identified as players E, F, and G). Then, player E received BPG training. Subsequent to an additional three rounds in competition (i.e., an extended baseline), player F experienced the BPG intervention. Player G received no BPG training.

Figure 2 presents the results using each player's median baseline score as their zero point (baseline). Relative to baseline, player E was expected to perform better (lower scores) during intervention I and intervention II (i.e., following his BPG training). Player F was expected to produce lower scores (i.e., improve) in intervention II. Player G was not expected to improve at all. Figure 2 depicts median performances for the three phases of the study for all three players. The only unexpected datum shown is player G's temporary gain during intervention I.

Although the findings are generally in accord with expectations, it should be noted that, like the 1977 data, these data are merely suggestive of potential beneficial effects caused by BPG. Considerable variability existed in all phases (hence the use of medians instead of means). Thus, the relatively small median changes observed are not dramatic or stable. However, self-report data, once again, provided additional highly positive corroborative support for these weak performance data (e.g., players E and F recommended BPG to six other players).

Regarding BPG's overall efficacy, we concluded, based on these small 1977 and 1978 studies, that additional evaluative research is necessary. The results obtained to date are favorable, but not overwhelmingly so. Most importantly, additional participants are needed to afford much better controls for non-specific treatment effects and to explore the stability of treatment effects.

Table 2. 1977 Golf Study: Self-report Evaluations of the Four Participants

Instructions for ratings: Use the following scale to evaluate how helpful (or harmful) Brain Power Golf was for you.

-3 Very Harmful	-2 Harmful	-1 Slightly Harmful	0 Neutral	+1 Slightly Helpful	+2 Helpful	+3 Very Helpful

	GOLFER			
	A*	B	C	D
Overall program	+3	+2	+2	+2
Relaxation component	+3	+2	+1	+2
Planning component	+3	+1	+2	+1
Imagery component	+1	+2	+3	+3
Positive self-monitoring component	+3	+2	+3	+1
Positive self-statements component	+3	+3	+1	0

*Golfer A was the experimental subject shown in Figure 1.

Selected Comments

Golfer A: "I think that for the first time that I can remember, a plan has been put forth to help improve the mental side of golf—and it's about time."
"This program could do more for the average golfer than five lessons from a professional."

Golfer B: "[The program] is unique and helpful. It makes golf much more enjoyable because it makes you much more relaxed."

Golfer C: "I like the overall program . . . and I believe it helped me."

Golfer D: "It helped quite a bit although my scores don't really show it. I expect the scores will be dropping soon."

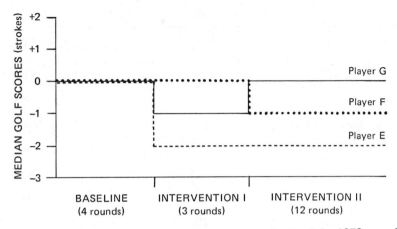

Figure 2. Median golf scores, relative to baselines, across phases of the 1978 experiment

GOLFERS' ATTENTIONAL STYLES

In addition to continued studies of BPG efficacy, more information is needed regarding essential cognitive-behavioral skills for golfers. In view of the widely recognized importance of attentional factors in golf, we administered Nideffer's (1976) Test of Attentional and Interpersonal Style (TAIS)[3] to the nine golfers on the 1978 University of Cincinnati golf team. Pearson product moment correlation coefficients were computed between mean 18-hole golf scores (based on 19 rounds for five players, 16 rounds for one player, 3 rounds for one player, and 2 rounds for one player)[4] and each of 17 TAIS subscales.

Table 3 shows that four coefficients surpassed the $p < .05$ level (approximately one significant correlation should be anticipated due to chance alone). The small sample size clearly mandates caution in interpreting these results. Nevertheless, the findings are provocative. Before interpreting them, the definitions of the TAIS scales involved need to be reviewed.

Nideffer (1976, p. 397) offers the following definitions for the four scales that yielded significant results:

> *Overloaded by External Stimuli (OET).* "The higher the score, the more individuals make mistakes because they become confused and overloaded with external stimuli."
> *Broad Internal Attentional Focus (BIT).* "High scores indicate that individuals see themselves as able to effectively integrate ideas and information from several different areas. They see themselves as analytical and philosophical."
> *Reduced Attentional Focus (RED).* "A high score on this scale indicates that the individuals make mistakes because they narrow their attention too much."
> *Obsessive (OBS).* "A high score indicates the person has a tendency to ruminate and worry about one particular thing without any real resolution or movement."

---

[3]See the article by Nideffer on pages 281-290. –Ed.
[4]Correlations were also computed omitting scores from golfers who only played in three or fewer rounds; the results were quite similar to those reported in the paper.

Table 3. Pearson Correlations between Scales of the Test of Attentional—and Interpersonal Style (TAIS) and Mean Golf Score (N = 9)

TAIS SCALE	ABBREVIATION	CORRELATION WITH $\bar{x}$ GOLF SCORE
Broad External Attentional Focus	BET	−06
Overloaded by External Stimuli	OET	−73*
Broad Internal Attentional Focus	BIT	+79**
Overloaded by Internal Stimuli	OIT	−25
Narrow Attentional Focus	NAR	−41
Reduced Attentional Focus	RED	−71*
Information Processing	INFP	+24
Behavior Control	BCON	−43
Control Scale	CON	+15
Self-esteem	SES	+28
Physical Orientation	P/O	−09
Obsessive	OBS	−69*
Extroversion	EXT	+10
Introversion	INT	+48
Intellectual Expression	IEX	+07
Negative Affective Expression	NAE	−28
Positive Affective Expression	PAE	+24

*$p < .05$, two-tailed
**$p < .02$, two-tailed

Considering that low scores indicate better golf skills, these significant correlations suggest that better golfers: (*a*) are extremely sensitive to external distractions (OET); (*b*) see themselves as non-analytic/philosophical (BIT); (*c*) tend to narrow their attention too much (RED); and (*d*) tend to worry about specific things a great deal (OBS).

Interpretation of these data should be tempered by understanding that the TAIS measures attention in daily life—not specifically on the golf course. Whether general attentional style determines attentional focus on the golf course awaits further experimentation. However, a very recent study of a tennis-specific TAIS suggests that specific attentional focusing in sports differs markedly from general attentional style (Van Schoyck, Grasha, and Bale 1978). Another interpretive qualifier is that this correlational data merely tells us which attentional style is associated with better golf performance. It does not reveal a cause and effect relationship between particular styles and golf scores.

Given appropriate cautionary considerations, these data present the better male college-level golfer as someone who considers himself finicky or highly fastidious in attentional style. He views himself as overly sensitive to external distractions to the point where he narrows his attention too much. Further, he tends to ruminate excessively. Perhaps these finicky tendencies are adaptive in a sport that requires hours and hours of practice on individual elements of the game (e.g., sand shots, putts, planned hooks, slices, or fades; shots from uphill, downhill, and half-buried lies). The only correlation that appears inconsistent with this portrait is the highly significant positive correlation between scores and Broad Internal Attention. Perhaps highly skilled athletes generally view themselves as action-oriented nonphilosophical types.

Certainly further study on golf-specific attentional skills and styles should prove illuminating. It would be particularly interesting to discover under what conditions the "finicky attentional style" appears most adaptive in reference to this particular sport and other sports.

REFERENCES

Bandura, A. 1977. Self-efficacy: Toward a unifying theory of behavioral change. *Psychological Review* 84:191-215.

Bernstein, D. A., and Borkovec, T. D. 1973. *Progressive relaxation training: A manual for therapists.* Champaign, Ill.: Research Press.

Greiner, J. M., and Karoly, P. 1976. Effects of self-control training on study activity and academic performance: An analysis of self-monitoring, self-reward, and systematic planning components. *Journal of Counseling Psychology* 23:495-502.

Hersen, M., and Barlow, D. H. 1976. *Single case experimental designs.* New York: Pergamon Press.

Jacobson, E. 1938. *Progressive relaxation.* Chicago: University of Chicago Press.

Kanfer, F. H. 1975. Self-management methods. In *Helping people change,* ed. F. H. Kanfer and A. P. Goldstein. New York: Pergamon Press.

Kazdin, A. E. 1973. Methodological and assessment considerations in evaluating reinforcement programs in applied settings. *Journal of Applied Behavior Analysis* 6:517-531.

———. 1974a. Covert modeling, model similarity, and reduction of avoidance behavior. *Behavior Therapy* 5:325-340.

———. 1974b. The effect of model identity and fear relevant similarity on covert modeling. *Behavior Therapy* 5:624-636.

———. 1974c. Reactive self-monitoring: The effects of response desirability, goal setting, and feedback. *Journal of Consulting and Clinical Psychology* 42:704-716.

Kirschenbaum, D. S., and Karoly, P. 1977. When self-regulation fails: Tests of some preliminary hypotheses. *Journal of Consulting and Clinical Psychology* 45:1116-1125.

Mahoney, M. J. 1977. Cognitive skills and athletic performance. In *Sports psychology: Background, issues, and current research,* ed. M. J. Mahoney. A symposium presented at the meeting of the Association for Advancement in Behavior Therapy, Atlanta, December 1977.

Meichenbaum, D. 1977. *Cognitive-behavior modification.* New York: Plenum.

Nicklaus, J. 1974. *Golf my way.* New York: Simon and Schuster.

Nideffer, R. M. 1976. Test of attentional and interpersonal style. *Journal of Personality and Social Psychology* 34:394-404.

Suinn, R. M. 1972. Behavior rehearsal training for ski racers. *Behavior Therapy* 3:519-520.

Van Schoyck, S.; Grasha, A. F.; and Bale, R. M. 1978. A tennis-specific test of attentional and interpersonal style. Unpublished manuscript, University of Cincinnati.

Psyching the College Athlete:
A Comprehensive Sports Psychology
Training Package

Philip R. Spinelli and Billy A. Barrios

Each year a great deal of energy is expended by college and university athletic programs to discover, pursue, and recruit promising young athletes to fill the ranks of numerous sports teams. Young men and women, having excelled on the playing fields of high schools throughout the country (indeed, the world!) are offered substantial scholarships to continue demonstrating such prowess in a variety of athletic events. And nothing, of course, raises the spirits of a coaching staff as much as experiencing the continued growth and development of these athletes into Olympic contenders and outstanding team members. On the other hand, nothing raises the blood pressure of these same trainers as much as investing in an athlete of great promise, catching momentary glimpses of talent (usually on the practice field), but being frustrated in all attempts to potentiate this talent into performance during the competitive moment. Many a coach has stood wringing his hands as the "Bombshell from Balboa High" fizzles out on the college playing field. "He just can't stand pressure" or "Poor attitude!" laments the frustrated trainer as mediocre performance continues in the face of fantastic potential.

Every coach recognizes the importance of the mental aspects of athletic performance. The competitor must be psyched up to just the right pitch prior to competition but must also "keep cool" during the heat of the event. While no coach needs a Ph.D. in psychology to fully appreciate the fact that what goes on inside the head of an athlete will greatly affect his/her performance, many coaches and athletes alike have been turning to psychologists in order to "get inside the head" and gain greater access to these elusive attitudes and feelings. It is not uncommon to find psychologists working directly with Olympic teams, professional football and baseball teams, as well as professional and amateur athletes on an individual basis. The reason for this, of course, is that athletic performance has been improved by the direct application of a variety of psychological principles and accompanying techniques that have served to sharpen concentration, reduce negative thinking, and enable the athlete to better cope with the intense stress of competition. What is in fact emerging is a new area of psychological specialization generally referred to as sports psychology, where specific psychological procedures are systematically introduced to athletes in an effort to give them greater control over cognitive and emotional factors that can either facilitate or block performance.

Philip R. Spinelli and Billy A. Barrios. Counseling center outreach: Sports psychology. *Journal of College Student Personnel* 20, 3 (May 1979):280. Copyright © 1979 American Personnel and Guidance Association. Reprinted with permission. This article is an expanded version of the journal article.

A SPORTS PSYCHOLOGY TRAINING PACKAGE

The purpose of this paper is to present some notions as to how a sports psychology program might be developed on a university campus, utilizing university resources and implemented by an athletic department. The ideas expressed here are drawn from the authors' shared experiences as psychologists working in the counseling center of a large western university. Numerous requests from coaches to work with individual athletes who were not progressing satisfactorily or, in several instances, a request to provide training to an entire team in stress reduction techniques prompted the authors to consider the development of a more comprehensive and coordinated system for offering sports psychology services. A Sports Psychology Outreach Team was formed and staffed by members of the University Counseling Center. The program seeks to relate to the university athlete and his/her training program in three ways:

1. to develop appropriate methods for assessing the college athlete with respect to cognitive style, level of stress, and behavioral response to training and competitive performance
2. to develop training modules that can be applied to groups (teams) that teach skills useful in anticipating and coping with problems common to competition, i.e., stress management
3. to provide the opportunity to work with individual athletes on special problems

Assessing "Mental Factors"

As previously mentioned, it is one thing to know that mental attitude greatly influences an athlete's performance, but quite another to do something with that knowledge. The reason for this, it would seem, is that until very recently *mental attitude* has been a wastebasket term that has been used to describe or explain any phenomenon not directly observable, and therefore trainable in the usual sense. Such diverse notions as motivation, confidence, nervousness, concentration, and the like have all been included under the general rubric *mental*. The first step of sports psychologists and others trying to work with the athlete's "head" has been the work of describing more precisely the mental processes that are significant in affecting competitive performance. It is only then that a useful assessment procedure can be developed.

Our outreach sports psychology program attempts to provide a comprehensive assessment component. Each athlete is evaluated in terms of cognitive style, stress response, and behavioral response as each relates to training and competitive performance situations. Cognitive style[1] refers to the specific ways that athletes talk to themselves as they approach an athletic event. Are their thoughts encouraging, "I'll give it my best shot," or discouraging, "I'll never make that jump"? The stress response refers to the level of tension that is present prior to and during competition. While optimal performance requires that the athlete be physiologically aroused and "psyched up," too much tension can have devastating effects in the forms of premature fatigue, impairment of judgement, and loss of concentration.[2] For this reason it is important to determine the extent to which the athlete experiences stress and, more importantly, how it is handled. And while it is true that the college athlete generally has a well-developed set of behavioral skills that enable him or her to perform at a high level, it is certainly not uncommon that modifications are necessary if the athlete is to excel. Bad

---

[1] See the article by Kirschenbaum and Bale on pages 334-343 and the article by Suinn on pages 26-36. —Ed.
[2] See the article by Oxendine on pages 103-111. —Ed.

habits need to be eliminated and/or new techniques developed. For this reason the program will often include a behavioral assessment of specific motor tasks that need to be present or modified. This is usually carried out in conjunction with the training staff and athlete on an individual basis. A comprehensive assessment tool that we have found useful in helping to evaluate the cognitive, emotional, and to some extent behavioral components of an athlete's response to competition is a modified version of a questionnaire developed by Mahoney and Avener (1977). This questionnaire identifies anxiety-provoking situations related to the athlete's competitive event as well as cognitive strategies utilized in preparing and coping with the stress of competition. Responses to certain key items on the questionnaire can be used to assist in individualizing the program. This paper-and-pencil instrument may be group administered and lends itself nicely as a preliminary screening method for identifying problems.

On the basis of findings from the assessment process and prior research, a training package was developed and is currently offered to university athletic teams upon request. The training program can be administered to an entire team or to individual athletes. In the following sections an example of the group application of the training program is presented. Each of the various components of the package is described, and details are provided with respect to the administration of the component to the specific athletic team involved. In the subsequent section an example of the individual application and assessment of the training package is presented.

Working with the Team

The assistant track coach responsible for the sprinters contacted the authors and requested assistance in enhancing the competitive performance of his athletes. A modified version of a questionnaire developed by Mahoney and Avener (1977) was completed by each of the athletes. Examination of responses to the questionnaire revealed that all of the sprinters were deficient in certain aspects of preparing and coping with the stress of competition. Since it was determined that each athlete could benefit from the training package, the program was administered to the entire team of sprinters.

The program was conducted during the training period prior to the beginning of the formal competitive season. Team members met in small groups twice a week for approximately five weeks. The groups were comprised of six to eight sprinters, and each session lasted 60 minutes. First, all athletes were trained in a cue-controlled relaxation technique (Paul 1966). This is a behavioral self-control procedure that allows a person to gain control over perceived tension during the early stages by eliciting a calm response to a previously conditioned signal. The athletes were instructed to perform a number of exercises which are aimed at relaxing the muscles of the body. These exercises consisted of tensing various muscle areas, focusing on that stress, releasing the tension, and then attending to the sensations associated with relaxation. Once the athletes achieved a state of relaxation, a cue-word such as *calm* or *relax* was subvocalized with each exhalation. In this way the behavior chain of taking a deep breath, exhaling, and saying the cue-word to oneself developed conditioned relaxation properties.

Athletes were then provided the opportunity to gain experience in utilizing this anxiety reduction technique through an imaginal practice coping procedure (Goldfried 1971). Each sprinter generated a series of situations, related to preparation and performance in a competitive event, which were associated with inordinate amounts of stress for the individual. Information from the assessment questionnaire and the coach facilitated the identification of the various situations. Each of these situations was then presented to the athlete in imaginal scenes. The athlete was instructed to imagine himself clearly in each scene, to begin experiencing the early onset of anxiety, and then to apply the cue-controlled relaxation technique (Suinn 1977). Even though the athletes individually constructed a list of anxiety-provoking situations, the degree of overlap among items was considerable. Common scenes which the sprinters received practice coping with were warming up, watching competitors loosening up, and walking towards and situating themselves into the starting blocks.

Most of the sprinters experienced negative or distracting thoughts which affected their ability to perform. Specifically, they were emitting self-critical thoughts which directed their attention away from the preparatory behaviors necessary for excellent performance. The self-statement modification (Meichenbaum and Cameron 1974) component of the training program is aimed at replacing negative/ critical thoughts with more adaptive task-oriented self-statements. Athletes monitored their self-statements for a two-week period. Performance-debilitating thoughts and the situations which elicited them were identified. A list of alternative, task-directed self-statements was generated. The athletes then imagined themselves in the various situations identified and practiced subvocalizing the adaptive statements.

A number of the sprinters expressed disappointment and concern over their poor starts. In order to facilitate the unlearning of bad techniques, the training program makes use of visual motor behavior rehearsal (Suinn 1972).[3] This procedure utilizes mental imagery and focuses the athletes' attention on specific motor sequences that are important in the execution of the desired skill. In the present case, sprinters vividly imagined setting themselves and "exploding" from the starting blocks the instant the gun was fired. The coach provided a detailed description of the proper sequence involved in executing a good start. This script was used for the visual motor behavior rehearsal training.

In the preceding section an example of the team application of the training package was provided. The following section presents a description of the administration of a modified version of the treatment program to an individual athlete. Also documented is an evaluation of the effectiveness of the training.

Individualizing the Program

Background. The client was an 18-year-old member of the university women's tennis team. Although she had received an athletic scholarship to compete for the university, the client expressed concern over the debilitating effects which anxiety was having upon her performance. She reported an inability to control the tension associated with events prior to competition and also the anxiety elicited by performance errors. The client requested treatment after she became aware that a continuation of anxiety-induced impairment of her athletic performance would result in her dismissal from the team. It should also be noted that the client's coach actively encouraged her to seek treatment in hopes of alleviating the subjectively experienced distress and consequently improving her athletic performance.

Assessment. In order to document the effectiveness of the treatment program, data were collected from variables in the cognitive and behavioral domains. Assessment sessions were conducted one week prior to treatment and one and one-half weeks after the termination of treatment. The self-report scales consisted of: the State-Trait Anxiety Inventory, state form (STAI-S) (Spielberger,

---

[3] See the article by Suinn on pages 306-315. —Ed.

Gorsuch, and Lushene 1968); a modified version of the S-R Inventory of Anxiousness (Endler, Hunt, and Rosenstein 1963); and an altered form of the Mahoney and Avener (1977) athletic questionnaire. The S-R Inventory of Anxiousness was modified by using three situations relating only to athletic competition. The situations, which were identified by the client as major problem areas, were: (1) warming up prior to a match; (2) after a series of poor shots or mistakes; and (3) after losing a critical point or the first set of the match. The client was asked to rate various aspects of her reactions to each situation, using response alternatives identical to those of the original instrument. The Mahoney and Avener (1977) questionnaire was altered in order to specifically gather information relevant to tennis (Spinelli and Barrios 1978b).[4] Responses to critical items on the questionnaire were used to assess: (1) the level of subjectively experienced anxiety at various stages of competition, (2) the extent of rumination over performance mistakes, (3) the frequency of self-reinforcement, (4) the frequency of self-punishment or criticism, and (5) the ability to cope with mistakes made during a competitive match. All items were rated on a scale of 0 to 10, with 0 representing none or not at all and 10 representing very much or very often. A measure of the effects of anxiety on the client's overt performance was based upon reports by her coach. Also the client maintained a behavioral diary one week prior to treatment and throughout the course of treatment. The client recorded evaluations of her daily practice sessions and match performances.

Treatment. The treatment program consisted of four components. Therapy sessions were conducted once per week for four consecutive weeks, with each session approximately 60 minutes in duration. The first two sessions were devoted to training the client in cue-controlled relaxation. The goal of the cue-controlled relaxation technique is to teach the client to achieve a state of relaxation in response to a self-produced cue-word, such as *calm* or *control.* The procedure consisted of two phases: first, the client was trained in deep muscle relaxation (Berstein and Borkovec 1973),[5] and, second, the relaxed state was paired with the cue-word. The cue-word association was formed by having the client focus on her breathing while subvocally repeating the cue-word with each exhalation. The therapist repeated aloud the cue-word in synchrony with the client's exhalations from 3 to 5 times; the client then continued this procedure for 15 more pairings. After a 60-second period in which the client was instructed to focus on general feelings associated with relaxation, the cue-word pairing was repeated another 20 times. The client was given tape recordings of relaxation instructions and was encouraged to practice both the relaxation exercises and the cue-word association procedure on a daily basis outside the therapy setting.

Following the second treatment session, the client was instructed to implement the technique outside of the therapy setting in situations which were minimally anxiety-arousing. This involved recognizing inappropriate increases in anxiety and then applying the cue-controlled procedure (i.e., exhaling and subvocalizing the cue-word *calm*).

In the third session, an anxiety hierarchy was constructed from information collected at the pretreatment assessment period. The client then engaged in a number of exercises designed to facilitate and provide practice in coping with anxiety and stress (Spinelli and Barrios 1978a). This procedure involved, first, relaxation induction and then having the client imagine clearly a hierarchy item. Once clarity of imagery was achieved, the client was instructed to begin to experience the onset of anxiety, to detect the early appearance of these physiological cues, and then to actively cope with

---

[4]The Mahoney-Avener questionnaire used with gymnasts is included at the end of this article. —Ed.
[5]See the article by Suinn on pages 306-315, the article by Zaremski on pages 238-246, and the article by Wenz and Strong on pages 328-333. —Ed.

the situation. Coping with the situation consisted of the client inhaling deeply, subvocalizing the cue-word upon exhalation, and finally imagining herself successfully reducing the tension and performing in an appropriate and competent manner. Since the client had identified negative and distracting thoughts as a factor which affected her ability to perform, positive and task-oriented self-statements were introduced at the conclusion of the coping sequence.

The entire third and fourth sessions were devoted exclusively to the presentation of hierarchy items and active attempts in the management of competition-related stress and anxiety. Upon completion of the fourth session, the client was instructed to role-play practice matches with her teammates as though they were actual competitive events. This involved imagining that her teammates were opponents from various universities. Preparatory behavior and performance during the matches, both on an overt and a covert level, were to stimulate as closely as possible those that the client would exhibit for actual competitive play. The function of these role-play matches was to provide the client with as much *in vivo* application of the coping procedures as possible.

Results and Discussion. The pre- and posttreatment scores for the various self-report measures are presented in Table 1. Inspection of Table 1 reveals a substantial decrease in the level of subjectively experienced anxiety and tension associated with athletic competition. Responses to critical items on the Spinelli and Barrios (1978*b*) questionnaire indicate reductions in the application of self-punishment/criticism and a concomitant increase in the use of self-reinforcement and instructional self-statements. The STAI-S was included as an index of generalized effects; and the pre- to posttreatment decrement in anxiety suggests that the treatment may have been effective in reducing tension associated with non-athletic situations. The client's behavioral diary and reports from her coach were consistent with the other measures in indicating reductions in self-report and behavioral indices of anxiety.

The results of the present case report suggest that the training program was successful in reducing competition-related anxiety. Also the findings lend some support to the claims that the treatment procedure teaches the client a technique or skill which can be utilized in a variety of anxiety-eliciting situations (Spinelli and Barrios 1978*a*). It should be noted, however, that the present report suffers, as do all case studies (Campbell and Stanley 1966; Paul 1969) from a number of plausible rival hypotheses. The results are to be viewed as suggestive and not as a critical empirical demonstration of efficacy.

CONCLUSION

What we have tried to reflect in the above comments is that there is a growing body of knowledge and an accompanying technology that has been found to be useful in gaining access to the mental aspects of sports competition in ways that can enhance performance. In addition we have suggested how a comprehensive model for delivering a sports psychology program to college athletes can be developed using the resources of a university counseling center. We have been gratified by the positive response to the program by the university athletic coaches that we have consulted with. Perhaps even more important has been the opportunity that has been afforded us to grapple with the enormously complex issues and problems inherent in the quest for excellence by a very special person—the college athlete.

Table 1. Pretreatment and Posttreatment
Scores on Dependent Measures

		PRE	POST
S-R Inventory of Anxiousness			
1.	Warming up for a match	39	27
2.	After a series of poor shots or mistakes	55	39
3.	After losing a crucial point or first set	50	38
Spinelli and Barrious questionnaire			
1.	Level of anxiety		
a.	1 week before a match	0	2
b.	24 hours before match	7	3
c.	1 hour before match	9	4
d.	In dressing room prior to match	10	5
e.	Warming up	9	5
f.	Prior to serving	10	5
g.	Prior to receiving	8	5
h.	During a tiebreaker	10	6
i.	After you have doublefaulted	10	8
2.	Ruminating about mistakes	10	7
3.	Extent of instructional self-talk	8	10
4.	Extent of self-punishment	10	6
5.	Extent of self-reinforcement	2	4
6.	Ability to cope	0	5
STAI-S		47	36

REFERENCES

Bernstein, D. A., and Borkovec, T. D. 1973. *Progressive relaxation training.* Champaign, Ill.: Research Press.

Campbell, D. T. and Stanley, J. C. 1966. *Experimental and quasi-experimental designs for research.* New York: Rand McNally.

Endler, N.S.; Hunt, J. McV.; and Rosenstein, A. J. 1962. An S-R inventory of anxiousness. *Psychological Monographs* 76 (whole no. 536).

Goldfried, M. R. 1971. Systematic desensitization as training in self-control. *Journal of Consulting and Clinical Psychology* 37:228-234.

Mahoney, M. J., and Avener, M. 1977. Psychology of the elite athlete: An exploratory study. *Cognitive Therapy and Research* 1:135-141.

Meichenbaum, D., and Cameron, R. 1974. The clinical potential of modifying what clients say to themselves. In *Self-control: Power to the person*, ed. M. J. Mahoney and C. E. Thoresen, pp. 236-290. Monterey, Calif.: Brooks/Cole.

Paul, G. L. 1966. *Insight versus desensitization in psychotherapy*. Palo Alto: Stanford University Press.

———. 1969. Behavior modification research: Design and tactics. In *Behavior therapy: Appraisal and status*, ed C. M. Franks, pp. 29-62. New York: McGraw-Hill.

Spielberger, C. D.; Gorsuch, R. L.; and Lushene, R. E. 1968. *Manual for the State-Trait Anxiety Inventory*. Palo Alto, Calif.: Consulting Psychologists Press.

Spinelli, P. R., and Barrios, B. A. 1978*a*. A self-control procedure for coping with anxiety. Unpublished manuscript, University of Utah.

———. 1978*b*. Sports psychology questionnaire. Unpublished questionnaire, University of Utah.

Suinn, R. M. 1972. Behavior rehearsal training for ski racers. *Behavior Therapy* 3:519-520.

———. 1977. *Manual, Anxiety Management Training*. Fort Collins, Colo.: Rocky Mountain Behavioral Sciences Institute.

APPENDIX
MAHONEY-AVENER GYMNAST QUESTIONNAIRE

The following questions* are designed to provide us with a better understanding of individual differences in athletes' training and competition strategies. Please answer them as accurately as possible, indicating your own personal patterns (whether or not they are what you might prefer or recommend for others). If you would like to see a copy of the results, put your mailing address below your name. Thank you for taking the time and effort to share this information with us.

Name_____ Date_____ Age____ Ht.___ Wt.___

Address (optional)_____ _____

When did you last compete in gymnastics?_____
  For what team?_____

What is the highest all-around score you ever received for *optional* routines?_____
  At what competition?_____ Date?_____

What is the highest all-around score you ever received for *compulsory* routines? (If you have not performed compulsories in competition, mark *NA*.)_____
  At what competition?_____ Date?_____

What is the highest all-around score you ever received for *combined* (optional plus compulsory) routines in the same meet?_____
  At what competition?_____ Date?_____

1. Relative to *all* other collegiate and postcollegiate gymnasts in the United States, how self-confident would you rate yourself? (Circle one)

   0   1   2   3   4   5   6   7   8   9   10
   Much Less   About   Much More
   Than Most   Average   Than Most

2. How many hours per week do you spend in training?_____

*Michael J. Mahoney 1978: personal communication. Used with permission.

3. How would you describe your overall lifestyle?

0   1   2   3   4   5   6   7   8   9   10
Very Structured   Very Unstructured
and Organized   and Disorganized

4. How often do you dream about some aspect of gymnastics?

0   1   2   3   4   5   6   7   8   9   10
Not at   Very
All   Frequently

a   If you do dream about gymnastics, who is the performer in your dream? (Circle one)

Yourself   Someone Else   Mixed

b.   Do you dream about *practice* sessions or an actual competitive *meet*?

Practice   Competition

c.   Are you usually *successful* or *unsuccessful* in your dream performance?

Successful   Unsuccessful   Mixed

d.   Do you dream more about *past* or *future* performances?

Past   Future   Mixed

e.   Does the frequency of your gymnastics dreams *increase* or *decrease* right before a meet?

Increase   Decrease   Neither

f.   When you dream about a competitive meet, what are you usually doing in the dream?

Dressing   Warming Up   Performing

g.   Would you rate your dreams as realistic or unrealistic in terms of how well you perform in them?

0   1   2   3   4   5   6   7   8   9   10
Too Tragic   Realistic   Too Perfect

5. Please rate your usual anxiety at each of the following moments:

		No Anxiety										Very Anxious
a.	One week prior to an important meet	0	1	2	3	4	5	6	7	8	9	10
b.	Twenty-four hours before the meet	0	1	2	3	4	5	6	7	8	9	10
c.	One hour before the meet	0	1	2	3	4	5	6	7	8	9	10
d.	In the dressing room prior to the meet	0	1	2	3	4	5	6	7	8	9·	10
e.	Warming up at the meet	0	1	2	3	4	5	6	7	8	9	10
f.	Chalking up prior to your *worst* (weakest) event	0	1	2	3	4	5	6	7	8	9	10
g.	Chalking up prior to your *best* (strongest) event	0	1	2	3	4	5	6	7	8	9	10

    h.   During the actual performance of   0   1   2   3   4   5   6   7   8   9   10
         your weakest event

    i.   During the actual performance of   0   1   2   3   4   5   6   7   8   9   10
         your strongest event

6.   Do you keep track of your points and standing during a meet?
                                 Yes   No   Sometimes

7.   Going into the final event would it *help* or *hinder* you to know that you need to score *above* your usual marks to do well in the meet?
                                 Help   Hinder   Neither

8.   Going into the final event, would it *help* or *hinder* you to know that you could score moderately *under* your usual marks and still do well in the meet?
                                 Help   Hinder   Neither

9a.   How close do you think you are at present to reaching your maximum athletic potential?
     0   1   2   3   4   5   6   7   8   9   10
     Very   Very
     Far Away   Close

9b.   How much do you think about gymnastics in everyday situations (outside of practice, meets, etc.)?
     0   1   2   3   4   5   6   7   8   9   10
     Very   Very
     Little   Much

10.   When you are competing, how much of your attention is focused on each of the following? (Please specify percentages and remember that they should total 100%.)

    a.   The audience   _____%
    b.   The movement I am currently executing   _____%
    c.   The movement I have just completed   _____%
    d.   The movement I will do next   _____%

11.   When you are competing, how often do you think about mistakes you made earlier in your routine?
     0   1   2   3   4   5   6   7   8   9   10
     Never   Very
                                                                       Often

12.   To what extent do you use visual imagery (mental pictures) in your training and competition?
     0   1   2   3   4   5   6   7   8   9   10
     Not At   Very
     All   Extensively

13. When you are trying to picture something mentally (e.g., a back flip), how much difficulty do you have in getting the image to do what you want it to? That is, is it easy or difficult for you to control your mental pictures?

0	1	2	3	4	5	6	7	8	9	10

Very Difficult — Very Easy

14. When you practice something mentally, do you "see" yourself as an external observer would (e.g., from a distance, with your entire body visible, like a movie character) or do you "see" things as you would normally (i.e., through your eye sockets, with such body parts as your face and neck unseen)? That is, in mental practice, do you try to get *inside* your body and experience the sensations involved or do you try to get *outside* your body and view yourself as a coach or trainer might?

0	1	2	3	4	5	6	7	8	9	10

Exclusively Inside — Equal Mixture — Exclusively Outside

15. How vivid or clear are your mental images?

0	1	2	3	4	5	6	7	8	9	10

Very Unclear — Very Vivid

16. To what extent do you "talk to yourself" (either silently or out loud) in your training and competition?

0	1	2	3	4	5	6	7	8	9	10

Not at All — Very Extensively

17. When you talk to yourself during your training or competition, how often do you

    a. Give yourself technical (coaching) *instructions* (e.g., "tuck tighter" or "you need better extension")?

0	1	2	3	4	5	6	7	8	9	10

Never — Very Often

    b. *Criticize* yourself (either directly or via swearing)?

0	1	2	3	4	5	6	7	8	9	10

Never — Very Often

    c. *Praise* yourself?

0	1	2	3	4	5	6	7	8	9	10

Never — Very Often

18. To what extent do you use *both* visual imagery (mental pictures) and private monologues (self-talk) in your training and competition?

0	1	2	3	4	5	6	7	8	9	10

Exclusively Imagery — Equal Use of Both — Exclusively Self-Talk

19. How would you rate your ability to concentrate your attention on a specific movement or sensation (to the extent that you can block out everything else)?

0	1	2	3	4	5	6	7	8	9	10

Very
Poor

Very
Good

20. When you make a mistake in a competitive routine, how difficult is it for you to recover psychologically during the remainder of the routine?

0	1	2	3	4	5	6	7	8	9	10

Not at
All

Very
Difficult

21. Which of the following has been most frequently responsible for your poorer performances? (Please *rank* these; 1 = most frequently responsible)

_____Injuries and illness
_____Poor judging
_____Nervous tension
_____Inadequate training or preparation

22. Which of the following is most important in terms of your feeling good about a performance? (Please rank these by placing a number beside them; 1 = most important).

_____How it compares with my own past performances
_____How it compares with the performances of the other gymnasts at the meet
_____How close it came to a perfect score

23. How often do you have doubts about your gymnastic abilities?

0	1	2	3	4	5	6	7	8	9	10

Never

Very
Often

24. When you are trying to "psych yourself up" for an event, do you emphasize *reassurance* (e.g., "this will be easy") or *challenge* (e.g., "you're going to have to work at it")?

0	1	2	3	4	5	6	7	8	9	10

Reassurance

Challenge

25. What percent of a gymnast's success is due to each of the following? (Please make sure that your percentages add up to 100).

a. Natural of innate ability _____%
b. Diligent training _____%
c. A positive mental attitude _____%
d. Good coaching _____%

Are there any strategies or skills which we have overlooked and which you believe might be important to study? If so, please note them below. Thank you again for sharing this information with us.

ISSUES IN SPORTS PSYCHOLOGY

<hr>
<hr>

Dr. Robert W. Titley, in this second article by him,[1] points out crucial ethical issues facing any consultant in sports psychology. He raises the question of to whom a consultant is reponsible—to the athlete as a performer, to the athlete as a person, to the coach as referral agent, or even to the team (which needs a win). Although recognizing that behavioral methods do not necessarily involve personal or emotional topics, the author discusses confidentiality and communication with the public news media.

Dr. Wayne Lanning has been a consultant to the U.S. Olympic Track and Field Development Committee and to collegiate basketball and track coaches and teams. He was a counseling psychologist at Indiana University and is now at the University of Wyoming. This article offers insights into the practical issues facing sports psychology consultants. The author discusses steps that can interfere with or enhance credibility of a consultant, such as what to do about establishing trust, and summarizes a variety of principles and observations derived from direct experiences with a team sport.

[1] Another article by Titley appears on page 321-327.

Ethics in a Highly Visible Environment: Consultation and Intervention with Athletes and Athletic Teams

Robert W. Titley

On November 15, 1975 an athlete at Colorado State University established a new NCAA major college football record by kicking a 63-yard field goal.[1] I had been serving in a consultative role with the football program at CSU and my work included assisting this particular athlete through the application of a muscle relaxation and imagery rehearsal technique based on learning theory and behavior modification principles (Suinn 1976).[2]

Following the game, a number of reporters were interviewing the athlete about his record-setting feat when he revealed to them that I had helped him in his training program. Local and state newspapers, and later national wire-service releases, mentioned the athlete's acknowledgment of my delivery of psychology assistance. Unfortunately, some reports were incomplete or misleading as to the nature of the assistance rendered. For example, one article stated I had "counseled" the young man after he had become "despondent" over having missed kicks in key situations in earlier games. The incompleteness and inaccuracies probably were due to the athlete not knowing quite how to explain how I had helped him, my reticence about giving information to the reporters, and misconceptions which journalists and others have about forms of intervention used by psychologists.

The highly publicized event, albeit a happy one for the athlete (and admittedly for me), pointed up the need for guidelines for the psychologist who consults with athletes and athletic teams—individuals and groups who alternately suffer and enjoy the unique vagaries of high visibility and public exposure.

Athletic coaches and athletes who seek psychological assistance are entitled to the full protection of the psychologist's principles and standards of ethics, the same degree of protection guaranteed any other client. This holds whether a coach wants advice on coaching methods, staff relationships, team morale, or the color of the locker room walls. This also holds whether a given individual athlete is sent for help by a coach, as opposed to a self-referral, and whether the intervention consists of simple advice, counseling, or psychotherapy or if it involves training the athlete in a behavior modification technique designed to improve motor performance.

---

[1] See the article by Titley on pages 321-327. —Ed.
[2] See the article by Suinn on pages 306-315. —Ed.

The fact that the organization and the participating athletes are in the public eye directly or via the media should not override any of the principles of confidentiality or any other ethical considerations. By way of contrast, it seems customary in the sports world for certain *medical* information, at least medical information which relates to an athlete's current ability to perform, to be released publicly by some coaches, physicians, and trainers—apparently a gray area of confidentiality regarding one's medical or physical condition. But should psychologists publicly reveal *psychological* information about teams or athletes? I believe not, and for reasons alluded to above.

The general public is not familiar with the kinds of services a psychologist might render a sports team or an athlete. For example, many people might automatically assume that if an athlete is being seen by a psychologist, it must be a "head" problem, and negative attributions and attitudes toward the athlete might result. Nevertheless, there should be no gray area in psychology, even in sports—as in any other setting the client's rights and the psychologist's responsibility must be sustained.

Yet, certain realities and problems exist in the consulting and intervention role of the sports psychologist.[3] The psychologist involved with a team or with certain athletes may have other, and sometimes conflicting, roles in the same general setting or location, e.g., a university. Athletes have other dimensions to their lives, and they may seek psychological help unrelated to their existence as athletes. Coaches are inevitably interested in the outcome of psychological intervention with athletes in their charge, for their own welfare may be directly at stake. Should the goals of intervention be the goals of the athlete, or the goals the coach has for the athlete, i.e., who is the client if the coach is the one who has "hired" the psychologist? Are behavior modification procedures designed merely to improve a specific normal motor behavior exempt from those rules of confidentiality governing personal counseling or psychotherapy? What about working with an athlete at the practice or game site in view of others? What constitutes a "public revelation" of the relationship by the athlete? Are certain case histories or search studies precluded from publication because any description of the problem and the outcome would immediately make the identity of the athlete known—via his or her publicized accomplishments and notoriety?

Although these problems and questions are related to general and specific ethical and professional standards applicable to all psychologist-client contacts, they illustrate certain aspects somewhat unique to the psychologist-athlete or psychologist-athlete-team relationship. Following are some suggested guidelines pertaining to these unique aspects.

THE DUAL ROLE PROBLEM

In some settings, the sports psychologist may be in more than one set of dual roles with athletes. In the college or university setting, for example, the psychologist may be on the staff of the counseling center and also a classroom teacher. A student who happens to be an athlete may come to the psychologist for assistance as an athlete, but may seek from the same person help with a personal matter unrelated to sports. In the same semester, the psychologist as teacher might look up from the podium and see the same student-athlete in the front row of the classroom.

In each case of psychologist-client contact, the role of both the psychologist and the athlete should be clarified through mutual discussion at the outset of the involvements.

[3]See the article by Lanning on pages 362-367. —Ed.

THE COACH AS THIRD PARTY

Coaches, especially in the collegiate ranks, appear to have a tradition-based authori'y to send players to see whomever they want them to see—a rather mandatory referral process. According to my experience, their motive generally seems to be a compromise between a genuine interest in the athlete's welfare and an equally genuine interest in their own welfare, i.e., winning.

In situations wherein a psychologist has contracted to serve an athletic program and the participating athletes, it should be the responsibility of the psychologist to inform the coaches in the organization as to the conditions under which an athlete will be seen and what information stemming from the contacts can and cannot be revealed to the coaching staff. The athlete should be given clear information at the outset as to the principles and guidelines of confidentiality and an agreement reached as to what kinds of information; if any, the athlete wants conveyed to the coaches. (Some athletes, as they view their own best interests, may *want* certain information passed on to their coaches by the psychologist. In some cases it might benefit the athlete if the coach were informed about certain psychological characteristics of his or her charge).

Regarding referral, the psychologist should insist that athletes not feel coerced into approaching the psychologist. Ideally, contacts should be by mutual agreement among the coach, the athlete, and the psychologist, when the athlete is a candidate for assistance directly related to his or her performance.

WHO IS THE CLIENT? WHO SETS THE GOALS?

The psychologist who has contracted as a consultant and deliverer of services to a program may be serving, on occasion, two clients—the coaches responsible for the program and the athletes.

Psychologists so involved should determine—first in an overall sense and subsequently in each specific case—whether the goals of the coaches and the athletes are congruent. These goals should also be congruent with the values and ethics of the psychologist. In some cases the psychologist might wish to avoid service or input to the organization or an athlete when an unresolvable incongruency appears to exist. However, in most cases congruence can be achieved and/or incongruencies resolved through mutual discussions.

PSYCHOLOGICAL TESTING, PSYCHOTHERAPY, AND BEHAVIOR MODIFICATION: DIFFERENT RULES?

The current wide application of behavior modification techniques used in various settings and the alleged non-personal nature of these modes, especially in their application to normal behaviors in normal people, can lead to laxity in certain ethical measures. Stolz, Wienckowski, and Brown (1975) emphasize the need for careful attention to such issues as voluntary and informed consent, goal setting, and other professional and ethical standards in the use of behavior modification techniques. Deeply emotional, cognitive, historical, or personal material is usually not involved in behavior modification, especially when the alteration or enhancement of a normal behavior in a normal person is the focus of treatment. Nevertheless, any client, including an athlete, receiving behavior modification should be afforded the same degree of ethical and professional considerations as the consumer of psychodynamic therapies or other services.

If behavioristic procedures are used with an entire team in a group setting, those who do not wish to participate should be allowed to so choose, and the psychologist should insist that the coaches accept this without retribution toward those who decline. Further, it is as much the responsibility of the sports psychologist to help coaches understand why some athletes reject psychological assistance as it is to help them understand why other athletes want and accept such help.

Additionally, the same ethics applicable to group or individual psychological testing should be adhered to in the use of tests with individual athletes or entire athletic teams. There is nothing about the world of sport which justifies any departure from these principles.

CONTACT IN THE PUBLIC SETTING

Unique to the psychologist-athlete relationship is that the psychologist might recommend, as part of the service, observation or even direct intervention at the practice site or contest setting. An example would be a behavior modification method such as the imaged motor rehearsal I utilize with some football players. In addition to training sessions in the confidential confines of my office, I believe that some on-the-field observation and instruction enhances the effectiveness of the method. As a consultant to a football program I have the privilege of unrestricted access to practice sessions, the locker room, and the sidelines during games, and I travel with the team. They have become accustomed to and accept my presence, even though it makes some of my work visible. This is in marked contrast to my other clinical practice—I do not observe, follow around, eat with, treat, or train any of my other clients in their natural habitats. When public setting contact seems justified as part of the service, the athlete and coaches should be apprised of this, and their consent obtained. However, even though the sports psychologist may be seen working in the practice, pre-game, or game settings and consent of the client has been obtained, there is no consent implied that permits the psychologist to announce publicly to anyone that a particular person or unit is the client, to describe the process being used, or to reveal any privileged information about a particular athlete or the team.

A CLIENT-ATHLETE HAS THE RIGHT TO REVEAL

As in any psychologist-client relationship, an individual client-athlete has the right to reveal anything he or she wishes about the fact, the nature, and the content of the contacts, but the psychologist does not share this privilege. If the athlete, however, reveals publicly that a psychologist has helped him or her, complicated circumstances may arise.

What constitutes a public revelation by the athlete? If the athlete merely tells a friend that a psychologist is working with him or her, that does not make it a matter of public record, nor would it become necessarily widely known. However, should an athlete reveal to the news media that "Dr. —— worked with me," then the psychologist may become subject to inquiries and questions from numerous formal and informal sources. However, before the psychologist acknowledges the contact and/or describes the method as it was directly applied to the particular athlete in an article, interview, or speech or in an informal reply to interested persons, permission to do so should be obtained from the athlete. Any such statements made, formal or informal, should be limited to a confirmation that the particular athlete was assisted and a general description of the method as it was used. Other information about the client, especially confidential and personal material, should never be discussed or mentioned.

PUBLICATION OF CASE HISTORIES OR RESEARCH REPORTS

Case histories and research findings are an important part of the professional literature in psychology, athletics, and physical education. It is an accepted ethical practice to conceal the identity of the clients or subjects in publications, but a contrary and unique situation often arises in sports psychology. It is difficult to publish a case history on an athlete who broke a NCAA football record and conceal his identity (Titley 1975). Or to mention only that the subject was a collegiate athlete and mention the sport speciality narrows it down considerably, especially if the author's institutional or organizational affiliation is known.

When a psychologist believes a case history should be part of the professional literature, permission should be obtained from the athlete and he or she should read and approve the manuscript prior to its submission for publication. If any aspect of psychological work with an identified or identifiable athletic organization or team is described in published material, permission for publication from those in charge of the program, whether or not they are mentioned by name in the publication, should be secured.

The authorized publication of work with identified or identifiable athletes or athletic organization does free the psychologist to then acknowledge, mention, or describe publicly elsewhere the work (but only with professional discretion) in speeches, interviews, or related publications or in replies to responsible inquiries. Nevertheless, such utterances and responses should be limited only to the content and facts in the original authorized publication.

CONCLUSION

Athletic programs as organizations, and coaches and athletes as individuals, when they become clients of the psychologist, should be afforded the same considerations and protection with respect to professional ethics as any client. Standard ethical principles apply, even though consultation and intervention may involve unique situations regarding dual roles, behavior modification procedures with a normal population displaying normal skills, and high public visibility. The client should be apprised of any special or unique situation which might arise in the course of the relationship, with the assurance that the client's welfare and best interest is always the foremost consideration.

REFERENCES

Stolz, S. B.; Wienckowski, L. A.; and Brown, B. S. 1975. Behavior modification: A perspective on critical issues. *American Psychologist* 30:1027-1048.

Suinn, R. M. 1976. Visual motor behavior rehearsal for adaptive behavior. In *Counseling methods,* ed. J. Krumbol·z and C. Thoresen. New York: Holt.

Titley, R. W. 1976. The loneliness of a long-distance kicker. *Athletic Journal,* September 1976, pp. 74-80.

Applied Psychology
in Major College Athletics

Wayne Lanning

Presently in the United States there are psychiatrists, physiologists, physical educationalists, clinical psychologists, educational psychologists, research psychologists, and even physicists all working within an area generally called sports psychology. The unifying principle among these diverse people is the conviction that maximum athletic performance is effected not only by one's physical attributes and skills but also by his/her psychological make-up. In American sports the focus for years has been on the development of technique and the physical skills. Only recently has some systematic attention been given to the impact of the psychological upon performance.[1] And yet, even under the new emphasis, the majority of effort has been toward discovering similarities and differences between athletes in different sports and between the great athlete and the average weekend athlete. Little systematic effort has been given by applied psychologists who work day-by-day with the coaches and athletes to incorporate the principles of the behavioral sciences into the process of coaching and competition. Those who have been involved usually are brought in as "consultants." Most of them follow the consultation models which have been developed for use in mental health settings or within the complex organizations of business and industry. Those models require the consultant to go into the athletic situation with his specialized package of skills and/or knowledge and impart it to the athletes or coaches. He typically does some specific training and then leaves the coaches and athletes to use the new skills in their competitions. An alternative approach is to have a psychologist become immersed in the system with the coaches and athletes and work day-by-day with them throughout the athletic season. The present article contains a description of a consulting model used with an NCAA championship basketball team.

In March 1976 the Indiana University basketball team culminated an undefeated season by winning the NCAA championship. During the following 1976-1977 basketball season I was invited by Coach Bob Knight to participate freely in his basketball program at Indiana University. He stated that he believed the mental part of athletic competition was four times as important as the physical, and he was interested in finding out what contributions a psychologist could make to his program. I was, therefore, given complete freedom to attend all practices, locker room settings, games, film sessions, planning meetings, and even team social functions during the course of the year. From that involvement certain distinct impressions and learning were acquired concerning the involvement of psychology and a psychological consultant in athletics.

---

[1] See the preceding articles in Part III, in the sections *Coaching Variables, Mental States*, and *Behavioral Strategies*. —Ed.

ESTABLISHING CREDIBILITY

There are certain issues involved in the establishment and continuation of any consultation relationship, but there are some which apply specifically to the athletic setting. Since the area of athletics is a unique world, any psychologist who ventures into it is immediately seen as an outsider and must demonstrate that he is credible within that world. One obvious factor in establishing credibility is the ability to discuss athletes in nontechnical jargon. For a psychologist to discuss with a coach one of the athletes in terms of "ego strength," "social introversion," and "depressive tendencies" is both self-defeating and unnecessary. It is more meaningful and useful to talk rather about a player's ability to bounce back from defeat or criticism, about his preference for being alone or with others, and about his tendency to feel helpless and guilty. To couch the information in nontechnical language is to provide the opportunity of being heard and understood.

Another factor that must be addressed quickly is the sterotypic view people have of psychologists as test-givers. It is true that we are trained to administer and interpret tests which provide us with considerable information about others, but to limit oneself to that role is to severely restrict the contribution that can be made within an overall program. Both coaches and athletes need to be instructed about the contributions that a psychologist can make to the program which are not necessarily tied to the objective testing role. He may also contribute in the area of learning styles, motivation, stress reduction, and the like.

The most critical issue to be dealt with in the establishment of credibility is the issue of trust.[2] The psychologist is an outsider and the moment he steps into a program to function as a consultant he disrupts an entire system. That disruption involves many people and if not understood can result in destruction of the consultation relationship.

The head coach will have questions and concerns about the role that the psychologist will have with the players. He will be concerned that the players do not use him for a crying towel upon whom they can lay all of their complaints and grievances. The sympathetic ear is not one of the functions to be served by the consultant. The head coach will also be concerned that the psychologist is able to understand enough of the entire system to comprehend the stresses and pressures which it places upon the athletes. Previous experience in intercollegiate athletics and/or coaching on the part of the psychologist will be helpful in this area. Of most importance, however, is the ability of the psychologist to provide new information for the coach in such a way that he is able to use it with the athletes in ways that had not been done before. The most critical role definition for the psychologist is the one perceived by the head coach. Considerable time and effort, therefore, must initially be given to that definition.

The assistant coaches can see the entry of a psychologist as being a threat to their relationship with the head coach or with the players. It is imperative that the consultant meet with the assistant coaches and inform them also about the nature of his role in the program. The head coach may have told them that another person is going to be involved for a period of time, but the consultant himself needs to personally respond to all questions that the assistants have, especially those which are implied. Can they be assured that they are in no way being replaced or bypassed?

It is obvious that the athletes themselves will have many questions about the role of the consultant. Just telling the players that a psychologist is going to be working with the program will generate confusion and anxiety. It seems most appropriate for the players to be instructed a bit in

---

[2] See the article by Titley on pages 357-361. —Ed.

the role that the mental part plays in their athletic performance and then tie in the consultant as someone who will be working with them and the coaches in that area. Over time they will become aware that the psychologist is not a spy for the coaches and that many things they discuss with him are not immediately transmitted to the coach. There is always a fine line to be walked about how much the coach needs to know from the consultant and what is to be kept in confidence. Only good professional judgment and ethics can finally determine the answer.

Many other people are also affected by the entry of a psychological consultant to the system. While this includes many diverse people it is probably the most critical group to deal with for continued success of the consultant. Included in this group are such people as other athletic personnel, newpaper reporters, team trainers and physicians, alumni, and friends of the program. Each one of those has a unique ability to hinder or help the relationship and contribution which a psychological consultant is able to establish with a given athletic program. Identification with the coach and his team is generally coveted and jealously guarded once one thinks he has obtained it. Even within the confines of the athletic department itself there is considerable jockeying to maintain or establish a position just a little bit closer to the operation. The psychologist, therefore, who is brought into the center of the operation, is an immediate threat to the position of a lot of people. They will attempt to use him for their own enhancement or attempt to undermine him in order to maintain their own perceived position. Just doing a good job with the task at hand is not enough to ensure the continuation of the relationship. In addition, one must be sensitive to the vested interests that others have and deal with those directly without getting caught in the struggle for positioning.

PSYCHOLOGICAL IMPLICATIONS FOR ATHLETIC PROGRAMS

In addition to the many issues involved in the establishment of credibility the year of involvement provided me with the opportunity to closely observe and work with a major college basketball program and learn much more about the role that psychology has in the ultimate performance of the athletes. The rest of this article is devoted to a brief discussion of some of the conclusions reached at the end of the year's involvement.

1. Each team and each program is unique. That sounds like an axiomatic statement, but many psychologists tend to do research with and draw conclusions about "college athletes." I had the opportunity to learn a great deal about major college basketball programs, and the one striking feature was that all the highly successful programs were very different. Each coach has his own basketball system that he tries to instill in his players. There are, of course, basic elements to the coaching of basketball that everyone uses, but beyond that each coach has his individual beliefs and philosophies about the game of basketball which he puts into practice with his team. He, therefore, must recruit young men who are both physically and psychologically able to implement the system of basketball which he teaches. A coach cannot just recruit superior high school athletes with the assurance that they will likely become superior college athletes. Many of the great high school athletes who were so disappointing in their college performances were recruited into the wrong system A high school athlete may have all the skills needed to become a world-class athlete but never succeed in the college he attends for a variety of reasons. The coach's system of basketball (or football or soccer, etc.) may place the greatest demands on the player's weakest skill. For example, a quick, good-shooting, free-lance guard may be asked to work within a system that requires a controlled, screening, passing, disciplined offense. He not only is asked to develop new physical skills, but the realization that he is not the star in a new system brings with it frustration and not a little bit of fear—fear that the basis for his acceptance and worth for so many years is slipping away. When that happens the athlete may pursue one of a number of courses. He may quit the team and transfer to a program that will maximize his strengths, and he can re-establish his basis of worth with a minimum of short-range trauma. He may also accept his role of diminished importance and invest himself in developing a new basis of worth through an academic program, a girl friend or campus parties. He may also recognize the need to learn new skills and redouble his efforts to contribute and develop and, thereby, stabilize his threatened basis of worth. Whichever alternative he chooses, however, is not a function of his physical skills as much as a function of his psychological makeup. All of the options are less desirable than the athlete who joins a new program and is able to use his strengths while developing. The others could all be considered recruiting errors which effect both the program and the individual. From a psychological point of view, many recruiting errors happen each year because not enough attention is given in recruiting to obtaining athletes who are both physically and emotionally suited to play within a given system. One athlete who transferred from Indiana University stated that he didn't know before he came that he would have to work so hard to play major college basketball. He, therefore, transferred to a school that was not a major successful program and where he could practice with a minimum of work. That transfer was undoubtedly better for the athlete and for the basketball program he left. More desirable for all would have been the realization *before* he was recruited that he didn't like to work hard. He then would not have become one of the "recruiting errors."

One of the tasks, therefore, which I set for myself during the year of involvement was to develop a psychological profile of the ideal basketball player at Indiana University. That was done by means of discussions with coaches and players, systematic observation of practice sessions, and testing of these who were successfully and unsuccessfully incorporated into the system. The discussions with coaches were designed to determine the expectations they had for a successful player in their specific system of basketball. The discussions with players then determined their reactions to those expectations. Discrepancies were sometimes found. For example, a few athletes stated that they didn't realize how demanding a major college program and schedule was. Most, however, said that they were able to adjust their expectations quite readily, and they were successful in the program, as opposed to the player mentioned above who transferred. The observation of practice sessions was conducted to determine the demands the system placed on the players and then used to establish the psychological characteristics necessary to meet those demands and be successful. Testing was conducted in an attempt to obtain some more objective data which would distinguish the successful athlete *in this system* from the unsuccessful one.

There is no question that a coach who recruits for a certain psychological profile as well as a physical profile will have fewer unsuccessful athletes in his program. That is far better both for the program and for the athlete.

2. Each player on a team is different and must be treated differently. This notion is foreign and abhorrent to most coaches, who believe firmly in treating everyone the same. They are convinced that it will avoid charges of favoritism and partiality against them. It will do that, but at the expense of some of their athletes and surely at the expense of the victory side of their won-lost record. Current research in the area of arousal and athletic performance clearly suggests that different people function optimally at different arousal levels. To "psych up" everyone the same before a game will decrease the performance level of some and increase the level of others. Comments by some contemporary and successful coaches that "you can never get a team too high" or "the more psyched-up they are, the better" may be typically fashionable, but they are in direct conflict with considerable evidence that shows quite the opposite is true. The very reason that some programs are consistently successful is that the coaches do *not* treat everyone on the team the same. For example, some players need to be externally motivated by a coach or another player in order to perform to their maximum level. Others have such high levels of internal drive that any attempt to externally motivate them further only results in decreased performance. The wise coach seeks to discover those differences and treats his players accordingly. While most coaches may not be able to discover all those differences themselves, they are able to utilize the skills of psychologists who can assist them.

3. Coaches need to deal with their players as more than just athletes. Since the psychological makeup of an athlete so greatly affects his performance, a coach must deal with his players regarding other areas of their life than athletics. Their family life, academic life, social life, and the rest all highly influence the mental approach the athlete has toward his sport. For a coach to ignore that is to ignore critical factors in the athlete's life. The athlete who has always pleased his parents by means of his athletic ability expects to be able to continue that in college. But when he finds himself on a team full of high school all-Americans it becomes more difficult to be as successful as before. Everyone on the team can't be the high scorer, the play-maker, or even a starter. Those who must assume new roles on the team may also have new tensions and pressures placed upon their relationships with their family.

In the same way, the athlete who is having girlfriend problems or academic problems will not perform the same for the team as he would without those problems. The coach needs to know his players as more than just athletes and accommodate this to factors in their lives external to their athletic role which greatly effect their athletic performance. A striking example of this occurred midway through the 1976-1977 basketball season. One of the young players on the team was beginning to struggle academically at the beginning of the second semester. His course requirements were demanding more time than he had left after all his other responsibilities were met. He was not in critical danger of failing, but he couldn't spread his energy so thinly and perform well at anything. Coach Knight discussed the situation with him and told him to take as much time as he needed away from basketball and to concentrate his energies on his studies. When (and if) the athlete felt he had them under control, then he should return to basketball practice. The athlete took two and a half weeks off in the middle of the basketball season and concentrated his energies on his studies. He then returned to the team and performed so well in practice that he started some of the games during the rest of the season. He has since maintained a commendable grade point average and contributed significantly to the success of the basketball team.

Numerous examples exist in all areas of an athlete's life but the point to be made is that a global view of an athlete is critical to have since all elements of his life may effect his performance as an athlete.

4. In team sports, the interaction effect of the coach and the player is a most critical element in maximizing the team performance. As mentioned above, each athletic program requires certain types of athletes to make it successful. Highly skilled people who do not fit into the system will not contribute to the success of the program. The system, however, is not a sterile objective approach to the game but rather something that the coaches teach to the players. Any time a teaching situation of that type occurs, the learning acquired is directly related to the compatibility of the interaction between the personality of the coaches and the players. Therefore, in the selection of athletes the personality of the coach must be considered as significantly as the personality of the player. There are many examples of players who were not successful with one team who, after joining a new team, became stars of the team. Part of the reason for that undoubtedly was the different demands the system placed upon the player, but part of the reason is also the different interaction effect that occurrred between the player and the coaches. Any activity that requires a superior/subordinate relationship such as coaching/playing will necessitate compatible personalities between the people involved. Since all of the compatibility cannot be guaranteed through the selection of athletes at recruitment time, accommodations must necessarily be made during the development of the coach-player relationship. Rigidity and interpersonal inflexibility on the part of either party will obviously impede the development of a working relationship between them.

5. Even the best coaches don't understand all the psychological implications of maximizing athletic performance. There is no question that the successful coaches, at least implicitly, use many sound psychological principles in their coaching. Few of them, however, are very systematic about it. That is not a criticism of coaches but rather a reflection of their training and traditions. Their job is to learn and understand as much as they can about the intricacies of the sport they are coaching. They are not trained as behavioral specialists, and any use of the psychological principles comes from an inherent sensitivity to other people rather than a systematic study of motivation, maximum performance, reactions to pressure, and the like. Since coaching has traditionally focused upon improving athletic technique and physical skills, most coaches emphasize those, usually at the expense of the equally critical psychological factors. The coaches and athletes who are most successful in the future will be those who systematically address themselves to the role that an athlete's psychological makeup contributes to his/her athletic performance.

6. A psychologist or behavioral specialist can be a valuable and productive resource for coaching staffs. Eastern European countries have for years been aware of the role that mental factors play in athletic performance. They have conducted expensive research into the area and more recently have even had sports psychologists working as members of the coaching cadre with their national teams. The United States has been much slower to recognize the value that an applied practicing psychologist can have in working with the athletes and coaches. To date most of our Olympic team efforts have been limited to uncoordinated instances of psychologists collecting date on the personality characteristics of our world-class athletes or conducting isolated workshops in such areas as imagery, stress reduction, anxiety management, and biofeedback. Full-time applied psychologists have not been used in our major athletic efforts even though the psychological aspects of maximum performance are largely undeveloped in relation to the physical.

As can be seen, the majority of knowledge in the physical area is known and developed. There is still the tip of the iceberg to explore, but progress will be slow and less easily applied. The psychological components, on the other hand, have just been touched and leave seven-eighths of the iceberg still to uncover and explore. While new efforts are being directed toward that part of the athlete's performance, even when the research psychologists have discovered some critical knowledge, it will still require an applied psychologist to help the coaches and athletes implement and use that new knowledge to maximize athletic performance in both team and individual sports. Perhaps when that all happens we will know more clearly just what a sports psychologist is, and maybe even the American Psychological Association will add one more division to their already confusing number. One thing is abundantly clear, however, and that is the fact that more systematic attention needs to be devoted to the psychological aspects of maximum athletic performance.